W9-ADJ-500

THE *POETRY* ANTHOLOGY

THE

POETRY

ANTHOLOGY

1912–1977

*Sixty-five Years of America's Most
Distinguished Verse Magazine*

EDITED BY

Daryl Hine & Joseph Parisi

HOUGHTON MIFFLIN COMPANY
BOSTON 1978

Permissions copy begins on page 529.

Library of Congress Cataloging in Publication Data
Main entry under title:

The Poetry anthology, 1912–1977.

   Includes index.
    1. American poetry—20th century.   I. Hine, Daryl.
II. Parisi, Joseph, date   III. Poetry (Chicago)
PS613.P64   811'.5'208   78-8042
ISBN 0-395-26548-7
ISBN 0-395-26874-5 pbk.

Printed in the United States of America

P 10 9 8 7 6 5 4 3

ACKNOWLEDGMENTS

For their aid at several stages in the preparation of this anthology, the editors are indebted to many people and institutions, of which we should like to thank in particular: Mr. Michael Goodkin, Mr. James Wells, and other Trustees of The Modern Poetry Association; Mr. Robert Rosenthal, Ms. Mary Janzen, and Mr. Sidney Huttner, for use of materials and facilities in the Department of Special Collections, University of Chicago Library; and to Mr. John Ashbery; Ms. Diana Haskell of the Newberry Library; Mr. James Laughlin; Ms. Patricia McDonald of the Witter Bynner Foundation; Mr. Charles A. Wagner of the Poetry Society of America; Dr. Ellen Williams and Ms. Patricia C. Willis, for help in locating poets or heirs of poets whose works appear in this book.

Except for obvious typographical errors which have been silently corrected, all poems in this anthology appear as they were first printed in *Poetry*. Several of these works, and their titles, were changed in subsequent publication. We regret that we were unable to reprint certain other poems for lack of permission from copyright holders. For assistance and good wishes of several poets and publishers, we are most grateful.

We should like to express, however inadequately, special thanks to our associates at *Poetry*: Mrs. Nadine Cummings, who assumed extra burdens during the long process of compiling this book, and Mrs. Helen Lothrop Klaviter, without whose tireless efforts with innumerable details, particularly corre-

v

spondence on permissions, the anthology would have been impossible. Their unfailing care, industry, and cheerfulness were a constant encouragement to the editors.

D.H.

J.P.

CONTENTS

ACKNOWLEDGMENTS • V
INTRODUCTION • XXXV

PART I
1912–1920
(Volumes 1–16)

Ezra Pound	To Whistler, American	3
William Butler Yeats	Fallen Majesty	4
Vachel Lindsay	General William Booth Enters into Heaven	4
H. D.	Epigram	6
Witter Bynner	Grieve Not for Beauty	6
Ezra Pound	*From* CONTEMPORANIA Tenzone	7
Francis Thompson	To My Friend	7
Ezra Pound	*From* LUSTRA I. "O helpless few in my country"	8
	III. Further Instructions	8
D. H. Lawrence	Green	9
	Illicit	10
Robert Frost	The Code — Heroics	10
Carl Sandburg	*From* CHICAGO POEMS Chicago	14

Sara Teasdale   From LOVE SONGS
           September Midnight 15

Edwin Arlington Robinson Eros Turannos 16
William Butler Yeats   To a Friend Whose Work
           Has Come to
           Nothing 17
           The Magi 18
Ezra Pound   ΤΟ ΚΑΛΌΝ 18
James Stephens   Dark Wings 18
D. H. Lawrence   Don Juan 19
Ezra Pound   The Coming of War:
           Actaeon 19

H. D.   Moonrise 20
Amy Lowell   Venus Transiens 21
Rupert Brooke   Nineteen-fourteen 21
William Carlos Williams Slow Movement 23
Marianne Moore   From POUTERS AND
           FANTAILS
           That Harp You Play
           So Well 24

T. S. Eliot   The Love Song of J.
           Alfred Prufrock 24

Harriet Monroe   The Pine at Timber-Line 28
Conrad Aiken   From DISCORDANTS
           IV. "Dead Cleopatra
           lies in a crystal
           casket" 29

Sara Teasdale   The Answer 30
T. S. Eliot   Aunt Helen 31
Richard Aldington   Images 31
John Hall Wheelock   Beethoven 32
Wallace Stevens   Sunday Morning 32
William Butler Yeats   The Hawk 35
           The Scholars 36

Edgar Lee Masters   In Memory of Bryan
           Lathrop 36

Ezra Pound	O Atthis	37
	The Lake Isle	37
Rabindranath Tagore	From EPIGRAMS	38
Harold Monro	From STRANGE MEETINGS	
	VII — Birth	38
T. S. Eliot	From OBSERVATIONS	
	La Figlia Che Piange	39
	Mr. Apollinax	40
	Morning at the Window	40
John Drinkwater	Invocation	41
Arthur Davison Ficke	From FOUR JAPANESE PAINTINGS	
	III. The Wave Symphony	41
William Carlos Williams	Marriage	42
Isaac Rosenberg	From TRENCH POEMS	
	Break of Day in the Trenches	42
Amy Lowell	From LACQUER PRINTS	
	Desolation	43
Carl Sandburg	From MY PEOPLE	
	In Tall Grass	44
James Joyce	Night Piece	44
Ezra Pound	From THREE CANTOS	
	I. "Hang it all, there can be but one Sordello!"	45
Jane Heap	From NOTES	
	II. "Where go the birds when the rain"	51
Sherwood Anderson	From MID-AMERICAN SONGS	
	A Visit	51
John Drinkwater	Reciprocity	51
James Joyce	On the Beach at Fontana	52
John Gould Fletcher	From CHICAGO NOTES	
	The Monadnock	52

Arthur Waley From CHINESE POEMS
                The Orphan   53
Ford Maddox Hueffer The Sanctuary   54
Edna St. Vincent Millay From FIGS FROM THISTLES
                First Fig   55
                Second Fig   55
                The Unexplorer   55
                Thursday   55
D. H. Lawrence Moonrise   56
William Carlos Williams Le Médecin Malgré Lui 56
Mark Turbyfill Benediction   57
Arthur Symons Dreams   58
Carl Sandburg From REDHAW WINDS
                Falltime   58
D. H. Lawrence Nostalgia   59
Ezra Pound From PROPERTIUS
                IV. "When, when,
                and whenever
                death closes our
                eyelids"   60
John Reed Proud New York   61
Emanuel Carnevali Walt Whitman   61
Edna St. Vincent Millay Recuerdo   62
Louis Untermeyer End of the Comedy   62
Conrad Aiken From MANY EVENINGS
                Multitudes Turn in
                Darkness   63
Vachel Lindsay The Horrid Voice of
                Science   63
Sara Teasdale Song   64
Wallace Stevens From PECKSNIFFIANA
                The Indigo Glass in
                the Grass   64
                Anecdote of the Jar   65
                The Curtains in the
                House of the
                Metaphysician   65
William Butler Yeats A Prayer for My Daughter 65

Malcolm Cowley	From THREE PORTRAITS	
	Danny	68
Alfred Kreymborg	To W.C.W.M.D.	69
H. L. Davis	From TO THE RIVER BEACH	
	Stalks of Wild Hay	70

PART II
1920–1930
(Volumes 17–36)

Agnes Lee	The Ilex Tree	73
Edmund Wilson, Jr.	Not Here	73
Winifred Bryher	From HELLENICS	
	Blue Sleep	73
Yvor Winters	Hawk's Eyes	74
Edgar Lee Masters	Keats to Fanny Brawne	74
Mortimer J. Adler	The Fearless	75
Elinor Wylie	Atavism	75
Arthur Davison Ficke	Perspective of Co-ordination	76
John Peale Bishop	The Hunchback	76
Marjorie Allen Seiffert	Cubist Portrait	77
Oscar Williams	The Golden Fleece	77
Glenway Wescott	The Poet at Night-fall	78
Wallace Stevens	From SUR MA GUZZLA GRACILE	
	Tea at the Palaz of Hoon	79
	Of the Manner of Addressing Clouds	79
	Of Heaven Considered as a Tomb	80
William Carlos Williams	The Lonely Street	80
Babette Deutsch	Tak for Sidst	81
Hervey Allen	Upstairs Downstairs	81
Osbert Sitwell	Maxixe	82
Harriet Monroe	In High Places	83

Louise Bogan	From BEGINNING AND END	
	Knowledge	83
Kay Boyle	Monody to the Sound of	
	Zithers	84
Ernest M. Hemingway	From WANDERINGS	
	Champs D'Honneur	84
	Chapter Heading	85
Malcolm Cowley	From HERE AND THERE	
	Nocturnal Landscape	85
Marion Strobel	Pastoral	86
Yvor Winters	Static Autumn	86
Robert Frost	The Flower-Boat	87
DuBose Heyward	The Equinox	87
Louis Zukofsky	Of Dying Beauty	88
Edgar Lee Masters	Mind Flying Afar	89
Lola Ridge	Chicago	90
Sara Teasdale	Epitaph	90
Morris Bishop	Dementia Praecox	90
Winifred Bryher	From THREE SONGS	
	Thessalian	91
Paul Eldridge	To a Courtesan a	
	Thousand Years	
	Dead	91
Robert McAlmon	From CONTRIBUTIONS	
	For Instance	92
Laura Riding Gottschalk	From BODY'S HEAD	
	Head Itself	93
Countee Cullen	For Amy Lowell	94
Edward Davison	The Owl	94
Archibald MacLeish	Ars Poetica	95
John Dos Passos	Crimson Tent	96
George H. Dillon	The Hard Lovers	97
Hart Crane	At Melville's Tomb	98
Malcolm Cowley	From BLUE JUNIATA	
	The Streets of Air	99
Mark Van Doren	Apple Hell	99

Kay Boyle   To a Seaman Dead on
                           Land   100
Léonie Adams   Counsel to Unreason   101
Robert Graves   In the Beginning Was a
                           Word   101
                         The Cool Web   102
Hortense Flexner   Contemporary   103
Louis Ginsberg   Hymn to Evil   103
Dorothy M. Richardson   Message   104
Hart Crane   O Carib Isle!   104
Richard Eberhart   From THINGS KNOWN
                           Under the Hill   106
Robinson Jeffers   From THE TRUMPET
                           V. — Grass on the
                             Cliff   107
Morton Dauwen Zabel   Journal to Stella   108
Elinor Wylie   Lament for Glasgerion   108
H. D.   Birds in Snow   109
Archibald MacLeish   From PUBLISHED
                           CORRESPONDENCE
                           Epistle to the
                             Rapalloan   110
Merrill Moore   From HOSPITAL POEMS
                           Transfusion   111
Stanley Kunitz   Prophecy on Lethe   111
Loren C. Eiseley   The Deserted Homestead   112
Margaret Mead   Misericordia   113
Dudley Fitts   Southwest Passage   113

PART III
1930–1940
(Volumes 37–56)

Edna St. Vincent Millay   Sonnet ("Women have
                             loved before as I love
                             now")   119

May Sarton · *From* WORDS ON THE WIND
Fruit of Loneliness · 119

Edward Dahlberg · Kansas City West Bottoms · 120

Basil Bunting · The Word · 121

Robert Fitzgerald · *From* MUTATIONS
Midsummer · 122

Louise Bogan · Hypocrite Swift · 123

Langston Hughes · Sailor · 124

Allen Tate · *From* THE ROOFTREE
Sonnets of the Blood
I. "What is this flesh
and blood
compounded of" · 124
II. "Near to me as my
flesh, my flesh and
blood" · 125
IV. "The times have
changed, there is not
left to us" · 125
VII. "The fire I praise
was once perduring
flame" · 126
IX. "Not power nor
the storied hand of
God" · 126
The Wolves · 127

Paul Frederic Bowles · Extract · 127

Cecil Day Lewis · Winter Night · 128

Basil Bunting · Fearful Symmetry · 129

J. V. Cunningham · Sonnet on a Still Night · 130

Robert Penn Warren · Watershed · 130

John Peale Bishop · Hunger and Thirst · 131

Marianne Moore · *From* PART OF A NOVEL,
PART OF A POEM, PART
OF A PLAY
The Hero · 132

R. P. Blackmur · Resurrection · 133

Theodore Roethke	Bound	134
Marianne Moore	No Swan So Fine	135
John Wheelwright	Canal Street	135
Hart Crane	From THE URN	
	Reliquary	136
	The Sad Indian	136
	Enrich My	
	Resignation	137
Charles Reznikoff	Winter Sketches	137
Robert Penn Warren	The Limited	139
Cecil Day Lewis	From THE MAGNETIC	
	MOUNTAIN	
	Condemned	139
Selden Rodman	Time of Day	140
Carl Rakosi	The Memoirs	141
John Peale Bishop	The Ancestors	142
R. P. Blackmur	From A LABYRINTH OF BEING	
	Sonnet ("Three	
	silences made him	
	a single word")	143
William Carlos Williams	From "THAT'S THE	
	AMERICAN STYLE"	
	4th of July	143
Robert Fitzgerald	Metaphysician	144
Kenneth Patchen	Empty Dwelling Places	145
Winfield Townley Scott	The First Reader	146
Josephine Miles	From LOCAL HABITATION	
	On Inhabiting an	
	Orange	146
S. Ichiyé Hayakawa	To One Elect	147
Basil Bunting	Fishermen	147
Marianne Moore	From IMPERIOUS OX,	
	IMPERIAL DISH	
	The Buffalo	148
William Butler Yeats	Meru	150
Mary Barnard	Shoreline	150
Louis Zukofsky	"Mantis"	152
Harold Rosenberg	Epos	154

Clifford Dyment | From SECRET IDIOM
Sanctuary | 155
Robert Penn Warren | From OCTOBER POEMS
The Garden | 155
Howard Blake | Argent Solipsism | 156
Marianne Moore | Pigeons | 157
Sydney Justin Harris | I Come to Bury Caesar | 160
Robert Frost | At Woodward's Gardens | 162
Frederic Prokosch | The Gothic Dusk | 164
Muriel Rukeyser | From NIGHT-MUSIC
Time Exposures | 165
D. S. Savage | Fall of Leaves | 166
Samuel French Morse | From FRACTURE OF LIGHT
Song in the Cold
Season | 167
Theodore Roethke | "Long Live the Weeds" | 168
Josephine Miles | Sunday | 168
Marianne Moore | Walking-Sticks and
Paperweights and
Watermarks | 170
William Empson | Reflection from Rochester | 173
William Carlos Williams | To an Elder Poet | 174
Louise Bogan | Putting to Sea | 175
Harriet Monroe | A Farewell | 176
W. H. Auden | Journey to Iceland | 177
Poem ("O who can ever
praise enough") | 179
Dylan Thomas | We Lying by Seasand | 179
Ronald Bottrall | Mating Answer | 180
George Barker | Sequence | 181
Delmore Schwartz | Poem ("Old man in the
crystal morning after
snow") | 182
Thomas Lanier Williams | My Love Was Light | 183

Elizabeth Bishop	TWO MORNINGS AND TWO EVENINGS	
	Paris, 7 A.M.	183
	A Miracle for Breakfast	184
	From the Country to the City	186
	Song	186
Robert Penn Warren	Bearded Oaks	187
Norman Rosten	Aesthetic	188
Janet Lewis	At Carmel Highlands	189
Delmore Schwartz	"In the naked bed, in Plato's cave"	189
Yvor Winters	A Nocturne for October 31st	190
Dylan Thomas	Four Poems	
	I. "When all my five and country senses see"	191
	II. "O make me a mask and a wall to shut from your spies"	191
	III. "Not from this anger, anticlimax after"	191
	IV. "The spire cranes. Its statue is an aviary"	192
Ronald Bottrall	Darkened Windows	192
Theodore Roethke	The Reckoning	193
e. e. cummings	")when what hugs stopping earth than silent is"	194
Parker Tyler	Anthology of Nouns	194
Peter De Vries	Mirror	195
Stephen Spender	The Marginal Field	195
Edna St. Vincent Millay	The Snow Storm	196
Brewster Ghiselin	Headland	197
W. H. Auden	Voltaire at Ferney	197

Wallace Stevens	The Sense of the Sleight-of-Hand Man	199
Randall Jarrell	The Ways and the Peoples	199
H. B. Mallalieu	Epilogue	200
Glenway Wescott	The Summer Ending	201
Roy Fuller	Sonnet ("The crumbled rock of London is dripping under")	202
Paul Engle	Moving In	202
Gertrude Stein	Stanzas in Meditation	203
William Empson	Bacchus III	204
Louis MacNeice	Perdita	205
Nicholas Moore	Untitled ("Fivesucked the feature of my girl by glory")	205
Peter Viereck	Graves Are Made to Waltz On	206
e. e. cummings	"anyone lived in a pretty how town"	206
Walter de la Mare	Things	208
	Antiques	208
John Frederick Nims	Parting: 1940	208
Edwin Muir	Then . . .	209

PART IV
1940–1950
(Volumes 57–76)

W. H. Auden	Poem ("He watched with all his organs of concern")	213
Karl Shapiro	Necropolis	213
William Carlos Williams	River Rhyme	214
Robinson Jeffers	The Bloody Sire	214
David Daiches	Ulysses' Library	215
Robert Penn Warren	Terror	216
Theodore Roethke	Second Shadow	218

Babette Deutsch	Memory	218
Roy Fuller	Soliloquy in an Air-Raid	219
Robert Finch	Words	221
Langston Hughes	Dust Bowl	221
Walter de la Mare	Immanent	222
Basil Bunting	To Violet	222
Edwin Muir	The Finder Found	222
Weldon Kees	Henry James at Newport	223
Geoffrey Grigson	The Professionals	224
John Malcolm Brinnin	At the Band Concert	224
Karl Shapiro	October 1	225
Julian Symons	Hart Crane	226
William Empson	Bacchus IV	227
A. M. Klein	Upon the Heavenly Scarp	228
Thomas James Merton	The Dark Morning	229
Robert Duncan	A Spring Memorandum	229
Alex Comfort	The Lovers	232
Theodore Spencer	Return	232
Louis Zukofsky	1892–1941	234
Louis MacNeice	The Springboard	235
e. e. cummings	"what if a much of a which of a wind"	236
Howard Nemerov	Sigmund Freud	236
Randall Jarrell	The Emancipators	237
Howard Moss	A Game of Chance	238
Theodore Roethke	Dolor	238
William Jay Smith	"Abruptly All the Palm Trees"	239
Dilys Bennett Laing	Eros out of the Sea	239
John Ciardi	First Snow on an Airfield	240
Randall Jarrell	Losses	241
Gwendolyn Brooks	"Still Do I Keep My Look, My Identity . . ."	242
Alan Dugan	Aside	242
Dylan Thomas	Poem in October	243
Francis King	Séance	245

John Ciardi	Journal	246
Robert Francis	Part for the Whole	246
P. K. Page	Stories of Snow	247
Francis C. Golffing	The Higher Empiricism	249
Kenneth Koch	Poem for My Twentieth Birthday	249
James Merrill	From "THEORY OF VISION" The Green Eye	249
John Nerber	Castaway	250
Theodore Roethke	The Return	251
Robert Lowell	The Ghost	252
Ezra Pound	From CANTO LXXX "Oh to be in England now that Winston's out"	254
John Malcolm Brinnin	Angel Eye of Memory	256
Yvor Winters	Night of Battle	257
Leslie A. Fiedler	From "THOU SHALT SURELY DIE . . ." No Ghost Is True	258
Muriel Rukeyser	Motive	259
James Merrill	The Broken Bowl	259
Dannie Abse	Near the Border of Insanities	260
Francis Scarfe	The Grotto	261
Alan Dugan	Niagara Falls	262
Kenneth Koch	Schoolyard in April	262
Paul Goodman	"Dreams Are the Royal Road to the Unconscious"	263
Karl Shapiro	The Dirty Word	264
Robert Lowell	The Fat Man in the Mirror	264
e. e. cummings	"if(touched by love's own secret)we,like homing"	266
Margaret Avison	The Party	266

Wallace Stevens	The Ultimate Poem Is Abstract	267
Weldon Kees	Small Prayer	268
Robert Graves	Return of the Goddess Artemis	268
Richard Wilbur	The Death of a Toad	268
W. S. Merwin	Variation on the Gothic Spiral	269
John Berryman	The Traveler	270
William Carlos Williams	Lear	270
Ruthven Todd	Upon This Rock	271
Randall Jarrell	The Sleeping Beauty: Variation of the Prince	272
Elizabeth Daryush	The Look	273
David Wagoner	Marsh Leaf	274
Paul Goodman	Stanzas	275
Gwendolyn Brooks	The Children of the Poor	275
V. R. Lang	The Suicide	277
George Barker	Ode Against St. Cecilia's Day	277
William Gibson	Circe	278
Wallace Stevens	*From* THINGS OF AUGUST	
	1. "These locusts by day, these crickets by night"	279
	3. "High poetry and low"	279
	8. "When was it that the particles became"	280
Harvey Shapiro	Provincetown, Mass.	281
John Berryman	The Cage	282
Delmore Schwartz	The Self Unsatisfied Runs Everywhere	283
	The Heart Flies Up, Erratic as a Kite	283

Babette Deutsch	The Poem	284
Paul Goodman	Little Ode	285
Richard Wilbur	"A World Without Objects Is a Sensible Emptiness"	285
Anthony Hecht	Alceste in the Wilderness	286

PART V
1950–1960
(Volumes 77–96)

Henry Rago	The Monster	291
Robinson Jeffers	The Beauty of Things	291
Anne Ridler	On a Picture by Michele Da Verona, of Arion as a Boy Riding upon a Dolphin	292
John Frederick Nims	Conclusion	292
Roy Marz	Vittoria Colonna	293
James Merrill	Hotel de l'Univers et Portugal	294
Robert Graves	The Foreboding	295
Muriel Rukeyser	The Place at Alert Bay	296
Kathy McLaughlin	Suicide Pond	297
Kathleen Raine	The Instrument	298
Parker Tyler	Nijinsky	298
William Burford	On the Apparition of Oneself	299
W. H. Auden	The Shield of Achilles	299
Louise Bogan	After the Persian	301
Marianne Moore	Then the Ermine:	303
J. V. Cunningham	Epigram	304
Patrick Anderson	Sestina in Time of Winter	304
William Jay Smith	Nightwood	305
Robert Graves	From the Embassy	306
Kenneth Pitchford	Lobotomy	306

Alan Dugan	Prison Song	307
George Barker	*From* SONNETS OF THE TRIPLE-HEADED MANICHEE	
	II. "Keelhauled across the star-wrecked death of God"	307
E. L. Mayo	The Word of Water	308
Richard Wilbur	Marginalia	308
Karl Shapiro	The Alphabet	309
Chester Kallman	A Romance	310
Joseph Warren Beach	Horatian Ode	310
Melvin Walker La Follette	Didactic Sonnet	311
W. S. Merwin	The Sapphire	311
Robert Francis	Cold	312
Randall Jarrell	Aging	313
Frank O'Hara	Chez Jane	313
Fairfield Porter	The Island in the Evening	314
Kenneth Patchen	O Now the Drenched Land Wakes	315
Norman MacCaig	Beach Talk	316
Thom Gunn	High Fidelity	317
Turner Cassity	Chronology	317
Edith Sitwell	Elegy for Dylan Thomas	318
David Jones	The Wall	320
Dylan Thomas	Out of a War of Wits	326
John Ashbery	Grand Abacus	327
Richard Howard	Landed: A Valentine	327
Stanley Kunitz	Goose Pond	328
Frank O'Hara	Radio	329
Galway Kinnell	Braemar	330
Sidney Goodsir Smith	Cokkils	330
Kenneth Koch	Permanently	331
Constance Urdang	Birth of Venus	332
Ruth Stone	Private Pantomime	332

Sylvia Plath — Metamorphosis — 333

Witter Bynner — *From* INSCRIPTIONS ON
CHINESE PAINTINGS
I. Lines to Do With
Youth — 333

Jay Macpherson — *From* THE ARK
Ark to Noah — 335
Ark Articulate — 335
Ark Astonished — 336

Robert Fitzgerald — Metaphysical — 336
Tom Scott — The Real Muse — 337
John Ashbery — To Redouté — 338
W. S. Merwin — The Highway — 339
Stanley Kunitz — The Approach to Thebes — 339
Thom Gunn — The Unsettled
Motorcyclist's Vision
of His Death — 340

Howard Moss — *From* KING MIDAS
The King's Speech — 342

Geoffrey Hill — Wreaths — 343
Robert Duncan — A Morning Letter — 344
Howard Nemerov — Holding the Mirror Up to
Nature — 345

Gil Orlovitz — Art of the Sonnet: LVI — 346
H. D. — In Time of Gold — 346
Margaret Avison — Stray Dog, Near Ecully — 347
William Stafford — Shepherd — 347
Vernon Watkins — Demands of the Muse — 348
Donald Hall — T. R. — 349
Denise Levertov — To the Snake — 350
W. S. Graham — The Constructed Space — 350
Frederick Bock — Aubade: The Desert — 351
Richard Hugo — Skykomish River Running — 352
A. R. Ammons — Close-Up — 353
Delmore Schwartz — *From* THE KINGDOM OF
POETRY
Swift — 354

Josephine Miles	Dream	356
T. Weiss	The Fire at Alexandria	356
John Logan	Lines for a Young Wanderer in Mexico	358
William Dickey	Teaching Swift to Young Ladies	359
James Dickey	The Landfall	359
Sylvia Plath	The Death of Myth-Making	361
Gwendolyn Brooks	*From* THE BEAN EATERS We Real Cool	362
Richard Eberhart	The Spider	362
Robert Duncan	Returning to Roots of First Feeling	363
Carl Sandburg	Alice Corbin Is Gone	364
X. J. Kennedy	Nude Descending a Staircase	364
Robert Creeley	Song	365
Frank O'Hara	In Favor of One's Time	366
James Merrill	Angel	366
William Stafford	After Plotinus	367

PART VI
1960–1970
(Volumes 97–116)

George Oppen	Population	371
A. R. Ammons	Gravelly Run	371
James Dickey	Inside the River	372
Philip Levine	*From* SIERRA KID He Faces the Second Winter	374
Carolyn Kizer	To a Visiting Poet in a College Dormitory	374
e. e. cummings	"how many moments must(amazing each"	375

Denise Levertov   The Illustration — A
                           Footnote   376
Horace Gregory   On a Celtic Mask by
                           Henry Moore   377
Richmond Lattimore   Remorse   377
Robert Mezey   Vetus Flamma   378
John Hollander   For the Passing of
                           Groucho's Pursuer   378
David Daiches   Notes for a History of
                           Poetry   379
Donald Justice   Poem ("Time and the
                           weather wear away")   380
Howard Nemerov   The Dragonfly   380
Edgar Bowers   The Astronomers of Mont
                           Blanc   381
James Dickey   After the Night Hunt   381
Turner Cassity   Technique on the Firing
                           Line   383
Sylvia Plath   Stars over the Dordogne   383
Philip Levine   The Reply   384
Anne Sexton   The Black Art   385
John Ciardi   Death's the Classic Look   386
Alan Dugan   From Heraclitus   387
Robert Duncan   After a Passage in
                           Baudelaire   387
William Meredith   Iambic Feet Considered as
                           Honorable Scars   389
James Merrill   The Mad Scene   389
John Ashbery   If the Birds Knew   390
Donald Davie   Autumn Imagined   391
John Berryman   From NINE DREAM SONGS
                           Snow Line   391
J. V. Cunningham   Miramar Beach   392
Ted Hughes   After Lorca   392
David Wagoner   The Words   393
Mac Hammond   In Memory of V. R. Lang   394

Philip Booth	Seeing Auden Off	394
Turner Cassity	The Gardens of Proserpine	395
Stevie Smith	Here Lies . . .	396
LeRoi Jones	Like Rousseau	396
Donald Justice	About My Poems	396
Donald Finkel	Metaphysic of Snow	397
Hayden Carruth	From CONTRA MORTEM	
	The Being	398
	The Little Death	398
	The Coming of Snow	399
	The Water	399
	The Leaves	400
	The Woman's Genitals	400
Anne Sexton	The Wedding Night	401
Gary Snyder	From THROUGH THE SMOKE HOLE	
	I. "There is another world above this one; or outside of this one"	402
Mona Van Duyn	"The Wish to Be Believed"	403
Charles Tomlinson	The Door	404
Barry Spacks	October	405
John Hollander	Swan and Shadow	406
Richard Howard	Secular Games	406
William Stafford	Priest Lake	408
W. S. Graham	The Beast in the Space	408
Michael Benedikt	Fraudulent Days	409
Robert Bly	Hurrying Away from the Earth	410
W. S. Merwin	Divinities	410
Karl Shapiro	From WHITE-HAIRED LOVER	
	"I swore to stab the sonnet with my pen"	411

Winfield Townley Scott	Uses of Poetry	411
Mark Van Doren	Slowly, Slowly Wisdom Gathers	412
Vernon Watkins	Cwmrhydyceirw Elegiacs	413
Charles Tomlinson	The Chances of Rhyme	413
William Heyen	The King's Men	414
Jim Carroll	The Distances	415
Maxine Kumin	The Masochist	417
Mona Van Duyn	Open Letter from a Constant Reader	417
James Dickey	Venom	418
A. D. Hope	The School of Night	419
Richard Howard	Aubade: Donna Anna to Juan, Still Asleep	420
Tom Clark	The Greeks	422
Michael Heffernan	The Table	422
John Koethe	Mission Bay	423
May Swenson	Fire Island	423
Denise Levertov	Invocation	424
Gilbert Sorrentino	Handbook of Versification	425
Chester Kallman	Dead Center	425
Dennis Trudell	Hotel in Paris	425
A. R. Ammons	Transaction	426
Stephen Dobyns	Counterparts	427
Jean Malley	Untitled	428
Marvin Bell	The Music of the Spheres	428
Thom Gunn	The Messenger	429
Michael Mott	Islanders, Inlanders	430
W. S. Merwin	Sunset after Rain	430
Wendell Berry	September 2	430
Mark McCloskey	Too Dark	431
Frank O'Hara	Homosexuality	431
Calvin Forbes	Gabriel's Blues	432
F. D. Reeve	Hope	433
Mark Strand	Black Maps	433
Charles Wright	Nightletter	435

PART VII
1970–1977
(Volumes 117–131)

A. R. Ammons	Play	439
David Lehman	For David Shapiro	439
Phoebe Pettingell	Ode on Zero	440
Andrew Hoyem	Circumambulation of Mt. Tamalpais	441
Thomas James	Reasons	441
Jon Anderson	In Sepia	442
James Merrill	The Black Mesa	443
Robert Bly	After Long Busyness	444
Louise Glück	The Magi	444
Katherine Hoskins	Baucis and Philemon	445
George Johnston	Indoors	445
John Glassco	For Cora Lightbody, R.N.	446
Erica Jong	Climbing You	447
David Wagoner	Lost	448
John Hollander	Hall of Ocean Life	448
Andrew Oerke	The Sun	449
W. H. Auden	Ode to the Medieval Poets	450
John Betjeman	Crematorium	451
Greg Kuzma	Poetry	451
Michael Newman	Negative Passage	452
Tom Disch	The Vowels of Another Language	452
Robert Siegel	Ego	453
Timothy Steele	Wait	454
Daisy Aldan	Stones: Avesbury	454
Jack Anderson	A Garden of Situations	455
Lisel Mueller	Historical Museum, Manitoulin Island	456
James McMichael	Terce	457
Kathleen Spivack	Dido: Swarming	458
David Wagoner	Muse	459

Hugh Seidman	N	459
Charles Wright	Negatives	460
Howard Nemerov	To D —, Dead by Her Own Hand	461
William Dickey	The Poet's Farewell to His Teeth	461
A. D. Hope	Parabola	462
James McAuley	Winter Drive	464
May Swenson	July 4th	464
Richard Eberhart	Plain Song Talk	465
Stephen Berg	Don't Forget	465
Sandra McPherson	Seaweeds	466
David Shapiro	About This Course	467
Geoffrey Grigson	Burial	467
Charles Martin	Leaving Buffalo	468
James Schuyler	Poem ("This beauty that I see")	469
Michael Magee	It Is the Stars That Govern Us	470
Ruth Fainlight	Fire-Queen	471
Brewster Ghiselin	Credo	472
Mark Jarman	The Desire of Water	472
Suzanne Noguere	Pervigilium Veneris	473
John Hollander	Breadth. Circle. Desert. Monarch. Month. Wisdom.	473
Horace Gregory	Death & Empedocles 444 B.C.	475
Thomas Cole	Spider	476
Stephen Sandy	Declension	476
David Ignatow	In a Dream	477
John Frederick Nims	Clock Without Hands	478
Richard Hugo	Last Days	478

Richard Howard	*From* COMPULSIVE QUALIFICATIONS	
	I. "Richard, May I Ask A Question? What Is An Episteme?"	479
	II. "Richard, What Do You Mean When You Say You're Writing Two-Part Inventions?"	479
	III. "Richard, May I Ask You Something? Is Poetry Involved With Evil?"	480
	XIII. "Richard, What Will It Be Like When *You* Ask The Questions?"	480
Sandra McPherson	Page	481
Stewart Lindh	Settler	482
Sandra M. Gilbert	The Fog Dream	482
Marya Zaturenska	Bird and the Muse	483
Jay Macpherson	*From* THE WAY DOWN They Return	484
Marilyn Hacker	Under the Arc de Triomphe: October 17	485
H. B. Mallalieu	Empedocles on Etna	485
David Bromwich	Wandsworth Common	486
John Ashbery	A Man of Words	487
David Wagoner	Elegy for Yards, Pounds, and Gallons	488
Robert Chatain	World of Darkness	489

Margaret Atwood | From SONGS OF THE TRANSFORMED

Siren Song — 490

Daryl Hine | Vowel Movements — 491
David Galler | Narcissus: To Himself — 495
Judith Minty | Look to the Back of the Hand — 496

David Mus | From THE JOY OF COOKING

Conserves — 496

Jack Anderson | Ode to Pornography — 497
Dannie Abse | Angels — 498
David Schloss | The Poem — 499
John N. Morris | The Mirror — 499
William Stafford | The Day You Are Reading This — 500

Gjertrud Schnackenberg | Signs — 500
Tom Disch | Homage to the Carracci — 501
J. D. McClatchy | The Pleasure of Ruins — 501
Charles Gullans | Satyr — 502
Jayanta Mahapatra | A Rain of Rites — 503
Jane Shore | An Astronomer's Journal — 504
Robert Pinsky | From ESSAY ON PSYCHIATRISTS

XIV. Their Speech, Compared with Wisdom and Poetry — 504

James Applewhite | Bordering Manuscript — 505
Peter Schjeldahl | A Younger Poet — 506
Charles O. Hartman | Inflation — 507
David Smith | Dome Poem — 507
Sandra McPherson | Sentience — 509
Howard Nemerov | Waiting Rooms — 509
Robin Fulton | The Waiting-Room — 510
Ben Howard | Winter Report — 511
Judith Moffett | Diehard — 512
Alfred Corn | Deception — 512

James Schuyler	"Can I Tempt You to a Pond Walk?"	513
David Bromwich	From the Righteous Man Even the Wild Beasts Run Away	514
Greg Kuzma	The Dump	515
Rika Lesser	Translation	516
Ezra Pound	Fragmenti	517
James Applewhite	To Earth	517
John Ashbery	The Ice-Cream Wars	518
Frank O'Hara	Princess Elizabeth of Bohemia, as Perdita	519
Diane Wakoski	The Ring	520
David Wagoner	The Death of the Moon	521
Philip Levine	Here and Now	521
Judith Moffett	Twinings Orange Pekoe	523
Sandra M. Gilbert	Elegy	524

LIST OF THE EDITORS • 527
CREDITS • 529
INDEX • 545

INTRODUCTION

In the history of periodicals, the position of *Poetry* is unique. Alone among literary magazines at the time of its founding in 1912 in devoting its pages exclusively to the publication and criticism of new verse, and still without serious rival, though it has had many imitators, it offers an uninterrupted monthly record of the poetic achievement, as well as some of the vagaries, fads, fashions and failures, of the last sixty-five years. It has stood, signally open to all movements and to every new voice, at the seldom still center of modern verse, reflecting, like a mirror or a stream, the temper of each period as infallibly as the taste of each successive editor. The following selection serially represents, in a résumé necessarily much abbreviated, some if not all of the splendors, and perhaps a few of the miseries, of *Poetry*'s remarkable career.

The inception of that career was not propitious. *Poetry*'s founding editor, Harriet Monroe, who continued to direct the magazine until her death in 1936, was at the time of the first issue a strong-minded literary spinster of fifty-two, virtually unknown outside her native Chicago, for which she had written years earlier a "Cantata" on the occasion of the dedication of Louis Sullivan's Auditorium Theater:

> Hail to thee, fair Chicago! On thy brow
>   America, thy mother, lays a crown.
> Bravest among her daughters brave art thou,
>   Most strong of all her heirs of high renown . . .

But this anachronistic celebrant of the public virtues, whose "Columbian Ode" had been sung by a choir of five thousand at the Exposition of 1892 was also a world traveler. She would die, alone, in the Andes, returning from a P.E.N. Congress in Buenos Aires. And it was on the Trans-Siberian Railway in 1910 that she conceived, if not the idea of *Poetry,* some notion of the need for "a magazine of verse," for she too saw that poetry was unique among the arts, and invidiously so, a sort of Cinderella. While the other arts all had audiences of sufficient size to provide a market and the possibility of patronage, serious poetry had none.

When Harriet Monroe set about trying to rectify this situation by founding a forum for poets, she confronted a further need, for literary and financial support. She sought two sorts of contributors, those of verse and those of cash.

The former she found through the public library and her wide reading of contemporary verse. She sent manifestoes and invitations to submit new work to all the living poets she could discover in print, few of whom then resided in Chicago or were known to her personally. The response was, if not overwhelming, encouraging. Poets in 1912, as they would now, agreed with her expressed need for a purely poetic showplace, a periodical devoted to their art only, where they need not appear, as they did in the infrequent instances when they appeared in periodical print at all, sandwiched between short stories, social criticism, and irrelevant advertisements — as poetry still appears in general magazines of wider circulation. The known, and even more generously, the unknown, sent their poems in response to Harriet Monroe's appeal — just as, unsolicited, they send them today. It is one of the permanent ironies, and delights, of literary-historical perspective that among these first contributors it is the known, even the celebrated, of those days who utterly fail to awaken recognition now; whereas many of the then unknown names of *Poetry*'s early issues are now the major reputations of modern literature and the glories of this anthology.

But lofty enterprises require equally altruistic support. *Poetry* has never quite been self-supporting, though the goal of financial independence, while never paramount, has not quite ceased to flicker like an *ignis fatuus* before the eyes of its anxious editors. Except for an occasional grant from a cultural foundation, the necessary assistance has come from private patrons, principally local ones. Frequent appeals during the magazine's long and prestigious career have been necessary to save it from extinction; it may be imagined how much more persuasive those which brought it into being had to be. *Poetry* began with a hundred guarantors, each committed to contributing fifty dollars a year for five years. These were solicited from among the moneyed class of Chicago by Harriet Monroe — who, though not wealthy herself, belonged by birth to that class — in persistent person, with a success her successors must envy. In addition, she had an advisory committee, whose advice was more valued in the planning of the magazine than in its direction. These were, at first, H. C. Chatfield-Taylor, a cultivated philanthropist who proposed the financial scheme for launching the magazine; Edith Wyatt, a poet; and Henry Blake Fuller, a novelist. It was a period of triple names, as is shown by many contributors to this and other magazines of the decade, and by some of Harriet Monroe's associates. Alice Corbin Henderson, whom Harriet Monroe regarded, with reason, as the most acute poetic and critical intelligence in Chicago — at the time when Chicago glowed with a brief literary luster never equaled since — played an incalculable role at the editor's right hand from the beginning, and even after her retirement to New Mexico in 1916. In later years, often while Harriet Monroe was away — the burdens of editorship and the constant care of fund raising had not caused her to forego globetrotting — some of the responsibilities of the magazine were assumed by, among others, Eunice Tietjens, Jessica Nelson North, Geraldine Udell, George Dillon, and Morton Dauwen Zabel, the last two of whom were to become editors in turn. In its happiest periods, *Poetry,* like heaven, has been a monarchy, albeit often a constitutional one; at its least distinguished it has sunk, if not to a democracy (in which Harriet Monroe, for one, had a passionate if paradoxical belief), then an oligarchy, and its contents sometimes exhibit the telltale traces of compilation by committee.

If *Poetry*'s financial horizons have been bounded, for the most part, by Chicago, its literary ones eminently have not. From the beginning, the scope of the magazine has been broad enough to include what became virtually the whole spectrum of modern verse. In the face of initial, often adverse, criticism by the literary establishment of the day, Harriet Monroe's magazine pioneered and persisted in printing those radical and experimental writers who were to create the new literature. There is no contemporary figure of any importance who did not publish in *Poetry*; and many who first appeared in these pages are responsible for forming, or reforming, the taste of our time.

One whose name figures, briefly, on the masthead during these early years and whose influence on *Poetry,* as on modern poetry in general, has been exaggerated out of proportion to the depth and duration of his association with it, is Ezra Pound. The Idaho iconoclast, then relocated in London, where he proclaimed himself in touch with "whatever is most dynamic in artistic thought, either here or in Paris," responded enthusiastically to Harriet Monroe's original appeal for contributors, and saw in the young magazine a vehicle for his ambitions and theories, despite his distaste for its Whitmanesque motto, "To have great poets there must be great audiences too." Not only was the new publication to be devoted to new verse (and Pound intended to see that it was *the* new verse); it paid. With an openness that may have looked deceptively like weakness, Harriet Monroe accepted the verse he sent her, not only his own, but that of Yeats, Tagore, Frost, Eliot, H. D., Richard Aldington, and Skipwith Cannell, along with Pound's offers of collaboration. He was styled Foreign Editor and, in an intermittent stream of hectoring letters, fought under this exotic banner to keep *Poetry* from becoming the provincial journal he feared it would degenerate into without his unceasing if distant vigilance. But in fact there was nothing weak, or provincial, about Harriet Monroe. Her taste, if, like all genuine taste, idiosyncratic, was both catholic and sure, as she stated in a declaration of editorial intent in the first volume:

> The Open Door will be the policy of this magazine — may the great poet we are looking for never find it shut, or half-shut, against his ample genius! To this end the editors hope to keep free of entangling alliances

> with any single class or school. They desire to print the best English verse which is being written today, regardless of where, by whom, or under what theory of art it is written. Nor will the magazine promise to limit its editorial comments to one set of opinions . . .

Apart from some of the new and outlandish poets Pound imported and imposed — and Harriet Monroe's resistance to Frost and "Prufrock" has been exaggerated by their promoter for his own purposes — his influence, which Harriet Monroe knew well how and when to resist, was manifested chiefly and historically in his puffing of something he liked to call Imagisme — and, later, Vorticism. The first term, which he was soon to repudiate as Amygism, once its principles had been appropriated, and distorted, by the equally ambitious Amy Lowell, had been invented to cover the work of a group of poets he had collected for an anthology: H. D., Aldington, F. S. Flint, James Joyce, Amy Lowell, and (of course) Pound himself. The precepts of this "movement" were enunciated, with typical clarity and arrogance, in the famous "A Few Don'ts by an Imagiste," a statement whose doctrinaire dogmatism seems as foreign to the proclaimed — and practiced — heterodox inclusiveness of *Poetry* as its essential principles are proper to all good writing. No one can read the mass of magazine verse of the time, including much of Harriet Monroe's and even Pound's, without feeling how much the corrective was needed. Unfortunately what seemed egregious and novel in the Imagiste program was not the laudable emphasis on clarity, precision, economy, and colloquialism, but the formal or informal implication of free verse, with which *Poetry* — fairly or unfairly — has been associated ever since. Many of the contributors to *Poetry,* including those introduced by Pound himself, wrote metered and sometimes rhymed verse; some still do. Yet the magazine is indelibly associated, by such formal conservatives as Robert Graves and A. D. Hope as well as the general poetry-reading public, with the cause of free verse, not a form at all but a sometimes studied absence of one which, perhaps because of the word "free," enjoys to this day a spurious, quasi-political glamour. It is instructive to look back to these early issues of

Poetry and see for how long the same conventions have been being defied, the same trammels cast off, the same molds smashed. How long can a revolution, particularly a revolution in taste, continue? How long can innovation remain new? We tend to forget how mutable a concept modernism is, how soon the self-consciously up-to-date begins to look old hat.

But modern verse, as we conceive it, was at the time of *Poetry*'s birth *in utero*. The temper of the age seemed inimical not merely to free verse but to all verse. Within a few years, largely thanks to *Poetry,* this was to change and the prevalent indifference to, and of, new poetry vanished before an indefinable but splendid phenomenon called a Poetry Renaissance.*
Among the new poets waiting to be discovered, who were introduced to a more appreciative, if not always larger, audience by *Poetry,* in addition to those unearthed by Pound, are several for whose discovery Harriet Monroe, and sometimes Alice Corbin Henderson, must be given credit. Notable are three popular, and populist, poets of the Middle West, Vachel Lindsay, Carl Sandburg, and Edgar Lee Masters; but also, and from our point of view more impressively, Marianne Moore, William Carlos Williams, and Wallace Stevens. In the following years, and throughout its sometimes threatened but still unbroken continuity of monthly publication, *Poetry* has continued to discover new poets who have in time become the dominant talents of their generation, as a glance at any of the numerous First Appearance issues of later years will show.

It was Alice Corbin Henderson who discovered, or rediscovered, Vachel Lindsay and Edgar Lee Masters. Harriet Monroe had misgivings about the former's "General William Booth Enters into Heaven," but was persuaded to publish it for its shock value and originality; the piece justified, at least in terms of publicity and popularity, this prudent maneuver. A laudatory review of Master's masterpiece *Spoon River Anthology* in 1915 by Alice Henderson introduced him to *Poetry*'s readers, and his work began to appear in the magazine immediately after. Carl Sandburg's *Chicago Poems,* appearing in Volume III (1914), like Lindsay's work caused a sensation at first unfavor-

* See Ellen Williams, *Harriet Monroe and the Poetry Renaissance* (Urbana: University of Illinois Press, 1977).

able, though they too would one day assume the status of classics, if not of clichés. Yet there seems to have been a feeling in the *Poetry* office that neither Lindsay nor Masters lived up to his early promise, and their later contributions were less enthusiastically accepted.

Marianne Moore also first appeared in *Poetry* — perhaps her first appearance anywhere — in 1915. But as a result of a critical symposium on her first book, *Poems*, in 1920, in which she was championed by Winifred Bryher and Yvor Winters and attacked by Pearl Andelson, who inscrutably compared her to Emily Dickinson, and by Harriet Monroe, who thus showed herself somewhat short of infallible, she did not publish here again until the Thirties.

Although *Poetry*, again, was the first American magazine to publish William Carlos Williams, and continued printing him in copious selections throughout his prolific career, his relations with *Poetry*'s editor, while friendly, were not unvexed. He resented her rejection of some of his work, for she knew how to pick and choose among the many manuscripts he sent her, and he balked at her practical criticism, and what he felt was her generally tepid tone even in acceptance. In his pique he was inclined to credit Pound with "hammering" his work into the magazine, over Harriet Monroe's objections. But there is no real evidence in this instance of the efficacy of Pound's influence, nor that Harriet Monroe was guided, in rejection or acceptance, by anything but her own independent judgment, however comforting it may have been to Williams to think otherwise.

It is clear, moreover, that even in the case of these important poets Harriet Monroe did not restrict her editorial activity to mere acceptance or rejection. She often suggested revisions in a given poem, and on occasion performed these revisions herself, to the annoyance of some poets but to the admitted improvement of many of the poems submitted to her. If her successors have proven less highhanded, it is not altogether clear that their tact has resulted in a more distinguished or interesting magazine.

But perhaps Harriet Monroe's greatest achievement as an editor, apart from having begun so soon and continued so long, is her discovery and patient, lonely encouragement of Wallace

Stevens. She tore apart in proof an issue of Volume V in 1914 — the Poems of War issue — to insert his "Phases," which she had picked out of a pile of unsolicited manuscripts. She published, the next year, her own rearranged and excised version of "Sunday Morning," showing that she had the great gift of admiring what she did not understand — a gift denied Pound, who detested Stevens — and she printed and prized his plays *Three Travellers Watch a Sunrise* and *Carlos Among the Candles.* Over the years she published him plentifully and often; and in her note on the group of poems by Stevens that opens Volume XIX and includes "Of Heaven Considered as a Tomb," Harriet Monroe regrets that he has not yet favored his readers, among whom she was certainly foremost, with a volume. She urged him to the publication of *Harmonium,* and at once favorably reviewed it. The Pounds of this world need no such exertions on their behalf, but it is for the Stevenses that editors such as Harriet Monroe perform a function for which we must be grateful.

Yet no magazine, however superior its aims or selective its policy, can avoid reflecting the general poetic temper of its period. Genius like that of Stevens or Marianne Moore must always seem exceptional to that temper, which is given temporary weight, and even appeal, by its novelty, or at least its currency. Much of what has appeared in *Poetry,* early and late, is mediocre, and seems more so today. Our inevitable myopia as participants in our own time limits our perspective with regard to the products of that time. It is easy to see how second-rate was the general level of literary achievement even in this, the most consistently and seriously excellent verse magazine of this century. It is impossible to be sure how the fresher splendors of our own day will fade or tarnish. Only knowledge of the historical modification of taste permits — no, forces — us to suspect that much of what we now admire will not seem so admirable in the future, while reputations marginal today, as Stevens's and Moore's seemed fifty years ago, may come to assume central importance.

The task of the anthologist, and what is more, the anthologist of *Poetry,* in this respect is difficult, and all the more so if one happens to have been an editor of the magazine, for to select an anthology of work much of which was produced long enough ago that its value seems certain is very different from selecting untried verse of whose merit he can and must be the sole judge. In both cases, of course, the object is to choose the best; but when the best has already been chosen, as it were, by time, the anthologist's only option is to determine how much of the best he should include. An anthology of this type — this anthology — cannot really be representative; certainly all the poems did appear in *Poetry* first, but so did much else that would be tedious to repeat in print. By the processes of condensation and selection, the consistent quality — the incidence of excellence — must naturally appear higher than it was. Yet whenever the richness of material allowed, an attempt has been made to present the context of the great, now famous poems that first appeared in *Poetry*. Many fine poems by authors not destined to what, prematurely, we call immortality also appeared here and still give pleasure; and it is these we have been most zealous to reprint, without apology or condescension, in an effort to provide a background to the giant reputations that grew in this nursery.

Prohibition would seem to have had its effect on *Poetry,* the contents of the years 1919 to 1932 are so dry, or, alternately, dilute. Most of the issue of December 1921 is devoted to an oratorio, "Resurgam," by an Evanston author, Louise Ayres Garnett. Harriet Monroe had the highest admiration for the work of Lew Sarett, who was born and brought up in Evanston, and joined the Advisory Board in 1922. She considered his "Box of Earth," which won *Poetry*'s Levinson Prize in 1921, superior to *The Waste Land,* published the same year in the *Dial.* Frost's "The Witch of Coos" strikes the contemporary reader as the only memorable, not to say readable, work besides Stevens's poems, in Volume XIX. The fledgling Yvor Winters at this time described Sandburg's later poetry as "a sort of plasmodial delerium," but Sandburg continued to be published in *Poetry.* So did a certain amount of "primitive" verse, cowboy ballads and Indian chants of varying degrees of inauthenticity. The Thirties saw the publication of Langston Hughes, Dudley Fitts, Ford Madox Ford (formerly Hueffer), Julian Huxley, C. Day Lewis, and Allen Tate, as well as a very curious review by Marianne Moore of *A Draft of XXX Cantos*. An Objectivist issue in 1931 was guest-edited by Louis Zukofsky.

After the unexpected and remote death in 1936 of Harriet Monroe, who had doubted, vocally and often, whether the magazine could continue under any direction but her own, *Poetry* was edited for one year only by the critic Morton Dauwen Zabel, who was responsible for a remarkable British issue edited by W. H. Auden and Michael Roberts. After that, except for service in the Second World War, George Dillon remained as editor, sometimes single-handed, sometimes with varying combinations of others on the editorial board, until his resignation in 1949. This is a dark and vexed period, for the historian as well as for the anthologist, and the only time at which *Poetry* has not borne the imprint of one absolute and responsible editor and of one man's or woman's taste. Some of Dillon's associates, who occasionally replaced him on the masthead, included figures not always associated with Chicago, or with poetry: Thornton Wilder, S. I. Hayakawa, and Peter De Vries. Despite some extraordinary issues, such as the British one just mentioned and St.-John Perse's introductory appearance with *Exil* in 1941, the general literary picture of *Poetry* at this period is not distinguished. Whole volumes, such as LXV (1944) offer little one could really want to read now. Chicago writers, such as Helen Carus, Marion Castleman, Marie Boroff, Jeremy Ingalls, Paul B. Newman, and Ellen Borden Stevenson — also a trustee of the magazine — abound: not even Nelson Algren's "Man with the Golden Arm" can dispell the gloom. At the same time *Poetry* remained a mirror, if not always a bright one, for the wider literature of the period, publishing, among the better known names, Dannie Abse, Elizabeth Bishop, John Malcolm Brinnin, John Ciardi, Oliver St. John Gogarty, Leslie Fiedler, John Howard Griffin, William Meredith, Nicolas Moore, George Barker, Henry Treece, Horace Gregory, and Marya Zaturenska. There was a special issue on postwar Romanticism in England, and a Canadian issue edited by E. K. Brown. Canadians figure in other issues and among the recipients of *Poetry*'s annual prizes: P. K. Page, A. M. Klein, F. R. Scott, and — a temporary Canadian — Patrick Anderson. *Poetry* continued to fulfill an essentially catholic and passive role.

George Dillon himself nursed a desire to "express the new and exciting life, the dynamic aspects of the city in writing" — an ambition that reminds us of Harriet Monroe at her most self-conciously modern, as well as of Theodore Dreiser and Ben Hecht; but his romantic and lyric gift could not cope with such material.

George Dillon was succeeded as editor by a young man who had been working in the office, Hayden Carruth, who in less than a year deleted *Poetry*'s explanatory subtitle, *A Magazine of Verse,* and, as if to prove his point, inverted the ancient practice of the magazine by publishing less verse than prose, until one issue, early in 1950, contained virtually no poetry at all. But this was a boom period for criticism: a critical supplement had been felt necessary in the late Forties, and *Poetry* had published a separate pamphlet, *A Guide to the New Criticism,* by William Elton. A second and final separate pamphlet was published by Carruth, a reply to the *Saturday Review* on the problem of awarding the Bollingen Prize to Ezra Pound — a controversy that still arouses strong feelings. Carruth's tenure was even briefer than that of Zabel, and no one figures on the masthead as editor until Karl Shapiro consented to fill that role in March 1950.

Karl Shapiro's standards were high and international in scope. *Poetry* has always been unusual among American magazines in its willingness to print foreign, or at least French, texts; though none of these has been reprinted in this anthology, whose province is not only the history of *Poetry* but, to an extent, of modern poetry in English as reflected in *Poetry*. In addition to more St.-John Perse, "O Vous Mers," and essays on modern Italian literature, Shapiro devoted an issue in 1951 to what he regarded as a new and promising phenomenon, the writing workshop — Paul Engle's at Iowa and Theodore Roethke's in Seattle. In general, Karl Shapiro had exactly those qualities of energy and taste, the broad view and the rigorous standards, that make for an excellent editor. His years, from 1950 to 1955, are very distinguished ones for *Poetry,* perhaps the richest since the *anni mirabiles* of the mid-Teens. The yearly awards, as always, provide an interesting index to what was being printed and prized in this period, and those of 1951 are still for the most part green laurels: Theodore Roethke, Randall Jarrell, Robinson Jeffers, James Merrill, Horace Gregory, M. B. Tolson. The prize list ten years later, in the middle of Henry Rago's editorship, contains no Chicago, and few American, names: Charles Tomlinson, A. Alvarez, David Jones, Kathleen Raine, Karl Shapiro, Robert Lowell, X. J. Kennedy, and Belle Randall.

Henry Rago succeeded Karl Shapiro in 1955; his tenure, until his death in 1969, is second in duration only to Harriet Monroe's. *Poetry* during these nearly fifteen years fulfilled a dictum of St.-John Perse that had appeared on the cover earlier in the Fifties, and defined a literary review as a river, faithfully mirroring the landscape that bordered it and following the current and trend of the times. Yet the catholicism of Rago's taste did not prevent his exhibiting certain predilections. He seems, from the space he gave certain fashionable poets both in the magazine and on its movie-marquee-like cover, to have picked favorites, on whom he was betting to win, place, or show. It is perhaps surprising, in view of Rago's sensitivity to the contemporary climate, that he printed little — if any — of the writings of the Beats. A lifelong attachment to Chicago did not diminish his attraction to the exotic, as evidenced in his publication of many British and French poets — a whole issue featuring Yves Bonnefoy, as well as frequent appearances by René Char — and the various guest-edited foreign issues, among them the Israeli, Greek, Japanese, and Indian. However, there are few surprises in these years. It is as if the magazine had been content to record and reflect taste rather than create or impose it.

The present editor, who, by the time this survey appears, will be the past editor, feels that the time is premature, nor is he the person, to categorize the years from 1969 to the present. Undoubtedly a change will be apparent, though it may be blurred by the very process of selection for the anthology — so different, in practice, from that of editing a monthly magazine — at the same time that an essential continuity has been preserved. There has been a bend in the stream; its flow however is uninterrupted. *Poetry*'s unique position has always made it controversial. With *Poetry,* as in Wilde's epigram about Society, it is those who cannot get in it who criticize most. Certain names, familiar and frequent here before, have figured less prominently or disappeared altogether; they have been replaced by others, at first less well known, but some of whom in less than a decade are already becoming celebrated. A rare and perhaps rash excursion into public affairs is reflected in the Vietnam War issue of September 1970, the overwhelmingly positive response to which was marred by some dissenting voices. A less controversial political gesture underlies the issue devoted to underground Soviet poetry in 1974. In addition to various issues given over to single long works, or the work of a single poet, there have been two issues of verse translation, from various tongues by various hands. But one basic principle has guided editorial judgment, in the preparation of this anthology as in that of the latest years of *Poetry:* a regard not for trends or reputations but for verse alone. We have sought — as Harriet Monroe sought at the magazine's outset — to find and print the best work available without regard to what theory it may illustrate or by whom it was written. *Poetry* publishes not poets but poems; this surely is what a magazine, or anthology, of verse exists to do.

DARYL HINE

PART I

1912–1920
(Volumes 1–16)

TO WHISTLER, AMERICAN

On the loan exhibit of his paintings at the Tate Gallery.

You also, our first great,
Had tried all ways;
Tested and pried and worked in many fashions,
And this much gives me heart to play the game.

Here is a part that's slight, and part gone wrong,
And much of little moment, and some few
Perfect as Dürer!

"In the Studio" and these two portraits,* if I had my choice!
And then these sketches in the mood of Greece?

You had your searches, your uncertainties,
And this is good to know — for us, I mean,
Who bear the brunt of our America
And try to wrench her impulse into art.

You were not always sure, not always set
To hiding night or tuning "symphonies";
Had not one style from birth, but tried and pried
And stretched and tampered with the media.

You and Abe Lincoln from that mass of dolts
Show us there's chance at least of winning through.

EZRA POUND

* "Brown and Gold — de Race."
   "Grenat et Or — Le Petit Cardinal."

FALLEN MAJESTY

Although crowds gathered once if she but showed her face
And even old men's eyes grew dim, this hand alone,
Like some last courtier at a gipsy camping place
Babbling of fallen majesty, records what's gone.
The lineaments, the heart that laughter has made sweet,
These, these remain, but I record what's gone. A crowd
Will gather and not know that through its very street
Once walked a thing that seemed, as it were, a burning cloud.

WILLIAM BUTLER YEATS

GENERAL WILLIAM BOOTH ENTERS INTO HEAVEN

(To be sung to the tune of "The Blood of the Lamb" *with indicated instruments.)*

Booth led boldly with his big bass drum.
    Are you washed in the blood of the Lamb?
The saints smiled gravely, and they said, "He's come."
    Are you washed in the blood of the Lamb?
Bass drums   Walking lepers followed, rank on rank,
Lurching bravos from the ditches dank,
Drabs from the alleyways and drug-fiends pale —
Minds still passion-ridden, soul-powers frail!
Vermin-eaten saints with mouldy breath,
Unwashed legions with the ways of death —
    Are you washed in the blood of the Lamb?

Every slum had sent its half-a-score
The round world over — Booth had groaned for more.
Every banner that the wide world flies
Bloomed with glory and transcendent dyes.
Banjo   Big-voiced lasses made their banjos bang!
Tranced, fanatical, they shrieked and sang,
    Are you washed in the blood of the Lamb?

Hallelujah! It was queer to see
Bull-necked convicts with that land make free!
Loons with bazoos blowing blare, blare, blare —
On, on, upward through the golden air.
Are you washed in the blood of the Lamb?

Booth died blind, and still by faith he trod,
Eyes still dazzled by the ways of God.
Booth led boldly and he looked the chief: Bass drums
Eagle countenance in sharp relief,   slower and
Beard a-flying, air of high command   softer
Unabated in that holy land.

Jesus came from out the Court-House door,
Stretched his hands above the passing poor.
Booth saw not, but led his queer ones there   Flutes
Round and round the mighty Court-House square.
Yet in an instant all that blear review
Marched on spotless, clad in raiment new.
The lame were straightened, withered limbs uncurled
And blind eyes opened on a new sweet world.

Drabs and vixens in a flash made whole!   Bass drums
Gone was the weasel-head, the snout, the jowl; louder and
Sages and sibyls now, and athletes clean,   faster
Rulers of empires, and of forests green!

The hosts were sandalled and their wings were fire —
Are you washed in the blood of the Lamb?
But their noise played havoc with the angel-choir.   Grand
Are you washed in the blood of the Lamb?   chorus —
Oh, shout Salvation! it was good to see   tambourines —
Kings and princes by the Lamb set free.   all
The banjos rattled, and the tambourines   instruments
Jing-jing-jingled in the hands of queens!   in full blast

And when Booth halted by the curb for prayer   Reverently
He saw his Master through the flag-filled air. sung — no
Christ came gently with a robe and crown   instruments

5

For Booth the soldier while the throng knelt down.
He saw King Jesus — they were face to face,
And he knelt a-weeping in that holy place.
     Are you washed in the blood of the Lamb?

NICHOLAS VACHEL LINDSAY

EPIGRAM

(After the Greek)

The golden one is gone from the banquets;
She, beloved of Atimetus,
The swallow, the bright Homonoea:
Gone the dear chatterer;
Death succeeds Atimetus.

H. D.,
"Imagiste."

GRIEVE NOT FOR BEAUTY

Grieve not for the invisible, transported brow
On which like leaves the dark hair grew,
Nor for the lips of laughter that are now
Laughing inaudibly in sun and dew,
Nor for those limbs that, fallen low
And seeming faint and slow,
Shall yet pursue
More ways of swiftness than the swallow dips
Among . . . and find more winds than ever blew
The straining sails of unimpeded ships!
Mourn not! — yield only happy tears
To deeper beauty than appears!

WITTER BYNNER

From CONTEMPORANIA

TENZONE

Will people accept them?
          (i.e. these songs).
As a timorous wench from a centaur
        (or a centurian),
Already they flee, howling in terror.
Will they be touched with the truth?
        Their virgin stupidity is untemptable.
I beg you, my friendly critics,
Do not set about to procure me an audience.

I mate with my free kind upon the crags;
        the hidden recesses
Have heard the echo of my heels.
        in the cool light,
        in the darkness.

              EZRA POUND

TO MY FRIEND

When from the blossoms of the noiseful day,
Unto the hive of sleep and hushèd gloom,
Throng the dim-wingèd dreams, what dreams are they
That with the wildest honey hover home?
O they that have, from many thousand thoughts,
Stolen the strange sweet of ever blossomy you —
A thousand fancies in fair-coloured knots
Which you are inexhausted meadow to.

Ah, what sharp heathery honey, quick with pain,
Do they bring home! It holds the night awake
To hear their lovely murmur in my brain,
And sleep's wings have a trouble for your sake.
Day and you dawn together; for, at end,
With the first light breaks the first thought — my Friend.

          FRANCIS THOMPSON

From LUSTRA

I

O helpless few in my country,
O remnant enslaved!

Artists broken against her,
A-stray, lost in the villages,
Mistrusted, spoken-against,

Lovers of beauty, starved,
Thwarted with systems,
Helpless against the control;

You who can not wear yourselves out
By persisting to successes,
You who can only speak,
Who can not steel yourselves into reiteration;

You of the finer sense,
Broken against false knowledge,
You who can know at first hand,
Hated, shut in, mistrusted:

Take thought.
I have weathered the storm,
I have beaten out my exile.

III FURTHER INSTRUCTIONS

Come, my songs, let us express our baser passions.
Let us express our envy for the man with a steady job and no
worry about the future.

You are very idle, my songs,
I fear you will come to a bad end.

You stand about the streets. You loiter at the corners and
    bus-stops,
You do next to nothing at all.
You do not even express our inner nobility,
You will come to a very bad end.

And I? I have gone half cracked.
I have talked to you so much
    that I almost see you about me,
Insolent little beasts! Shameless! Devoid of clothing!

But you, newest song of the lot,
You are not old enough to have done much mischief.
I will get you a green coat out of China
With dragons worked upon it.
I will get you the scarlet silk trousers
From the statue of the infant Christ at Santa Maria Novella;

Lest they say we are lacking in taste,
Or that there is no caste in this family.

                                    EZRA POUND

GREEN

    The dawn was apple-green,
    The sky was green wine held up in the sun,
    The moon was a golden petal between.

    She opened her eyes, and green
    They shone, clear like flowers undone,
    For the first time, now for the first time seen.

                        D. H. LAWRENCE

ILLICIT

In front of the sombre mountains, a faint, lost ribbon of
    rainbow,
And between us and it, the thunder;
And down below, in the green wheat, the laborers
Stand like dark stumps, still in the green wheat.

You are near to me, and your naked feet in their sandals,
And through the scent of the balcony's naked timber
I distinguish the scent of your hair; so now the limber
Lightning falls from heaven.

Adown the pale-green, glacier-river floats
A dark boat through the gloom — and whither?
The thunder roars. But still we have each other.
The naked lightnings in the heavens dither
And disappear. What have we but each other?
The boat has gone.

D. H. LAWRENCE

THE CODE — HEROICS

There were three in the meadow by the brook,
Gathering up windrows, piling haycocks up,
With an eye always lifted toward the west,
Where an irregular, sun-bordered cloud
Darkly advanced with a perpetual dagger
Flickering across its bosom. Suddenly
One helper, thrusting pitchfork in the ground,
Marched himself off the field and home. One stayed.
The town-bred farmer failed to understand.

What was there wrong?
                    Something you said just now.
What did I say?
                    About our taking pains.

To cock the hay? — because it's going to shower?
I said that nearly half an hour ago.
I said it to myself as much as you.

You didn't know. But James is one big fool.
He thought you meant to find fault with his work.
That's what the average farmer would have meant.
James had to take his time to chew it over
Before he acted; he's just got round to act.

He *is* a fool if that's the way he takes me.

Don't let it bother you. You've found out something.
The hand that knows his business won't be told
To do work faster or better — those two things.
I'm as particular as anyone:
Most likely I'd have served you just the same:
But I know you don't understand our ways.
You were just talking what was in your mind,
What was in all our minds, and you weren't hinting.
Tell you a story of what happened once.
I was up here in Salem, at a man's
Named Sanders, with a gang of four or five,
Doing the haying. No one liked the boss.
He was one of the kind sports call a spider,
All wiry arms and legs that spread out wavy
From a humped body nigh as big as a biscuit.
But work! — that man could work, especially
If by so doing he could get more work
Out of his hired help. I'm not denying
He was hard on himself: I couldn't find
That he kept any hours — not for himself.
Day-light and lantern-light were one to him:
I've heard him pounding in the barn all night.
But what he liked was someone to encourage.
Them that he couldn't lead he'd get behind
And drive, the way you can, you know, in mowing —
Keep at their heels and threaten to mow their legs off.
I'd seen about enough of his bulling tricks —

We call that bulling. I'd been watching him.
So when he paired off with me in the hayfield
To load the load, thinks I, look out for trouble!
I built the load and topped it off; old Sanders
Combed it down with the rake and said "O.K."
Everything went right till we reached the barn
With a big take to empty in a bay.
You understand that meant the easy job
For the man up on top of throwing down
The hay and rolling it off wholesale,
Where, on a mow, it would have been slow lifting.
You wouldn't think a fellow'd need much urging
Under those circumstances, would you now?
But the old fool seizes his fork in both hands,
And looking up bewhiskered out of the pit,
Shouts like an army captain, "Let her come!"
Thinks I, D'ye mean it? "What was that you said?"
I asked out loud so's there'd be no mistake.
"Did you say, let her come?" "Yes, let her come."
He said it over, but he said it softer.
Never you say a thing like that to a man,
Not if he values what he is. God, I'd as soon
Murdered him as left out his middle name.
I'd built the load and knew just where to find it.
Two or three forkfuls I picked lightly round for
Like meditating, and then I just dug in
And dumped the rackful on him in ten lots.
I looked over the side once in the dust
And caught sight of him treading-water-like,
Keeping his head above. "Damn ye," I says,
"That gets ye!" He squeaked like a squeezed rat.

That was the last I saw or heard of him.
I cleaned the rack and drove out to cool off.
As I sat mopping the hayseed from my neck,
And sort of waiting to be asked about it,
One of the boys sings out, "Where's the old man?"
"I left him in the barn, under the hay.
If you want him you can go and dig him out."

They realized from the way I swobbed my neck
More than was needed, something must be up.
They headed for the barn — I stayed where I was.
They told me afterward: First they forked hay,
A lot of it, out into the barn floor.
Nothing! They listened for him. Not a rustle!
I guess they thought I'd spiked him in the temple
Before I buried him, else I couldn't have managed.
They excavated more. "Go keep his wife
Out of the barn."
                    Some one looked in a window;
And curse me, if he wasn't in the kitchen,
Slumped way down in a chair, with both his feet
Stuck in the oven, the hottest day that summer.
He looked so mad in back, and so disgusted
There was no one that dared to stir him up
Or let him know that he was being looked at.
Apparently I hadn't buried him
(I may have knocked him down), but just my trying
To bury him had hurt his dignity.
He had gone to the house so's not to face me.
He kept away from us all afternoon.
We tended to his hay. We saw him out
After a while, picking peas in the garden;
He couldn't keep away from doing something.

Weren't you relieved to find he wasn't dead?

No! — and yet I can't say: it's hard to tell.
I went about to kill him fair enough.

You took an awkward way. Did he discharge you?

Discharge me? No! He knew I did just right.

ROBERT FROST

13

From CHICAGO POEMS

CHICAGO

Hog Butcher for the World,
Tool Maker, Stacker of Wheat,
Player with Railroads and the Nation's Freight Handler;
Stormy, husky, brawling,
City of the Big Shoulders:

They tell me you are wicked and I believe them, for I have seen
  your painted women under the gas lamps luring the farm
  boys.
And they tell me you are crooked and I answer: Yes, it is true
  I have seen the gunman kill and go free to kill again.
And they tell me you are brutal and my reply is: On the faces
  of women and children I have seen the marks of wanton
  hunger.
And having answered so I turn once more to those who sneer
  at this my city, and I give them back the sneer and say to
  them:
Come and show me another city with lifted head singing so
  proud to be alive and coarse and strong and cunning.
Flinging magnetic curses amid the toil of piling job on job, here
  is a tall bold slugger set vivid against the little soft cities;
Fierce as a dog with tongue lapping for action, cunning as a
  savage pitted against the wilderness,
    Bareheaded,
    Shoveling,
    Wrecking,
    Planning,
    Building, breaking, rebuilding,
Under the smoke, dust all over his mouth, laughing with white
  teeth,
Under the terrible burden of destiny laughing as a young man
  laughs,
Laughing even as an ignorant fighter laughs who has never lost
  a battle,

Bragging and laughing that under his wrist is the pulse, and
   under his ribs the heart of the people,
                Laughing!
Laughing the stormy, husky, brawling laughter of Youth, half-
   naked, sweating, proud to be Hog Butcher, Tool Maker,
   Stacker of Wheat, Player with Railroads and Freight Handler
   to the Nation.

CARL SANDBURG

From LOVE SONGS

SEPTEMBER MIDNIGHT

Lyric night of the lingering Indian Summer,
Shadowy fields that are scentless but full of singing,
Never a bird, but the passionless chant of insects,
     Ceaseless, insistent.

The grasshopper's horn, and far-off, high in the maples,
The wheel of a locust leisurely grinding the silence
Under a moon waning and worn, broken,
     Tired with summer.

Let me remember you, voices of little insects,
Weeds in the moonlight, fields that are tangled with asters,
Let me remember, soon will the winter be on us,
     Snow-hushed and heavy.

Over my soul murmur your mute benediction,
While I gaze, O fields that rest after harvest,
As those who part look long in the eyes they lean to,
     Lest they forget them.

SARA TEASDALE

EROS TURANNOS

She fears him, and will always ask
    What fated her to choose him;
She meets in his engaging mask
    All reasons to refuse him;
But what she meets and what she fears
Are less than are the downward years,
Drawn slowly to the foamless weirs
    Of age, were she to lose him.

Between a blurred sagacity
    That once had power to sound him,
And Love, that will not let him be
    The seeker that she found him,
Her pride assuages her, almost,
As if it were alone the cost.
He sees that he will not be lost,
    And waits, and looks around him.

A sense of ocean and old trees
    Envelops and allures him;
Tradition, touching all he sees
    Beguiles and reassures him;
And all her doubts of what he says
Are dimmed with what she knows of days,
Till even prejudice delays,
    And fades — and she secures him.

The falling leaf inaugurates
    The reign of her confusion;
The pounding wave reverberates
    The crash of her illusion;
And home, where passion lived and died,
Becomes a place where she can hide, —
While all the town and harbor side
    Vibrate with her seclusion.

We tell you, tapping on our brows,
    The story as it should be, —

As if the story of a house
  Were told, or ever could be;
We'll have no kindly veil between
Her visions and those we have seen, —
As if we guessed what hers have been
  Or what they are, or would be.

Meanwhile, we do no harm; for they
  That with a god have striven,
Not hearing much of what we say,
  Take what the god has given;
Though like waves breaking it may be,
Or like a changed familiar tree,
Or like a stairway to the sea,
  Where down the blind are driven.

EDWIN ARLINGTON ROBINSON

TO A FRIEND WHOSE WORK HAS COME TO NOTHING

Now all the truth is out,
Be secret and take defeat
From any brazen throat,
For how can you compete,
Being honor bred, with one
Who were it proved he lies
Were neither shamed in his own
Nor in his neighbors' eyes;
Bred to a harder thing
Than Triumph, turn away
And like a laughing string
Whereon mad fingers play
Amid a place of stone,
Be secret and exult,
Because of all things known
That is most difficult.

WILLIAM BUTLER YEATS

THE MAGI

Now as at all times I can see in the mind's eye,
In their stiff, painted clothes, the pale unsatisfied ones
Appear and disappear in the blue depths of the sky
With all their ancient faces like rain-beaten stones,
And all their helms of silver hovering side by side,
And all their eyes still fixed, hoping to find once more,
Being by Calvary's turbulence unsatisfied,
The uncontrollable mystery on the bestial floor.

WILLIAM BUTLER YEATS

TO ΚΑΛÒN

Even in my dreams you have denied yourself to me,
You have sent me only your handmaids.

EZRA POUND

DARK WINGS

Sing while you may, O bird upon the tree!
    Although on high, wide-winged above the day,
Chill evening broadens to immensity,
    Sing while you may.

On thee, wide-hovering too, intent to slay,
    The hawk's slant pinion buoys him terribly —
Thus near the end is of thy happy lay.

The day and thee and miserable me
    Dark wings shall cover up and hide away
Where no song stirs of bird or memory:
    Sing while you may.

JAMES STEPHENS

DON JUAN

It is Isis the mystery
Must be in love with me.

Here this round ball of earth,
Where all the mountains sit
Solemn in groups,
And the bright rivers flit
Round them for girth:

Here the trees and troops
Darken the shining grass;
And many bright people pass
Like plunder from heaven:
Many bright people pass
Plundered from heaven.

But what of the mistresses,
What the beloved seven?
— They were but witnesses,
I was just driven.

Where is there peace for me?
It is Isis the mystery
Must be in love with me.

D. H. LAWRENCE

THE COMING OF WAR: ACTAEON

An image of Lethe,
             and the fields
Full of faint light
             but golden,
Gray cliffs,
        and beneath them
A sea

Harsher than granite,
   unstill, never ceasing;
High forms
   with the movement of gods,
Perilous aspect;
    And one said:
"This is Actaeon."
     Actaeon of golden greaves!

Over fair meadows,
Over the cool face of that field,
Unstill, ever moving,
Host of an ancient people,
The silent cortège.

       EZRA POUND

MOONRISE

Will you glimmer on the sea?
Will you fling your spear-head
on the shore?
What note shall we pitch?

We have a song,
on the bank we share our arrows —
the loosed string tells our note:

O flight,
bring her swiftly to our song.
She is great,
we measure her by the pine-trees.

       H. D.

VENUS TRANSIENS

Tell me,
Was Venus more beautiful
Than you are,
When she topped
The crinkled waves,
Drifting shoreward
On her plaited shell?
Was Botticelli's vision
Fairer than mine;
And were the painted rosebuds
He tossed his lady
Of better worth
Than the words I blow about you
To cover your too great loveliness
As with a gauze
Of misted silver?

For me,
You stand poised
In the blue and buoyant air,
Cinctured by bright winds,
Treading the sunlight.
And the waves which precede you
Ripple and stir
The sands at my feet.

AMY LOWELL

NINETEEN-FOURTEEN

PEACE

Now, God be thanked who has matched us with his hour,
    And caught our youth, and wakened us from sleeping!
With hand made sure, clear eye, and sharpened power,
    To turn, as swimmers into cleanness leaping,

Glad from a world grown old and cold and weary;
    Leave the sick hearts that honor could not move,
And half-men, and their dirty songs and dreary,
    And all the little emptiness of love!
Oh! we, who have known shame, we have found release
  there,
    Where there's no ill, no grief, but sleep has mending,
      Naught broken save this body, lost but breath;
Nothing to shake the laughing heart's long peace there,
    But only agony, and that has ending;
      And the worst friend and enemy is but Death.

THE DEAD

These hearts were woven of human joys and cares,
    Washed marvellously with sorrow, swift to mirth.
The years had given them kindness. Dawn was theirs,
    And sunset, and the colors of the earth.
These had seen movement, and heard music; known
    Slumber and waking; loved; gone proudly friended;
Felt the quick stir of wonder; sat alone;
    Touched flowers and furs, and cheeks. All this is ended
There are waters blown by changing wings to laughter
And lit by the rich skies, all day. And after,
    Frost, with a gesture, stays the waves that dance
And wandering loveliness. He leaves a white
    Unbroken glory, a gathered radiance,
A width, a shining peace, under the night.

THE SOLDIER

If I should die, think only this of me:
    That there's some corner of a foreign field
That is for ever England. There shall be
    In that rich earth a richer dust concealed;
A dust whom England bore, shaped, made aware,
    Gave, once, her flowers to love, her ways to roam,
A body of England's, breathing English air,
    Washed by the rivers, blest by suns of home.

And think, this heart, all evil shed away,
    A pulse in the eternal mind, no less
        Gives somewhere back the thoughts by England
           given;
Her sights and sounds; dreams happy as her day;
    And laughter, learnt of friends; and gentleness,
        In hearts at peace, under an English heaven.

RUPERT BROOKE

SLOW MOVEMENT

All those treasures that lie in the little bolted box whose tiny
    space is
Mightier than the room of the stars, being secret and filled with
    dreams:
All those treasures — I hold them in my hand — are straining
    continually
Against the sides and the lid and the two ends of the little box
    in which I guard them;
Crying that there is no sun come among them this great while
    and that they weary of shining;
Calling me to fold back the lid of the little box and to give them
    sleep finally.

But the night I am hiding from them, dear friend, is far more
    desperate than their night!
And so I take pity on them and pretend to have lost the key to
    the little house of my treasures,
For they would die of weariness were I to open it, and not be
    merely faint and sleepy
As they are now.

WILLIAM CARLOS WILLIAMS

From POUTERS AND FANTAILS

THAT HARP YOU PLAY SO WELL

O David, if I had
Your power, I should be glad —
    In harping, with the sling,
    In patient reasoning!

Blake, Homer, Job, and you,
Have made old wine-skins new.
    Your energies have wrought
    Stout continents of thought.

But, David, if the heart
Be brass, what boots the art
    Of exorcising wrong,
    Of harping to a song?

The sceptre and the ring
And every royal thing
    Will fail. Grief's lustiness
    Must cure that harp's distress.

MARIANNE MOORE

THE LOVE SONG OF J. ALFRED PRUFROCK

S' io credessi che mia risposta fosse
A persona che mai tornasse al mondo,
Questa fiamma staria senza piú scosse.
Ma perciocchè giammai di questo fondo
Non tornò vivo alcum, s' i' odo il vero,
Senza tema d'infamia ti rispondo.

Let us go then, you and I,
When the evening is spread out against the sky
Like a patient etherized upon a table;

Let us go, through certain half-deserted streets,
The muttering retreats
Of restless nights in one-night cheap hotels
And sawdust restaurants with oyster-shells:
Streets that follow like a tedious argument
Of insidious intent
To lead you to an overwhelming question . . .

Oh, do not ask, "What is it?"
Let us go and make our visit.

In the room the women come and go
Talking of Michelangelo.

   The yellow fog that rubs its back upon the window panes,
The yellow smoke that rubs its muzzle on the window panes,
Licked its tongue into the corners of the evening,
Lingered upon the pools that stand in drains,
Let fall upon its back the soot that falls from chimneys,
Slipped by the terrace, made a sudden leap,
And seeing that it was a soft October night,
Curled once about the house, and fell asleep.

   And indeed there will be time
For the yellow smoke that slides along the street,
Rubbing its back upon the window panes;
There will be time, there will be time
To prepare a face to meet the faces that you meet;
There will be time to murder and create,
And time for all the works and days of hands
That lift and drop a question on your plate:
Time for you and time for me,
And time yet for a hundred indecisions,
And for a hundred visions and revisions,
Before the taking of a toast and tea.

In the room the women come and go
Talking of Michelangelo.

And indeed there will be time
To wonder, "Do I dare?" and, "Do I dare?" —
Time to turn back and descend the stair,
With a bald spot in the middle of my hair —
(They will say: "How his hair is growing thin!")
My morning coat, my collar mounting firmly to the chin,
My necktie rich and modest, but asserted by a simple pin —
(They will say: "But how his arms and legs are thin!")
Do I dare
Disturb the universe?
In a minute there is time
For decisions and revisions which a minute will reverse.

For I have known them already, known them all:
Have known the evenings, mornings, afternoons,
I have measured out my life with coffee spoons;
I know the voices dying with a dying fall
Beneath the music from a farther room.
        So how should I presume?

And I have known the eyes already, known them all —
The eyes that fix you in a formulated phrase.
And when I am formulated, sprawling on a pin,
When I am pinned and wriggling on the wall,
Then how should I begin
To spit out all the butt-ends of my days and ways?
        And how should I presume?

And I have known the arms already, known them all —
Arms that are braceleted and white and bare
(But in the lamplight, downed with light brown hair!)
    Is it perfume from a dress
    That makes me so digress?
Arms that lie along a table, or wrap about a shawl.
    And should I then presume?
    And how should I begin?

                    .   .   .   .   .

        Shall I say, I have gone at dusk through narrow streets,
26   And watched the smoke that rises from the pipes
        Of lonely men in shirtsleeves, leaning out of windows? . . .

I should have been a pair of ragged claws
Scuttling across the floors of silent seas.

                    .   .   .   .   .

    And the afternoon, the evening, sleeps so peacefully!
Smoothed by long fingers,
Asleep . . . tired . . . or it malingers,
Stretched on the floor, here beside you and me.
Should I, after tea and cakes and ices,
Have the strength to force the moment to its crisis?
But though I have wept and fasted, wept and prayed,
Though I have seen my head (grown slightly bald) brought in
        upon a platter,
I am no prophet — and here's no great matter;
I have seen the moment of my greatness flicker,
And I have seen the eternal Footman hold my coat, and
        snicker,
    And in short, I was afraid.

    And would it have been worth it, after all,
After the cups, the marmalade, the tea,
Among the porcelain, among some talk of you and me,
Would it have been worth while
To have bitten off the matter with a smile,
To have squeezed the universe into a ball
To roll it toward some overwhelming question,
To say: "I am Lazarus, come from the dead,
Come back to tell you all, I shall tell you all" —
If one, settling a pillow by her head,
    Should say: "That is not what I meant at all;
        That is not it, at all."

    And would it have been worth it, after all,
Would it have been worth while,
After the sunsets and the dooryards and the sprinkled streets,
After the novels, after the teacups, after the skirts that trail
        along the floor —
And this, and so much more? —
It is impossible to say just what I mean!
But as if a magic lantern threw the nerves in patterns on a   27
    screen:

Would it have been worth while
If one, settling a pillow or throwing off a shawl,
And turning toward the window, should say: "That is not it
    at all,
      That is not what I meant, at all."

     . . . . .

   No! I am not Prince Hamlet, nor was meant to be;
Am an attendant lord, one that will do
To swell a progress, start a scene or two,
Advise the prince: withal, an easy tool,
Deferential, glad to be of use,
Politic, cautious, and meticulous;
Full of high sentence, but a bit obtuse;
At times, indeed, almost ridiculous —
Almost, at times, the Fool.

I grow old . . . I grow old . . .
I shall wear the bottoms of my trowsers rolled.

   Shall I part my hair behind? Do I dare to eat a peach?
I shall wear white flannel trowsers, and walk upon the beach.
I have heard the mermaids singing, each to each.
I do not think that they will sing to me.

I have seen them riding seaward on the waves,
Combing the white hair of the waves blown back
When the wind blows the water white and black.

We have lingered in the chambers of the sea
By seagirls wreathed with seaweed red and brown,
Till human voices wake us, and we drown.

     . . . . .

T.S.ELIOT

THE PINE AT TIMBER-LINE

   What has bent you,
   Warped and twisted you,

Torn and crippled you? —
What has embittered you,
O lonely tree?

You search the rocks for a footing,
      dragging scrawny roots;
You bare your thin breast to the storms,
      and fling out wild arms behind you;
You throw back your witch-like head,
      with wisps of hair stringing the wind.

You fight with the snows,
You rail and shriek at the tempests.
Old before your time, you challenge the cold stars.

Be still, be satisfied!
Stand straight like your brothers in the valley,
The soft green valley of summer down below.

Why front the endless winter of the peak?
Why seize the lightning in your riven hands?
Why cut the driven wind and shriek aloud?

Why tarry here?

HARRIET MONROE

From DISCORDANTS

IV

Dead Cleopatra lies in a crystal casket,
Wrapped and spiced by the cunningest of hands.
Around her neck they have put a golden necklace,
Her tatbebs, it is said, are worn with sands.

Dead Cleopatra was once revered in Egypt —
Warm-eyed she was, this princess of the south.
Now she is very old and dry and faded,
With black bitumen they have sealed up her mouth.

29

Grave-robbers pulled the gold rings from her fingers,
Despite the holy symbols across her breast;
They scared the bats that quietly whirled above her.
Poor lady! she would have been long since at rest

If she had not been wrapped and spiced so shrewdly,
Preserved, obscene, to mock black flights of years.
What would her lover have said, had he foreseen it?
Had he been moved to ecstasy, or tears?

O sweet clean earth from whom the green blade cometh! —
When we are dead, my best-beloved and I,
Close well above us that we may rest forever,
Sending up grass and blossoms to the sky.

                                        CONRAD AIKEN

THE ANSWER

When I go back to earth
And all my joyous body
Puts off the red and white
That once had been so proud,
If men should pass above
With false and feeble pity,
My dust will find a voice
To answer them aloud:

"Be still, I am content,
Take back your poor compassion —
Joy was a flame in me
Too steady to destroy.
Lithe as a bending reed
Loving the storm that sways her —
I found more joy in sorrow
Than you could find in joy."

                                        SARA TEASDALE

AUNT HELEN

Miss Helen Slingsby was my maiden aunt,
And lived in a small house near a fashionable square
Cared for by servants to the number of four.
Now when she died there was silence in heaven
And silence at her end of the street.
The shutters were drawn and the undertaker wiped his feet —
He was aware that this sort of thing had occurred before.
The dogs were handsomely provided for,
But shortly afterwards the parrot died too.
The Dresden clock continued ticking on the mantelpiece,
And the footman sat upon the dining table
Holding the second housemaid on his knees —
Who had always been so careful while her mistress lived.

T. S. ELIOT

IMAGES

I

Like a gondola of green scented fruits
Drifting along the dank canals at Venice,
You, O exquisite one,
Have entered my desolate city.

II

The blue smoke leaps
Like swirling clouds of birds vanishing. *hyperbole*
So my love leaps forth towards you,
Vanishes and is renewed.

III

A rose-yellow moon in a pale sky
When the sunset is faint vermilion
In the mist among the tree-boughs,
Art thou to me.

IV

As a young beech-tree on the edge of a forest
Stands still in the evening,
Yet shudders through all its leaves in the light air
And seems to fear the stars —
So are you still and so tremble.

V

The red deer are high on the mountain,
They are beyond the last pine trees.
And my desires have run with them.

VI

The flower which the wind has shaken
Is soon filled again with rain;
So does my mind fill slowly with misgiving
Until you return.

RICHARD ALDINGTON

BEETHOVEN

Behold the tormented and the fallen angel
    Wandering disconsolate the world along,
That seeks to atone with inconsolable anguish
    For some old grievance, some remembered wrong;
To storm heaven's iron gates with angry longing,
    And beat back homeward in a shower of song!

JOHN HALL WHEELOCK

SUNDAY MORNING

I

Complacencies of the peignoir, and late
Coffee and oranges in a sunny chair,

And the green freedom of a cockatoo
Upon a rug, mingle to dissipate
The holy hush of ancient sacrifice.
She dreams a little, and she feels the dark
Encroachment of that old catastrophe,
As a calm darkens among water-lights.
The pungent oranges and bright, green wings
Seem things in some procession of the dead,
Winding across wide water, without sound.
The day is like wide water, without sound,
Stilled for the passing of her dreaming feet
Over the seas, to silent Palestine,
Dominion of the blood and sepulcher.

II

She hears, upon that water without sound,
A voice that cries, "The tomb in Palestine
Is not the porch of spirits lingering;
It is the grave of Jesus, where he lay."
We live in an old chaos of the sun,
Or old dependency of day and night,
Or island solitude, unsponsored, free,
Of that wide water, inescapable.
Deer walk upon our mountains, and the quail
Whistle about us their spontaneous cries;
Sweet berries ripen in the wilderness;
And, in the isolation of the sky,
At evening, casual flocks of pigeons make
Ambiguous undulations as they sink,
Downward to darkness, on extended wings.

III

She says, "I am content when wakened birds,
Before they fly, test the reality
Of misty fields, by their sweet questionings;
But when the birds are gone, and their warm fields
Return no more, where, then, is paradise?"

There is not any haunt of prophecy,
Nor any old chimera of the grave,
Neither the golden underground, nor isle
Melodious, where spirits gat them home,
Nor visionary South, nor cloudy palm
Remote on heaven's hill, that has endured
As April's green endures; or will endure
Like her remembrance of awakened birds,
Or her desire for June and evening, tipped
By the consummation of the swallow's wings.

IV

She says, "But in contentment I still feel
The need of some imperishable bliss."
Death is the mother of beauty; hence from her,
Alone, shall come fulfilment to our dreams
And our desires. Although she strews the leaves
Of sure obliteration on our paths —
The path sick sorrow took, the many paths
Where triumph rang its brassy phrase, or love
Whispered a little out of tenderness —
She makes the willow shiver in the sun
For maidens who were wont to sit and gaze
Upon the grass, relinquished to their feet.
She causes boys to bring sweet-smelling pears
And plums in ponderous piles. The maidens taste
And stray impassioned in the littering leaves.

V

Supple and turbulent, a ring of men
Shall chant in orgy on a summer morn
Their boisterous devotion to the sun —
Not as a god, but as a god might be,
Naked among them, like a savage source.
Their chant shall be a chant of paradise,
Out of their blood, returning to the sky;
And in their chant shall enter, voice by voice,

The windy lake wherein their lord delights,
The trees, like seraphim, and echoing hills,
That choir among themselves long afterward.
They shall know well the heavenly fellowship
Of men that perish and of summer morn —
And whence they came and whither they shall go,
The dew upon their feet shall manifest.

WALLACE STEVENS

THE HAWK

Call down the hawk from the air —
Let him be hooded or caged
Till the yellow eye has grown mild.
For larder and spit are bare,
The old cook enraged,
The scullion gone wild.

I will not be clapped in a hood,
Nor a cage, nor alight upon wrist,
Now I have learnt to be proud
Hovering over the wood
In the broken mist
Or tumbling cloud.

What tumbling cloud did you cleave,
Yellow-eyed hawk of the mind,
Last evening, that I, who had sat
Dumbfounded before a knave
Should give to my friend
A pretence of wit?

WILLIAM BUTLER YEATS

THE SCHOLARS

Bald heads forgetful of their sins,
Old, learned, respectable bald heads
Edit and annotate the lines
That young men, tossing on their beds,
Rhymed out in love's despair
To flatter beauty's ignorant ear.

They'll cough in the ink to the world's end;
Wear out the carpet with their shoes
Earning respect; have no strange friend;
If they have sinned nobody knows:
Lord, what would they say
Should their Catullus walk that way!

WILLIAM BUTLER YEATS

IN MEMORY OF BRYAN LATHROP

Who bequeathed to Chicago a School of Music.

So in Pieria, from the wedded bliss
Of Time and Memory, the Muses came
To be the means of rich oblivion,
And rest from cares. And when the Thunderer
Took heaven, then the Titans warred on him
For pity of mankind. But the great law,
Which is the law of music, not of bread,
Set Atlas for a pillar, manacled
His brother to the rocks in Scythia,
And under Aetna fixed the furious Typhon.
So should thought rule, not force. And Amphion,
Pursuing justice, entered Thebes and slew
His mother's spouse; but when he would make sure
And fortify the city, then he took
The lyre that Hermes gave, and played, and watched
The stones move and assemble, till a wall
Engirded Thebes and kept the citadel

Beyond the reach of arrows and of fire.
What other power but harmony can build
A city, and what gift so magical
As that by which a city lifts its walls?
So men, in years to come, shall feel the power
Of this man moving through the high-ranged thought
Which plans for beauty, builds for larger life.
The stones shall rise in towers to answer him.

EDGAR LEE MASTERS

O ATTHIS

Thy soul
Grown delicate with satieties,
Atthis.

O Atthis,
I long for thy lips.

I long for thy narrow breasts,
Thou restless, ungathered.

EZRA POUND

THE LAKE ISLE

O God, O Venus, O Mercury, patron of thieves,
Give me in due time, I beseech you, a little tobaccco-shop,
With the little bright boxes
            piled up neatly upon the shelves
And the loose fragrant cavendish
            and the shag,
And the bright Virginia
            loose under the bright glass cases,
And a pair of scales
            not too greasy,
And the *volailles* dropping in for a word or two in passing,
For a flip word, and to tidy their hair a bit.

37

O God, O Venus, O Mercury, patron of thieves,
Lend me a little tobacco-shop,
            or install me in any profession
Save this damn'd profession of writing,
            where one needs one's brains all the time.

EZRA POUND

From EPIGRAMS

The echo always mocks the sound — to conceal that she is his debtor.

The arrow thinks it is free, for it moves, and the bow is bound, for it is still. The bow says to the arrow, "Your freedom depends on me."

The world speaks truth. We take its meaning wrong and call it a liar.

The flute knows it is the breath that gives birth to its music. The breath knows it is nothing. And he who plays on the flute is not known.

Death threatens to take his son, the thief his wealth, and his detractors his reputation. "But who is there to take away my joy?" asks the poet.

Death belongs to life as birth does, even as walking contains the raising of the foot as much as the laying of it down.

RABINDRANATH TAGORE

From STRANGE MEETINGS

VII — BIRTH

One night when I was in the House of Death
A shrill voice penetrated root and stone,

And the whole earth was shaken under ground:
I woke and there was light above my head.

Before I heard that shriek I had not known
The region of Above from Underneath,
Alternate light and dark, silence and sound,
Difference between the living and the dead.

HAROLD MONRO

From OBSERVATIONS

LA FIGLIA CHE PIANGE

Stand on the highest pavement of the stair —
Lean on a garden urn —
Weave, weave, weave the sunlight in your hair —
Clasp your flowers to you with a pained surprise —
Fling them to the ground and turn
With a fugitive resentment in your eyes:
But weave, weave the sunlight in your hair.

So I would have had him leave,
So I would have had her stand and grieve,
So he would have left
As the soul leaves the body torn and bruised,
As the mind deserts the body it has used.
I should find
Some way incomparably light and deft,
Some way we both should understand,
Simple and faithless as a smile and shake of the hand.

She turned away, but with the autumn weather
Compelled my imagination many days —
Many days and many hours:
Her hair over her arms and her arms full of flowers —
And I wonder how they should have been together!

I should have lost a gesture and a pose.
Sometimes these cogitations still amaze
The troubled midnight and the noon's repose.

MR. APOLLINAX

When Mr. Apollinax visited the United States
His laughter tinkled among the teacups.
I thought of Fragilion, that shy figure among the birch trees,
And of Priapus in the shrubbery
Gaping at the lady in the swing.
In the palace of Mrs. Phlaccus, at Professor Channing-
     Cheetah's,
His laughter was submarine and profound
Like the old man of the sea's
Hidden under coral islands
Where worried bodies of drowned men drift down in the
     green silence, dropping from fingers of surf.
I looked for the head of Mr. Apollinax rolling under a chair,
Or grinning over a screen
With seaweed in its hair.
I heard the beat of centaurs' hoofs over the hard turf
As his dry and passionate talk devoured the afternoon.
"He is a charming man," "But after all what did he mean?"
"His pointed ears — he must be unbalanced,"
"There was something he said which I might have
     challenged."
Of dowager Mrs. Phlaccus, and Professor and Mrs. Cheetah
I remember a slice of lemon, and a bitten macaroon.

MORNING AT THE WINDOW

They are rattling breakfast plates in basement kitchens,
And along the trampled edges of the street
I am aware of the damp souls of housemaids
Hanging despondently at area gates.

The brown waves of fog toss up to me
Twisted faces from the bottom of the street,

And tear from a passerby with muddy skirts
An aimless smile that hovers in the air
And vanishes along the level of the roofs.

T. S. ELIOT [SIC]

INVOCATION

As pools beneath stone arches take
　　Darkly within their deeps again
Shapes of the flowing stone, and make
　　Stories anew of passing men,

So let the living thoughts that keep,
　　Morning and evening, in their kind,
Eternal change in height and deep,
　　Be mirrored in my happy mind.

Beat, world, upon this heart, be loud
　　Your marvel chanted in my blood.
Come forth, O sun, through cloud on cloud
　　To shine upon my stubborn mood.

Great hills that fold above the sea,
　　Ecstatic airs and sparkling skies,
Sing out your words to master me —
　　Make me immoderately wise.

JOHN DRINKWATER

From FOUR JAPANESE PAINTINGS

III THE WAVE SYMPHONY

A Screen by Sotatsu

Around islands of jade and malachite
And lapis-lazuli and jasper,

41

Under golden clouds,
Struggle the grey-gold waves.

   The waves are advancing,
Swirling, eddying; the pale waves
Are leaping into foam, and retreating —
And straining again until they seem not waves
But gigantic crawling hands.
The waves clutch at the clouds,
The near and golden clouds;
They rise in spires over the clouds,
And over the pine-branch set against the clouds.
And around the islands,
Jasper and jade,
Their rhythms circle and sweep and re-echo
With hollow and foam-crest,
Infinitely interlacing their orbits and cycles
That join and unravel, and battle and answer,
From tumult to tumult, from music to music,
Crest to trough, foam-height to hollow,
Peace drowning passion, and passion
Leaping from peace.

ARTHUR DAVISON FICKE

MARRIAGE

   So different, this man
And this woman:
A stream flowing
In a field.

WILLIAM CARLOS WILLIAMS

From TRENCH POEMS

BREAK OF DAY IN THE TRENCHES

The darkness crumbles away —
It is the same old Druid Time as ever.

Only a live thing leaps my hand —
A queer sardonic rat —
As I pull the parapet's poppy
To stick behind my ear.
Droll rat, they would shoot you if they knew
Your cosmopolitan sympathies
(And God knows what antipathies).
Now you have touched this English hand
You will do the same to a German —
Soon, no doubt, if it be your pleasure
To cross the sleeping green between.
It seems you inwardly grin as you pass:
Strong eyes, fine limbs, haughty athletes,
Less chanced than you for life;
Bonds to the whims of murder,
Sprawled in the bowels of the earth,
The torn fields of France.
What do you see in our eyes
At the boom, the hiss, the swiftness,
The irrevocable earth buffet —
A shell's haphazard fury.
What rootless poppies dropping? . . .
But mine in my ear is safe,
Just a little white with the dust.

ISAAC ROSENBERG

From LACQUER PRINTS

DESOLATION

Under the plum-blossoms are nightingales;
But the sea is hidden in an egg-white mist,
And they are silent.

AMY LOWELL

From MY PEOPLE

IN TALL GRASS

Bees and a honeycomb in the dried head of a horse in a pasture
    corner — a skull in the tall grass and a buzz and a buzz of
    the yellow honey-hunters.

And I ask no better a winding sheet
                        over the earth and under the sun.

Let the bees go honey-hunting with yellow blur of wings in the
    dome of my head, in the rumbling, singing arch of my
    skull.

Let there be wings and yellow dust and the drone of dreams of
    honey — who loses and remembers? — who keeps and
    forgets?

In a blue sheen of moon over the bones and under the hanging
    honeycomb the bees come home and the bees sleep.

CARL SANDBURG

NIGHT PIECE

Gaunt in gloom
The pale stars their torches,
Enshrouded, wave.
Ghost-fires from heaven's far verges faint illume —
Arches on soaring arches —
Night's sin-dark nave.

Seraphim
The lost hosts awaken
To service, till
In moonless gloom each lapses, muted, dim,
Raised when she has and shaken
Her thurible.

And long and loud
To night's nave upsoaring,
A star-knell tolls —
As the bleak incense surges, cloud on cloud,
Voidward from the adoring
Waste of souls.

JAMES JOYCE

From THREE CANTOS

I

Hang it all, there can be but one *Sordello!*
But say I want to, say I take your whole bag of tricks,
Let in your quirks and tweeks, and say the thing's an art-form,
Your *Sordello,* and that the modern world
Needs such a rag-bag to stuff all its thought in;
Say that I dump my catch, shiny and silvery
As fresh sardines flapping and slipping on the marginal
    cobbles?
(I stand before the booth, the speech; but the truth
Is inside this discourse — this booth is full of the marrow of
    wisdom.)
Give up th' intaglio method.
                  Tower by tower
Red-brown the rounded bases, the plan
Follows the builder's whim. Beaucaire's slim gray
Leaps from the stubby base of Altaforte —
Mohammed's windows, for the Alcazar
Has such a garden, split by a tame small stream.
The moat is ten yards wide, the inner court-yard
Half a-swim with mire.
Trunk hose?
            There are not. The rough men swarm out
In robes that are half Roman, half like the Knave of Hearts;
And I discern your story:
              Peire Cardinal

45

Was half forerunner of Dante. Arnaut's that trick
Of the unfinished address,
And half your dates are out, you mix your eras;
For that great font Sordello sat beside —
'Tis an immortal passage, but the font? —
Is some two centuries outside the picture.
Does it matter?

        Not in the least. Ghosts move about me
Patched with histories. You had your business:
To set out so much thought, so much emotion;
To paint, more real than any dead Sordello,
The half or third of your intensest life
And call that third *Sordello;*
And you'll say, "No, not your life,
He never showed himself."
Is't worth the evasion, what were the use
Of setting figures up and breathing life upon them,
Were 't not *our* life, your life, my life, extended?
I walk Verona. (I am here in England.)
I see Can Grande. (Can see whom you will.)
      You had one whole man?
And I have many fragments, less worth? Less worth?
Ah, had you quite my age, quite such a beastly and
     cantankerous age?
You had some basis, had some set belief.
Am I let preach? Has it a place in music?

      I walk the airy street,
See the small cobbles flare with the poppy spoil
'Tis your "great day," the Corpus Domini,
And all my chosen and peninsular village
Has made one glorious blaze of all its lanes —
Oh, before I was up — with poppy flowers.
Mid-June: some old god eats the smoke, 'tis not the saints;
And up and out to the half-ruined chapel —
Not the old place at the height of the rocks,
But that splay, barn-like church the Renaissance
Had never quite got into trim again.
As well begin here. Began our Catullus:

"Home to sweet rest, and to the waves' deep laughter,"
The laugh they wake amid the border rushes.
This is our home, the trees are full of laughter,
And the storms laugh loud, breaking the riven waves
On "north-most rocks"; and here the sunlight
Glints on the shaken waters, and the rain
Comes forth with delicate tread, walking from Isola Garda —
                         Lo soleils plovil,
As Arnaut had it in th' inextricable song.
The very sun rains and a spatter of fire
Darts from the "Lydian" ripples; *"locus undae,"* as Catullus,
    "Lydiae,"
And the place is full of spirits.
Not *lemures,* not dark and shadowy ghosts,
But the ancient living, wood-white,
Smooth as the inner bark, and firm of aspect,
And all agleam with colors — no, not agleam,
But colored like the lake and like the olive leaves,
Glaukopos, clothed like the poppies, wearing golden greaves,
Light on the air.
Are they Etruscan gods?
The air is solid sunlight, *apricus,*
Sun-fed we dwell there (we in England now);
It's your way of talk, we can be where we will be,
Sirmio serves my will better than your Asolo
Which I have never seen.
                    Your "palace step"?
My stone seat was the Dogana's curb,
And there were not "those girls," there was one flare, one
    face.
'Twas all I ever saw, but it was real. . . .
And I can no more say what shape it was . . .
But she was young, too young.
                         True, it was Venice,
And at Florian's and under the north arcade
I have seen other faces, and had my rolls for breakfast, for
    that matter;
So, for what it's worth, I have the background.
                    And you had a background,

Watched "the soul," Sordello's soul,
And saw it lap up life, and swell and burst —
"Into the empyrean?"
So you worked out new form, the meditative,
Semi-dramatic, semi-epic story,
And we will say: What's left for me to do?
Whom shall I conjure up; who's my Sordello,
My pre-Daun Chaucer, pre-Boccacio,
    As you have done pre-Dante?
Whom shall I hang my shimmering garment on;
Who wear my feathery mantle, *hagoromo;*
Whom set to dazzle the serious future ages?
Not Arnaut, not De Born, not Uc St. Circ who has writ out
  the stories.
Or shall I do your trick, the showman's booth, Bob
  Browning,
Turned at my will into the Agora,
Or into the old theatre at Arles,
And set the lot, my visions, to confounding
The wits that have survived your damn'd *Sordello?*
(Or sulk and leave the word to novelists?)
What a hodge-podge you have made there! —
Zanze and *swanzig,* of all opprobrious rhymes!
And you turn off whenever it suits your fancy,
Now at Verona, now with the early Christians,
Or now a-gabbling of the "Tyrrhene whelk."
"The lyre should animate but not mislead the pen" —
That's Wordsworth, Mr. Browning. (What a phrase! —
That lyre, that pen, that bleating sheep, Will Wordsworth!)
That should have taught you avoid speech figurative
     And set out your matter
As I do, in straight simple phrases:
    Gods float in the azure air,
Bright gods, and Tuscan, back before dew was shed,
It is a world like Puvis'?
     Never so pale, my friend,
'Tis the first light — not half light — Panisks
And oak-girls and the Maenads
48 Have all the wood. Our olive Sirmio

Lies in its burnished mirror, and the Mounts Balde and Riva
Are alive with song, and all the leaves are full of voices.
"Non è fuggito."

      "It is not gone." Metastasio
Is right — we have that world about us,
And the clouds bow above the lake, and there are folk upon
   them
Going their windy ways, moving by Riva,
By the western shore, far as Lonato,
And the water is full of silvery almond-white swimmers,
The silvery water glazes the up-turned nipple.
How shall we start hence, how begin the progress?
Pace naif Ficinus, say when Hotep-Hotep
Was a king in Egypt —
  When Atlas sat down with his astrolabe,
   He, brother to Prometheus, physicist —
    Say it was Moses' birth-year?
Exult with Shang in squatness? The sea-monster
Bulges the squarish bronzes.
(Confucius later taught the world good manners,
Started with himself, built out perfection.)
     With Egypt!
Daub out in blue of scarabs, and with that greeny turquoise?
Or with China, *O Virgilio mio,* and gray gradual steps
Lead up beneath flat sprays of heavy cedars,
Temple of teak wood, and the gilt-brown arches
Triple in tier, banners woven by wall,
Fine screens depicted, sea waves curled high,
Small boats with gods upon them,
Bright flame above the river! Kwannon
Footing a boat that's but one lotus petal,
With some proud four-spread genius
Leading along, one hand upraised for gladness,
Saying, "'Tis she, his friend, the mighty goodess! Paean!
Sing hymns ye reeds,
     and all ye roots and herons and swans be glad,
Ye gardens of the nymphs put forth your flowers."
What have I of this life,
    Or even of Guido?   **49**

Sweet lie! — Was I there truly?
Did I know Or San Michele?
Let's believe it.
Believe the tomb he leapt was Julia Laeta's?
Friend, I do not even — when he led that street charge —
I do not even know which sword he'd with him.
Sweet lie, "I lived!" Sweet lie, "I lived beside him."
And now it's all but truth and memory,
Dimmed only by the attritions of long time.

"But we forget not."
No, take it all for lies.
I have but smelt this life, a whiff of it —
The box of scented wood
Recalls cathedrals. And shall I claim;
Confuse my own phantastikon,
Or say the filmy shell that circumscribes me
Contains the actual sun;
confuse the thing I see
With actual gods behind me?
Are they gods behind me?
How many worlds we have! If Botticelli
Brings her ashore on that great cockle-shell —
His Venus (Simonetta?),
And Spring and Aufidus fill all the air
With their clear-outlined blossoms?
World enough. Behold, I say, she comes
"Apparelled like the spring, Graces her subjects,"
(That's from *Pericles*).
Oh, we have worlds enough, and brave *décors,*
And from these like we guess a soul for man
And build him full of aery populations.
Mantegna a sterner line, and the new world about us:
Barred lights, great flares, new form, Picasso or Lewis.
If for a year man write to paint, and not to music —
O Casella!

EZRA POUND

(To be continued)

From NOTES

II

Where go the birds when the rain *hyperbole*
Roars and sweeps and fells the grain,
When tortured trees groan with pain,
And the storm-worn night is old —
Driven forth from their slumber cold,
Where go the birds?

JANE HEAP

From MID-AMERICAN SONGS

A VISIT

Westward the field of the cloth of gold. It is fall. See the
    corn. How it aches.
Lay the golden cloth upon me. It is night and I come through
    the streets to your window.
The dust and the words are all gone, brushed away. Let me
    sleep.

SHERWOOD ANDERSON

RECIPROCITY

I do not think that skies and meadows are
Moral, or that the fixture of a star
Comes of a quiet spirit, or that trees
Have wisdom in their windless silences.
Yet these are things invested in my mood
With constancy, and peace, and fortitude;
That in my troubled season I can cry
Upon the wide composure of the sky,
And envy fields, and wish that I might be
As little daunted as a star or tree.

JOHN DRINKWATER

51

ON THE BEACH AT FONTANA

Wind whines and whines the shingle,
The crazy pier-stakes groan;
A senile sea numbers each single
Slime-silvered stone.

From whining wind and colder
Grey sea I wrap him warm,
And touch his fine-boned boyish shoulder
And trembling arm.

Around us fear, descending,
Darkness of fear above;
And in my heart how sweet unending
Ache of love.

JAMES JOYCE

From CHICAGO NOTES

THE MONADNOCK

Pylon for some incomplete gateway
Through which the high priests of the sun
Might blow their trumpets in the morning,
Strong red and yellow buttress,
What breed of desert dwellers
Left you here in the midst of the city,
To mock with your severity
The gaudy frippery of more bright façades,
To smolder like a polished block
Of dark Egyptian stone?

JOHN GOULD FLETCHER

From CHINESE POEMS

THE ORPHAN

To be an orphan,
To be fated to be an orphan,
How bitter is this lot!
When my father and mother were alive
I used to ride in a fine carriage
Driving four horses;
But when my father and mother died,
My brother and his wife made of me a merchant.
In the South I travelled to the Nine Rivers
And in the East as far as Ch'i and Lu.
At the end of the year when I came home
I dared not tell them what I had suffered —
Of the lice and vermin in my head,
Of the dust in my face and eyes.
My brother told me to get ready the dinner;
My sister-in-law told me to see after the horses.
I was always going up into the hall
And running down again to the parlor.
My tears fell like a shower of rain.
In the morning they sent me to draw water;
I didn't get back till night-fall.
My hands were all sore,
And I hadn't any shoes;
I walked the cold earth
Treading on the thorns and brambles.
As I stopped to pull out the thorns,
How bitter my heart was! —
My tears fell and fell
And I went on sobbing and sobbing.
In winter I have no great-coat,
Nor in summer thin clothes.
It is no pleasure to be alive;
I had rather quickly leave this earth
And go beneath the Yellow Springs.
The April winds blow

And the grass grows so green:
In the third month, silk worms and mulberries;
In the sixth month, the melon-harvest.
I went out with the melon-cart,
And just as I was coming home
The melon-cart turned over.
The people who came to help me were few,
But the people who ate the melons were many.
All they left me was the stalks;
I took them home as fast as I could.
My brother and sister-in-law were harsh;
They asked me all sorts of awful questions.
Why does every one in the village blame me?
I want to write a letter and send it
To my father and mother under the earth
And tell them I can't go on any longer
Living with my brother and my sister-in-law.

Anonymous — First Century B.C.
ARTHUR WALEY

THE SANCTUARY

Shadowed by your dear hair, your dear kind eyes
Look on wine-purple seas, whitened afar
With marble foam, where the dim islands are.
We sit forgetting. For the great pines rise
Above dark cypress to the dim white skies
So clear and black and still — to one great star.
The marble dryads and the veined white jar
Gleam from the grove. Glimmering, the white owl flies
In the dark shade. . . .
                        If ever life was harsh
Here we forget — or ever friends turned foes.
The sea cliffs beetle down above the marsh
And through sea-holly the black panther goes.
And in the shadows of this secret place
Your kind, dear eyes shine in your dear, dear face.

FORD MADOX HUEFFER

From FIGS FROM THISTLES

FIRST FIG

My candle burns at both ends;
    It will not last the night:
But ah, my foes, and oh, my friends —
    It gives a lovely light!

SECOND FIG

Safe upon the solid rock the ugly houses stand:
Come and see my shining palace built upon the sand!

THE UNEXPLORER

There was a road ran past our house
    Too lovely to explore.
I asked my mother once — she said
That if you followed where it led
    It brought you to the milk-man's door.
    (That's why I have not traveled more.)

THURSDAY

And if I loved you Wednesday,
    Well, what is that to you?
I do not love you Thursday —
    So much is true.

And why you come complaining
    Is more than I can see.
I loved you Wednesday — yes — but what
    Is that to me?

EDNA ST. VINCENT MILLAY

MOONRISE

And who has seen the moon, who has not seen
Her rise from out the chamber of the deep
Flushed and grand and naked, as from the chamber
Of finished bridegroom, seen her rise and throw
Confession of delight upon the wave,
Littering the waves with her own superscription
Of bliss, till all her lambent beauty shakes towards us
Spread out and known at last: and we are sure
That beauty is a thing beyond the grave,
That perfect, bright experience never falls
To nothingness, and time will dim the moon
Sooner than our full consummation here
In this odd life will tarnish or pass away.

D. H. LAWRENCE

LE MÉDECIN MALGRÉ LUI

Oh I suppose I should
Wash the walls of my office,
Polish the rust from
My instruments and keep them
Definitely in order;
Build shelves in
The little laboratory;
Empty out the old stains,
Clean the bottles
And refill them; buy
Another lens; put
My journals on edge instead of
Letting them lie flat
In heaps — then begin
Ten years back and
Gradually
Read them to date,

Cataloguing important
Articles for ready reference.
I suppose I should
Read the new books.
If to this I added
A bill at the tailor's
And the cleaner's
And grew a decent beard
And cultivated a look
Of importance —
Who can tell? I might be
A credit to my Lady Happiness
And never think anything
But a white thought!

WILLIAM CARLOS WILLIAMS

BENEDICTION

Let no blasphemer till the sacred earth
Or scatter seed upon it,
Lest fruit should fail
And weed-scars sting its fineness.

Send him here who loves its beauty
And its brownness.

He will plow the earth
As a dancer dances —
Ecstatically.

Let no blasphemer till the sacred earth
Or scatter seed upon it.

MARK TURBYFILL

DREAMS

I

To dream of love, and, waking, to remember you:
As though, being dead, one dreamed of heaven, and woke in
hell.
At night my lovely dreams forget the old farewell:
Ah! wake not by his side, lest you remember too!

II

I set all Rome between us: with what joy I set
The wonder of the world against my world's delight!
Rome, that hast conquered worlds, with intellectual might
Capture my heart, and teach my memory to forget!

ARTHUR SYMONS

From REDHAW WINDS

FALLTIME

Gold of a ripe oat straw, gold of a southwest moon,
Canada-thistle blue and flimmering larkspur blue,
Tomatoes shining in the October sun with red hearts,
Shining five and six in a row on a wooden fence,
Why do you keep wishes shining on your faces all day long,
Wishes like women with half-forgotten lovers going to new
cities?
What is there for you in the birds, the birds, the birds, crying
down on the north wind in September — acres of birds
spotting the air going south?

Is there something finished? And some new beginning on the
way?

CARL SANDBURG

NOSTALGIA

The waning moon looks upward, this grey night
Sheers round the heavens in one smooth curve
Of easy sailing. Odd red wicks serve
To show where the ships at sea move out of sight.

This place is palpable me, for here I was born
Of this self-same darkness. Yet the shadowy house below
Is out of bounds, and only the old ghosts know
I have come — they whimper about me, welcome and
    mourn.

My father suddenly died in the harvesting corn,
And the place is no longer ours. Watching, I hear
No sound from the strangers; the place is dark, and fear
Opens my eyes till the roots of my vision seem torn.

Can I go nearer, never towards the door?
The ghosts and I, we mourn together, and shrink
In the shadow of the cart-shed — hovering on the brink
For ever, to enter the homestead no more.

Is it irrevocable? Can I really not go
Through the open yard-way? Can I not pass the sheds
And through to the mowie? Only the dead in their beds
Can know the fearful anguish that this is so.

I kiss the stones. I kiss the moss on the wall,
And wish I could pass impregnate into the place.
I wish I could take it all in a last embrace.
I wish with my breast I could crush it, perish it all.

D. H. LAWRENCE

From PROPERTIUS

IV

When, when, and whenever death closes our eyelids,
Moving naked over Acheron
   Upon the one raft, victor and conquered together,
Marius and Jugurtha together,
        One tangle of shadows.

Caesar plots against India —
Tigris and Euphrates shall from now on flow at his bidding,
Tibet shall be full of Roman policemen,
The Parthians shall get used to our statuary
       and acquire a Roman religion:

One raft on the veiled flood of Acheron,
       Marius and Jugurtha together.
Nor at my funeral either will there be any long trail,
       bearing ancestral lares and images;
No trumpets filled with my emptiness;
Nor shall it be on an Attalic bed.
       The perfumed cloths shall be absent.
A small plebeian procession —
       Enough, enough, and in plenty.
There will be three books at my obsequies
Which I take, my not unworthy gift, to Persephone.

You will follow the bare scarified breast;
Nor will you be weary of calling my name, nor too weary
       To place the last kiss on my lips
When the Syrian onyx is broken.

      "He who is now vacant dust
        Was once the slave of one passion" —
Give that much inscription —
       "Death, why tardily come?"

You, sometime, will lament a lost friend,
        for it is a custom —
This care for past men —
  Since Adonis was gored at Idalia, and the Cytherean
Ran crying with out-spread hair.
          In vain you call back the shade;
In vain, Cynthia, vain call to unanswering shadow —
      small talk comes from small bones.

EZRA POUND

PROUD NEW YORK

By proud New York and its man-piled Matterhorns,
The hard blue sky overhead and the west wind blowing,
Steam-plumes waving from sun-glittering pinnacles,
And deep streets shaking to the million-river —

  Manhattan, zoned with ships, the cruel
    Youngest of all the world's great towns,
  Thy bodice bright with many a jewel,
    Imperially crowned with crowns . . .

Who that has known thee but shall burn
  In exile till he come again
To do thy bitter will, O stern
  Moon of the tides of men!

JOHN REED

WALT WHITMAN

Noon on the mountain! —
And all the crags are husky faces powerful with love for the
    sun;
All the shadows
Whisper of the sun.

EMANUEL CARNEVALI   61

RECUERDO

We were very tired, we were very merry —
We had gone back and forth all night on the ferry.
It was bare and bright, and smelled like a stable —
But we looked into a fire, we leaned across a table,
We lay on a hill-top underneath the moon;
And the whistles kept blowing, and the dawn came soon.

We were very tired, we were very merry —
We had gone back and forth all night on the ferry;
And you ate an apple, and I ate a pear,
From a dozen of each we had bought somewhere;
And the sky went wan, and the wind came cold,
And the sun rose dripping, a bucketful of gold.

We were very tired, we were very merry,
We had gone back and forth all night on the ferry.
We hailed, "Good-morrow, mother!" to a shawl-covered
     head,
And bought a morning-paper, which neither of us read;
And she wept, "God bless you!" for the apples and pears,
And we gave her all our money but our subway fares.

EDNA ST. VINCENT MILLAY

END OF THE COMEDY

Eleven o'clock, and the curtain falls.
The cold wind tears the strands of illusion;
The delicate music is lost
In the blare of home-going crowds
And a midnight paper.

The night has grown martial;
It meets us with blows and disaster.
Even the stars have turned shrapnel,
Fixed in silent explosions.

And here at our door
The moonlight is laid
Like a drawn sword.

LOUIS UNTERMEYER

From MANY EVENINGS

MULTITUDES TURN IN DARKNESS

The half-shut doors through which we heard that music
Are softly closed. Horns mutter down to silence,
The stars wheel out, the night grows deep.
Darkness settles upon us; a vague refrain
Drowsily teases at the drowsy brain.
In numberless rooms we stretch ourselves and sleep.

Where have we been? What savage chaos of music
Whirls in our dreams? We suddenly rise in darkness,
Open our eyes, cry out, and sleep once more.
We dream we are numberless sea-waves, languidly foaming
A warm white moonlit shore;

Or clouds blown windily over a sky at midnight,
Or chords of music scattered in hurrying darkness,
Or a singing sound of rain . . .
We open our eyes and stare at the coiling darkness,
And enter our dreams again.

CONRAD AIKEN

THE HORRID VOICE OF SCIENCE

"There's machinery in the
    butterfly;
  There's a mainspring to the
    bee;
There's hydraulics to a daisy,
    And contraptions to a tree.

63

"If we could see the birdie
    That makes the chirping sound
With x-ray, scientific eyes,
    We could see the wheels go
      round."

And I hope all men
Who think like this
Will soon lie
Underground.

VACHEL LINDSAY

SONG

Let it be forgotten, as a flower is forgotten,
    Forgotten as a fire that once was singing gold.
Let it be forgotten forever and ever —
    Time is a kind friend, he will make us old.

If anyone asks, say it was forgotten
    Long and long ago —
As a flower, as a fire, as a hushed footfall
    In a long forgotten snow.

SARA TEASDALE

From PECKSNIFFIANA

THE INDIGO GLASS IN THE GRASS

Which is real —
This bottle of indigo glass in the grass,
Or the bench with the pot of geraniums, the stained mattress
    and the washed overalls drying in the sun?
Which of these truly contains the world?

64   Neither one, nor the two together.

ANECDOTE OF THE JAR

I placed a jar in Tennessee,
And round it was, upon a hill.
It made the slovenly wilderness
Surround that hill.

The wilderness rose up to it,
And sprawled around, no longer wild.
The jar was round upon the ground
And tall and of a port in air.

It took dominion everywhere.
The jar was gray and bare.
It did not give of bird or bush,
Like nothing else in Tennessee.

THE CURTAINS IN THE HOUSE OF THE METAPHYSICIAN

It comes about that the drifting of these curtains
Is full of long motions; as the ponderous
Deflations of distance; or as clouds
Inseparable from their afternoons;
Or the changing of light, the dropping
Of the silence, wide sleep and solitude
Of night, in which all motion
Is beyond us, as the firmament,
Up-rising and down-falling, bares
The last largeness, bold to see.

WALLACE STEVENS

A PRAYER FOR MY DAUGHTER

I

Once more the storm is howling, and half hid
Under this cradle-hood and coverlid
My child sleeps on. There is no obstacle

65

But Gregory's Wood and one bare hill
Whereby the haystack and roof-levelling wind,
Bred on the Atlantic, can be stayed;
And for an hour I have walked and prayed
Because of the great gloom that is in my mind.

II

I have walked and prayed for this young child an hour,
And heard the sea-wind scream upon the tower,
And under the arches of the bridge, and scream
In the elms above the flooded stream;
Imagining in excited reverie
That the future years had come
Dancing to a frenzied drum
Out of the murderous innocence of the sea.

III

May she be granted beauty, and yet not
Beauty to make a stranger's eye distraught,
Or hers before a looking-glass; for such,
Being made beautiful overmuch,
Consider beauty a sufficient end,
Lose natural kindness, and maybe
The heart-revealing intimacy
That chooses right, and never find a friend.

IV

Helen, being chosen, found life flat and dull,
And later had much trouble from a fool;
While that great Queen that rose out of the spray,
Being fatherless, could have her way,
Yet chose a bandy-legged smith for man.
It's certain that fine women eat
A crazy salad with their meat
Whereby the Horn of Plenty is undone.

V

In courtesy I'd have her chiefly learned;
Hearts are not had as a gift, but hearts are earned
By those that are not entirely beautiful.
Yet many, that have played the fool
For beauty's very self, has charm made wise;
And many a poor man that has roved,
Loved and thought himself beloved,
From a glad kindness cannot take his eyes.

VI

May she become a flourishing hidden tree,
That all her thoughts may like the linnet be,
And have no business but dispensing round
Their magnanimities of sound;
Nor but in merriment begin a chase,
Nor but in merriment a quarrel.
Oh, may she live like some green laurel
Rooted in one dear perpetual place.

VII

My mind, because the minds that I have loved,
The sort of beauty that I have approved,
Prosper but little, has dried up of late,
Yet knows that to be choked with hate
May well be of all evil chances chief.
If there's no hatred in a mind
Assult and battery of the wind
Can never tear the linnet from the leaf.

VIII

An intellectual hatred is the worst,
So let her think opinions are accursed.
Have I not seen the loveliest woman born
Out of the mouth of Plenty's horn,

Because of her opinionated mind
Barter that horn and every good
By quiet natures understood
For an old bellows full of angry wind?

IX

Considering that, all hatred driven hence,
The soul recovers radical innocence
And learns at last that it is self-delighting,
Self-appeasing, self-affrighting,
And that its own sweet will is heaven's will,
She can, though every face should scowl
And every windy quarter howl
Or every bellows burst, be happy still.

X

And may her bridegroom bring her to a house
Where all's accustomed, ceremonious;
For arrogance and hatred are the wares
Peddled in the thoroughfares.
How but in custom and in ceremony
Are innocence and beauty born?
Ceremony's a name for the rich horn,
And custom for the spreading laurel tree.

WILLIAM BUTLER YEATS

From THREE PORTRAITS

DANNY

You marched off southward with the fire of twenty,
Proud of the uniform that you were wearing.
The girls made love to you, and that was plenty;
The drums were beating and the horns were blaring.

From town to town you fought, and bridge to bridge,
Thinking: "So this is Life; so this is Real."
And when you swept up Missionary Ridge,
Laughing at death, you were your own ideal.

But when you limped home, wounded and unsteady,
You found the world was new to you; your clutch
On life had slipped, and you were old already.
So who can blame you if you drink too much,

Or boast about your pride when no one sees,
Or mumble petulant inanities?

MALCOLM COWLEY

TO W. C. W. M. D.

There has been
Another death.
This time
I bring it to you.
You are kind,
Brutal,
You know
How to lower
Bodies.
I ask only
That the rope
Isn't silk,
(Silk doesn't break)
Nor thread,
(Thread does.)
If it lifts
And lowers
Common things,
It will do.

ALFRED KREYMBORG

69

From TO THE RIVER BEACH

STALKS OF WILD HAY

I can shake the wild hay, and wet seed sticks to my hand.
The white lower stalks seem solid. Yellow flowers
Grow in the sun, with dog fennel, near apple trees.
White petals carry to this water. So plants breed.
But I, the man who would have put up his life
Against less pleasure than yours, against your black hair
And your deep mouth, ask that no man my friend
Find me in this wild hay now or tonight
To remind me how worthless this was which was so dear.
It is late for me to see grass-stalks my first time,
And for this trouble of spirit to come to an end.

H. L. DAVIS

PART II

1920–1930

(Volumes 17–36)

THE ILEX TREE

What spirit touched the faded lambrequin,
And slept? The doorway's lintel, ambered, rosed
With age, overlooks a stunted ilex tree
Grown in the middle path. Its branches guard
The house in silence, or with green dark gesture
Spreading protection, whisper pleadingly:
"The past is asleep behind the lambrequin.
Do not go in. The door is closed."

AGNES LEE

NOT HERE

Not here! — not here! I have been here too many years,
    Have stumbled about the darkened room for a door,
Seeing only the phantom shafts the moonlight clears,
    The broken bars of silver along the floor.

I can hear the women's laughter, a song half blown
    Away by the wind; through all the dust I can smell
A garden wet with the rain. And I am alone.
    Not here, old shadows — I know you, all too well!

EDMUND WILSON, JR.

From HELLENICS

BLUE SLEEP

Aphrodite!
Aphrodite of the blue sleep, the bird–black sea,
I thank you that at last my body is at peace.

I toss these flowers from the flowers, your feet,
From the pear buds of your ankles,
The white hyacinths of your limbs.

The love-hour is ended.
Swallow-wings, dreams of a spiked iris,
Gipsy your eyes.

The hollows under your knees are sweet with love.
Your knees are quince-blossoms, bent back by the rain.

Blue of your eyes,
Blue of the Greek seas that has no name,
Am I lifted
To the porch of Aphrodite on your wings?

W. BRYHER

HAWK'S EYES

As a gray hawk's eyes
Turn here and away,
So my course turns
Where I walk each day.

YVOR WINTERS

KEATS TO FANNY BRAWNE

Fanny! If in yours arms my soul could slip —
Arms that my love first fancied — not the grave!
Cities of Hate and Madness round me rave;
And Love with anguished finger at the lip
Fares shelterless! These have my fellowship —
Memory and Loneliness! What's left? To brave
Death! But before it Tragedy: not to crave
You changed or truly seen! The hemlock drip
Of rains upon half-lived or ruined springs,

Where you dance, smiling, numbs me now, and soothes
Hopes that once sought a beauty gone before.
Losses have stripped me! But the vanishings
Of winter winds leave me to starry truths —
Who once desired you, but desire no more!

EDGAR LEE MASTERS

THE FEARLESS

As Winter, fleeing,
Leaves the shreds of its ermine
To be crunched into murk,
The fearless leave
Their names.

MORTIMER J. ADLER

ATAVISM

I always was afraid of Somes's Pond:
Not the little pond, by which the willow stands,
Where laughing boys catch alewives in their hands
In brown, bright shallows; but the one beyond.
There, when the frost makes all the birches burn
Yellow as cow-lilies, and the pale sky shines
Like a polished shell between black spruce and pines,
Some strange thing tracks us, turning where we turn.

You'll say I dream it, being the true daughter
Of those who in old times endured this dread.
Look! Where the lily-stems are showing red
A silent paddle moves below the water,
A sliding shape has stirred them like a breath;
Tall plumes surmount a painted mask of death.

ELINOR WYLIE

75

1921

PERSPECTIVE OF CO-ORDINATION

The circles never fully round, but change
In spiral gropings — not, as on a wall,
Flat-patterned, but back into space they fall,
In depth on depth of indeterminate range.
Where they begin may be here at my hand
Or there far lost beyond the search of eye;
And though I sit, desperately rapt, and try
To trace round-round the line, and understand
The sequence, the relation, the black-art
Of their continuance, hoping to find good
At least some logic of part-joined-to-part,
I judge the task one of too mad a mood:
And prophecy throws its shadow on my heart,
And Time's last sunset flames along my blood.

ARTHUR DAVISON FICKE

THE HUNCHBACK

I saw a hunchback climb over a hill,
Carrying slops for the pigs to swill.

The snow was hard, the air was frore,
And he cast a bluish shadow before.

Over the frozen hill he came,
Like one who is neither strong nor lame;

And I saw his face as he passed me by,
And the hateful look of his dead-fish eye:

His face, like the face of a wrinkled child
Who has never laughed or played or smiled.

I watched him till his work was done;
And suddenly God went out of the sun,

76

Went out of the sun without a sound
But the great pigs trampling the frozen ground.

The hunchback turned and retracked the snows;
But where God's gone, there's no man knows.

JOHN PEALE BISHOP

CUBIST PORTRAIT

She is purposeless as a cyclone; she must move
Either by chance or in a predestined groove,
Following a whim not her own, unable to shape
Her course. From chance or God even she cannot escape!

Think of a cyclone sitting far-off with its head in its hands,
Motionless, drearily longing for distant lands
Where every lonely hurricane may at last discover
Its own transcendent, implacable, indestructible lover!

What is a cyclone? Only thin air moving fast
From here to yonder, to become silent emptiness at last.

MARJORIE ALLEN SEIFFERT

THE GOLDEN FLEECE

I know that life is Jason,
And that beauty is the witch-maiden helping him.
I know that the soft, luminous night of stars
Is the golden fleece he is seeking.
I know that in the beginning
He sowed the boulders, the teeth of dead ages,
And the innumerable armored cities have arisen.
I know that he has thrown among them love and desire,
And they have warred and shall war with each other until the
    end.
And if you doubt the least word I have said,

77

1921

Come out on the dark beach some strange summer night
And watch the huge quivering serpent of the ocean
Still coiled around the trunk of the tree of paradise.

OSCAR WILLIAMS

THE POET AT NIGHT-FALL

I see no equivalents
For that which I see,
Among words.

And sounds are nowhere repeated,
Vowel for vocal wind
Or shaking leaf.

Ah me, beauty does not enclose life,
But blows through it —
Like that idea, the wind,

Which is unseen and useless,
Even superseded upon
The scarred sea;

Which goes and comes
Altering every aspect —
The poplar, the splashing crest —

Altering all, in that moment
When it is not
Because we see it not.

But who would hang
Like a wind-bell
On a porch where no wind ever blows?

GLENWAY WESCOTT

From SUR MA GUZZLA GRACILE

TEA AT THE PALAZ OF HOON

Not less because in purple I descended
The western day through what you called
The loneliest air, not less was I myself.

What was the ointment sprinkled on my beard?
What were the hymns that buzzed beside my ears?
What was the sea whose tide swept through me there?

Out of my mind the golden ointment rained,
And my ears made the blowing hymns they heard.
I was myself the compass of that sea:

I was the world in which I walked, and what I saw
Or heard or felt came not but from myself;
And there I found myself more truly and more strange.

OF THE MANNER OF ADDRESSING CLOUDS

Gloomy grammarians in golden gowns,
Meekly you keep the mortal rendezvous,
Eliciting the still sustaining pomps
Of speech which are like music so profound
They seem an exaltation without sound.
Funest philosophers and ponderers,
Their evocations are the speech of clouds.
So speech of your processionals returns
In the casual evocations of your tread
Across the stale, mysterious seasons. These
Are the music of meet resignation; these
The responsive, still sustaining pomps for you
To magnify, if in that drifting waste
You are to be accompanied by more
Than mute bare splendors of the sun and moon.

OF HEAVEN CONSIDERED AS A TOMB

What word have you, interpreters, of men
Who in the tomb of heaven walk by night,
The darkened ghosts of our old comedy?
Do they believe they range the gusty cold,
With lanterns borne aloft to light the way,
Freemen of death, about and still about
To find whatever it is they seek? Or does
That burial, pillared up each day as porte
And spiritous passage into nothingness,
Foretell each night the one abysmal night,
When the host shall no more wander, nor the light
Of the steadfast lanterns creep across the dark?
Make hue among the dark comedians,
Halloo them in the topmost distances
For answer from their icy Elysée.

WALLACE STEVENS

THE LONELY STREET

School is over. It is too hot
to walk at ease. At ease
in light frocks they walk the streets
to while the time away.
They have grown tall. They hold
pink flames in their right hands.
In white from head to foot,
with sidelong, idle look —
in yellow, floating stuff,
black sash and stockings —
touching their avid mouths
with pink sugar on a stick —
like a carnation each holds in her hand —
they mount the lonely street.

WILLIAM CARLOS WILLIAMS

TAK FOR SIDST

To C. S.

"Good-bye," you said, and your voice was an echo,
    a promise.
You turned to go, a grey iron ghost.
The night took you.
Insubstantial as air, stronger than iron,
You were here and had gone.
Your voice was an omen, an echo.

BABETTE DEUTSCH

UPSTAIRS DOWNSTAIRS

The judge, who lives impeccably upstairs
With dull decorum and its implication,
Has all his servants in to family prayers
And edifies *his* soul with exhortation.
Meanwhile, his blacks live wastefully downstairs;
Not always chaste, they manage to exist
With less decorum than the judge upstairs,
And find withal a something that he missed.

This painful fact a Swede philosopher,
Who tarried for a fortnight in our city,
Remarked one evening at the meal, before
We paralyzed him silent with our pity;
Saying the black man, living with the white,
Had given more than white men could requite.

HERVEY ALLEN

MAXIXE

Los enanitos
Se enojaren

(Old Mexican Song)

The Mexican dwarfs can dance for miles,
Stamping their feet and scattering smiles;
Till the loud hills laugh and laugh again
At the dancing dwarfs in the golden plain,
Till the bamboos sing as the dwarfs dance by
Kicking their feet at a jagged sky,
That, torn by leaves and gashed by hills,
Rocks to the rhythm the hot sun shrills.
The bubble sun sketches shadows that pass
To noiseless jumping-jacks of glass
So long and thin, so silent and opaque,
That the lions shake their orange manes, and quake,
And a shadow that leaps over Popocatepetl
Terrifies the tigers, as they settle
Cat-like limbs cut with golden bars
Under bowers of flowers that shimmer like stars.
Buzzing of insects flutters above,
Shaking the rich trees' treasure-trove
Till the fruit rushes down, like a comet whose tail
Thrashes the night with its golden flail.
The fruit hisses down with a plomp from its tree,
Like the singing of a rainbow as it dips into the sea.
Loud red trumpets of great blossoms blare
Triumphantly like heralds who blow a fanfare;
Till the humming-bird, bearing heaven on its wing,
Flies from the terrible blossoming,
And the humble honey-bee is frightened by the fine
Honey that is heavy like money, and purple like wine;
While birds that flaunt their pinions like pennons
Shriek from their trees of oranges and lemons,
And the scent rises up in a cloud, to make
The hairy swinging monkeys feel so weak
That they each throw down a bitten cocoanut or mango.

Up flames a flamingo over the fandango;
Glowing like a fire, and gleaming like a ruby,
From Guadalajara to Guadalupe
It flies; in flying drops a feather . . .
And the snatching dwarfs stop dancing and fight together.

OSBERT SITWELL

IN HIGH PLACES

My mountains, God has company in heaven —
Crowned saints who sing to him the sun-long day.
He has no need of speech with you — with you,
Dust of his foot-stool! No, but I have need.
Oh, speak to me, for you are mine as well —
Drift of my soul. I built you long ago;
I reared your granite masonry to make
My house of peace, and spread your flowered carpets,
And set your blue-tiled roof, and in your courts
Made musical fountains play. Ah, give me now
Shelter and sustenance and liberty,
That I may mount your sky-assailing towers
And hear the winds communing, and give heed
To the large march of stars, and enter in
The spirit-crowded courts of solitude.

HARRIET MONROE

From BEGINNING AND END

KNOWLEDGE

Now that I know
That passion warms little
Of flesh in the mold,
And treasure is brittle,

I'll lie here and learn
How, over their ground,
Trees make a long shadow
And a light sound.

LOUISE BOGAN

MONODY TO THE SOUND OF ZITHERS

I have wanted other things more than lovers . . .
I have desired peace, intimately to know
The secret curves of deep-bosomed contentment,
To learn by heart things beautiful and slow.

Cities at night, and cloudful skies, I've wanted;
And open cottage doors, old colors and smells a part;
All dim things, layers of river-mist on river —
To capture Beauty's hands and lay them on my heart.

I have wanted clean rain to kiss my eyelids,
Sea-spray and silver foam to kiss my mouth.
I have wanted strong winds to flay me with passion;
And, to soothe me, tired winds from the south.

These things have I wanted more than lovers . . .
Jewels in my hands, and dew on morning grass —
Familiar things, while lovers have been strangers.
Friended thus, I have let nothing pass.

KAY BOYLE

From WANDERINGS

CHAMPS D'HONNEUR

Soldiers never do die well;
Crosses mark the places —
Wooden crosses where they fell,
Stuck above their faces.

Soldiers pitch and cough and twitch —
    All the world roars red and black;
Soldiers smother in a ditch,
    Choking through the whole attack.

CHAPTER HEADING

For we have thought the longer thoughts
    And gone the shorter way.
And we have danced to devils' tunes,
    Shivering home to pray;
To serve one master in the night,
    Another in the day.

ERNEST M. HEMINGWAY

From HERE AND THERE

NOCTURNAL LANDSCAPE

I said: "The moon is obviously a boat
That rocks in the sunken pool as the waters swell.
Let us tiptoe hand in hand to the moon, and float
Inside its rim, as in a coracle.

"Look how she sways," I said, "like a ballet-dancer
That pirouettes to the edge of the stage and back.
We are watching the moon's performance."
                      She did not answer —
Her eyes fixed me and held me in their track.

"I am held," I said, "by the sanity of eyes
From becoming God or a chattering baboon;
From burning these peacock yews, which otherwise
Would shade the cast-iron panthers from the moon —

"From the sight of the waning moon which in July
Reflects its light in the metal eyes of the panthers.
They follow it down the alleys of the sky
Till they find a water poisoned by ailanthus,

85

"A pool like this one, black against the moon,"
I said.
      But her steel eyes held me in their track.
I might have gone quite mad, like the metal panthers,
And followed the moon; but her cold eyes held me back.

Her eyes were fixed and mad, like mine and the panthers'.

MALCOLM COWLEY

PASTORAL

This is a place of ease:
Beauty has come to rest,
Color is gentle in the trees,
The willow leaves look
Timidly down, more timidly back from the brook.

Beauty has come to rest:
Sweet as a sleepy-bell
The breeze swings within the close-pressed
Shadows, and the sun
Falls in little sprays, to be picked by anyone!

MARION STROBEL

STATIC AUTUMN

Inimitably quick
To taut deceit, I
Note a bird
Amid the autumn,

And my glossy bitch
Shatters leaves
Like water,
And the air

Is resonant
With pain.
I wait like one
Who has stood here before

With sunken head
In dropping leaves.

YVOR WINTERS

THE FLOWER-BOAT

The fisherman's swapping a yarn for a yarn
Under the hand of the village barber;
And here in the angle of house and barn
His deep-sea dory has found a harbor.

At anchor she rides the sunny sod
As full to the gunnel of flowers growing
As ever she turned her home with cod
From Georges Bank when winds were blowing.

And I judge from that Elysian freight
That all they ask is rougher weather,
And dory and master will sail by fate
To seek for the Happy Isles together.

ROBERT FROST

Written at the age of 20.
Published in *The Youth's Companion*.

THE EQUINOX

Heavy with salt, and warm
And damp from the Caribbean,
Like a wrestler's body
Muscled under its sweat;

Sounding a deep alarm
That shrills to a paean,
It charges the shuddering spit
Where the rivers have met.

Under its whirling cloak
The hummocks and houses are shrunken
To figures of fear
In the blue-green daylight-dark.
Only a dwarfed sea-oak
Leans truculent, drunken,
Brandishing terrible arms
That wind-bludgeons leave stark.

From the demoniac vault.
Gargantuan sledges
Crash to the huddling roofs
Until frail timbers start.
Then, thundering to the assault
Like surf on the ledges,
The weight of the wind drives through
And rends them apart.

Now the palmettoes that lash
On the southernmost beaches,
Thrill to the shout of the storm,
And sing through the rain.
Remembering typhoons that smash
Along tropical reaches,
They batter the winds with great hands,
And are happy again.

DUBOSE HEYWARD

OF DYING BEAUTY

"Spare us of dying beauty," cries out Youth,
"Of marble gods that moulder into dust —
Wide-eyed and pensive with an ancient truth
That even gods will go as old things must."

Where fading splendor grays to powdered earth,
And time's slow movement darkens quiet skies,
Youth weeps the old, yet gives new beauty birth
And molds again, though the old beauty dies.
Time plays an ancient dirge amid old places
Where ruins are a sign of passing strength,
As is the weariness of aged faces
A token of a beauty gone at length.
Yet youth will always come self-willed and gay —
A sun-god in a temple of decay.

LOUIS ZUKOFSKY

MIND FLYING AFAR

What a moment of strange dreaming! Quickly
All my vision girdled earth, and showed me
Temples in far India, tombs in Persia,
Down the Appian Way; and over Florence,
Home of Dante, wandering-place of Browning.
And how strange, how prying was this vision! —
For the coffin of old Landor opened;
Showed me what was left of that imperious
Proud and lonely singer of stern beauty.
There he lay, gone down to bits of nothing —
Just a few stray hairs, a piece of shoulder;
Nothing else of him who wrote these verses:
"Proud word you never spoke, but in some future
Day you shall not keep from speaking these words —
Over my open volume you will linger;
You will say in reading: 'This man loved me.'"

Who was she, and where is gone her beauty?
In what place of cypress or of willows,
In what separation from her poet,
Lies the woman, never speaking proud words?
Only there, over his treasured volume,
"This man loved me," tears upon the pages!

EDGAR LEE MASTERS

89

CHICAGO

Your faith is in what you hold,
Monster, with your back against the lakes.
You gather the cities close, with iron reins
Knotted in your frozen grip.
But your sleepily savage eyes, like a white bull's,
Turn neither to the East nor West.
Sometimes a sickness takes you —
Convulsive movements pass along your length. . . .
I think there is a giant child that kicks in you,
Where your blood is running like a river under its ice.

LOLA RIDGE

EPITAPH

Serene descent, as a red leaf's descending
    When there is neither wind nor noise of rain,
But only autumn air and the unending
    Drawing of all things to the earth again.

So be it, let the snow fall deep and cover
    All that was drunken once with light and air.
The earth will not regret her tireless lover,
    Nor he awake to know she does not care.

SARA TEASDALE

DEMENTIA PRAECOX

They put him here because God came at night
    And bade him prophesy and cry aloud;
As Jonah boomed against the Ninevite,
    Turning to God that stiff-necked folk and proud.

And to this revelation was he bidden:
    "Peace and good-will, and joy to all mankind!

Since God is Joy, let joy no more be chidden!
  Be glad, ye lepers! And rejoice, ye blind!"

He found men heedless to his admonitions,
  Courtiers of sorrow, husbands of despair.
Now this sane man, tended by mad physicians,
  Bellows of joy into the sodden air.

MORRIS BISHOP

From THREE SONGS

THESSALIAN

Bind your straight hair,
Thessalian,
For the winds pursue you
And the leaves.

The lake breeze would have you for a wrestler,
It would dust you with sand in the marshes,
Wash sedges and lilies to your feet;

Test your shoulders,
Whether they or the rushes were more supple,
Whether they or the larches were more sweet.

Bind back your hair,
Thessalian,
The fists of the wind are clenched.

WINIFRED BRYHER

TO A COURTESAN A THOUSAND YEARS DEAD

Be of good cheer, spirit of Myrrha!
Though you scattered your kisses shamelessly —
Confetti thrown out of open windows —

Though virtuous wives died, forgotten and hated,
And virgins could not find pure husbands,
Though your small silver sword, with exquisite handle
Studded with diamonds from the crowns of kings,
Pierced the heart of the saint who forgave you,
Be of good cheer!
Your delicate body hidden in the ebony coffin —
A white breast covered by black wings —
Has turned to water, and joined the rain
That pattered on you like little hammers.

Now you are a bit of foam that sizzles
Upon the peak of a wave in mid-ocean.

PAUL ELDRIDGE

From CONTRIBUTIONS

FOR INSTANCE

Vegetables

and jewelry, rightly displayed,
have an equal amount of fascination.

Carrots, for instance,
piled —
ferntops, bodies, and hair roots
so bound together in bunches —
bunches laid in rows
of oblong heaps with magnitude,
are sufficient to arrest any seeing eye.

Cabbages with a purplish tinge,
when of grandeur, with widespread petals,
as they rest in heaps
catching the dawn's first filtering of sunlight,
compare satisfyingly with roses enmassed,

with orchids, sunflowers, tulips,
or variegated flowers
extravagantly scattered.

While as to onions,
little can excel their decorative effect
when green tubes, white bulbs, and grey hair roots
rest in well arranged, paralleled piles
about which buxom women congregate,
laughing and chattering in wholesome vulgarity.

Crispness,
a cool indifference to the gash of knives,
to the crush of kind,
or to any destiny whatsoever,
has granted the vegetables an arrogance of identity
one would be foolhardy to strive after
with heated impressionable imagination.

Vegetables,
given their color,
scent and freshness,
too easily attain a cool supremacy of being
for our fumbling competition.

ROBERT MCALMON

From BODY'S HEAD

HEAD ITSELF

If it were set anywhere else but so,
Rolling in its private exact socket
Like the sun set in a joint on a mountain,
I think I should not love it half as much.
But here, waving and blowing on my neck,
Of no particular kind of shape or geometry,
Its own original,

Flying my hair like a field of corn-silk
Tangled on the neglected side of a hill,
My head is at the top of me
Where my face turns an inner courage
Toward what's outside of me
And meets the challenge of difference in other things
Bravely, minutely,
By being what it is.

From this place of high preferment
I, the idol of the head,
Send all the streams of sense running down
To explore the savage half-awakened land,
Tremendous continent of this tiny isle,
And civilize it as well as they can.

LAURA RIDING GOTTSCHALK

FOR AMY LOWELL

She leans across a golden table,
Confronts God with an eye
Still puzzled by the standard label
All flesh bears: *Made to die!*
And questions Him — if he is able
To reassure her Why.

COUNTEE CULLEN

THE OWL

Beyond the inmost barriers of the brain,
Hid by the tree of thought's most secret bough,
While suns and moons of mood arise and wane,
Patience, the owl, considers wisdom now.
Her twin dark-closing eyes in safety keep
The present and the past, and for the rest
Shadow and silence blend themselves with sleep,

Nestled against the oval of her breast.
Still motionless she ages, growing wise,
And day by day dreams on and never stirs;
Nor till the last leaf falls before her eyes,
And the bare winter ends that peace of hers,
Will she burst up into the startled night
Wailing, on wings widespread for sudden flight.

EDWARD DAVISON

ARS POETICA

A poem should be palpable and mute
As a globed fruit;

Dumb
As old medallions to the thumb;

Silent as the sleeve-worn stone
Of casement ledges where the moss has grown —

A poem should be wordless
As the flight of birds.

A poem should be motionless in time
As the moon climbs;

Leaving, as the moon releases
Twig by twig the night-entangled trees —

Leaving, as the moon behind the winter leaves,
Memory by memory the mind.

A poem should be motionless in time
As the moon climbs.

A poem should be equal to:
Not true.

For all the history of grief
An empty doorway and a maple leaf;

For love
The leaning grasses and two lights above the sea —

A poem should not mean,
But be.

ARCHIBALD MACLEISH

CRIMSON TENT

The wind blows up the tent like a balloon.
The tent plunges tugging at pegged ropes,
About to wrench loose and soar
Above wormwood-carpeted canyons
And flinty saw-tooth hills
Up into the driven night
And the howling clouds.
Tight
As a worm curls wickedly
Round the stamen of a fuchsia,
A man curls his hands round a candle.
The flame totters in the wind,
Flares to lick his hands,
To crimson the swaying walls.
The hands cast shadows on the crimson walls.

The candle-light shrinks and flaps wide.
The shadows are full of old tenters —
Men curious as to the fashion of cities,
Men eager to taste new-tasting bread,
Men wise to the north star and to the moon's phases,
To whom East and West
Are cloaks pulled easily tight,
Worn jaunty about the shoulders:
Herodotus, Thales, Democritus,
Heraclitus who watched rivers.

Parian–browed tan–cheeked travellers,
Who sat late in wine-shops to listen,
Rose early to sniff the wind of harbors
And see the dawn kindle the desert places,
And went peering and tasting —
Through seas and wastes and cities,
Held up to the level of their grey cool eyes
Firm in untrembling fingers —
The slippery souls of men and of gods.

The candle has guttered out in darkness and wind.
The tent holds firm against the buffeting wind,
Pegged tight, weighted with stones.
My sleep is blown up with dreams
About to wrench loose and soar
Above wormwood-carpeted canyons
And flinty saw-tooth hills,
Up into the driven night
And the howling clouds.

Perhaps when the light clangs
Brass and scarlet cymbals in the east
With drone and jangle of great bells,
Loping white across the flint-strewn hills,
Will come the seeking tentless caravans
That Bilkis leads untired,
Nodding in her robes
On a roaring dromedary.

JOHN DOS PASSOS

THE HARD LOVERS

Now austere lips are laid
Sternly on lips: implicit
In each bold body, dread
Of the outrageous visit.

97

As wind in a tall tide
Flooding the frantic trees,
Love, long withheld by pride,
Breaks coldly over these.

Their heritage is peace;
They root in a strong languor;
Like wind-assaulted trees
They bend in terrible anger.

They coldly clash — if either
Yields any tenderness
It is that they together
Share deeply one distress.

GEORGE H. DILLON

AT MELVILLE'S TOMB

Often beneath the wave, wide from this ledge,
The dice of drowned men's bones he saw bequeath
An embassy. Their numbers, as he watched,
Beat on the dusty shore and were obscured.

And wrecks passed without sound of bells,
The calyx of death's bounty giving back
A scattered chapter, livid hieroglyph,
The portent wound in corridors of shells.

Then in the circuit calm of one vast coil,
Its lashings charmed and malice reconciled,
Frosted eyes there were that lifted altars:
And silent answers crept across the stars.

Compass, quadrant and sextant contrive
No farther tides. . . . High in the azure steeps
Monody shall not wake the mariner.
This fabulous shadow only the sea keeps.

HART CRANE

From BLUE JUNIATA

THE STREETS OF AIR

All night waiting, in an empty house
under dry electric moons, they cast
no shadow, a man striding impatiently
sucking a dry pipe, waiting
an empty sacrificial vessel waiting
without patience to be filled with God.

He said,
      — There was a scratching at my door
the noise of some one fingering the latch
once, but I opened and only found the night
empty of sound, empty —
      The images of drouth
in a parched land growing, acacias in the sand
with thorns and thornlike leaves that cast no shadow,
dry leaves silently moving in the sun.

A wall rose there, of hewn enormous stones
laid without mortar and a gateway, barred
and skies closed in.
      But you shall hear the thunder
of bursting walls, the gates of night swing wide,
and journeys will be set toward the thunder.

Your path shall be the empty streets of air.

                       MALCOLM COWLEY

APPLE HELL

Apples, bright on the leafless bough
In the high noon sun, with the sky above you,
Time will turn; for the white sky falls,
And long red shadows soon will shove you

Eastward, downward, into the room
Where the moon hangs low like a smoking lamp;
Walls lean in; and the studded ceiling
Shines no more; and the bins grow damp.

Apples, yellow on the naked limb,
Although you burn till the air be gold,
Time is tarnish. Skies are falling,
Noon is dead, and the day grows old.

MARK VAN DOREN

TO A SEAMAN DEAD ON LAND

Bitten to dust are the savage feathers of fire,
And the foam lies in rusted chains on the sand.
The black weeds of the sea and the conch's spire
Are brittle as bird-claws upon my hand.

My ear on the drum of the dune is hollow
Under the sabres of clanging grass —
Stark for the thunder of sails to follow,
And the throb of wings when the dark gulls pass.

Ah, but the land has silenced you,
Your blood thinning down in dew on an inland plain.
Ah, but the loud sea would have rended you
On coral stalks and the straight white horns of rain.

The sea would have pierced you with the salt of its pace,
Boomed down your sails and the ribs of your bark on stones,
Given me touch of you in the bitter foam on my face
And the sea-mist coiled like silk about your bones.

KAY BOYLE

COUNSEL TO UNREASON

These lover's inklings which our loves enmesh,
Lost to the cunning and dimensional eye,
Though tenemented in the selves we see,
Not more perforce than azure to the sky,
Were necromancy-juggled to the flesh,
And startled from no daylight you or me.

For trance and silverness those moons commend,
Which blanch the warm life silver-pale; or look
What ghostly portent mist distorts from slight
Clay shapes; the willows that the waters took
Liquid and brightened in the water's bend,
And we, in love's reflex, seem loved of right.

Then no more think to net forthwith love's thing,
But cast for it by spirit sleight-of-hand,
Then only in the slant glass contemplate,
Where lineament outstripping line is scanned.
Then on the perplexed text leave pondering —
Love's proverb is set down transliterate.

LÉONIE ADAMS

IN THE BEGINNING WAS A WORD

The difficulty was, it was
Simple, as simple as it seemed;
Needing no scrutinizing glass,
No intense light to be streamed

Upon it. It said what it said
Singly, without backthought or whim,
With all the strictness of the dead,
Past reason and past synonym.

But they, too dull to understand,
Laboriously improvised
A mystic allegory, and
A meaning at last recognized:

A revelation and a cause,
Crowding the cluttered stage again
With saints' and sinners' lies and laws
For a new everlasting reign.

ROBERT GRAVES

THE COOL WEB

Children are dumb to say how hot the sun is,
How hot the scent is of the summer rose,
How dreadful the black wastes of evening sky,
How dreadful the tall soldiers drumming by.

But we have speech that cools the hottest sun,
And speech that dulls the hottest rose's scent.
We spell away the overhanging night,
We spell away the soldiers and the fright.

There's a cool web of language winds us in
Retreat from too much gladness, too much fear:
We grow sea-green at last, and coldly die
In brininess and volubility.

But if we let our tongues lose self-possession,
Throwing off language and its wateriness
Before our death, instead of when death comes;
Facing the brightness of the children's day,
Facing the rose, the dark sky and the drums —
We shall go mad no doubt, and die that way.

ROBERT GRAVES

CONTEMPORARY

We shall be called harsh names by men unborn,
Since we have seen no glory in his face.
Our blindness shall not save us from the scorn
Of those who bend above the guarded case,
Where under glass his crowded note-book shines
(Pages we turn — dismiss with comment smug),
Become a thing a flaming dream enshrines,
The miracle we greeted with a shrug.

For now as always, tortured and alone,
Behind a paltry door he makes his fight;
Great thoughts sit down to dinner with a bone,
And beauty starves and sings and trims the light.
But no man comes — no man with praise for bread.
We shall be better friends when he is dead.

HORTENSE FLEXNER

HYMN TO EVIL

Heavenly Evil, holy One,
You whose work is never done,
Any visage, any name
Cannot cloak your single aim.
Watch a leaf in autumn flit —
Resurrection flames from it.
Death, as anybody knows,
Feeds the roots of any rose.
Gasping of an insect scales
Into notes of nightingales.
Crushing agonies alone
Melt into the diamond-stone
Till some earthquake lets us see
Long-imprisoned jewels free.
Motes of dust, in catching rays,
Comb a sunset from the blaze.

Rills will run to meet your shocks,
Sucking melody from rocks.
Darkness, beating on your bars,
Brightens into foam of stars.

Any visage, any name
Cannot cloak your single aim;
Anywhere in matter hide,
You are still the spirit's guide.
Fire or prism, mire or stone,
All are you and you alone.
Blest and mighty Evil, you —
Holy is the deed you do!

LOUIS GINSBERG

MESSAGE

Seeing in flight along the lifting wind,
Like sudden birds peopling an empty sky,
Those last crisped leaves so long you had passed by —
Where dark they hung that had been fire behind
The pasture whose scant blossoms kept in mind
Our summer now grown gold for memory —
Did you remember as you saw them pass,
Flutter and sink, sully the silvered grass,
That each forsaken stem bears, fast asleep,
An eager bud to tell the tale of spring?
Will you forget, hearing the darkness weep,
How each hour moves toward their awakening?

DOROTHY M. RICHARDSON

O CARIB ISLE!

The tarantula rattling at the lily's foot,
Across the feet of the dead, laid in white sand
Near the coral beach; the small and ruddy crabs
Stilting out of sight, that reverse your name —

And above, the lyric palsy of eucalypti, seeping
A silver swash of something unvisited. . . .
    Suppose
I count these clean enamel frames of death,
Brutal necklaces of shells around each grave
Laid out so carefully. This pity can be told . . .

And in the white sand I can find a name, albeit
In another tongue. Tree-name, flower-name
    deliberate,
Gainsay the unknown death. . . . The wind,
Sweeping the scrub palms, also is almost kind.

But who is a Captain of this doubloon isle
Without a turnstile? Nought but catchword crabs
Plaguing the hot groins of the underbrush? Who
The commissioner of mildew throughout the
    senses?
His Carib mathematics dull the bright new
    lenses.

Under the poinciana, of a noon or afternoon
Let fiery blossoms clot the light, render my
    ghost,
Sieved upward, black and white along the air —
Until it joins the blue's comedian host.

Let not the pilgrim see himself again
Bound like the dozen turtles on the wharf
Each twilight — still undead, and brine caked in
    their eyes,
— Huge, overturned: such thunder in their
    strain!
And clenched beaks coughing for the surge
    again!

Slagged of the hurricane — I, cast within its
    flow,
Congeal by afternoons here, satin and vacant . . .

You have given me the shell, Satan — the ember,
Carbolic, of the sun exploded in the sea.

HART CRANE

From THINGS KNOWN

UNDER THE HILL

When darkness crept and grew
The hushed wide earth lay still.
I listened; I thought I knew
The vibrance under the hill.
If I were now just dead
I could not make less sound.
I slowly bent my head
Intently to the ground.
I listened again. My feet
Took root within the soil;
Earth grew within me, sweet
In my limbs. I knew the soil
Had claimed my body whole.
I listened. There came no sound
Across the darkening knoll
Or over the matted ground.

I had become a thing
Of earth. My face felt air
As leaves feel winds that bring
A sudden cool. My hair
Was grass, my flesh was sand —
Strange that it happened there
Upon the solid land!
My blood turned water. My bone
Took on the strength of stone.

Mixed with earth and sky,
I bore all things to die.
I caused the twig to sprout
And every flower come out.
Flaming the earth with spring
I made each robin sing,
Then sent the long heat down
Tinging green leaves with brown.
I made the summer old
With singing autumn gold,
And stilled all things that grow,
And covered the world with snow.

When darkness crept and grew
The hushed wide earth lay still.
Being earth, at last I knew
The vibrance under the hill.

RICHARD EBERHART

From THE TRUMPET

V — GRASS ON THE CLIFF

Under the house, between the road the sea-cliff, bitter wild
    grass
Stands narrowed between the people and the storm.
The ocean winter after winter gnaws at its earth, the wheels and
    the feet
Summer after summer encroach and destroy.
Stubborn green life, for the cliff-eater I cannot comfort you,
    ignorant which color,
Gray-blue or pale-green, will please the late stars;
But laugh at the other, your seed shall enjoy wonderful venge-
    ances and suck
The arteries and walk in triumph on the faces.

ROBINSON JEFFERS

JOURNAL TO STELLA

Our cherished dualism gone?
Six seasons saw it wasting, for
The frames were broken, seals undone,
And ribbons raveled on the floor.

The gradual fear, the growing dread,
Have found their end in casual lust.
We ate the honeyed heart of bread
But threw away the bitter crust.

Compacts like ours have always lent
Their glamour to an obvious deed,
Greater than treaty bought in Ghent
Or charter signed at Runnymede.

The alleys stretch without a torch,
Low darkness creeps around the room;
We tried to sweep our narrow porch
But fingers trembled on the broom.

Pray, though the night seem strange and long
And spectral gatepost forms appear,
That yet the first grey streak grow strong
Before man's laughter hunts our fear!

MORTON DAUWEN ZABEL

LAMENT FOR GLASGERION

The lovely body of the dead,
Wherein he laid him down to rest,
Is shrunken to corruption's thread;
The blood which delicately dressed
The flying bone, the sighing breast,
One with nothingness is made.

The darling garment is outworn;
Its fabric nourishes the moth.
The silk wherein his soul was born,
Woven of flesh and spirit both,
Is crumpled to a pitiful cloth.
His soul lies naked and forlorn.

So one that walks within the air,
Who loves the ghost below the ground,
Rejoices fervently to wear
A body shaken and unsound;
A brow divided by a wound;
A throat encircled by a care.

Shall I go warm above the cold
Wherein he sleeps without a shroud
Or shred of beauty left to fold
About the poor soul's solitude?
The vanishing dust of my heart is proud
To watch me wither and grow old.

ELINOR WYLIE

BIRDS IN SNOW

See
how they trace,
across the very-marble
of this place,
bright sevens and printed fours,
elevens and careful eights,
abracadabra
of a mystic's lore
or symbol
outlined
on a wizard's gate.

Like plaques of ancient writ
our garden flags now name
the great and very-great;
our garden flags acclaim
in carven hieroglyph,
here king and kinglet lie,
here prince and lady rest,
mythical queens sleep here
and heroes that are slain

in holy righteous war.
Hieratic, slim and fair,
the tracery written here
proclaims what's left unsaid
in Egypt of her dead.

H. D.

From PUBLISHED CORRESPONDENCE

EPISTLE TO THE RAPALLOAN

Ezra, whom not with eye nor with ear have I ever
(But nevertheless as one by a rhyme-beat, one
By the break of his syllables, one by a slow breath) known,
By doubts that in common between us two deliver
Better your face to me than the photograph,
Which besides they say lies — they say, that is, you were
        never
The beautiful boy with the sullen mouth, the giver
Of ambiguous apples — Ezra, you that could laugh

When the rest of them followed your hearse in five-years-
        ago's mud,
When the rest of them talked of the promise of youth cut off
By a fever, a flush in the cheek, an ironical cough
(That did in truth, they were right enough there, bring
blood),

Ezra, I've read again your *Sixteen Cantos:*
  There's a word for my praise — if there's a rhyme for
    cantos!

ARCHIBALD MACLEISH

From HOSPITAL POEMS

TRANSFUSION

The scene is set now: in a silent room
Is Woman exsanguinated on a bed;

Enter the cult in mask and white cloth clad
Bearing borrowed blood in a red cup
The first tall foremost priest holds and lifts up;

The arm is cleansed — a needle in the vein,
Then rosy color fast returns again.

Averted is proximity of doom
And joyous the new blood enters avenues
Of old veins to dispel the bluish hues
On face and finger, joyous as a bride-groom,

The new blood enters in the trembling room
That is the heart's first chamber whence it flows
And does the miracles men say it does.

MERRILL MOORE

PROPHECY ON LETHE

Echo, the beating of the tide,
Infringes on the blond curved shore;
Archaic weeds from sleep's green side
Bind skull and pelvis till the four
Seasons of the blood are unified.

1929

Anonymous sweet carrion,
Blind mammal floating on the stream
Of depthless sound, completely one
In the cinnamon-dark of no dream: —
A pod of silence, bursting when the sun

Clings to the forehead, will surprise
The gasping turtle and the leech
With your strange brain blooming as it lies
Abandoned to the bipeds on the beach;
Your jelly-mouth and, crushed, your polyp eyes.

STANLEY J. KUNITZ

THE DESERTED HOMESTEAD

The wind is desolate in the fields;
And round the house at night
The autumn smoulder of decay
Creeps like a blight.

His standing corn with mildew rusts
Forsaken on the hill.
The wild will cover up the road
Now his hands are still.

Only a sparrow, like a leaf,
Skips along the eaves,
Half lonely for a human voice
In the hush of leaves.

This ending that is old as earth
Sorrow cannot break.
Our doors are open to the wind,
And the wind will take.

The jeweled phrase is worthless here.
The blackbird and the crow,

Bleak criers over windswept land,
Alone may sow

Dark syllables across the wind;
Or, in the ruined field,
Deride the hackneyed misery —
Earth's only yield.

LOREN C. EISELEY

MISERICORDIA

Summer, betray this tree again!
Bind her in winding sheets of green;
With empty promises unlock her lips;
Sift futile pollen through her finger-tips.
Curve those tense hands, so tightened in disdain,
To eager chalices for falling rain.
Break and elaborate that frozen line
With golden tendril and swift sinuous vine.
Summer, in mercy blur this bare delight
Of chiselled boughs against the winter night!

MARGARET MEAD

SOUTHWEST PASSAGE

I remember partly
There was a river, a dark foreflowing song
Of silence. There was a way
Irremeably downward. There was
Loss also in that selfless flood, submerging
Desire with all desired

(I would not know
That hour again, I would not live tolling
Future suns to arise from these dead
Embers of morning:

                    I tell you, I have lost
Irrevocable things: innocence, my standing before you;
Faith, my strength in you; and I have heard the cry
Of them that ride on hopeless croiseries,
And I have hid my face)

Long roads Long roads from the world's end:
Morning was open; the way called,
Youth was brave, the heart careless, fair
And free the ascent; but at noon
Freshness was gone from the sky, the young winds burned
Stalely, heaviness dragged on the heart; thereafter
The sullen roads wound crazily
Through vacant lands, through cruel meaningless wastes,
Urgent, futile, to converge at last

In this: the shrine empty,
The sought chalice dry,
Long roads in vain.

It is vague now, it is almost forgotten now

I remember only
I slept: and it was after waking with sleep drifting
From roof to quiet roof, and I arose
And dressed and joined numberless mute faces turning
        westward;
Voicelessly the night drew down sliding cold stars,
The road lambent with barbs of brittle flame,
And we marched on, and terribly the years
Marched with us: Long roads
Long roads back to the western rim of the world,
Long roads in vain, until

                    (I would not remember,
I would not know again, only
I would cross over)

There was a river
Irremeable, darkflowing, sweetly profound.
No memory troubled that other distant shore.
And all we knelt, I knelt, at the river's brim,
And my eyelids were wet
In Lethe

DUDLEY FITTS

PART III

1930–1940
(Volumes 37–56)

SONNET

Women have loved before as I love now;
At least, in lively chronicles of the past —
Of Irish waters by a Cornish prow
Or Trojan waters by a Spartan mast
Much to their cost invaded — here and there,
Hunting the amorous line, skimming the rest,
I find some woman bearing as I bear
Love like a burning city in the breast.
I think however that of all alive
I only in such utter, ancient way
Do suffer love; in me alone survive
The unregenerate passions of a day
When treacherous queens, with death upon the tread,
Heedless and wilful, took their knights to bed.

EDNA ST. VINCENT MILLAY

From WORDS ON THE WIND

FRUIT OF LONELINESS

Now for a little I have fed on loneliness
As on some strange fruit from a frost-touched vine —
Persimmon in its yellow comeliness,
Or pomegranate-juice color of wine,
The pucker-mouth crab apple, or late plum —
On fruit of loneliness have I been fed.
But now after short absence I am come
Back from felicity to the wine and bread.
For, being mortal, this luxurious heart

Would starve for you, my dear, I must admit,
If it were held another hour apart
From that food which alone can comfort it —
I am come home to you, for at the end
I find I cannot live without you, friend.

MAY SARTON

KANSAS CITY WEST BOTTOMS

The nickelplate moon
Is low over the wires
Like a Queensboro
Electric lamp.
The lights along the street
Are fragments of
A shooting star.

The evening is a lonely wind
In my bones
And the sidewalks are
Thick fog inside me.
Down below
The lanterns at the
Railroad crossing
Are blue on my lips.
A caboose is stalled somewhere,
And the Long Island train
Rattles along the tracks
Like a talmudic student
In a chaider.

And after the night has
Rolled up into a piece of
Stage celluloid,
The Kansas City west bottoms

Returns and stirs up
The hossfly stockyards,
The strawy cool livery-stables,
The bluffs,
And the belly-stabbing
Hobo-pariah box-car '20's.

EDWARD DAHLBERG

THE WORD

Nothing
substance utters or time
stills or restrains
joins the design and the

supple measure deftly
as thought's intricate polyphonic
score dovetails with the tread
sensuous things
keep in our consciousness.

Celebrate man's craft
and the word spoken in shapeless night, the
sharp tool paring away
waste and the forms
cut out of mystery!

When the tight string's note
passes ear's reach, or red rays or violet
fade, strong over unseen
forces the word
ranks and enumerates . . .

Mimes the clouds condensed
and the hewn hills and the bristling forests,
steadfast corn in its season
and the seasons

in their due array,
life of man's own body
and death. . . .
            The sound thins into melody,
discourse narrowing, craft
failing, design
petering out;

ears heavy to breeze of speech and
thud of the ictus.

Appendix: Iron
    Molten pool, incandescent spilth of
    deep cauldrons — and brighter nothing is —
    cast and cold, your blazes extinct and
    no turmoil nor peril left you,
    rusty ingot, bleak paralyzed blob!

BASIL BUNTING

From MUTATIONS

MIDSUMMER

The adolescent night, breath of the town,
Porch-swings and whispers, maple leaves unseen
Deploying moonlight quieter than a man dead
After the locusts' song. These homes were mine
And are not now forever, these on the steps
Children I think removed to many places,
Lost among hushed years, and so strangely known.

This business is well ended. If in the dark
The firefly made his gleam and sank therefrom
Yet someone's hand would have him, the wet grass
Bed him no more. . . . From corners of the lawn
The dusk-white dresses flutter and are past . . .
Before our bed-time there were things to say
Remembering tree-bark, crickets, and the first star.

After, and as the sullenness of time
Went on from summer, here in a land alien
Made I my perfect fears and flower of thought.
Sleep being no longer swift in the arms of pain,
Revisitations are convenient with a cough
And there is something I would say again
If I had not forever, if there were time.

ROBERT FITZGERALD

HYPOCRITE SWIFT

After Reading Swift's Journal to Stella

Hypocrite Swift now takes an eldest daughter.
He lifts Vanessa's hand. *Cudsho, my dove!*
Drink Wexford Ale and quaff down Wexford water,
But never love.

He buys new caps; he and Lord Stanley ban
Hedge-fellows who have neither wit nor swords.
He turns his coat; Tories are in; Queen Anne
Makes twelve new lords.

The town mows hay in hell; he swims in the river;
His giddiness returns; his head is hot.
Berries are clean, while peaches damn the giver,
(Though grapes do not).

Mrs. Vanhomrigh keeps him safe from the weather.
Preferment pulls his periwig askew.
Pox take belittlers; do the willows feather?
God keep you.

Stella spells ill; Lords Peterborough and Fountain
Talk politics; the Florence wine went sour.
Midnight: two different clocks, here and in Dublin,
Give out the hour.

On walls at court, long gilded mirrors gaze.
The parquet shines; outside the snow falls deep.
Venus, the Muses stare above the maze.
Now sleep.

Dream the mixed, fearsome dream. The satiric word
Dies in its horror. Wake, and live by stealth.
The bitter quatrain forms, is here, is heard,
Is wealth.

What care I; what cares saucy Presto? Stir
The bed-clothes, hearten up the perishing fire.
Hypocrite Swift sent Stella a green apron
And dead desire.

LOUISE BOGAN

SAILOR

He sat upon the rolling deck
Half a world away from home,
And smoked a Capstan cigarette
And watched the blue waves tipped with foam.

He had a mermaid on his arm,
An anchor on his breast,
And tattooed on his back he had
A blue bird in a nest.

LANGSTON HUGHES

From THE ROOFTREE

SONNETS OF THE BLOOD

I

What is this flesh and blood compounded of
But water seething with convulsive lime?
This prowling strife of cells, sharp hate and love,
Wears the long claw of flesh-devouring time.

We who have seen the makers of our bone
Bemused with history, then make more dust
Pausing forever, and over their dust a stone,
We know the chastened look of men who must
Confess the canker gnawing the flesh flower
And are made brothers by mortality;
That is our treason to the murderous hour —
To think of brothers, hard identity
Not made of ash and lime by time undone
Nor poured out quite when the life-blood has run.

II

Near to me as my flesh, my flesh and blood,
And more mysterious, you are my brother;
The light vaulting within your solitude
Now studied burns lest you that rage should smother.
It is a flame obscure to mortal eyes
(Most like the fire that warms the deepest grave,
For the cold grave's the deepest of our lies)
Of which our blood's the long indentured slave.
The fire that burns most secretly in you
Does not expand you hidden and alone,
For the same blaze consumes not one, but two,
Me also, the same true marrow and bone
Contrived and seasoned in a house of strife
Built far back in the fundaments of life.

IV

The times have changed, there is not left to us
The vice of privilege, the law of form —
Who of our kin was pusillanimous
And took the world so easy, so by storm?
Why none, unless we count it arrogance
To cultivate humility in pride,
To look but blushingly and half-askance
On boots and spurs that went the devil's ride.
There was, remember, that Virginian
Who took himself to be brute nature's law

125

And cared not what men thought him, a tall man
Who meditated calmly what he saw
Until he freed his negroes, lest he be
Too strict with nature and then they less free.

VII

The fire I praise was once perduring flame
Till it snuffs with our generation, out —
No matter, it's all one, it's but a name
Not as late honeysuckle half so stout,
So think upon it how the fire burns blue
Its hottest, when the fury's all but spent;
Thank God the fuel is low, we'll not renew
Such length of flame into our firmament;
Think too the rooftree crackles and will fall
On us, who saw the sacred fury's height
Seated in her great chair with the black shawl
From head to feet, burning with motherly light
More spectral than November eve could mix
With sunset, to blaze on her pale crucifix.

IX

Not power nor the storied hand of God
Shall keep us whole in this dissevering air,
Which is a stink upon this pleasant sod
So foul, the hovering buzzard sees it fair.
I ask you therefore will it end tonight
And the moth tease again his windy flame,
Or spiders eating their loves hide in the night
At last, drowsy with self-devouring shame?
This is the house of Atreus where we live —
Which one of us the Greek, perplexed with crime,
Questions the future that with his lucid sieve
Strains off the appointed particles of time;
It is not spoken now, for time is slow,
Which brother, you or I, shall swiftly go.

ALLEN TATE

THE WOLVES

There are wolves in the next room waiting
With heads bent low, thrust out, breathing
At nothing in the dark: between them and me
A white door patched with light from the hall
Where it seems never (so still is the house)
A man has walked from the front door to the stair.
It has all been forever; a beast claws the floor.
I have brooded on angels and archfiends
But no man has ever sat where the next room's
Crowded with wolves, and for the honor of man
I affirm that never have I before. Now while
I have looked for the evening star at a cold window
And whistled when Arcturus spilt his light,
I've heard the wolves scuffle, and said: So this
Is man; so — and what better conclusion is there —
The day will not follow night, and the heart
Of man has a little dignity, but less patience
Than a wolf's, and a duller sense that cannot
Smell its own mortality. (This and other
Meditations will be suited to other times
After dog silence howls my epitaph.)
Now remember courage, go to the door,
Open it and see whether coiled on the bed
Or cringing by the wall a savage beast,
Maybe with golden hair, with deep eyes
Like a bearded spider on a sunlit floor,
Will snarl — and man can never be alone.

ALLEN TATE

EXTRACT

Mica shines on the beach
and the frogs drone all night in the jungle.
In the valley the twigs clink under the falling snow.

The salamanders chant a pebble-song on the hill-road
and the storm advances between the mountains.

127

Astrea, convince me that resolution means
an elegy, and say but one word.

The night sky,
now white, now black,
performs a mute miracle
above the lowering sleet-storm.

The light-house sways at the edge of the farthest cliff,
and a crab crawls into a yellowed skull at low tide.
Give me your hand here on the sand dune
and explain to me the wisdom
of winter.

The gulls disappear into the north-east,
and the ocean groans darkly grey in the half-light.

PAUL FREDERIC BOWLES

WINTER NIGHT

For Charles Fenby

This evening holds her breath
And makes a crystal pause;
The streams of light are frozen,
Shining above their source.

Now if ever might one
Break through the sensual gate;
Seraph's wing glimpse far-glinting.
Is it, is it too late?

We look up at the sky.
Yes, it is mirror clear;
Too well we recognise
The physiognomy there.

Friend, let us look to earth,
Be stubborn, act and sleep.

Here at our feet the skull
Keeps a stiff upper lip;

Feeling the weight of winter,
Grimaces underground;
But does not need to know
Why spirit was flesh-bound.

CECIL DAY LEWIS

FEARFUL SYMMETRY

Muzzle and jowl and beastly brow,
bilious glaring eyes, tufted ears,
recidivous criminality in the slouch,
        — This is not the latest absconding bankrupt
but a "beautiful" tiger imported at great expense from
                        Kuala Lumpur.

7 photographers, 4 black-and-white artists and an R. A.
are taking his profitable likeness;
28 reporters and an essayist
are writing him up.
Several ladies think he is a darling
especially at mealtimes, observing
that a firm near the Docks advertizes replicas
full-grown on approval for easy cash payments.

Felis Tigris (Straights Settlements) (Bobo) takes exercise
up and down his cage before feeding,
in a stench of excrements of great cats
indifferent to beauty or brutality.
He is said to have eaten several persons,
but of course you can never be quite sure of these things.

BASIL BUNTING

SONNET ON A STILL NIGHT

The brittle streets, with midnight walking flung
from curb to curb in rime-resounding fall,
now (pausing) still reverberate the tall
tension of the mind to friendship strung.

And over chimes that toll the twelve gone hours
from where the city lights its sky-hung pall,
your words, that speed pronouncement, shatter all
the twinging chill with noise like frozen flowers.

Oh, take the car, and coming to the city,
follow the head-waiter's evening smile;
glance quickly down the glass-reflecting aisle;
hang up your coat; then stretch your feet out straightly
and finger bread where there had been but lately
the far-heard chime of bells in sullen file.

J. V. CUNNINGHAM

WATERSHED

From this high place all things flow:
Land of divided streams, of water spilled
Eastward, westward without memento;
Land where the morning mist is curled
Like smoke about the ridgepole of the world.
The mist is furled.

The sunset hawk now rides
The tall light up the climbing deep of air.
Beneath him swings the rooftree that divides
The east and west. His gold eyes scan
The crumpled shade on gorge and crest,
And streams that creep and disappear, appear,
Past fingered ridges and their shrivelling span.
Under the broken eaves men take their rest.

Forever, should they stir, their thought would keep
This place. Not love, happiness past, constrains,
But certitude. Enough, and it remains;
Though they who thread the flood and neap
Of earth itself have felt the earth creep,
In pastures hung against the rustling gorge
Have felt the shudder and the sweat of stone,
Knowing thereby no constant moon
Sustains the hill's lost granite surge.

ROBERT PENN WARREN

HUNGER AND THIRST

Shrieks in dark leaves. The rumpled owl
disgorges undigested bones
and feathered bits of lesser fowl.

When black obese flies are few,
starved spiders have been seen to drink
gold mornings in a round of dew.

The charlatan beneath his tent
with a wide flourish of the hand
consumes a fiery element.

There have been soldiers, too, who drank
a yellow water from steel casques
not minding how the sunlight stank.

And some had fed on air that sang
from skulls where under hollow darks
dust sneered to show a horny fang.

And Ugolino's horrible hunger
we too have known, and known too well
the strength that stretches famine longer.

We too have known within our cell
voices entreat us that we feed
on flesh whose bone we loved too well.

JOHN PEALE BISHOP

From PART OF A NOVEL, PART OF A POEM, PART OF A PLAY

THE HERO

Where there is personal liking we go.
    Where the ground is sour; where there are
    weeds of beanstalk height,
    snakes' hyperdermic teeth, or
    the wind brings the "scarebabe voice"
    from the neglected yew set with
    the semi-precious cats' eyes of the owl —
awake, asleep, "raised ears extended to fine points," and so
on — love won't grow.

We do not like some things and the hero
    doesn't; deviating head-stones
    and uncertainty;
    going where one does not wish
    to go; suffering and not
    saying so; standing and listening where something
    is hiding. The hero shrinks
as what it is flies out on muffled wings, with twin yellow
eyes — to and fro —

with quavering water-whistle note, low,
    high, in basso-falsetto chirps
    until the skin creeps.
    Jacob when a-dying, asked
    Joseph: Who are these? and blessed
    both sons, the younger most, vexing Joseph. And
    Joseph was vexing to some.
Cincinnatus was; Regulus; and some of our fellow
men have been, though

devout, like Pilgrim having to go slow
   to find his roll; tired but hopeful —
   hope not being hope
   until all ground for hope has
   vanished; and lenient, looking
   upon a fellow creature's error with the
   feelings of a mother — a
woman or a cat. The decorous frock-coated Negro
by the grotto

answers the fearless sightseeing hobo
   who asks the man she's with, what's this,
   what's that, where's Martha
   buried, "Gen-ral Washington
   there; his lady, here"; speaking
   as if in a play — not seeing her; with a
   sense of human dignity
and reverence for mystery, standing like the shadow
of the willow.

Moses would not be grandson to Pharaoh.
   It is not what I eat that is
   my natural meat,
   the hero says. He's not out
   seeing a sight but the rock
   crystal thing to see — the startling El Greco
   brimming with inner light — that
covets nothing that it has let go. This then you may know
as the hero.

MARIANNE MOORE

RESURRECTION

   I did not see the frigate Constitution,
   her yards cock-billed and bare as if she still
   lay unretrieved and rotting at her pier,
   towed all the summer port to port,
   a lubber's sport
   to every ignorant patrioteer.

She should have had the same sea-burial
my great-grandfathers had that fought on her;
the inconsolable sea closing above her
with no sound but the scream of skittering gulls
and the wind dying where her sails had been.

Instead there are a thousand in her shrouds
swarming to set the sails that are not there.

R. P. BLACKMUR

BOUND

Negative tree, you are belief
Engendered by an iron grief,

A variously compounded fact
Denied the favor of swift act.

With terrible precision, you
Can split an aging rock in two;

Yet in your dumb profusion there
Is quiet, positive and clear.

You are a timeless sorrow thrust
Beyond the dreamlessness of dust.

You are a bird, securely bound,
That sings the song of voiceless ground,

And builds a nest in sterile stone,
Yet breeds no kin of flesh and bone.

You are a bird denied, the blood
Of earth in flying attitude.

THEODORE ROETHKE

NO SWAN SO FINE

"No water so still as the
   dead fountains of Versailles." No swan,
with swart blind look askance
and ambidextrous legs, so fine
   as the chintz china one with fawn-
brown eyes and toothed gold
   collar on to show whose bird it was.

Lodged in the Louis Fifteenth
   candelabrum-tree of cockscomb-
tinted buttons, dahlias,
sea-urchins and everlastings,
   it perches on the branching foam
of polished sculptured
flowers — at ease and tall. The king is dead.

MARIANNE MOORE

CANAL STREET

Variations after Longfellow and Lowell

City, whose streets are wavering reflections
of leaning palaces and strips of sky,
Byzantine water-lily where the Wingèd
Lion nested; your seed-pod domes have scattered
seeds of dome-capped towers over our cities,
constructed of steel flames, whose streets are shade.

(Each tower is a web spun by a spider
efficient, diligent.) And through our caves of trade
aromas blow of pollen dust (choking,
exuberant) from your malicious dead —
the human principalities and powers,
your named and nameless who are mixed with fate.

JOHN WHEELWRIGHT   135

From THE URN

RELIQUARY

Tenderness and resolution!
What is our life without a sudden pillow,
What is death without a ditch?

The harvest laugh of bright Apollo
And the flint tooth of Sagitarius,
Rhyme from the same Tau (closing cinch by cinch)
And pocket us who, somehow, do not follow:
As though we know those who are variants,
Charms that each by each refuse the clinch
With desperate propriety, whose name is writ
In wider letters than the alphabet.
Who is now left to vary the Sanscrit
Pillowed by
My wrist in the vestibule of Time? Who
Will hold it — wear the keepsake, dear, of time —
Return the mirage on a coin that spells
Something of sand and sun the Nile defends?

THE SAD INDIAN

Sad heart, the gymnast of inertia, does not count
Hours, days — and scarcely sun and moon.
The warp is in his woof, and his keen vision
Spells what his tongue has had, and only that —
How more? But the lash, lost vantage and the prison
His fathers took for granted ages since — and so he looms

Farther than his sun-shadow, farther than wings —
Their shadows even — now can't carry him.
He does not know the new hum in the sky
And — backwards — is it thus the eagles fly?

ENRICH MY RESIGNATION

Enrich my resignation as I usurp those far
Feints of control, hear rifles blown out on the stag
Below the aeroplane, and see the fox's brush
Whisk silently beneath the red hill's crag —
Extinction stirred on either side
Because love wonders, keeps a certain mirth.

Die, O centuries, die, as Dionysus said,
Yet live in all my resignation.
It is the moment, now, when all
The heartstrings spring, unlaced.
Here is the peace of the fathers.

HART CRANE

WINTER SKETCHES

I

Now that black ground and bushes —
saplings, trees,
each twig and limb — are suddenly white with snow,
and earth becomes brighter than the sky,

that intricate shrub
of nerves, veins, arteries —
myself — uncurls
its knotted leaves
to the shining air.

Upon this wooded hillside,
pied with snow, I hear
only the melting snow
drop from the twigs.

II SUBWAY

In steel clouds
to the sound of thunder
like the ancient gods:
our sky, cement;
the earth, cement;
our trees, steel;
instead of sunshine,
a light that has no twilight,
neither morning nor evening,
only noon.

Coming up the subway stairs, I thought the moon
only another street-light —
a little crooked.

III

From the middle of the pool
in the concrete pavement a fountain
in neat jets; the wind scatters it
upon the water. The untidy trees
drop their leaves upon the pavement.

IV

Along the flat roofs beneath our window,
in the morning sunshine,
I read the signature of last night's rain.

V

The squads, platoons, and regiments
of lighted windows,
ephemeral under the evening star —

feast, you who cross the bridge
this cold twilight
on these honeycombs of light, the buildings of Manhattan.

CHARLES REZNIKOFF

THE LIMITED

Since there's no help, come, let them kiss and part —
The Pullman step's as good as any place.
It's certain love can scarcely learn the art
To read the mind's construction in the face.
And so he tips the grim white-coated groom,
Consigns her bags to that black hand of doom;
Then slick as death the velvet pistons start,
Like fat blood in a drowning swimmer's heart.

White Proserpine whirled in the cloudy car
While brightness drops from star and star:
Proven — ah, sad sorites of the year —
For him who turns like that mute Orpheus
Again to thrust by all the vulgar dead.
But in his heart the summer's wrath shall roam
With burning eyes, as in the vacant house
The cold and dry-foot cat whose tread
Wheels from last week's newspaper to the broom.

ROBERT PENN WARREN

From *THE MAGNETIC MOUNTAIN*

CONDEMNED

Tempt me no more; for I
Have known the lightning's hour,
The poet's inward pride,
The certainty of power.

Bayonets are closing round.
I shrink; yet I must wring
A living from despair
And out of steel a song.

Though song, though breath be short,
I'll share not the disgrace

Of those that ran away
Or never left the base.

Comrades, my tongue can speak
No comfortable words,
Calls to a forlorn hope,
Gives work and not rewards.

Oh keep the sickle sharp
And follow still the plough:
Others may reap, though we
See not the winter through.

Father, who endest all,
Pity our broken sleep;
For we lie down with tears
And waken but to weep.

And if our blood alone
Will melt this iron earth,
Take it. It is well spent
Easing a saviour's birth.

C. DAY LEWIS

TIME OF DAY

I ask for the strength to follow through my life
This seasonal growth of day!

After the first dark moment of the awakening,
The sun and the first taste of coffee leap in the blood.
Broad is the orb of the world —
The steps on the stone by the window seem to spring.
Damp and sweet is the air,
While a voice that calls with a rising note and laughter
Seems to be more a body than air or sound.

Late in the morning everything seems to wait;
There is a pause,
A cloud covers the sun,
Laborers think of the long afternoon,
And then the soul considers its years of anguish,
Marking its time, questions its existence.

Late in the afternoon comes another pause;
Then is the body most aware of its being,
Flesh is a burning voice to the gray twilight,
Vision a mad lust,
Death is a painful joy;
Many cry and wait long for an answer
Sweet is the will to give. . . .

Finally in the deep dark silence,
Out of a life gone that seems a dream,
Out of defeat and evil,
Weakness and lost faith and curbed desire,
Sleep and a great peace not distant —

Comes a moment when the mind, no longer
Bound to its intimate self, confesses dreams;
Doubt and desire fade
Into the night, and mind
At the last silence cries for the unknown day.

SELDEN RODMAN

THE MEMOIRS

A cutter risen from the mollusks, it is a god
with a god carved on the stempiece
arriving in Detroit with Jesuits,
feluccas, pinnaces and brigantines,
the mainsail hauled out on a little tackle.

Here cometh what hath broken your legs . . .
the king of France, the Secretary for the Latin
Tongue, the Lord High Butler of England
with coronation jewels, and the chandlers.

They have broken me for the last time.
I spit on them all.
They lie on the high poop all the night
with open eye, with wenches, singing
in radium like Chaucer and the smale fowles.

A sail in Atlantis in the morning, a Sappho
of a sloop slapping the buss ship London
white and anchored as a living clam.
Michigan freshwater walnut trees.
The memoirs —
                           canvas, cable, chain, tar, paint.

CARL RAKOSI

THE ANCESTORS

The house leaks and leans. Night's roof-timbers glut
   To rain on those wide planks the dead have thinned
With their loud feet. Still, though the door is shut,
   We sit to shudder in the rising wind.

A great bed in the chamber off the hall
   Whispers its curtains. White its counterpane
And white the faces that have lain there, all
   Corrupt in silence, noble, skulled by rain.

Why should the wind rise now? It never rose
   Like this before! Where will the worse than poor
Porch their unsheltered beards and pierce their clothes
   This night with rain? Where contemplate their store

Of pitiless thoughts? Where sleep? On nights like these,
   Whose spacious wars living and dead exhume,
What calm to send the mind on the stone ease
   Of passions rivalling the sculptured tomb!

JOHN PEALE BISHOP

From A LABYRINTH OF BEING

SONNET

Three silences made him a single word:
the footloose lover's agony of eye,
the heartfast husband's peace; these joined the third,
the straight silence of something about to die
that something else, no different, might live.
They sat in silence on their separate chairs
knowing that silence would be positive
when they should climb their nightly good-night stairs.

He spoke it first. Is it ourselves that go
from us? ourselves that to ourselves add up,
because this child shall be, to zero? No —
(her voice was from a void that broke) we stop:
we are not us; not dear and dear: we are
to this child's sun the silent morning star.

R. P. BLACKMUR

From "THAT'S THE AMERICAN STYLE"

4TH OF JULY

I

The ship moves
but its smoke
moves with the wind
faster than the ship

143

— thick coils of it
through leafy trees
pressing
upon the river

II

The heat makes
this place of the woods
a room
in which two robins pain

crying
distractedly
over the plight of
their unhappy young

III

During the explosions
at dawn, the celebrations
I could hear
a native cuckoo

in the distance
as at dusk, before
I'd heard
a night hawk calling

WILLIAM CARLOS WILLIAMS

METAPHYSICIAN

His logic unperturbed, exacting new
Tribute in turbulence, a tithe of motion:

Runners by whose feet daylight is shaken,
Moths, mantles wind-wrought, released sharply
Against throned columns, shafts closing in air —

Attend. Time's clear device in each man's eye
Makes shadows what he sees, and streets shadows
Wherein we move, impelled or quieted.

We have been out to see the latest signs
Unbent from heaven, and these who staring walk
Beside us are not blind, and all who see
Through this low draft of shade will be undone.

Thus to lie one night with his back broken
And dream at dawn the idol in the stone.

ROBERT FITZGERALD

EMPTY DWELLING PLACES

Forever the little thud of names, falling,
Disappearing, baying at the moon for the last time —
Quiet obscure little names, leaving no trace
But the ash-flecked aroma of stale fragmentary careers.
Names that once clothed the pound of blood in a body,
That stood for lungs, and love-possible limbs,
And voices, voices rich in faith and friendly
To the sweep and surge of curious spying years.
In the brisk procession of sub-tunneled fame
The little names settle in the ooze of silent unhurried
        nothingness.

In the night the head on the pillow turns,
And a little changed hurt settles on the course
Of his dearest striving, a wrong music flooding
Forbidden chambers, with no semblance of comfort even
        in the words.
                My name is . . .
                (over and over) —
                my name is . . .
I swear to you I knew it once.

KENNETH PATCHEN

THE FIRST READER

There grows no rootless flower.
There are nowhere
Blossoms lacking air.
Even the fertile stone
Feeds and is nourished;
No thing blooms alone.
Even the black night air,
Thronged with jostling moonlit
Bubbles ballooning
Up from the restless brain,
Secret and flourished . . .
Even the black night cone
Sways from the flesh and bone
Over the bubbling brain;
Never the dream alone.

WINFIELD TOWNLEY SCOTT

From LOCAL HABITATION

ON INHABITING AN ORANGE

All our roads go nowhere.
Maps are curled
To keep the pavement definitely
On the world.

All our footsteps, set to make
Metric advance,
Lapse into arcs in deference
To circumstance.

All our journeys nearing Space
Skirt it with care,
Shying at the distances
Present in air.

Blithely travel-stained and worn,
Erect and sure,
All our travelers go forth,
Making down the roads of Earth
Endless détour.

JOSEPHINE MILES

TO ONE ELECT

They come not within the tall woods,
neither they nor their enemies;
their commerce is but chaffering in
futilities.

We are the proud, the light-hearted —
we are they who have felt
the shattering of the farther stars; but we
are also they who have knelt.

Into the tall woods then,
where the fretful come not!
Unleash your hounds and shout! We are they
whom the gods harm not.

S. ICHIYÉ HAYAKAWA

FISHERMEN

Mesh cast for mackerel
by guess and the sheen's tremor —
imperceptible if you haven't the knack —
a difficult job,

hazardous and seasonal:
many shoals all of a sudden,
it would tax the Apostles to take the lot;
then drowse for months,

nets on the shingle,
a pint in the tap.
Likewise the pilchards come unexpectedly,
startle the man on the cliff.

"Remember us to the teashop girls.
Say we have seen no legs better than theirs,
we have the sea to stare at —
its treason, copiousness, tedium."

BASIL BUNTING

From IMPERIOUS OX, IMPERIAL DISH

THE BUFFALO

Black in blazonry means
prudence; and niger, unpropitious. Might
hematite-
    black incurved compact horns on a bison
        have significance? The
    soot brown tail-tuft on
        a kind of lion-

    tail; what would that express?
And John Steuart Curry's Ajax pulling
grass — no ring
    in his nose — two birds standing on his back?
        though prints like this cannot
    show if they were black
        birds, nor the color

    of the back. The modern
ox does not look like the Augsburg ox's
portrait. Yes,
    the great extinct wild Aurochs was a beast
        to paint, with stripe and six-
    foot horn-spread — decreased
        to Siamese-cat-

Brown Swiss size, or zebu
shape with white plush dewlap and warmblooded
hump; to red-
    skinned Hereford or to piebald Holstein. Yet
        some would say the sparse-haired
    buffalo has met
            human notions best —

        unlike the elephant,
both jewel and jeweler in the hairs
that he wears —
    no white-nosed Vermont ox yoked with its twin
        to haul the maple sap,
    up to their knees in
            snow; no freakishly

        Over-Drove Ox drawn by
Rowlandson, but the Indian buffalo,
albino-
    footed, standing in the mud-lake, with a
        day's work to do. No white
    Christian heathen, way-
            laid by the Buddha,

        serves him so well as the
buffalo — as mettlesome as if check-
reined — free neck
    stretching out, and snake-tail in a half twist
        on the flank; nor will so
    cheerfully assist
            the Sage sitting with

        feet at the same side, to
dismount at the shrine; nor are there any
ivory
    tusks like those two horns which when a tiger
        coughs, are lowered fiercely
    and convert the fur
            to harmless rubbish.

       The Indian buffalo
led by bare-leggèd herd-boys to a hay
hut where they
    stable it, need not fear comparison
      with bison, with the twins,
   nor with anyone
      of ox ancestry.

MARIANNE MOORE

MERU

Civilization is hooped together, brought
Under a rule, under the semblance of peace
By manifold illusion; but man's life is thought
And he, despite his terror, cannot cease
Ravening through century after century,
Ravening, raging and uprooting that he may come
Into the desolation of reality:
Egypt and Greece, good-bye, and good-bye, Rome.

Hermits upon Mount Meru or Everest
Caverned in night under the drifted snow,
Or where that snow and winter's dreadful blast
Beat down upon their naked bodies, know
That day brings round the night, that before dawn
His glory and his monuments are gone.

WILLIAM BUTLER YEATS

SHORELINE

The sea has made a wall for its defence
Of falling water. Those whose impertinence
Leads them to its moving ledges
It rejects. Those who surrender
It will with the next wave drag under.

Sand is the beginning and the end
Of our dominion.

The way to the dunes is easy and not steep.
The shelving sand is stiffened in the rain
And loosened again in the sun's fingers.
Children, lustful of the glistening hours,
Drink and are insatiate. Wind under the eyelids,
Confusion walling the ears, they bend
And balance, warmed by secure and ordered blood
In the cold wash of the beach.

          And after,
They walk with rigid feet the planked street of the town.
They miss the slipping texture of the sand
And a sand pillow under the hollow instep.
They are unmoved by fears
That breed in darkening kitchens at sun–down
Following storm; and they rebel
Against cold waiting in the wind and rain
For the late sail.

The harbor town is backed by its fertile valley.
Seines, drying, scallop the waterfront.
Wharf ladders descend to the green swell.
Did you, as I did, feel
A supple braid that dragged against your hips,
Thick as a ship's cable,
And watch the light that slips
And clings along the moving channel wave?

          Did you, as I,
Condemn the coastal fog and long for islands
Seen from a sail's shadow?

          The dunes lie
More passive to the wind than water is.

This, then, the country of our choice.
It is infertile, narrow, prone
Under a dome of choral sound:
Water breaking upon water.

Litter of bare logs in the drift —
The sea has had its sharp word with them. The smudged
    odor
Of wild roses, wild strawberries on the dune shoulder
Stains as with color the salt stench of the sea.
It is a naked restless garden that descends
From the crouched pine
To shellfish caught in flat reflecting sands.

We lose the childish avarice of horizons. The sea ends
Against another shore. The cracked ribs of a wreck
Project from the washed beach.
Under the shell-encrusted timbers
Dripping brine
Plucks at the silence of slant chambers
Opening seaward. What moving keel remembers
Such things as here are buried under sand?

The transitory ponds and smooth bar slide
Easily under the advancing tide,
Emerging with the moon's
Turning.

        Clear lagoons
Behind the shattered hulk, thin
Movements of sea grass on the dune rim
Bending against cloud, these things are ours.
Submissive to the sea and wind,
Resistful of all else, sand
Is the beginning and the end
Of our dominion.

MARY BARNARD

"MANTIS"

Mantis! praying mantis! since your wings' leaves
And your terrified eyes, pins, bright, black and poor
Beg — "Look, take it up" (thoughts' torsion)! "save it!"

I who can't bear to look, cannot touch, — You —
You can — but no one sees you steadying lost
In the cars' drafts on the lit subway stone.

Praying mantis, what wind-up brought you, stone
On which you sometimes prop, prey among leaves
(Is it love's food your raised stomach prays?), lost
Here, stone holds only seats on which the poor
Ride, who rising from the news may trample you —
The shops' crowds a jam with no flies in it.

Even the newsboy who now sees knows it
No use, papers make money, makes stone, stone,
Banks, "it is harmless," he says moving on — You?
Where will he put *you*? There are no safe leaves
To put you back in here, here's news! too poor
Like all the separate poor to save the lost.

Don't light on my chest, mantis! do — you're lost,
Let the poor laugh at my fright, then see it:
My shame and theirs, you whom old Europe's poor
Call spectre, strawberry, by turns; a stone —
You point — they say — you lead lost children — leaves
Close in the paths men leave, saved, safe with you.

Killed by thorns (once men), who now will save you
Mantis? what male love bring a fly, be lost
Within your mouth, prophetess, harmless to leaves
And hands, faked flower — the myth is: dead, bones, it
Was assembled, apes wing in wind: On stone,
Mantis, you will die, touch, beg, of the poor.

Android, loving beggar, dive to the poor
As your love would even without head to you,
Graze like machined wheels, green, from off this stone
And preying on each terrified chest, lost
Say, I am old as the globe, the moon, it
Is my old shoe, yours, be free as the leaves.

Fly, mantis, on the poor, arise like leaves
The armies of the poor, strength: stone on stone
And build the new world in your eyes, Save it!

LOUIS ZUKOFSKY

EPOS

for Ezra Pound

A language on which the sun flows
for the first time! The page is
exceptionally white; and
image and gesture
(pantomimic, verbal, and musical),
blue and yellow and a touch of
orange occupy the whole
adjacent air.

Picture:
A Japanese murder:
Blue knife, orange bowels (exposed),
and the actors appropriately restrained.
   It is a ballet light
as one moment,
the early ages, days of gold,
in costumes
of all men's ingenuity.

Fit tongue
for tracers of new calendars,
consultors
of lately polished stars;
for whom the singular
is all surface; space
is filled to the world's extremes;
and neither rains nor twilights blur the winds.

HAROLD ROSENBERG

From SECRET IDIOM

SANCTUARY

Not far beyond the town wild flowers grow
In the delicate shooting grass, the blades
Like swords pacific turning from the hand,
Not watchful, hostile, flowers' champions.
The wind rehearses themes at leisure here,
And birds sing in the sun, yet every hour
A train roars through the cutting, shakes the air
In haste, gives tongue like hound on scent of prey.

Man plays his own retreat, builds sanctuary
Not seen by eyes within the alien walls,
Where he can scrawl his thought in private log,
And exercise his secret idiom,
Though road drill give no peace, and omnibus
Bullies a passage through congested ways.

CLIFFORD DYMENT

From OCTOBER POEMS

THE GARDEN

On a fine day in early autumn

How kind, how secretly, the sun
Has blessed this garden frost has won,
And touched again, as once it used,
The furlèd boughs by frost bemused.
Though summered brilliance had but room
For blossom, now the leaves will bloom
Their time, and take from a milder sun
The unreviving benison.

No marbles whitely gleam among
These paths where gilt the late pear hung;

But branches interlace to frame
An avenue of stately flame
Where yonder, far more chill and pure
Than marble, gleams the sycamore,
Of argent torse and cunning shaft
Propped nobler than the sculptor's craft.

The hand that crooked upon the spade
Here plucked the peach, and thirst allayed;
Here lovers paused upon the kiss,
Instructed of what ripeness is.
Where all who came might stand to try
The grace of this green empery.
Now jay and cardinal debate,
Like twin usurpers, the ruined state.

Then he who sought, not love but peace,
In such rank plot could take no ease:
Now poised between the two alarms
Of summer's lusts and winter's harms,
For him alone these precincts wait
With sacrament that could translate
All things that fed luxurious sense
From appetite to innocence.

ROBERT PENN WARREN

ARGENT SOLIPSISM

Now is a bursting in me. Now a fugue
Sprouts in that heart where othertime you broke
Each outbound note of callower crescendo.
For the sky is in this skull and flings
Blue paradigms beyond this breathing's ken.
To be an equanimity like stone,
So quiet as the ether between stars,
Needing no thing nor hoping, where to hope
Must breed a pain that seeps through every vein.

These pontiff syllables may mean to you
No more than pretty sounds of winds that slide
With pointless whimpers through garrets glazed with dust.
But these are words affirming spring and green
Shoots in an earth no other self will sense.
I formulate for wind and ornament . . .
You are intent on damask or noon curls
With which birth donored you, withholding wisps
Of thought that ivy and unite disparate brains.

Never to hope. Never to need your trees.
Never to tread the cobbles under lamps
Shedding their perpendicular inane,
Clinging to nothing which is surely grey
Substance floating in bone beneath your waves . . .
Needing no self beyond a self I know.

HOWARD BLAKE

PIGEONS

Older than the ancient Greeks, than
        Solomon, the pigeon family is a
        ramifying one, a
        banyan of banyans; to begin
with, bluish slate,
        but with ability. Modesty cannot dull
        the lustre of the pigeon
        swift and sure, coming quickest and
straightest just after a storm. The great
        lame war hero Cher Ami, the
        Lost Battalion's gallant bird; and
        Mocker with one eye
            destroyed, delivering his despatch
        to his superiors; and Sergeant Dunn,
        civilian pigeon who flew eight
        hundred sixty-eight miles
        in four days and six hours;
            and destined to hatch

in France, Spike, veteran of
the division in which Mocker
          served — exceptional messenger.
"Rarely was confidence misplaced" a newspaper
says. Dastardly comment
          inexactly phrased, as used of Her-
mes, Ariel, or Leander —
pigeons of the past. Neither was confidence
misplaced in the Javan-
Sumatran birds the Dutch had had
brought from Baghdad.
          Mysterious animal with a magnetic
feel by which he traces back-
ward his transportation outward,
even in a fog at sea, though glad
          to be tossed near enough the loft
          or coop to get back the same day.
"Home on time without
          his message." What matter since he has
got back. Migrating always in the same
direction, bringing all letters
to the same address, see-
ing better homes than his,
          he is not Theudas
boasting himself to be some-
body, this anonymous post-
          man who, as soon as he could fly,
was carrying valentines and messages of
state; or soberer news —
          "So please write me and believe that I
am yours very truly;" fine words
those. An instrument not just an instinctive
individual, this
dove, that lifts his right foot over
the alighting-
          board to rejoin his ungainly pin-clad dark-skinned
brood as domestic turtle-
          doves might; two. Invariably
two. The turtle, a not exciting

bird — in Britain shy, detected
by its constantly heard coo, with-
out a song but not
      without a voice — does well to stay far
out of sight; but the Pelew pigeon with
black head, metallic wasp-lustred
grass-green breast and purple
legs and feet, need not; nor
      need the Nicobar,
novel, narrow-feathered dove.
And one should see the Papuan
      fancrests with six-sided scale which
coats the foot; "not much is known about these splendid
birds" hid in unimag-
      inably weak lead-colored ostrich-
plumes a third of an inch long, and
needle-fine cat-whisker-fibred battleship-
gray lace. The Samoan
tooth-billed pigeon fortunately
survives also —
      saved from destruction by no longer feeding on
the ground, a bird with short legs
and heavy bill, remarkable
because related to the dodo.
      Didus ineptus; man's remorse
enshrines it now, abundant still
in sixteen-one. "A
      little bigger than our swans, these birds
want wings and lay but one egg" the traveller
said — "defenceless unsuspicious
things, with a cry like the
cry of a Gosling." *Il*
      dóudo (the words
mean simple one) — extinct as
the Solitaires which having "raised
      their young one do not disunite."
A new pigeon cannot compensate, but we have
it. With neat-cered eye, long
      face, trim form and posture, this delight-

ful bird outdoes the dashingly
black and white Dalmatian dog and map-freckled
pony that Indians dress
with feathers seriatim down
the mane and tail; —
a slender Cinderella deliberately
pied, so she on each side is
the same, an all-feather piebald,
cuckoo-marked on a titanic scale
taking perhaps sixteen birds to
show the whole design, as in chess
played with men and hors-
es. Yes, the thus medievally
two-colored sea-pie-patterned semi-swan-
necked magpie-pigeon, gamecock-legged
with long-clawed toes, and all
extremes — head neck back tail
and feet — coal black, the
rest snow white, has a surpris-
ing modernness and fanciness
and stateliness and . . . Yes indeed;
developed by and humbly dedicated to
the Gentlemen of the
Feather Club, this is a dainty breed.

MARIANNE MOORE

I COME TO BURY CAESAR

(Being a litany, an anecdote, and an adolescent assertion of bravado)

"No! I am not Prince Hamlet, nor was meant to be . . ."

T. S. Eliot

There were five of us within the room
(Bach's polytechnics beat upon the limpid air) —
Eliot stretched in a chintz-covered chair,
While Pound sat around
Sipping a sloe gin fizz
And disseminating Italian gloom
That was peculiarly his.

The hounds of spring were snarling at the door,
(If you will pardon an apparent digression)
And Farefield, with an expression
Not quite like anything I had ever seen before,
Turned to us and casually said,
"I've just been accepted by *Poetry*,"
Eliot laughed, and Isaac turned quite red,
And I smiled stiffly, clearing the burned
Charcoal fumes from my dolichocephalic head,
Holding Ellen Terry at an arm's length,
(Ellen Terry is Clara's doll, and quite a sturdy wench).

"Quite possible," I replied,
"With Harriet out of town."
But all the same I could have died,
Comme çi, comme ça, just like that,
(Holding Ellen Terry in my arms
All spruced up in a satin gown
And a purple picture hat.)

"I call it *Heil, Hamlet,*" he announced proudly,
Smoothing the sleek
Black curls back of his left ear.

"How unique!" —
I giggled and coughed loudly,
For fear
That I might not be able to keep countenance,
And apprehension
Lest Pound and Eliot snap the tension
And attempt to execute a dance,
"Here we go round the prickly pear
At five o'clock in the morning."

Meanwhile Isaac had regained his poise,
And sneered sedately at the boys,
(Although Eliot is growing quite bald,
And Pound is going, with middle-aged intent,
To over-prepare another event.)

Then, from the conservatory
where nothing is conserved,
Clara called,
Restoring the equilibrium of the firmament.
"A friend at last," I thought,
And rushed into the conservatory,
where nothing is conserved.

But in some queer fashion we had all deserved
To have Farefield tell us that *Poetry* had bought
Heil, Hamlet.

The dinner, of course, was a fiasco
Even Lasco, (the incorrigible showman)
Sensed that the scene was definitely extra-Roman.
For Caesar-Farefield lay inert upon the floor,
And Brutus-I knelt down to tie an errant lace,
And Casca-Isaac's face
Was a study in anthropology;
And Pound and Eliot, intending no malice,
In delicate rages delicately tore
Their respective pages
From dear Harriet's (not to forget Alice),
Intellectual
But highly ineffectual
Anthology. . . .

Ambition should be made of much
sterner stuff.

Q. E. D.

SYDNEY JUSTIN HARRIS

AT WOODWARD'S GARDENS

A boy, presuming on his intellect,
Once showed two little monkeys in a cage
A burning-glass they could not understand,
And never could be made to understand.

1936

Words are no good: to say it was a lens
For gathering solar rays would not have helped.
But let him show them how the weapon worked.
He made the sun a pin-point on the nose
Of first one, then the other, till it brought
A look of puzzled dimness to their eyes
That blinking could not seem to blink away.
They stood, arms linked together, at the bars
And exchanged troubled glances over life.
One put a thoughtful hand up to his nose
As if reminded — or as if perhaps
Within a million years of an idea.
He got his purple little knuckles stung.
The already known had once more been confirmed
By psychological experiment;
And that were all the finding to announce
Had the boy not presumed too close and long.
There was a sudden flash, a monkey snatch,
And the glass was the monkey's, not the boy's.
Precipitately they retired back-cage
And instituted an investigation . . .
On their part, but without the needed insight.
They bit the glass and listened for the flavor,
They broke the handle and the binding off it;
Then, none the wiser, frankly gave it up,
And having hid it in their bedding straw
Against the day of prisoners' ennui,
Came dryly forward to the bars again
To answer for themselves.

        Who said it mattered —
What monkeys did or didn't understand?
They might not understand a burning-glass.
They might not understand the sun itself.
It's knowing what to do with things that counts.

ROBERT FROST

163

THE GOTHIC DUSK

The Gothic dusk extends her serpent shadow:
Ruined the hamlets on the northern shore,
Ruined the walls of the entrancing cities,
Ruined the walls of the unhappy craftsmen,
Ruined the walls against the sea.
The walls of the Sunday-adoring village have vanished,
The walls of the liberal saints and the holy three.

Loathed and alone the gardens of the merchants,
The lawns of the limp and academic old;
Black the long halls of the philosophers,
Lovers of history, darlings of tradition,
And the Platonic grove.
Gaunt lie the pillared pools, defiled the fountains —
Fruits of a subtle and individual love.

That is the boundary of the dark; but daylight
Rolls like a flood across the Alaskan coast.
White the Illyrian plains and the Pontic ridges;
Down from Montana pour the enormous rivers
Out of their granite night.
The boys are chanting on the edge of Syria;
Slowly the swamps of Mexico grow bright.

And further southward still the sun's dominion:
The darkening bodies on the foam-white sand;
White on the sand the terraces and towers,
Sparkling like foam the sails upon the water
And the watery music across the bay;
And beyond, the excited whispers of the prophets,
The domes of the hopeful glittering into day.

Yet over the daylight lands the eagles are desperate,
The ground is trembling, the gradual clouds assume
Those shapes half-visionary half-remembering.
Quick is the voice of the cricket, vast the ascending
Voice of the ocean in the shell

Tells the observant North and its dreary forests
How the dreams of the young grew potent, and how they fell.

And "Listen!" whisper the Alps and whistle the Andes,
"Be strong! — the revengeful past will rise like a storm,
Breathe on our dreams, ask the intolerable question,
Demand the end of our quaint perverted idols.
Be strong, be brave as you will —
The ghosts will arrive, the tempests will be indifferent,
The streets will flicker, the asylums will be still."

FREDERIC PROKOSCH

From NIGHT-MUSIC

TIME EXPOSURES

When the exposed spirit, busy in daytime,
searches out night, only renewer,
that time plants turn to. The world's table.
When any single thing's condemned again.
The changeable spirit finds itself out,
will not employ Saint Death, detective,
does its own hunting, runs at last to night.
Renewer, echo of judgment, morning-source, music.

Dark streets that light invents, one black tree standing,
struck by the street-light to raw electric green,
allow one man at a time to walk past, plain.
Cities lose size. The earth is field,
and ranging these countries in sunset, we make quiet,
living in springtime, wish for nothing, see
glass bough, invented green, flower-sharp day
crackle into orange and be subdued to night.

The mind, propelled by work, reaches its evening:
slick streets, dog-tired, point the way to sleep.

1936

We drive out to the suburbs, bizarre lawns
flicker a moment beside the speeding cars.
Speed haunts our ground, throws counties at us under
night, a black basin always spilling stars.

Waters trouble our quiet, vanishing down
reaches of hills whose image legend saves:
the foggy Venus hung above the flood
rising, rising, from the sea, with her arms full of waves
as ours are full of flowers.

Down polished airways a purple dove descending
sharp on the bodies of those so lately busy apart,
wing-tip on breast-tip, the deep body of feathers
in the breast-groove along the comforted heart.

The head inclined offers with love clear miles
of days simple in sun and action, bright
air poised about a face in ballet strictness
and pure pacific night.

But in our ears brute knocking at all doors,
factories bellow mutilation, and we live needy still
while strength and hours run
checkless downhill.

MURIEL RUKEYSER

FALL OF LEAVES

Soon, summer's drum will shake the earth no longer,
will raise no blood to bubble in the throat
of beast or bird. Now at the turning season
of divided winds, when autumn's tapestries
fall into rust, and winter clamps the sap
of trees to soil, I watch the sliding Thames,
think of the ragged lives that hopelessly

confront me now, cold in the fall of leaves
and decaying winds. Their blood fumbles through flesh
frayed and grown sick with living; deciduous
they drift like leaves from square to square, denied
society's thinning sap; loosed from the tree
almost without remorse, till finally,
shredded by rain and cold they crumble, sink

and are forgotten. This is the penalty
of our adolescence, while man's brain is still
confused with dreams, and the once urgent blood,
hesitant on the brink of faith, withdraws,
falters, unchanneled to determined fingers.

D. S. SAVAGE

From FRACTURE OF LIGHT

SONG IN THE COLD SEASON

December narrows our day to a thread of light:
winter begins: the calendar's page is turned:
the fox goes to earth: the owl descends: and the wind
has shaped rain to crystal — no one changes the night.

We shall not escape darkness: death is the end
of our birth: a myth sharpens truth in our eyes,
and water is melted to air and the fire dies out
in wet ground; smoke drifts and the ashes ascend.

Even the lengthening days, this increase of sun
fuses a triple warning of wind and the snow;
until it is unbound from ice, and the broken tree flowers —
so, till the blue-white brook begins to run.

And March lifts up the clear untarnished stalk —
the hand gropes on the breast, rewinds the clock.

SAMUEL FRENCH MORSE   167

"LONG LIVE THE WEEDS"

Hopkins

Long live the weeds that overwhelm
My narrow vegetable realm! —
The bitter rock, the barren soil
That force the son of man to toil;
All things unholy, marked by curse,
The ugly of the universe.
The rough, the wicked, and the wild
That keep the spirit undefiled.
With these I match my little wit
And earn the right to stand or sit,
Hope, look, create, or drink and die:
These shape the creature that is I.

THEODORE ROETHKE

SUNDAY

I

We have moving over us, over head and spire,
A sky entire:
From west to east the deep celestial drift,
The lurch and lift.
Being Sunday goers we go soberly,
But look to see
How soberly too the very dust and day
Proceed away.
We close up the white doors, sing the hymn out,
Contest with doubt,
Foster the faith that quietly still outside
Earth will abide.

II

Heaven said hello, it being Sunday;
It being a warm day and hilly place,
Heaven came down unto the picnickers.

Bright white egg-shells lay in grass,
Pickles and thistles were for spice,
Soft to offer and to pass.

It was a good picnic, being so attended;
Being a warm day, it warmed the voice;
Both talk and angel-cake large, soft, and ready.

Heaven made the mild address;
Using with hesitance such small device,
Sounding so fond, familiar, did rejoice.

III

Oceans every seventh day
Reunite with ancient kin,
Seize the feet and pull away,
Lick the salt upon the skin.

And the divers in the deep,
And the waders wild and blown,
Stop to think before they sleep
By what tokens they were known:

How rubber caps and water-wings,
In weeks so lately made and blessed,
Should aid the first created things
To meet upon their day of rest.

JOSEPHINE MILES

WALKING-STICKS AND PAPERWEIGHTS
AND WATERMARKS

Walking among sceptre-headed
weeds and daisies swayed, by wind, they said,
    "Don't scatter your
stick, on account of the souls." Led
from sun-spotted
    paths, we went "where leafy trees meet
    overhead and noise of traffic is unknown" —
the mind exhilarated
        by life all round, so stirringly

alive. The root-handled cudgel
with the bark left on, the woodbine smell-
    ing of the rain,
the very stones, have life. Little
scars on church-bell
    tongues put there by the Devil's claws —
    authentic phantoms, ghosts, and witches, transformed
into an invisible
        fabric of inconsistency

motheaten by self-subtractives —
now as outright murderers and thieves,
    thrive openly.
An epigraph before it leaves
the wax, receives
    to give, and giving must itself
    receive, "difficulty is ordained to check
poltroons," and courage achieves
        despaired of ends. Oppositely

jointed against indecision,
the three legs of the triskelion
    meeting in the
middle between triangles, run
in unison
        without assistance. Yet, trudging

      on two legs that move contradictorily,
irked by ghosts and witches, one
        does not fear to ask for beauty

that is power devoid of fear.
A bold outspoken gentleman, cheer-
    ful, plodding, to-
the-point, used to the atmosphere
of work — who here
    appropriate to the thought of
    permanence, says, "this is my taste, it might not
be another man's" — makes clear
        that stark sincere unflattery,

sine cera, is both farthest
from self-defensiveness and nearest;
    as when a seal
without haste, slowly is impressed
and forms a nest
    on which the raised device reversed,
    shows round. It must have been an able workman,
studious and self-possessed,
        a liker of solidity,

who gave a greenish Waterford
glass fool's cap with summit curled down toward
    itself as the
glass grew, the look of tempered sword-
steel, and three-ore-d
    fishscale-burnished antimony-
    tin-and-lead's smoky water-drop type-metal
smoothness emery-armored
        against rust. Its subdued glossy

splendor leaps out at the eye as
form dramatizes thought, in the glass
    witchball and air-
twist cane. This paperweight, in mass
a stone, surpass-

ing it in tint, enlarges the
fine chain-lines in the waterleaf weighted by
its hardened raindrop surface.
    The paper-mould's similarly

once unsolid waspnest-blue, snow-
white, or seashell-gray rags, seen through, show
    sheepcotes, turkey-
mills, acorns, and anvils. "Stones grow,"
then stop, and so
    do gardens. "Plants grow and live; men
    grow and live and think." *Utilizey la poste
aerienne*, trade will follow
        the telephone. The post's jerky

cancellings ink the stamp, relet-
tering stiltedly, as a puppet-
    acrobat walks
about with high steps on his net,
an alphabet
    of words and animals where the
    wire-embedded watermark's more integral
expressiveness had first set
        its alabaster effigy.

In bark silverer than the swan,
esparto grass, or so-called Titan
    parchment tougher
than Hercules' lion-skin — Span-
ish, Umbrian,
    eastern, open, and jewelled crowns,
    corroborate the dolphin, crane, and ox; sealed
with wax by a pelican
        studying affectionately

a nest's three-in-one cartwheel tri-
legged face. "For those we love, live and die"
    the motto says.
And we do. Part pelican, I,
doubting the high-

way's wide giant trivia where
   three roads meet in artificial openness,
am obliged to justify
      outspoken cordiality.

Firm-feathered juniper springing
from difficult ground, the sky trembling
   with power, the rain
falling upon the bird singing,
modest printing,
   on honest paper properly
   trimmed, are gifts addressed to memory, and a
gift is permanent, shining
      like the juniper's trinity

of spines. An unburdensomely
worthy officer of charity,
   the evergreen
with awlshaped leaves in whorls of three —
successively
   firm. "On the first day of Christmas
   my true love he sent unto me, part of a
bough of a juniper-tree,"
      javelin-ed consecutively.

MARIANNE MOORE

REFLECTION FROM ROCHESTER

But wretched Man is still in arms for fear.

"From fear to fear, successively betrayed" —
By making risks to give a cause for fear
(Feeling safe with causes, and from birth afraid),

By climbing higher not to look down, by mere
Destruction of the accustomed because strange
(Too complex a loved system, or too clear),

By needing change but not too great a change
And therefore a new fear . . . man has achieved
All the advantage of a wider range,

Successfully has the first fear deceived,
Thought the wheels run on sleepers. This is not
The law of nature it has been believed.

Increasing power (it has increased a lot)
Embarrasses "attempted suicides,"
Narrows their margin; policies that got

"Virility from war" get much besides;
The mind, as well in mining as in gas
War's parallel, now less easily decides

On a good root-confusion to amass
Much safety from irrelevant despair.
Mere change in numbers made the process crass.

We now turn blank eyes for a pattern there
Where first the race of armaments was made;
Where a less involute compulsion played.
"For hunger or for love they bite and tear."

WILLIAM EMPSON

TO AN ELDER POET

To be able
and not to do it —

Still as a flower.

No flame,
a flower spent
with heat —

lovely flower
        hanging
in the rain.

    Never!

  Soberly —

  whiter than day —

  Wait forever
shaken by the rain —
      forever!

WILLIAM CARLOS WILLIAMS

PUTTING TO SEA

Who, in the dark, has cast the harbor-chain?
This is no journey to a land we know.
The autumn night receives us, hoarse with rain;
Storm flakes with roaring foam the way we go.

Sodden with summer, stupid with its loves,
The country which we leave, and now this bare
Circle of ocean which the heaven proves
Deep as its height, and barren with despair.

Now this whole silence, through which nothing breaks,
Now this whole sea, which we possess alone,
Flung out from shore with speed a missile takes
When some hard hand, in hatred, flings a stone.

The Way should mark our course within the night,
The streaming System, turned without a sound.
What choice is this — profundity and flight —
Great sea? Our lives through we have trod the ground.

Motion beneath us, fixity above.

"O, but you should rejoice! The course we steer
Points to a beach bright to the rocks with love,
Where, in hot calms, blades clatter on the ear;

And spiny fruits up through the earth are fed
With fire; the palm trees clatter; the wave leaps.
Fleeing a shore where heart-loathed love lies dead
We point lands where love fountains from its deeps.

Through every season the coarse fruits are set
In earth not fed by streams." Soft into time
Once broke the flower: pear and violet,
The cinquefoil. The tall elm tree and the lime

Once held out fruitless boughs, and fluid green
Once rained about us, pulse of earth indeed.
There, out of metal, and to light obscene,
The flamy blooms burn backward to their seed.

With so much hated still so close behind
The sterile shores before us must be faced;
Again, against the body and the mind,
The hate that bruises, though the heart is braced.

Bend to the chart, in the extinguished night,
Mariners! Make way slowly; stay from sleep;
That we may have short respite from such light.
And learn, with joy, the gulf, the vast, the deep.

LOUISE BOGAN

A FAREWELL

Good-bye! — no, do not grieve that it is over,
  The perfect hour;
That the winged joy, sweet honey-loving rover,
  Flits from the flower.

Grieve not — it is the law. Love will be flying —
　Yes, love and all.
Glad was the living — blessed be the dying.
　Let the leaves fall.

HARRIET MONROE

JOURNEY TO ICELAND

And the traveller hopes: let me be far from any
Physician. And the ports have names for the sea,
　　The citiless, the corroding, the sorrow.
　　And North means to all Reject.

And the great plains are forever where the cold fish is hunted,
And everywhere. The light birds flicker and flaunt.
　　Under the scolding flag the lover
　　Of islands may see at last,

Faintly, his limited hope; and he nears the glitter
Of glaciers, the sterile immature mountains, intense
　　In the abnormal day of this world, and a river's
　　Fan-like polyp of sand.

Then let the good citizen here find marvels of nature:
The horse-shoe ravine, the issue of steam from a cleft
　　In the rock, and rocks, and waterfalls brushing the
　　Rocks, and among the rocks birds.

And the student of prose and conduct places to visit:
The site of the church where a bishop was put in a bog,
　　The bath of a great historian, the rock where an
　　Outlaw dreaded the dark.

Remember the doomed man thrown by his horse and crying
"Beautiful is the hill-side; I will not go":
　　The old woman confessing: "He that I loved the
　　Best, to him I was worst."

For Europe is absent. This is an island and therefore
Unreal. And the steadfast affections of its dead can be bought
      By those whose dreams accuse them of being
      Spitefully alive. And the pale

From too much passion of kissing feel pure in its deserts.
Can they? For the world is, and the present, and the lie.
      And the narrow bridge over the torrent, and the
      Small farm under the crag

Are the natural setting for the jealousies of a province;
And the weak vow of fidelity is formed by the cairn:
      And within the indigenous figure on horseback
      On the bridle-path down by the lake

The blood moves also by crooked and furtive inches,
Asks all your questions: "Where is the homage? When
      Shall justice be done? O who is against me?
      Why am I always alone?"

Present then the world to the world with its mendicant
    shadow:
Let the suits be flash, the minister of commerce insane:
      Let jazz be bestowed on the huts, and the beauty's
      Set cosmopolitan smile.

For our time has no favourite suburb. No local features
Are those of the young for whom all wish to care;
      The promise is only a promise, the fabulous
      Country impartially far.

Tears fall in all the rivers. Again the driver
Pulls on his gloves and in a blinding snowstorm starts
      On his deadly journey, and again the writer
      Runs howling to his art.

                              W. H. AUDEN

POEM

O who can ever praise enough
      The world of his belief?
  Harum–scarum childhood plays
  In the meadows near his home,
  In his woods Love knows no wrong,
  Travellers ride their placid ways,
  In the cool shade of the tomb
  Age's trusting footfalls ring.
O who can paint the vivid tree
      And grass of phantasy?

But to create it and to guard
      Shall be his whole reward.
  He shall watch and he shall weep,
  All his father's love deny,
  To his mother's womb be lost,
  Eight nights with a wanton sleep,
  But upon the ninth shall be
  Bride and victim to a ghost,
And in the pit of terror thrown
      Shall bear the wrath alone.

W. H. AUDEN

WE LYING BY SEASAND

We lying by seasand, watching yellow
And the grave sea, mock who deride
Who follow the red rivers, hollow
Alcove of words out of cicada shade,
For in this yellow grave of sand and sea
A calling for color calls with the wind
That's grave and gay as grave and sea
Sleeping on either hand.
The lunar silences, the silent tide
Lapping the still canals, the dry tide-master

Ribbed between desert and water storm,
Should cure our ills of the water
With a one-colored calm;
The heavenly music over the sand
Sounds with the grains as they hurry
Hiding the golden mountains and mansions
Of the grave, gay seaside land.
Bound by a sovereign strip, we lie,
Watch yellow, wish for wind to blow away
The strata of the shore and leave red rock;
But wishes breed not, neither
Can we fend off the rock arrival,
Lie watching yellow until the golden weather
Breaks, O my heart's blood, like a heart and hill.

DYLAN THOMAS

MATING ANSWER

Sun cheers us for a pin-point, flicks, then westers
To bury us, cheating our blind feet with molehills;
Light's razor edge, moveless as hawk, neither sears nor seals
The proud flesh that breeds anguish of mining festers.
Echoing earth-throbs presage the bustle and whirr
Of hive, mound, ant-empire, the insect pace that steals
Root from flower, eye from socket, ravishes, uncouples
Soul from body. Stubbed on iron bars our hands fumble
The alone, the lonely dark of self, clay meeting clay.
Then mating answers and suddenly free-winged in air
With gannet-speed we hurricane nestward, brake
The long confident swoop with webs, pinions, legs
At the cliff-face ledge and flutter humble
Down to soft welcoming feathers, warm eggs.

RONALD BOTTRALL

SEQUENCE

I

The wave approaching and the wave returning,
The grave is broken, and the phoenix burning,
The myrtle blossoms from the twisted pillar,
Love illuminates a scene of pallor:
Inevitably to life consigned
The flame consuming, the by flame consumed,
Eternally eternally bud and blossom
Evolve the particulars of doom.

II

The paralyzed bird within the autumn tree
Amber and dumb, I love the silent bird,
The palace mounted promontory
Blazing like birth above dirty world,
Apples at hand, the apples at the thigh
Love plucked, the girl in feathery garters
Carefully disrobing by open waters;
Though bird is silent life is the word.

III

The ghost I dog through Twickenham turns round
I see the bridge involved with its bowels;
The Richmond lady gathering spring flowers
Reveals the ache of time like rhododendron
Red in her bosom. The boy with the bright hair
Shows me his guts with the tame mice there.
And in my turn I bare the quick of soul,
They leap in, to sleep in the dark hole.

IV

Henceforth wandering with my womb
Heavy with ghost, the Richmond lady, boy;

I hang at finger the bird for toy,
The flower wear as a wonder wound;
Objects revolve as I proceed
About my breast like a solar system;
With the bleeding eye I bleed,
Event is staged hysteria.

V

The wave approaching and the wave returning,
The grave is broken, and the phoenix burning,
The myrtle blossoms from the twisted pillar,
Love illuminates a scene of pallor:
Thus inevitably to life consigned,
The flame consuming, the by flame consumed,
Eternally eternally bud and blossom
Evolve the particulars of doom.

GEORGE BARKER

POEM

Old man in the crystal morning after snow,
Your throat swathed in a muffler, your bent
Figure building the snow man which is meant
For the grandchild's target,
                              do you know
This fat cartoon, his eyes pocked in with coal
Nears you each time your breath smokes the air,
Lewdly grinning out of a private nightmare?
He is the white cold shadow of your soul.

You build his comic head, you place his comic hat;
Old age is not so serious, and I
By the window sad and watchful as a cat,
Build too this poem of old age and of snow,
And weep: you are my snow man and I know
I near you, you near him, all of us must die.

DELMORE SCHWARTZ

MY LOVE WAS LIGHT

My love was light the old wives said —
Light was my love and better dead!

My love was of such little worth
Stones were but wasted on her tomb;
She left no kettle by the hearth,
No crying child nor silent loom.

My love drank wine the old wives said
And danced her empty days away;
She baked no bread, she spun no thread,
She shaped no vessels out of clay. . . .

But how should old wives understand
Eternally my heart must grieve,
The cup remembering in her hand,
The dance her ghostly feet still weave. . . .

My love was light the old wives said —
Light was my love and better dead!

THOMAS LANIER WILLIAMS

TWO MORNINGS AND TWO EVENINGS

PARIS, 7 A.M.

I make a trip to each clock in the apartment:
Some hands point histrionically one way
And some point others, from the ignorant faces.
Time is an Etoile; hours diverge
So much that days are journeys round their suburbs,
Circles surrounding stars, overlapping circles.
The short, half-tone scale of winter weathers
Is a spread pigeon's wing.
Winter lives under a pigeon's wing, a dead wing with damp 183
    feathers.

Look down into the courtyard. All the houses
Are built this way, with ornamental urns
Set on the mansard roof-tops where the pigeons
Take their walks. It is like introspection
To stare inside, or retrospection,
A star inside a rectangle, a recollection:
This hollow square could easily have been there
— The childish snow-forts, built in flashier winters,
Could have reached these proportions and been houses;
The mighty snow-forts, four, five, stories high,
Withstanding spring as sand-forts do the tide,
Their walls, their shape, could not dissolve and die,
Only be overlapping in a strong chain, only be stone,
Be grayed and yellowed now like these.

Where is the ammunition, the piled-up balls
With the star-splintered hearts of ice?

This sky is no carrier-warrior-pigeon
Escaping endless intersecting circles.
It is a dead one, or the sky from which a dead one fell.
The urns have caught his ashes or his feathers.
When did the star dissolve, or was it captured
By the sequence of squares and squares and circles, circles?
Can the clocks say: is it there below
About to tumble in snow.

A MIRACLE FOR BREAKFAST

> *"Miracles enable us to judge of
> doctrine, and doctrine enables us
> to judge of miracles."*

At six o'clock we were waiting for coffee,
Waiting for coffee and the charitable crumb
That was going to be served from a certain balcony,
— Like kings of old, or like a miracle.
It was still dark. One foot of the sun
Steadied itself on a long ripple in the river.

The first ferry of the day had just crossed the river.
It was so cold we hoped the coffee
Would be very hot, seeing that the sun
Was not going to warm us; and that the crumb
Would be a loaf each buttered, by a miracle.
At seven a man stepped out on the balcony.

He stood for a minute alone on the balcony
Looking over our heads towards the river.
A servant handed him the makings of the miracle,
Consisting of one lone cup of coffee
And one roll, which he proceeded to crumb,
His head, so to speak, in the clouds — along with the sun.

Was the man crazy? What under the sun
Was he trying to do, up there on his balcony!
Each man received one rather hard crumb,
Which some flicked scornfully into the river,
And, in a cup, one drop of the coffee.
Some of us stood around, waiting for the miracle.

I can tell what I saw next; it was not a miracle.
A beautiful villa stood in the sun
And from its doors came the smell of hot coffee.
In front, a baroque white plaster balcony
Added by birds, who nest along the river,
— I saw it with one eye close to the crumb —

And galleries and marble chambers. My crumb
My mansion, made for me by a miracle,
Through ages, by insects, birds, and the river
Working the stone. Every day, in the sun,
At breakfast time I sit on my balcony
With my feet up, and drink gallons of coffee.

We licked up the crumb and swallowed the coffee.
A window across the river caught the sun
As if the miracle were working, on the wrong balcony.

FROM THE COUNTRY TO THE CITY

The long, long legs,
League-boots of land, that carry the city nowhere,
    Nowhere; the lines
That we drive on (the satin-stripes on harlequin's
    Trousers, tights);
His tough trunk dressed in tatters, scribbled over with
    Nonsensical signs;
His shadowy, tall dunce-cap; and best of all his
    Shows and sights,
His brain appears, throned in "fantastic triumph,"
    And shines through his hat
With jewelled works at work at intermeshing crowns,
    Lamé with lights.
As we approach, wickedest clown, your heart and head,
    We can see that
Glittering arrangement of your brain consists, now,
    Of mermaid-like,
Seated, ravishing sirens, each waving her hand-mirror;
    And we start at
Series of slight disturbances up in the telephone wires
    On the turnpike.
Flocks of short, shining wires seem to be flying sidewise.
    Are they birds?
They flash again. No. They are vibrations of the tuning-fork
    You hold and strike
Against the mirror-frames, then draw for miles, your dreams,
    Out country-wards.
We bring a message from the long black length of body:
    "Subside," it begs and begs.

SONG

Summer is over upon the sea.
The pleasure yacht, the social being,
That danced on the endless polished floor,
Stepped and side-stepped like Fred Astaire,
Is gone, is gone, docked somewhere ashore.

The friends have left, the sea is bare
That was strewn with floating, fresh green weeds.
Only the rusty-sided freighter
Goes past the moon's marketless craters
And the stars are the only ships of pleasure.

ELIZABETH BISHOP

BEARDED OAKS

The oaks, how subtle and marine!
Bearded, and all the layered light
Above them swims; and thus the scene,
Recessed, awaits the positive night.

So, waiting, we in the grass now lie
Beneath the langorous tread of light;
The grasses, kelp-like, satisfy
The nameless motions of the air.

Upon the floor of light, and time,
Unmurmuring, of polyp made,
We rest; we are, as light withdraws,
Twin atolls on a shelf of shade.

Ages to our construction went,
Dim architecture, hour by hour;
And violence, forgot now, lent
The present stillness all its power.

The storm of noon above us rolled,
Of light the fury, furious gold,
The long drag troubling us, the depth:
Unrocked is dark, unrippling, still.

Passion and slaughter, ruth, decay
Descended, whispered grain by grain,
Silted down swaying streams, to lay
Foundation for our voicelessness.

187

All our debate is voiceless here,
As all our rage is rage of stone;
If hopeless hope, fearless is fear,
And history is thus undone.

(Our feet once wrought the hollow street
With echo when the lamps were dead
At windows; once our headlight glare
Disturbed the doe that, leaping, fled.)

That cagèd hearts make iron stroke
I do not love you now the less,
Or less that all that light once gave
The graduate dark should now revoke

So little time we live in Time,
And we learn all so painfully,
That we may spare this hour's term
To practice for Eternity.

ROBERT PENN WARREN

AESTHETIC

Flight is the bird's value:
starting parallel with water, rising
breaks his definite shadow, high
he soars over the evening's valley.

We know him by motion: his beauty
is parting from pond, sharp wheel
of the white belly burnished in dusk,
the untiring path into the hills.

Movement alone is his great honor.

NORMAN ROSTEN

AT CARMEL HIGHLANDS

Below the gardens and the darkening pines
The living water sinks among the stones,
Sinking yet foaming till the snowy tones
Merge with the fog drawn landward in dim lines.
The cloud dissolves among the flowering vines,
And now the definite mountain-side disowns
The fluid world, the immeasurable zones.
Then white oblivion swallows all designs.
But still the rich confusion of the sea,
Unceasing voice, sombre and solacing,
Rises through veils of silence past the trees;
In restless repetition bound, yet free,
Wave after wave in deluge fresh releasing
An ancient speech, hushed in tremendous ease.

JANET LEWIS

In the naked bed, in Plato's cave,
Reflected headlights slowly slid the wall,
Carpenters hammered beneath the shaded window,
Wind troubled the window curtains all night long.
A fleet of trucks strained uphill, grinding,
Their freights, as usual, hooded by tarpaulin.
The ceiling lightened again, the slanting diagram
Slid slowly off. Hearing the milkman's chop,
His striving up the stair, the bottle's chink,
I rose from bed, lit a cigarette,
And walked to the window. The stony street bestowed
The stillness in which buildings stand upon
The street-lamp's vigil, and the horse's patience.
The winter sky's pure capital
Turned me back to bed with exhausted eyes.

Strangeness grew in the motionless air. The loose
Film greyed. Shaking wagons, hooves' waterfalls

Sounded far off, increasing, louder and nearer.
A car coughed, starting up. Morning, softly
Melting the air, lifted the half-covered chair
From underseas, kindled the mirror
Upon the wall. The bird called tentatively, whistled,
Bubbled and whistled, so! Perplexed, still wet
With sleep, affectionate, hungry and cold. So, so,
O son of man, the ignorant night, the rumors
Of building and movement, the travail
Of early morning, the mystery of beginning
Again and again,
                          while history is unforgiven.

DELMORE SCHWARTZ

A NOCTURNE FOR OCTOBER 31ST

The night was faint and sheer;
Immobile, road and dune.
Then, for a moment, clear,
A plane moved past the moon.

O spirit cool and frail,
Hung in the lunar fire!
Spun wire and brittle veil!
And trembling slowly higher!

Pure in each proven line!
The balance and the aim,
Half empty, half divine!
I saw how true you came.

Dissevered from your cause,
Your function was your goal.
Oblivious of my laws,
You made your calm patrol.

YVOR WINTERS

FOUR POEMS

I

When all my five and country senses see,
The fingers will forget green thumbs and mark
How through the halfmoon's vegetable eye
In the ten planted towers of their stalk
Love in the frost is pared and wintered by,
The whispering ears will watch love drummed away
Down wind and shell to a discordant beach,
And, lashed to syllables, the eyed tongue talk
How her sweet wounds are mended bitterly.
My nostrils see her breath burn like a bush.

My one and noble heart has witnesses
In all love's countries, that will watch awake;
And when blind sleep falls on the spying senses,
The heart is sensual, though five eyes break.

II

O make me a mask and a wall to shut from your spies
Of the sharp, enamelled eyes and the spectacled claws
Rape and rebellion in the nurseries of my face,
Gag of a dumbstruck tree to block from bare enemies
The bayonet tongue in this undefended prayerpiece,
The present mouth, and the sweetly blown trumpet of lies,
Shaped in old armor and oak the countenance of a dunce
To shield the glistening brain and blunt the examiners,
And a tear-stained widower grief drooped from the lashes
To veil belladonna and let the dry eyes perceive
Others betray the lamenting lies of their losses
By the curve of the nude mouth or the laugh up the sleeve.

III

Not from this anger, anticlimax after
Refusal struck her loins and the lame flower

Bent like a beast to lap the singular floods
In a land without weather,
Shall she receive a bellyfull of weeds
And bear those tendril hands I touch across
The agonised, two seas.

Behind my head a square of sky sags over
The circular smile tossed from lover to lover
And the golden ball spins out of the skies;
Not from this anger after
Refusal struck like a bell under water
Shall her smile breed that mouth, behind the mirror,
That burns along my eyes.

IV

The spire cranes. Its statue is an aviary.
From the stone nest it does not let the feathery
Carved birds blunt their striking throats on the salt gravel,
Pierce the spilt sky with diving wing in weed and heel
An inch in froth. Chimes cheat the prison spire, pelter
In time like outlaw rains on that priest, water,
Time for the swimmers' hands, music for silver lock
And mouth. Both note and plume plunge from the spire's
    hook.
Those craning birds are choice for you, songs that jump
    back
To the built voice, or fly with winter to the bells,
But do not travel down dumb wind like prodigals.

DYLAN THOMAS

DARKENED WINDOWS

Seepage of time rots judgment, makes it slip
Where once it moved master; the mildewing years
Blur for the teetering soul its precipitous fears
And wind our wounds into a coil of sleep.

Old triumphs of summer ardour are tasted
As memories of a great vintage on the tongue —
Steps that lead to a cellar, to the white waste
Nights when desire fails in the hungry.

The distant fountain we have left unheard,
The unexplored, but visible island,
Ferment in the fusty brain as murder
Secret, unacknowledged, soon to be branded.

The satisfied heart is coffined in its treasure;
Only the vigilant eye and unfaltering hand
Can dare to reject the little that is sure
For the hazardous cliff-face and the promised land.

RONALD BOTTRALL

THE RECKONING

All profits disappear: the gain
Of ease, the hoarded, secret sum;
And now grim digits of old pain
Return to litter up our home.

We hunt the cause of ruin, add,
Subtract, and put ourselves in pawn;
For all our scratching on the pad,
We cannot trace the error down.

What we are seeking is a fare
One way, a chance to be secure:
The lack that keep us what we are,
The penny that usurps the poor.

THEODORE ROETHKE

)when what hugs stopping earth than silent is
more silent than more than much more is or
total sun oceaning than any this
tear jumping from each most least eye of star

and without was if minus and shall be
immeasurable happenless unnow
shuts more than open could that every tree
or than all life more death begins to grow

end's ending then these dolls of joy and grief
these recent memories of future dream
these perhaps who have lost their shadows if
which did not do the losing spectres mime

until out of merely not nothing comes
only one snowflake(and we speak our names

E. E. CUMMINGS

ANTHOLOGY OF NOUNS

FOR THE NOUN C. BL.

The collapsible lover, the spider in iniquitousness
Up to the neck, the skyrocketing belly of the soldier
The elderly beautiful screen star, the avenue
Of the undeveloped city, focus of dreams as they are

The beauty of the classic catalogue of poets
Its deathwhite pages, the yawn in the middle of eternity
The broken sequence and the murmur of psychology
Drink's paradise of compliments, the heart in the street

Like a yellowing cur or a darkening stranger;
The rhyme to go with the Christ Child and His manger
The confidence stored beneath the fingernails, leaving
At cock's crow, the blue Sunday and the red-ripe job

These are sober phrases beyond the mind's deceiving
I said the lover, the lover and the spider iniquitous
The collapse of the attacked at the attacker's range
Said the result in the starry bowels of the soldier

Woman commanding and decayed, I said the blossom of
Spring on the outskirts, the verity of vision within name
Initiation by example and correction and I said death
The inattention of pupils in the teleological tangle

The mask of Freud exposed in the jungle of flattery
The mislaid heart, found and mislaid and knocked down again
For reassurance I mentioned a day of the week, and its color
How far can the noun expand, lacking the lust of the verb?

PARKER TYLER

MIRROR

Before this fever of the almost cold
Fierce things are gnawing on the sweated palm
And howl along taut sinews that behold
The awful tempest of the almost calm.
But not for long the paroxysmal hands
Like spiders writhing on the twisted sheet;
Time now abruptly cuts his flow of sands,
So simply deals him silence and defeat.
Now spent and vanquished in the bursting gloom
The limbs are quiet on the tortured bed;
The hands are rested in the raging room
And relaxation marks the fallen head
Whom peace has dealt his everlasting grace.
And when I turn they see death in my face.

PETER DE VRIES

THE MARGINAL FIELD

On the chalk cliff edge struggles the final field
Of barley smutted with tares and marbled
With veins of rusted poppy as though the plough had bled.

195

1939

The sun is drowned in bird-wailing mist
The sea and sky meet outside distinction
The landscape glares and stares — white poverty
Of gaslight diffused through frosted glass.

This field was the farmer's extremest thought
And its flinty heart became his heart
When he drove below the return it yields
The wage of the labourer sheeted in sweat.
Here the price and the cost cross on a chart
At a point fixed on the margin of profit
Which opens out in the golden fields

Waving their grasses and virile beards
On the laps of the dripping valleys and flushing
Their pulsing ears against negative skies.
Their roots clutch into the flesh of the soil,
As they fall to the scythe they whisper of excess
Heaped high above the flat wavering scale
Near the sea, beyond the wind-scarred hill

Where loss is exactly equalled by gain
And the roots and the sinews wrestle with stone
On the margin of what can just be done
To eat back from the land the man the land eats.
Starved outpost of wealth and final soldier,
Your stretched-out bones are the frontier of power
With your mouth wide open to drink in lead.

                                    STEPHEN SPENDER

THE SNOW STORM

No hawk hangs over in this air:
The urgent snow is everywhere.
The wing adroiter than a sail
Must lean away from such a gale,

196

Abandoning its straight intent,
Or else expose tough ligament
And tender flesh to what before
Meant dampened feathers, nothing more.

Forceless upon our backs there fall
Infrequent flakes hexagonal,
Devised in many a curious style
To charm our safety for a while,
Where close to earth like mice we go
Under the horizontal snow.

EDNA ST. VINCENT MILLAY

HEADLAND

The traveling sky goes landward, the blind mass
Of headland thrusts a black snout in the sea.
The indifferent violence of the working water,
The winter southwind turning the gulls, stirring
The shell-fed headland grass — these passionless
Elements feed passion and make our lives —
The lashed shelves, the basalt in the foam,
The sea-rocks dolphin-dark the green wave frays.

BREWSTER GHISELIN

VOLTAIRE AT FERNEY

Perfectly happy now, he looked at his estate.
An exile making watches glanced up as he passed
And went on working; where a hospital was rising fast,
A joiner touched his cap; an agent came to tell
Some of the trees he'd planted were progressing well.
The white alps glittered. It was summer. He was very great.

Far off in Paris where his enemies
Whispered that he was wicked, in an upright chair

1939

A blind old woman longed for death and letters. He would
      write,
"Nothing is better than life". But was it? Yes, the fight
Against the false and the unfair
Was always worth it. So was gardening. Civilize.

Cajoling, scolding, scheming, cleverest of them all,
He'd had the other children in a holy war
Against the infamous grown-ups; and, like a child, been sly
And humble, when there was occasion for
The two-faced answer or the plain protective lie,
But, patient like a peasant, waited for their fall.

And never doubted, like D'Alembert, he would win:
Only Pascal was a great enemy, the rest
Were rats already poisoned; there was much, though, to be
      done,
And only himself to count upon.
Dear Diderot was dull but did his best;
Rousseau, he'd always known, would blubber and give in.

Night fell and made him think of women: Lust
Was one of the great teachers; Pascal was a fool.
How Emilie had loved astronomy and bed;
Pimpette had loved him too, like scandal; he was glad.
He'd done his share of weeping for Jerusalem: As a rule,
It was the pleasure-haters who became unjust.

Yet, like a sentinel, he could not sleep. The night was full of
      wrong,
Earthquakes and executions: Soon he would be dead,
And still all over Europe stood the horrible nurses
Itching to boil their children. Only his verses
Perhaps could stop them: He must go on working: Overhead,
The uncomplaining stars composed their lucid song.

                                        W. H. AUDEN

THE SENSE OF THE SLEIGHT-OF-HAND MAN

One's grand flights, one's Sunday baths,
One's tootings at the weddings of the soul
Occur as they occur. So bluish clouds
Occurred above the empty house and the leaves
Of the rhododendrons rattled their gold,
As if some one lived there. Such floods of white
Came bursting from the clouds. So the wind
Threw its contorted strength around the sky.
Could you have said the bluejay suddenly
Would swoop to earth? It is a wheel, the rays
Around the sun. The wheel survives the myths.
The fire eye in the clouds survives the gods.
To think of a dove with an eye of grenadine
And pines that are cornets, so it occurs,
And a little island full of geese and stars:
It may be that the ignorant man, alone,
Has any chance to mate his life with the life
That is the sensual, pearly spouse, the life
That is fluent in even the wintriest bronze.

WALLACE STEVENS

THE WAYS AND THE PEOPLES

What does the storm say? What the trees wish,
If they can manage to wish it. I am the king of the dead,
Says the hero strongly to his won field.
And it's true, too. Nobody hears him.

And wisdom has sorts — ones even the intelligent
Can understand if they wish; love is the limit that love
Approaches and approaches. And the skinny digger
Picks up among the caves the partial shard

She loves better than all our brilliance. On it the leopard,
In ochre and not foreshortened, manages quietly

After its own millennia, the quick
Stare of the dead one, in that dawn, among its deer.

Remember, each cupful of air has its vector,
And the backward seedling can always say:
It may be so; and I certainly vary;
And it's you who're taking the great wind's way —

And it knows what it says will always be taken
As the simple answer of the helpless love
Of the dwarfs in the forest for the glittering virgin
Who is dying and glass on her marvelous bier.

RANDALL JARRELL

EPILOGUE

Phoenix on the hot sirocco's breath
Above Necropolis his mummied dead,
Their names in granite over-riding death,

Over our legendary home has spread
His feathered silence: and no welcome light
Could pierce the solemn darkness his wings shed.

The garden and the trees are out of sight,
The guest is isolated in her room,
The host unable to be there that night.

Did the sirocco or the red simoom,
The phoenix wings, the shadow that they cast,
Blind guest and host, obliterate the tomb?

The darkness and the dreamed-of house are past,
Nor will the carvings on the granite last.

H. B. MALLALIEU

THE SUMMER ENDING

Lick your lips, X. darling, it may be the last —
The last seedy sunshine feather deflowered bowers
Idling thighs of light bedded in grasses,
As long as we live, at least the last for hours.
Storm is formulating, black and blue and proud.
Is it end, is it interim, how can you tell
When the weather changes? It works fast;
The leaf the nest the balm bombed by cloud.
Which is the way love also alas passes:
Jealousy then conscience then unfaithful habit.
Hush, we were fortunate formerly, never say farewell.
See there, the nauseated boughs, under them weeping rabbit.

Of summery love-affair, perhaps before long no wonder
Amid annual drama the bond between us may ripely snap.
Air! glare less beautifully, or else hurry up, thunder!
X. dear, ex-dear, give me a kiss before it really rains.
Thanks, and for all my felicity in recent years, thanks.
Say safe things, say this is nothing but breathing-spell, oh
Nonsense, it is a labyrinth of stale atmospheres, a trap.
See how vegetable, animal, with soft paw salutes its fellow —
Whereas this glassy afternoon we are only bright-eyed brains,
Perfervid, like a pair of fighting-fish in twin tanks.

The sky looks liverish, then brownly wrinkles, then weeps,
Heaves a sigh: which sigh dampened with single drops
As we inhale it, slides into the lung like a dagger.
Warlike little winds in the dust arm and stamp,
Shrub throbs, the recumbent light's flesh creeps,
Green giants, oaks, on lame shadows all stagger,
The honeycombed horizon festers, and unfinished crops
In whipped warm fields lie down and implore.
Love with its over-exercised senses in fond cramp
Leaves us worse off than we were before.

What was all of a piece, now our intellects acutely part.
Through the pink of each cheek, the form loosely voluminous,   201

Each beholds the bone of the other's beloved head.
The healing concupiscent fit may not occur again in us.
I hiss in disappointment, your discipline of me is blunder —
As lightning lets fly in sensitive tree its golden witticism
And laggard along after it comes the thunder:
Nagging or warning, domestic, like a palpitating heart.
The hot sod under us creaks, reminiscent of the laborious bed
On which our young characters grew as in a cradle.
Now our kiss grows brotherly but love remains fatal.
Now lover hits lover, in loathing, in fright of criticism.

GLENWAY WESCOTT

SONNET

The crumbled rock of London is dripping under
Clouds of mechanical rain, and other cities
Lie frozen round their rivers and the thunder:
For these new decades open of silent pities,
The poet dead by green enormous sculpture,
Roads sanded for expressionless invaders
And empty as flame the heavens for the vulture.
Here walk with open lips the pale persuaders
Of doom, over the concrete near the river,
Shadowed by trusts on whose retreating faces
The glassy light and crimson vapors quiver.
This town is full of ghosts: successive bases
Lost to the living send their last battalion.
There is no face tonight that is not alien.

ROY FULLER

MOVING IN

Don't wait for the wind to blow you through the door,
If you need help, here is my hand, I said.
Don't let my walking on the hollow floor
Frighten you, only the dark air is dead.

202

People more than things can fill a house.
Sit by me on these boxes in the gloom,
Here, with our crumbs of living, like a mouse,
While the fire burns the strangeness from the room.

You answered: Something makes me want to hide
In open air from walls where cobwebs cling.
It's here in me and not with you inside,
Neither an emptiness the years have made,
Nor a house bare of any human thing,
But being afraid that I will be afraid.

PAUL ENGLE

STANZAS IN MEDITATION

I

Full well I know that she is there
Much as she will she can be there
But which I know which I know when
Which is my way to be there then
Which she will know as I know here
That it is now that it is there
That rain is there and it is here
That it is here that they are there
They have been here to leave it now
But how foolish to ask them if they like it
Most certainly they like it because they like what they have
But they might easily like something else
And very probably just as well they will have it
Which they like as they are very likely not to be
Reminded that it is more than ever necessary
That they should never be surprised at any one time
At just what they have been given by taking what they have
Which they are very careful not to add with
And they may easily indulge in the fragrance
Not only of which but by which they know
That they tell them so.

203

1940

IV

The whole of this last end is to say which of two.

V

Thank you for hurrying through.

VI

Why am I if I am uncertain reasons may inclose.
Remain remain propose repose chose.
I call carelessly that the door is open
Which if they can refuse to open
No one can rush to close.
Let them be mine therefor.
Everybody knows that I chose.
Therefor if therefor before I close.
I will therefor offer therefor I offer this.
Which if I refuse to miss can be miss is mine.
I will be well welcome when I come.
Because I am coming.
Certainly I come having come.

These stanzas are done.

GERTRUDE STEIN

BACCHUS III

The god who fled down with a standard yard
(Surveying with that reed which was his guard
He showed St. John the New Jerusalem;
It was a sugarcane containing rum
And hence the fire on which these works depend)
Taught and quivered strung upon the bend
An outmost crystal a recumbent flame
(He drinks all cups the tyrant could acclaim;

He still is dumb, illimitably wined,
Burns still his nose and liver for mankind) . . .
It is an ether, such an agony.
In the thin choking air of Caucasus
He under operation lies forever
Smelling the chlorine in the chloroform.
The plains around him flood with the destroyers
Pasturing the stallions in the standing corn.

WILLIAM EMPSON

PERDITA

The glamour of the end attic, the smell of old
Leather trunks — Perdita, where have you been
Hiding all these years? Somewhere or other a green
Flag is waving under an iron vault
And a brass bell is the herald of green country
And the wind is in the wires and the broom is gold.

Perdita, what became of all the things
We said that we should do? The cobwebs cover
The labels of Tyrol. The time is over-
Due and in some metropolitan station
Among the clank of cans and the roistering files
Of steam the caterpillars wait for wings.

LOUIS MAC NEICE

UNTITLED

Fivesucked the features of my girl by glory
And the trumpet drummer, in a field of scars,
Works in a brothel band, who is my champion,
The streetwalk soldier slipping to the wars.

By the shorewind he blows, a rumsicked line,
Tearing down the cloth of battle from the story,

And the drugend way is tempted by his rattle,
The sickness in the throat, the killjoy fury,

Who, teaser in the field, shapes crackled hands,
Joints fingercharge into his silver tone:
Blow, boy, against the brothel bones of war
And save us God's inscription in the bone.

NICHOLAS MOORE

GRAVES ARE MADE TO WALTZ ON

Tunes fainter on winds waywarder than others
When from the frozen swamp the evil crystals glow,
Lure us to our disowned deep-buried banished brothers,
Our dark-souled scowling brothers,
Who pound warm fists against their jails of snow.

Waltz with decorum — one step lax or lacking,
One slip on our own graves of many deaths ago,
Betrays us: ever nearer the tune of tough ice cracking,
The hungry snarl of cracking,
And hands reach out to drag us down below.

PETER VIERECK

anyone lived in a pretty how town
(with up so floating many bells down)
spring summer autumn winter
he sang his didn't he danced his did.

Women and men (both little and small)
cared for anyone not at all
they sowed their isn't they reaped their same
sun moon stairs rain

children guessed (but only a few
and down they forgot as up they grew

autumn winter spring summer)
that noone loved him more by more

when by now and tree by leaf
she laughed his joy she cried his grief
bird by snow and stir by still
anyone's any was all to her

someones married their everyones
laughed their cryings and did their dance
(sleep wake hope and then) they
said their nevers they slept their dream

stars rain sun moon
(and only the snow can begin to explain
how children are apt to forget to remember
with up so floating many bells down)

one day anyone died i guess
(and noone stooped to kiss his face)
busy folk buried them side by side
little by little and was by was

all by all and deep by deep
and more by more they dream their sleep
noone and anyone earth by april
wish by spirit and if by yes.

Women and men (both dong and ding)
summer autumn winter spring
reaped their sowing and went their came
sun moon stars rain

E. E. CUMMINGS

THINGS

Things are the mind's mute looking-glass —
That vase of flowers, this work-box here,
When false love flattered me, alas,
Glowed with a beauty crystal clear.

Now they are hostile. The tulip's glow
Burns with the mockery of despair;
And when I open the box, I know
What kind of self awaits me there.

WALTER DE LA MARE

ANTIQUES

Those quaint old worn-out words!
    Fashions in miniature:
Pious, amiable, reserved, serene,
    Modest, sedate, demure!
Mental poke-bonnets, — and no less effete,
Why, even their meanings now are obsolete.

WALTER DE LA MARE

PARTING: 1940

Not knowing in what season this again
Not knowing when again the arms outyearning
Nor the flung smile in eyes not knowing when.

Not sure beyond all doubt of full return
Not sure of time now nor the film's reversal
This all done opposite, the waif regathered.

We bag in hand with wandering steps and slow
Through suburbs take our solitary way
Not knowing in what season this again.

Not that all clouds are garrisoned and stung
Not that horizons loom with coppered legions
Not that the year is dark with weird condition.

All who parted in all days looked back
Saw the white face, the waving. And saw the sea.
Not knowing in what season this again.

For well they knew, the parters in all evenings,
Druids and hunters and the launched Phoenicians:
The blood flows one imposed way, and no other.

JOHN FREDERICK NIMS

THEN . . .

There were no men and women then at all,
But the flesh lying alone,
And angry shadows fighting on a wall
Which now and then sent out a groan
Stifled in lime and stone,
And sweated now and then like tortured wood
Big drops that looked yet did not look like blood.

And yet as each drop came a shadow faded
And left the wall.
There was a lull
Until another in its shadow arrayed it,
Came, fought and left a blood-mark on the wall.
And that was all; the blood was all.

If women had been there they might have wept
For the poor blood, unowned, unwanted,
Blank as forgotten script.
The wall was haunted
By mute maternal presences whose sighing
Fluttered the fighting shadows and shook the wall
As if that fury of death itself were dying.

EDWIN MUIR   209

PART IV

1940–1950
(Volumes 57–76)

POEM

He watched with all his organs of concern
How princes walk, what wives and children say;
Reopened old graves in his heart to learn
What laws the dead had died to disobey;

And came reluctantly to his conclusion:
"All the arm-chair philosophers are false,
To love another adds to the confusion,
The song of pity is the devil's waltz."

And bowed to fate and was successful, so
That soon he was the king of all the creatures:
Yet, shaking in an autumn nightmare, saw,

Approaching down an empty corridor,
A figure with his own distorted features
That wept, and grew enormous, and cried Woe.

W. H. AUDEN

NECROPOLIS

Even in death they prosper; even in the death
Where lust lies senseless and pride fallow
The mouldering owners of rents and labor
Prosper and improve the high hill.

For theirs is the stone whose name is deepest cut;
Theirs the facsimile temple, theirs
The iron acanthus and the hackneyed Latin,
The boxwood rows and all the birds.

And even in death the poor are thickly herded
In intimate congestion under streets and alleys.
Look at the standard sculpture, the cheap
Synonymous slabs, the machined crosses.

Yes, even in death the cities are unplanned.
The heirs govern from the marble centers;
They will not remove. And the ludicrous angels,
Remains of the poor, will never fly
But only multiply in the green grass.

KARL J. SHAPIRO

RIVER RHYME

The rumpled river
takes its course
lashed by rain

This is that now
that tortures
skeletons of weeds

and muddy waters
eat their
banks the drain

of swamps a bulk
that writhes and fat-
tens as it speeds.

WILLIAM CARLOS WILLIAMS

THE BLOODY SIRE

It is not bad. Let them play.
Let the guns bark and the bombing-plane
Speak his prodigious blasphemies.

It is not bad, it is high time,
Stark violence is still the sire of all the world's values.

What but the wolf's tooth chiseled so fine
The fleet limbs of the antelope?
What but fear winged the birds and hunger
Gemmed with such eyes the great goshawk's head?
Violence has been the sire of all the world's values.

Who would remember Helen's face
Lacking the terrible halo of spears?
Who formed Christ but Herod and Caesar,
The cruel and bloody victories of Caesar?
Violence has been the sire of all the world's values.

Never weep, let them play,
Old violence is not too old to beget new values.

ROBINSON JEFFERS

ULYSSES' LIBRARY

Here in the cool and book-infested den,
Hid from the Irish sun by storied shelves,
They tread, seeking no truth, loving themselves.
Each waits his hour, the devils whisper "When?"
(God yawns to hear the lewd travail of men.)
The mincing mind of Best politely delves
Into dull sins of genius. Trapped by spells,
They lend an ear who scorn to borrow pen.
But circling Stephen's heart lie armored elves
Striking unfatal wounds, for love is blind
And blithely digs its populated Hells.
There Self keeps Stephen-Hamlet from his kind,
Laughs like a frightened nun at cap and bells,
And turns the shrieking mill-wheels of his mind.

DAVID DAICHES

TERROR

"I Voluntari Americani Presso Eserciti Stranieri
Non Perdono La Cittadinanza."

Il Messaggero, Roma,
Sabato, 27 Gennaio, 1940, XVIII, S. Giovanni Crisostomo

Not picnics or pageants or the improbable
Powers of air whose tongues exclaim dominion
And gull the great man to follow his terrible
Star, suffice; not the window-box, or the bird on
The ledge, which mean so much to the invalid,
Nor the joy you leaned after, as by the tracks the grass
In the emptiness after the lighted Pullmans fled,
Suffices; nor faces which, like distraction, pass
Under the street-lights, teasing to faith or pleasure,
Suffice you, born to no adequate definition of terror.

For yours, like a puppy, is darling and inept,
Though his cold nose brush your hand while you laugh at his
      clowning;
Or the kitten you sleep with, though once or twice while you
      slept
It tried to suck your breath, and you dreamed of drowning,
Perjured like Clarence, sluiced from the perilous hatches;
But never of lunar wolf-waste or the arboreal
Malignancy, with the privy-breath, which watches
And humps in the dark; but only a dream after all.
At the worst, you think, with a little twinge of distress,
That contagion may nook in the comforting fur you love to
      caress.

Though some, unsatisfied and sick, have sought
That immitigable face, whose smile is ice,
And fired their hearts like pitch-pine, for they thought
Better flame than the damp worm-tooth of compromise:
So Harry L. I knew, whose whores and gin
Had dwindled to a slick smile in the drug store
But for the absurd contraption of a plane,
Which flung on air the unformulable endeavor

While heart bled speed to lave the applauded name.
The crash was in an old cornfield; not even flame.

So some, whose passionate emptiness and tidal
Lust swayed toward the debris of Madrid,
And left New York to loll in their fierce idyll
Among the olives, where the snipers hid;
And now the North, to seek that visioned face
And polarize their iron of despair,
Who praise no beauty like the boreal grace
Which greens the dead eye under the rocket's flare.
They fight old friends, for their obsession knows
Only the immaculate itch, not human friends or foes.

They sought a secret which, perhaps, the Moor,
Hieratic, white-robed, pitiless, might teach,
Who duped and dying but for pride, therefore
Hugged truth which cause or conscience scarcely reach.
As Jacob all night with the angelic foe,
They wrestled him who did not speak, but died,
And wrestle now, by frozen fen and floe,
New Courier in fury sanctified;
And seek that face which, greasy, frost-breathed, furred,
Bends to the bomb-sight over bitter Helsingfors.

Blood splashed on the terrorless intellect creates
Corrosive fizzle like the spattered lime,
And its enseamed stew but satiates
Itself, in that lewd and faceless pantomime.
You know, by radio, how hotly the world repeats,
When the brute crowd roars or the blunt boot-heels resound
In the Piazza or the Wilhelmplatz,
The crime of Onan, spilled upon the ground;
You know, whose dear hope Alexis Carrel kept
Alive in a test-tube, where it monstrously grew, and slept.

But it is dead, and you now, guiltless, sink
To rest in lobbies, or pace gardens where
The slow god crumbles and the fountains prink,
Nor heed the criminal king, who paints the air

With discoursed madness and protruding eye,
Nor give the alarm, nor ask tonight where sleeps
That head which hooped the jewel Fidelity,
But like an old melon now, in the dank ditch, seeps;
But crack nuts, while the conscience-striken stare
Kisses the terror; for you see an empty chair.

ROBERT PENN WARREN

SECOND SHADOW

Cast on the field from their full height,
The oak leaves turn upon our sight.
Sun doubles them upon the land,
Their shade is wider than a hand,
The shadows move from left to right.

A hundred years, to this same sound,
The tree repeats its daily round,
The drama of revolving shade.
A hundred years its leaves are laid
In rich profusion on the ground.

But man a second shadow throws
Beyond the visible he knows:
The mind, untrammeled, can outfly
The nets of mutability
And shake the shade that hugs him close.

THEODORE ROETHKE

MEMORY

Cities are walled. It is a cruel land
And private as a dream. Nothing alive
Will grow there, yet great ghostly acres thrive
On a sound, an odor: one blown pinch of sand
Erects a cape, and soon the seas arrive.
But nothing alters there. Beyond return,

Joys lost, like meteors, cross the indifferent night
And fall away. While fixed, nailed to the sight,
Sharp as midsummer stars, that blind and burn,
More disant moments lend their chilling light.
Retired as the face of one who died,
The landscape lies. The structures, being old,
Keep griefs too awkward for one life to hold;
The rooms are many-mirrored, not for pride.
Yet there delight blooms in remorseless cold.

BABETTE DEUTSCH

SOLILOQUY IN AN AIR-RAID

The will dissolves, the heart becomes excited,
Skull suffers formication; moving words
Fortuitously issue from my hand.
The winter heavens, seen all day alone,
Assume the color of aircraft over the phthisic
Guns.

But who shall I speak to with this poem?

Something was set between the words and the world
I watched today; perhaps the necrotomy
Of love or the spectre of pretense; a vagueness;
But murdering their commerce like a tariff.

Inside the poets the words are changed to desire,
And formulations of feeling are lost in action
Which hourly transmutes the basis of common speech.
Our dying is effected in the streets,
London an epicentrum; to the stench
And penny prostitution in the shelters
Dare not extend the hospital and bogus
Hands of propaganda.

Ordered this year:
A billion tons of broken glass and rubble,

1941

Blockade of chaos, the other requisites
For the reduction of Europe to a rabble.
Who can observe this save as a frightened child
Or careful diarist? And who can speak
And still retain the tones of this civilization?

The verse that was the speech of observation, —
Jonson's cartoon of the infant bourgeoisie,
Shakespeare's immense assertion that man alone
Is almost the equal of his environment,
The Chinese wall of class round Pope, the Romantic
Denunciation of origin and mould, —
Is sunk in the throat between the opposing voices:

I am the old life, which promises even less
In the future, and guarantees your loss.

And I the new, in which your function and
Your form will be dependent on my end.

Kerensky said of Lenin: *I must kindly*
Orientate him to what is going on.
Watching the images of fabulous girls
On cinema screens, the liberal emotion
Of the slightly inhuman poet wells up in me,
As irrelevant as Kerensky. It is goodbye
To the social life which permitted melancholy
And madness in the isolation of its writers,
To a struggle as inconclusive as the Hundred
Years' War. The air, as welcome as morphia,
This *rich ambiguous aesthetic air*
Which now I breathe, is an effective diet
Only for actors: in the lonely box
The author mumbles to himself, the play
Unfolds spontaneous as the human wish,
As autumn dancing, vermilion on rocks.

ROY FULLER

WORDS

There are words that can only be said on paper.
It is fortunate they are few. All others shrink
On paper to the thinness of dried ink
And fade at the mind into forgotten vapour.

There are words that can only be said once
And have all been said before that fact is plain.
In a sense no word can ever be said again
And none can be said again in the same sense.

There are words that have to be said or written,
Answers and questions, times to be observed,
But most words die in a cause they have not served
Or bite forever what never should be bitten.

And then there are the words that are left unsaid
And the undetectable words used in their stead.

ROBERT FINCH

DUST BOWL

The land wants me to come back
To a handful of dust in autumn,
To a raindrop
In the palm of my hand
In spring.
The land wants me to come back
To a broken song in October,
To a snowbird on the wing.
The land wants me to come back.

LANGSTON HUGHES

IMMANENT

The drone of airplane neared, and dimmed away,
The child beyond high-tide mark still toiled on;
Salt water welled the trench that in his play
He'd dug to beleaguer his grey fortress stone.
Lovely as Eros, and half-naked too,
He heaped dried beach-drift, kindled it, and lo!
The furious furnace roared, the sea-winds blew —
Vengeance divine; and death to every foe!
Young god! and not ev'n Nature eyed askance
The fire-doomed Empire of a myriad Ants.

WALTER DE LA MARE

TO VIOLET

with prewar poems

These tracings from a world that's dead
Take for my dust-smothered Pyramid.
Count the sharp study and long toil
As pavements laid for worms to soil.
You, without knowing it, might tread
The grass where my foundation's laid;
Your, or another's, house be built
Where my mossed, weathered stones lie spilt;
And this unread memento be
The only lasting part of me.

BASIL BUNTING

THE FINDER FOUND

Will you, sometime, who have sought so long, and seek
Still in the slowly darkening searching-ground,
Catch sight some ordinary month or week

Of that rare prize you hardly thought you sought —
The gatherer gathered and the finder found,
The buyer who would buy all himself well bought —
And perch in pride in the buyer's hand, at home,
And there, the prize, in freedom rest and roam?

EDWIN MUIR

HENRY JAMES AT NEWPORT

And shores and strands and naked piers,
Sunset on waves, orange laddering the blue,
White sails on headlands, cool
Wide curving bay, dim landward distances
Dissolving in the property of local air.

Viterbo, Bagdad, Carcassonne —
They play upon the mind, the eyes again,
Although these back verandas, resolutely prim,
Say *Quakers, Roger Williams* — murmurs of the past —
While special staircase ghosts return,
Known voices in the old brown rooms:
"People don't do those things."
The pictures huddle in the frames.

Removed from those blank days
In which the margin is consumed,
The palace sites stare seaward, pure, *blasé*,
Remember the detached, the casually disqualified,
The mild cosmopolites whose ivory dream
Found no successors, quietly embalmed.
They nursed nostalgia on the sun-warmed rocks,
Exquisite, sterile, easily distressed,
Thought much of Paris, died
While he lived out their deaths.

Shores, strands, white sails and naked piers,
Wide curving bay and landward distances.

Thoughts of the dispossessed on summer afternoons.
The sails are tattered and the shrubs are dead.
The stone-walled fields are featureless.

WELDON KEES

THE PROFESSIONALS

Amateur and muddled, as their sex goes
Tired, symbols, like trousered scars
Forgotten, pavements for their shoes, wristwatches
For their time, calendars for months,
Stars, comets, even the sparkler
Sirius and Wordsworth's planet hidden,
Men push in their cheques, dole out the rent
And tax, in August sniff the sea.

Professionally, the bird sings
Through fight or love, the new leaved willow
Bends, the children swing in blue
And green, and the wet clouds extend.

GEOFFREY GRIGSON

AT THE BAND CONCERT

Tropic tonight, burning, filled with fast trains,
The sunset spills its brazen lake on lawns
Alive with families; the girls are here,
The easy, light, and lecherous who stare
One nervous millimetre past your eyes
Before excitement rockets out and dies.

The children imitate our violence
With toy maneuvers by the iron fence,
While chronic women bless each others' ills
And tell and retell nothing to themselves;
Like an impending chorus, men in hats
Repeat the blunders of the diplomats.

When, thrilling, sudden, anthem speaks its phrase,
The strollers halt, and lollers sternly rise;
Glazed in that music, paralyzed, they stare
Like stone-eyed heroes in a public square;
While, like a faminous hand, the stillness locks
All but the voices of the birds and dogs.

Music undoes them. Though the earth may send
Its evening shadows into night and bind
The suburbs in wistaria, these lost
Will turn their purpose to the drums at last;
In no endeavor of their own, but in
The iron service of the tribal man.

The curt baton returns them to their lives:
And these are still their children and their wives,
And these the attitudes of evening when,
In parks and alley rooms, the citizen,
Denied his common power, schemes the peace
Of days potential, like discovered seas.

JOHN MALCOLM BRINNIN

OCTOBER I

That season when the leaf deserts the bole
And half-dead see-saws through the October air
Falling face-downward on the walks to print
The decalcomania of its little soul —
Hardly has the milkman's sleepy horse
On wooden shoes echoed across the blocks
When with its back jaws open like a dredge
The van comes lumbering up the curb to someone's door and
       knocks.

And four black genii muscular and shy
Holding their shy caps enter the first room
Where someone hurriedly surrenders up
The thickset chair, the mirror half awry,

225

Then to their burdens stoop without a sound.
One with his bare hands rends apart the bed,
One stuffs the china-barrel with stale print,
Two bear the sofa toward the door with dark funereal tread.

The corner lamp, the safety eye of night,
Enveloped in the sun blinks and goes blind
And soon the early risers pick their way
Through kitchenware and pillows bolt upright.
The bureau on the sidewalk with bare back
And wrinkling veneer is most disgraced,
The sketch of Paris suffers in the wind;
Only the bike, its nose against the wall, does not show haste.

Two hours — the movers mop their necks and look,
Filing through dust and echoes back and forth.
The halls are hollow and all the floors are cleared
Bare to the last board, to the most secret nook;
But on the street a small chaos survives
That slowly now the leviathan ingests,
And schoolboys and stenographers stare at
The truck, the house, the husband in his hat who stands and
      rests.

He turns with miserable expectant face
And for the last time enters. On the wall
A picture-stain spreads from the nail-hole down.
Each object live and dead has left its trace.
He leaves his key; but as he quickly goes
This question comes behind: Did someone die?
Is someone rich or poor, better or worse?
What shall uproot a house and bring this care into his eye?

KARL J. SHAPIRO

HART CRANE

He jumped, seeing an island like a hand,
And where he lived the hands were all unfriendly.

The island rose to take him: at the end
He saw all things unclearly.

Even the sea had become strange to him: he entered
To trace the visionary company of love, the voice
He heard an instant in the wind, that said
There was no hand, no choice.

And the complete vision of love or the swelling sea
Was what he could never attain; he always wanted
To live near bridges; envied the sailors, free
And happy, never tainted

By the terrible life of the city and the dark failures
That broke his heart. He entered the sea, his fall
Made the steamer go round and round like a dog in circles,
And the island became a wall.

JULIAN SYMONS

BACCHUS IV

The herm whose length measured degrees of heat
(Small lar that sunned itself in Mercury
And perked one word there that made space ends meet)
Fluttered his snake too lightly in to see
(Most fertile thief, and journal to inquire)
The mortal Eden forming and the fire.
A smash resounding in its constancy.
This burst the planet bacchus in the sky.
Thence dry lone asteroids took heart to be.
So soon the amalgam with mercury
This plumbing; given with it free, the house
Not built with hands: the silver crucible
Butt-armed: the sovereigns: eats into flaked sloughs
Paste for the backs of mirrors, there he lies.
Leper scales fall always from his eyes.

WILLIAM EMPSON   227

UPON THE HEAVENLY SCARP

I

And on that day, upon the heavenly scarp,
The hosannas ceased, the hallelujahs died,
And music trembled on the silenced harp.
An angel, doffing his seraphic pride,
Wept; and his tears so bitter were, and sharp,
That where they fell, the blossoms shriveled and died.

II

Another with such voice intoned the psalm
It sang forth blasphemy against the Lord.
O that was a very imp in angeldom
Who, thinking evil, said no evil word —
But only pointed, at each *Te Deum*,
Down to the earth, and its unspeakable horde.

III

The Lord looked down, and saw the cattle-cars:
Men ululating to a frozen land.
He saw a man tear at his flogged scars,
And saw a babe look for its blown-off hand.
Scholars, he saw, sniffing their bottled wars,
And doctors who had genuises unmanned.

IV

The gentle violinist whose fingers played
Such godly music, washing a gutter, with lye,
He saw. He heard the priest who called his aid.
He heard the agnostic's undirected cry.
Unto him came the odor Hunger made,
And the odor of blood before it is quite dry.

V

The angel who wept looked into the eyes of God.
The angel who sang ceased pointing to the earth.
A little cherub who'd spied the earthly sod
Went mad, and flapped his wings in crazy mirth.
And the good Lord said nothing, but with a nod
Summoned the angels of Sodom down to earth.

A. M. KLEIN

THE DARK MORNING

This is the black day when
Fog rides the ugly air:
Water wades among the buildings
To the prisoner's curled ear.

Then rain, in thin sentences,
Slakes him like danger,
Whose heart is his Germany
Fevered with anger.

This is the dark day when
Locks let the enemy in
Through all the coiling passages of
(Curled ear) my prison!

THOMAS JAMES MERTON

A SPRING MEMORANDUM

The year has run thin through the turning room of my mind
to have its spring in this desert's prison. The tree
from my heart, quick and green, dies at the throat's door
in the black and cannibal sun. As I turn back
the dust shifts and the glaring landscape bleaches the root.

1942

We lie on our bellies in the white blaze. The eye tires,
and the black target — the spot of a man's lung plate,
or, as the sinister thought dictates, the soft navel eye,
the beautiful inner chamber of his body — bursts,
shivers upon the level edge of the front sight. In this way
we are made strangely innocent killers. Gonzales,
Daniel García and I talk in a quiet moment
before mess, remembering the September fiestas,
the flowers' whirl in the sun's eye, or recall
from a waltz-time the mid-summer saxophones,
the earlier weddings. We speak of the Mexican cities;
sprawling, white unbelievable refuge, beyond us,
or at night we hear from some other barracks,
distant as the freedom of hills, a Texas guitar
and the prisoner's blues. If I had those wings
this bird would fly homeward, up from this guard-house,
over the hill. There is between us this desire
to be free, a silent territory in the cell; slow
to the kill, deliberate, the last shadow lifts
and we stand at attention in the mechanized day.

.   .   .   .

The eye and the hand which trembled
when it first took the pistol grow steady
and directed to murder. In his two dimensions
the flat man is easily shot: a small triangle.
He might have been loved.
It would have been harder.
                                    Abstracted, his heart
may be plotted and a new gas devised
to deaden the nerve ends.

Dead.

Like the smell of wild apples
Like the smell of geranium
Like the smell of the hive broken open:
it is human to murder.

.   .   .   .

Look! I am not native. I am a fox caught,
baited, clamped. I will claw my way free
from my own flesh, spring the lock at the wrist
leap out, away, power-dive to the darkness,
bleed to the wood, to run the red river
out of this body. I am not of this kind.
Green bark was my mother. My father is
Death, the most wild and the free way.
                              I am not of this kind,
Inventors of cages, of nets, traps. Marches
hut two three four. Their white hairy God
stalks toward the Dead-thing, smells God-corpse
and grinning devours the rotten Sun.

.   .   .   .

Or, because I love you, can there be life then
putting out branches to cover these wounds.
The Always, our dream of tomorrow, to be
more real than this country: consider,
the leaves of light that appear forever, here,
even in this wilderness, tormented by God.
Enormous worm, turning upon Himself in His cyst
disturbing the night with His love, who
has seen Him? I found at the trunk of his tree
a discarded body like dry paper, called,
Child of the Earth. Where
has He gone? The Never, suddenly realized,
has come to destroy us, to eat up our love.
Terrible Calendar of Days, is this
more bearable because we dream, or love
because the life roots are stubborn? The Again
is the sap rising under the horn-hided tree
to force out each bud to the hungry day.

ROBERT DUNCAN

THE LOVERS

Across the round field under the dark male tower
drift the two horses, the chestnut and the black,
aloof and quiet as two similar clouds —

alike and distant, heads towards the wind,
and the grass a green pool under moving clouds
under the sickle gulls, the screaming grey eyed girls.

Only by night around the standing tower
the stallion's white teeth in the brown mare's shoulder
those eight hooves fly like thunder in the wind,
like water falling under the night's drum.

ALEX COMFORT

RETURN

I

Summer is come, and evening spreads its gold
Slowly through broadening twilights into dark.
The daffodils that waningly danced to May
Are pinched with withered brown to empty stalks,
Their thin leaves sprawled to green; and chestnut flowers,
Once rose-splashed candles thrust against the sun,
Have scattered all their petals to the ground,
And, with the burgeoned world, have swelled to shade.

This what I see, walking along the streets
Of the mellow, tired city in late spring,
Wishing that I were crossing winter fields
So faintly splashed with green that every blade
Of grass against cold wind that dared be new
Was in itself an answer against death,

Was Dionysius heard beyond the hills
Piping the tentative spring to all his world;
Wishing cold winds like those, now only blown
Across the fields of thought, were blowing still
To check the spring against the spring's own urge,
And scatter fragile snow that only falls
To warm, in melting, its own grave of flowers.

II

But the will's weak, shallow the thought which calls
Back from the past one hour, much more a spring,
Which would renounce this fullness of the year
For its harsh childhood crossed by difficult winds,
Which thinks the seed more luscious than its fruit,
And fruit itself mere promise of decay.
Therefore I would not think of wind-swept hills,
Nor look for strenuous comfort out of snow;
But would accept this lushness and this warmth
For what they are, nor seek to find in green
The athletic beauty of its youth now gone.

III

And yet the mind, leashed like all else to time,
Forced to accept against its wish the place
And troublesome accidents implied by Now,
Must, if it be itself, revolve again
To those past hours when its own will appeared
The master not the slave, and push back days,
Like heavy curtains, once more to reveal
The illusion of its power, the taste of joy.

And so I am haunted by those upland hills,
Haunted by voices and their bass of music,
Blown close — blown far — by tides of April winds.
And I would banish summer from these lawns,
Banish the brown-tipped lilac flowers, the leaves,

233

Strip all reproaches from my haunted mind,
To feel again cold wind sharp on the cheek,
To know achievement promised, not fulfilled,
And the corrupted year once more a child.

THEODORE SPENCER

1892–1941

To be moved comes of want, though want be complete
as understanding. Cast, the statue rests, stopped:
a bronze — not "Grief" — the drapery should take in
body and head. The working eyes discarded.

Characterless lips, straight nose, sight, form no due
(are none too great sculpture) to portrait or you.
At the seat of government, but a cab's jaunt
from the evergreens raised about the statue,

people count, climb the steps of the Capitol.
Shrubs, close to hands, that age at the visitor's
curved bench derive no clue from its smooth stone or
its simplicity or animal foot ends.

Nor shows the headstone back of the figure's seat
more than a blank emblem of two wreaths entwined,
bare in Eighteen Ninety Two, of our country.
Dark forearm not draped, hand modelled to the chin:

a lady of Nineteen Forty One met by
chance, asked where you could be found, took us three here,
left quickly, said, "The two of them lie there"

(I am one alive while two see here with me)

under the circle of purposeful gravel
feet must skirt or cross to come near the figure

over the gravel as on no other plot, in
"the cemetery known as Rock Creek": the name

gravel, those under. "One's instinct abhors time."

LOUIS ZUKOFSKY

THE SPRINGBOARD

He never made the dive — not while I watched.
High above London, naked in the night
Perched on a board. I peered up through the bars
Made by his fear and mine but it was more than fright
That kept him crucified among the budding stars.

Yes, it was unbelief. He knew only too well
That circumstances called for sacrifice
But, shivering there, spreadeagled above the town,
His blood began to haggle over the price
History would pay if he were to throw himself down.

If it would mend the world, that would be worth while
But he, quite rightly, long had ceased to believe
In any Utopia or in Peace-upon-Earth;
His friends would find in his death neither ransom nor
    reprieve
But only a grain of faith — for what it was worth.

And yet we know he knows what he must do.
There above London where the gargoyles grin
He will dive like a bomber past the broken steeple,
One man wiping out his own original sin
And, like ten million others, dying for the people.

LOUIS MAC NEICE

what if a much of a which of a wind
gives the truth to summer's lie;
bloodies with dizzying leaves the sun
and yanks immortal stars awry?
Blow king to beggar and queen to seem
(blow friend to fiend: blow space to time)
— when skies are hanged and oceans drowned,
the single secret will still be man

what if a keen of a lean wind flays
screaming hills with sleet and snow:
strangles valleys by ropes of thing
and stifles forests in white ago?
Blow hope to terror; blow seeing to blind
(blow pity to envy and soul to mind)
— whose hearts are mountains, roots are trees,
it's they shall cry hello to the spring

what if a dawn of a doom of a dream
bites this universe in two,
peels forever out of his grave
and sprinkles nowhere with me and you?
Blow soon to never and never to twice
(blow life to isn't: blow death to was)
— all nothing's only our hugest home;
the most who die, the more we live

E. E. CUMMINGS

SIGMUND FREUD

Each house had its ghost. Graves opened to his voice,
The dead lived in him by his gray consent:
He was, by their constraint upon his choice,
Orpheus of all the lonesome, spent

His evenings charting out a private hell,
The spaceless realm that all the puzzled caught,

The swamps that made their frightful towns unwell:
He chained his life to theirs, was like them lost.

Perhaps unwillingly he did this, became
Laureate of those who were afraid.
For himself assumed them as a native guise,
Entered their warring lands as one of them,
Employed their rhetoric and blague to raid
The towers of their most strategic lies.

HOWARD NEMEROV

THE EMANCIPATORS

When you ground the lenses and the moons swam free
From that great wanderer; when the apple shone
Like a sea-shell through your prism, voyager;
When, dancing in pure flame, the Roman mercy,
Your doctrines blew like ashes from your bones;

Did you think, for an instant, past the numerals
Jellied in Latin like bacteria in broth,
Snatched for by holy Europe like a sign?
Past sombre tables inched out with the lives
Forgotten or clapped for by the wigged Societies?

You guessed this? The earth's face altering with iron,
The smoke ranged like a wall against the day?
The equations metamorphose into use: the free
Drag their slight bones from tenements to vote
To die with their children in your factories.

Man is born in chains; yet everywhere we see him dead.
On your earth they sell nothing but our lives.
You knew that what you died for was our deaths?
You learned, those years, that all men wish is Trade?
It was you who understood; it is we who change.

RANDALL JARRELL   237

A GAME OF CHANCE

Death, the friend behind phenomenon,
Coughs up his flowers in a gay pastiche,
Distributes favors to the party guests
And makes an all-inclusive speech.

He is that skier whom the winter snow
Bleeds for; his eminence of height
Is heaven-wise, tricking his foe
Before the owls and the night.

His tinkle hides behind the bark of trees
When the lottery of leaves is ill-begun;
He sighs the dangerous whisper at the frieze
Of fountains tipping in the summer sun.

Death is that slipshod saviour early come
To dereliction and the drowned dream;
And you will bow beneath his skillful thumb,
The legendary victim of his fame.

He claws to heaven with a corkscrew sound,
A hawk-foot-screamer swooping for the dead;
Death is your lover and your body bends
To meet his dark, possessive head.

HOWARD MOSS

DOLOR

I have known the inexorable sadness of pencils,
Neat in their boxes, dolor of pad and paper-weight,
All the misery of manila folders and mucilage,
Desolation in immaculate public places,
Lonely reception room, lavatory, switchboard,
The unalterable pathos of basin and pitcher,
Ritual of multigraph, paper-clip, comma,
Endless duplication of lives and objects.

And I have seen dust from the walls of institutions,
Finer than flour, alive, more dangerous than silica,
Sift, almost invisible, through long afternoons of tedium,
Dropping a fine film on nails and delicate eyebrows,
Glazing the pale hair, the duplicate gray standard faces.

THEODORE ROETHKE

"ABRUPTLY ALL THE PALM TREES"

Abruptly all the palm trees rose like parasols,
and sunlight danced, and green to greenness gave.
Birds flew forth and cast like waterfalls
shadow upon shade.

Where the crab with its linoleum colors crawls,
and coral combs the crystal-caverned sea,
we stood, our blood as bright and fringed as shawls
before the beautiful, progressing leaf.

Abruptly all the palm trees rose like parasols,
and green was the green which green to greenness gave.
Dimension crumbled, Time lay down its walls.
And all the world went wading towards the wave.

WILLIAM JAY SMITH

EROS OUT OF THE SEA

The sleepless ghost perpetually striving
out of the mythical and the actual foam:
Venus and the invertebrate contriving
to make the dry land and the air their home,
obscure their own statistics. Does all vigor
climb from a seashell to a cindered star?
Who can tell me, while the spine grows bigger,
what the intention and the limits are?

239

Toward a faint mark at the far side of dying
see how the boy spins upward from his own
wet element of dream and, suddenly crying,
sets his finned foot upon the arid stone.
Does the child's body, like a luminous symbol,
bottle the marvel, make the boundary tight
and absolute? But childhood, small as a thimble,
looses its genie to the ends of night.

DILYS BENNETT LAING

FIRST SNOW ON AN AIRFIELD

A window's length beyond the Pleiades
Wintering Perseus grounds his bow on haze
And midnight thickens on the fall of snow.
Now on the sound of sleepers past their days
The barracks turns to myth, and none shall die
But widen and grow beautiful a while
And then be written on a Grecian sky.

Look, the burnt mountain whitens, and the trees
Grow cavernous. And the field's lights are spread
Spangling on the daubed and rushing air
That fills with drone of engines overhead.
And see: the constellations of the running-lights,
Crossed on the beacon's arm, bring home the planes
That almost layered the hills with trilobites.

As near as a chance: A winter's memory
Of seconds not too soon that might have been
Fossils at impact with the shrouded stone.
Here on the ground, the noise of a machine
Above the falling snow at season's turn —
Memory crossed with moment — and again
Tomorrow's manual of guns to learn.

JOHN CIARDI

LOSSES

It was not dying: everybody died.
It was not dying: we had died before
In the routine crashes — and our fields
Called up the papers, wrote home to our folks,
And the rates rose, all because of us.
We died on the wrong page of the almanac,
Scattered on mountains fifty miles away;
Diving on haystacks, fighting with a friend,
We blazed up on the lines we never saw.
We died like aunts or pets or foreigners.
(When we left high school nothing else had died
For us to figure we had died like.)

In our new planes, with our new crews, we bombed
The ranges by the desert or the shore,
Fired at towed targets, waited for our scores —
And turned into replacements and woke up
One morning, over England, operational.
It wasn't different: but if we died
It was not an accident but a mistake
(But an easy one for anyone to make).
We read our mail and counted up our missions —
In bombers named for girls, we burned
The cities we had learned about in school —
Till our lives wore out; our bodies lay among
The people we had killed and never seen.
When we lasted long enough they gave us medals;
When we died they said, "Our casualties were low."

They said, "Here are the maps"; we burned the cities.

It was not dying — no, not ever dying;
But the night I died I dreamed that I was dead,
And the cities said to me: "Why are you dying?
We are satisfied, if you are; but why did I die?"

RANDALL JARRELL

"STILL DO I KEEP MY LOOK, MY IDENTITY . . ."

Each body has its art, its precious prescribed
Pose, that even in passion's droll contortions, waltzes,
or push of pain — or when a grief has stabbed
Or hatred hacked — is its and nothing else's.
Each body has its pose. No other stock
That is irrevocable perpetual,
And its to keep. In castle or in shack.
With rags or robes. Through good, nothing, or ill.
And even in death a body, like no other
On any hill or plain or crawling cot
Or gentle for the lilyless hasty pall
(Having twisted, gagged, and then sweet-ceased to bother),
Shows the old personal art, the look. Shows what
It showed at baseball. What it showed in school.

                              GWENDOLYN BROOKS

ASIDE

Under the El on Sunday afternoon
the paper on the pavement swirls
around the feet of little girls
in white anklets and black latticed shoes.

Prayers given, comics are to come,
and ballasted by bibles they
walk do not run home from
church. Among the entirely grey

cement, newspapers, and girders
their identical red hats are
the only color.
                    On murders,
wrecks, disease and war
their heels make sober solitary
sounds appropriate to Sunday.

ALAN DUGAN

POEM IN OCTOBER

It was my thirtieth year to heaven
Woke to my hearing from harbor and neighbor wood
And the mussel pooled and the heron —
Priested shore
The morning beckon
With water praying and call of seagull and rook
And the knock of sailing boats on the net webbed wall
Myself to set foot
That second
In the still sleeping town and set forth.

My birthday began with the water —
Birds and the birds of the winged trees flying my name
Above the farms and the white horses
And I rose
In rainy autumn
And walked abroad in a shower of all my days.
High tide and the heron dived when I took the road
Over the border
And the gates
Of the town closed as the town awoke.

A springful of larks in a rolling
Cloud and the roadside bushes brimming with whistling
Blackbirds and the sun of October
Summery
On the hill's shoulder,
Here were fond climates and sweet singers suddenly
Come in the morning where I wandered and listened
To the rain wringing
Wind blow cold
In the wood faraway under me.

Pale rain over the dwindling harbor
And over the sea wet church the size of a snail
With its horns through mist and the castle
Brown as owls,

But all the gardens
Of spring and summer were blooming in the tall tales
Beyond the border and under the lark full cloud.
There could I marvel
My birthday
Away but the weather turned around.

It turned away from the blithe country
And down the other air and the blue altered sky
Streamed again a wonder of summer
With apples
Pears and red currants
And I saw in the turning so clearly a child's
Forgotten mornings when he walked with his mother
Through the parables
Of sun light
And the legends of the green chapels

And the twice told fields of infancy
That his tears burned my cheeks and his heart moved in mine.
These were the woods the river and sea
Where a boy
In the listening
Summertime of the dead whispered the truth of his joy
To the trees and the stones and the fish in the tide.
And the mystery
Sang alive
Still in the water and singing birds.

And there could I marvel my birthday
Away but the weather turned around. And the true
Joy of the long dead child sang burning
In the sun.
It was my thirtieth
Year to heaven stood there then in the summer noon
Though the town below lay leaved with October blood.
O may my heart's truth
Still be sung
On this high hill in a year's turning.

DYLAN THOMAS

SÉANCE

The automatic fingers write. Tonight
We huddle round the table. Hands and features
Are green beneath the flicker of the light.
The pencil shakes, and bites into the future.

Then from the mouth, as from a rumbling cavern,
Reverberate the syllables of doom.
The body jerks away. In dense and driven
Rigor of ecstasy the fingers drum.

Anguish of drowning flesh! To see the blue
And swollen lips! The eye-balls burst, the skin
Sweats salt. "Speak, speak to those who question you!"
The lamplight thickens, and the voice begins:

"I see blood drying on a fissured rock
While all about the dark birds wheel and hover,
Image of death, image of all the black
Terrors of death that shall beset the lover.

"I see you in an empty room, while far
Away in unimagined valleys move
The bright and transitory shapes of war.
I see the endlessness and ache of love.

"I see the petrifaction of your lust,
Hands tearing, tearing ceaselessly at stone.
It is a stony image that you kiss.
You are alone, you always are alone."

". . . You always are alone!" The murmur ceases,
The body tumbles sideways in the chair.
Beneath the light the green, distorted faces
Recoil in attitudes of mute despair.

Whose is the voice that fills the shadowed room?
Who drowns beneath the revelatory wind?
Mine are the swollen lips that speak of doom,
And mine the stiff and automatic hand.

FRANCIS KING

JOURNAL

I grow accustomed to a new disguise:
Day after day with triggers at our thumb
We sit upon the calculated skies
Arranged upon the metal of a theorem.
Costumed in miracle we walk the wind,
Divide the sea, rain fire, but heal no blind.

Under the wing of omen Jericho
Falls in a blast of engines and we pass
Above the lame whose cure no engines know
Except to open craters in the grass,
Woven forever to the whistling graph
A bomb makes toward an epitaph.

Too nearly amateur at death by fire
We have our gift by borrowing, not by birth.
Yet we divine that we may mount still higher
And never be divided from the earth.
Opening whatever sky, the theorem turns:
We are the bomb, the crater, and what burns.

Compelled to our momentum which is Law,
We wait for mathematics to be right,
Improve our art, log what we did and saw,
And track the sun by day, the stars by night.
Yet though our engines master in our stead,
We fail the sick, but still may raise the dead.

JOHN CIARDI

PART FOR THE WHOLE

When others run to windows or out of doors
To catch the sunset whole, he is content
With any segment anywhere he sits.

From segment, fragment, he can reconstruct
The whole, prefers to reconstruct the whole,
As if to say, I see more seeing less.

A window to the east will serve as well
As window to the west, for eastern sky
Echoes the western sky. And even less —

A patch of light that picture-glass happens
To catch from window-glass, fragment of fragment,
Flawed, distorted, dulled, nevertheless

Gives something unglassed nature cannot give:
The old obliquity of art, and proves
Part may be more than whole, least may be best.

                                        ROBERT FRANCIS

STORIES OF SNOW

Those in the vegetable rain retain
an area behind their sprouting eyes
held soft and rounded with the dream of snow
precious and reminiscent as those globes —
souvenir of some never nether land —
which hold their snow storms, circular, complete,
high in a tall and teakwood cabinet.

In countries where the leaves are large as hands,
where flowers protrude their fleshy chins
and call their colors
an imaginary snow storm sometimes falls
among the lilies.
And in the early morning one will waken
to think the glowing linen of his pillow
a northern drift, will find himself mistaken
and lie back weeping.

And there the story shifts from head to head,
of how, in Holland, from their feather beds
hunters arise and part the flakes and go
forth to the frozen lakes in search of swans —
the snow light falling white along their guns,
their breath in plumes.
While tethered in the wind like sleeping gulls
ice boats wait the raising of their wings
to skim the electric ice at such a speed
they leap the jet strips of the naked water,
and how these flying, sailing hunters feel
air in their mouths as terrible as ether.
And on the story runs, that even drinks
in that white landscape dare to be no color
how, flasked and water clear, the liquor slips
silver against the hunters' moving hips.
And of the swan in death, these dreamers tell
of its last flight and how it falls, a plummet,
pierced by the freezing bullet
and how three feathers, loosened by the shot
descend like snow upon it.
While hunters plunge their fingers in its down
deep as a drift, and dive their hands
up to the neck of the wrist
in that warm metamorphosis of snow
as gentle as the sort that woodsmen knew
who, lost in the white circle, fell at last
and dreamed their way to death.

And stories of this kind are often told
in countries where great flowers bar the roads
with reds and blues which seal the route to snow —
as if, in telling, raconteurs unlock
the color with its complement and go
through to the area behind the eyes
where silent, unrefractive whiteness lies.

P. K. PAGE

THE HIGHER EMPIRICISM

O Visionary who adjust your lens
Till it is focused on a wheel of fire,
What spotless lover would you find in space?
Let wisdom guide you to the market-place,
There to be broken on the wheel of sense
And burnt by adequate objects of desire.

FRANCIS C. GOLFFING

POEM FOR MY TWENTIETH BIRTHDAY

Passing the American graveyard, for my birthday
the crosses stuttering, white on tropical green,
the years' quick focus of faces I do not remember . . .

The palm trees stalking like deliberate giants
for my birthday, and all the hot adolescent memories
seen through a screen of water . . .

For my birthday thrust into the adult and actual:
expected to perform the action, not to ponder
the reality beyond the fact,
the man standing upright in the dream.

KENNETH KOCH

From "THEORY OF VISION"

THE GREEN EYE

Come child, and with your sunbeam gaze assign
Green to the garden as a metaphor
For contemplation, seeking to declare
Whether by green you specify the green
Of orchard sunlight, blossom, bark, or leaf,
Or green of an imaginary life.

249

1946

A mosaic of all possible greens becomes
A premise in your eye, whereby the limes
Are green as limes faintly by midnight known,
As foliage in a thunderstorm, as dreams
Of fruit in barren countries; claims
The orchard as a metaphor of green.

Aware of change as no barometer
You may determine climates at your will;
Spectrums of feeling are accessible
If orchards in the mind will persevere
On their hillsides original with joy.
Enter the orchard differently today:

When here you bring your earliest tragedy,
Your goldfish, upside-down and rigidly
Floating on weeds in the aquarium,
Green is no panorama for your grief
Whose raindrop smile, dissolving and aloof,
Ordains an unusual brightness as you come:

The brightness of a change outside the eye,
A question on the brim of what may be,
Attended by a new, impersonal green.
The goldfish dead where limes hang yellowing
Is metaphor for more incredible things,
Things you shall live among, things seen, things known.

JAMES MERRILL

CASTAWAY

He was impoverished, possessing a full island,
Miles of rough contours and desert plains
Whose birds were prehistoric, yet seemed like men
Illusory in the distance of the desert;
Or amid ledges where the wild goats browsed
Clambering to slip, and thus to startle sound
Into the cavern of his vacant ear:
The footstep of a man moving amid bushes.

At first he clung to the smooth wave of the shore,
Thinking, marooned, his loneliness a joke
Played by his shipmates who tiring would return
To laugh and clap him on the shoulder,
An anecdote for the fo'c'sles of his time,
An allusion which would follow like a dog —
But who could be serious leaving him to starve,
Exiling to the island of himself?

The sea became a whirlpool, spilling around
His island which lay at the bottom of the funnel,
And he took refuge in the higher hills
To forget gradually himself as man;
His beard grew; clothed in his uncured skins
His language and intelligence wavered
Until, as he became more agile and suspicious,
He too, at last, became no more than goat.

JOHN NERBER

THE RETURN

I circled on leather paws
In the darkening corridor,
Crouched closer to the floor,
Then bristled like a dog.

As I turned for a backward look,
The muscles in one thigh
Sagged like a frightened lip.

A cold key let me in
That self-inflicted lair;
And I lay down with my life,
With the rags and rotting clothes,
With a stump of scraggy fang
Bared for a hunter's boot.

THEODORE ROETHKE

THE GHOST

(After Sextus Propertius)

A ghost is someone: death has left a hole
For the lead-colored soul to beat the fire:
    Cynthia leaves her dirty pyre
    And seems to coil herself and roll
        Under my canopy,
Love's stale and public playground, where I lie
And fill the run-down empire of my bed.
I see the street, her potter's field, is red
And lively with the ashes of the dead;

But she no longer sparkles off in smoke:
It is the body carted to the gate
    Last Friday, when the sizzling grate
    Left its charred furrows on her smock
        And ate into her hip.
A black nail dangles from her finger-tip
And Lethe oozes from her nether lip.
Her thumb-bones rattle on her brittle hands,
As Cynthia stamps and hisses and demands:

"Sextus, has sleep already washed away
Your manhood? You forget the window-sill
    My sliding wore to slivers? Day
    Would break before the Seven Hills
        Saw Cynthia retreat
And climb your shoulders to the knotted sheet.
You shouldered me and galloped on bare feet
To lay me by the crossroads. Have no fear:
Notus, who snatched your promise, has no ear.

"But why did no one call in my deaf ear?
Your calling would have gained me one more day.
    Sextus, although you ran away
    You might have called and stopped my bier
        A second by your door.
No tears drenched a black toga for your whore

When broken tilestones bruised her face before
The Capitol. Would it have strained your purse
To scatter ten cheap roses on my hearse?

"The State will make Pompilia's Chloris burn:
I knew her secret when I kissed the skull
     Of Pluto in the tainted bowl.
    Let Nomas burn her books and turn
       Her poisons into gold;
The finger-prints upon the potsherd told
Her love. You let a slut, whose body sold
To Thracians, liquify my golden bust
In the coarse flame that crinkled me to dust.

"If Chloris' bed has left you with your head,
Lover, I think you'll answer my arrears:
     My nurse is getting on in years,
    See that she gets a little bread —
       She never clutched your purse;
See that my little humpback hears no curse
From her close-fisted friend. But burn the verse
You bellowed half a lifetime in my name:
Why should you feed me to the fires of fame?

"I will not hound you, much as you have earned
It, Sextus: I shall reign in your four books —
     I swear this by the Hag who looks
    Into my heart where it was burned:
       Propertius, I kept faith;
If not, may serpents suck my ghost to death
And spit it with their forked and killing breath
Into the Styx where Agamemnon's wife
Founders in the green circles of her life.

"Beat the sycophant ivy from my urn,
That twists its binding shoots about my bones
     Where apple-sweetened Anio drones
    Through orchards that will never burn
       While honest Herakles,
My patron, watches. Anio, you will please

Me if you whisper upon sliding knees:
'Propertius, Cynthia is here:
She shakes her blossoms when my waters clear.'

"You cannot turn your back upon a dream,
For phantoms have their reasons when they come:
    We wander midnights: then the numb
    Ghost wades from the Lethean stream;
        Even the foolish dog
Stops its hell-raising mouths and casts its clog;
At cock-crow Charon checks us in his log.
Others can have you, Sextus; I alone
Hold: and I grind your manhood bone on bone."

ROBERT LOWELL

From CANTO LXXX

Oh to be in England now that Winston's out
    Now that there's room for doubt
        And the bank may be the nation's
        And the long years of patience
        And labour's vacillations
May have let the bacon come home,
        To watch how they'll slip and slide
        watch how they'll try to hide
            the real portent

        To watch a while from the tower
            where dead flies lie thick over the old charter
        forgotten, oh quite forgotten
        but confirming John's first one,
    and still there if you climb over attic rafters;
to look at the fields; are they tilled?
is the old terrace alive as it might be
with a whole colony
        if money be free again?

Chesterton's England of has-been and why-not,
or is it all rust, ruin, death duties and mortgages
and the great carriage yard empty
             and more pictures gone to pay taxes

     When a dog is tall but
     not so tall as all that
     that dog is a Talbot
              (a bit long in the pasterns?)
When a butt is ½ as tall as a whole butt
That butt is a small butt
          Let backe and side go bare
and the old kitchen left as the monks had left it
and the rest as time has cleft it.

[Only shadows enter my tent
              as men pass between me and the sunset,]
beyond the eastern barbed wire
    a sow with nine boneens
matronly as any duchess at Claridge's
and for that Christmas at Maurie Hewlett's
Going out from Southampton
they passed the car by the dozen
     who would not have shown weight on a scale
                  riding, riding
                     for Noel the green holly
     Noel, Noel, the green holly
     A dark night for the holly

That would have been Salisbury plain, and I have not thought
     of the Lady Anne for this twelve years
          Nor of Le Portel
How tiny the panelled room where they stabbed him
          In her lap, almost, La Stuarda
     Si tuit li dolh ehl planh el marrimen
          for the leopards and broom plants

Tudor indeed is gone and every rose,
Blood-red, blanch-white that in the sunset glows

Cries: "Blood, Blood, Blood!" against the gothic stone
Of England, as the Howard or Boleyn knows.

Nor seeks the carmine petal to infer;
Nor is the white bud Time's inquisitor
Probing to know if its new-gnarled root
Twists from York's head or belly of Lancaster;

Or if a rational soul should stir, perchance,
Within the stem or summer shoot to advance
Contrition's utmost throw, seeking in thee
But oblivion, not thy forgiveness, FRANCE.

as the young lizard extends his leopard spots
    along the grass-blade seeking the green midge half an ant-
    size
and the Serpentine will look just the same
and the gulls be as neat on the pond
and the sunken garden unchanged
and God knows what else is left of our London
    my London, your London
and if her green elegance
    remains on this side of my rain ditch
    puss lizard will lunch on some other T-bone

sunset grand couturier.

EZRA POUND

ANGEL EYE OF MEMORY

Turning, returning on world winds that know
The unraveled matter of a time ago,
My bondsman angel with spread-eagle eye
Reminds my wounds, unwinds my memory;
Within a cleft of sleep
Where the abhorred affections, arm in arm,
Lion and tamer come,
The ways I went, the days I could not keep

Stand still: wrapt in perfect ice I lie
Creating love out of a masque of clay
And see my arms, like vines, embrace a city.

O lion locked in yesterday, O lost
And by the years' five-shuttered cages last
Of all my lives, be fed on memory
Though, starved, you waken and go free;
Of your own flesh and blood,
The hand that froze mid-air, the heart that sank,
Make present meat and drink
That by your providence the sweet ghost laid
In love's misfitting batter at the door
Closed fast upon the only traveler
Hand would warm at, heart be lifted for.

Indentured angel, show me where I go
Though in long dwelling I imprison you;
In ponds of sleep, in pools of sense, over
Whatever solvent water you will hover,
Trouble the seines whose turning
Pictures on the water's winding wheel
Show now and always how all
Traveling is a leaving no returning
Though hands like spindrift fall awash before
Wheel, gear, piston rod and wild propeller
Rifle the air to make farewell forever.

JOHN MALCOLM BRINNIN

NIGHT OF BATTLE

Europe: 1944
as considered from a great distance

Impersonal the aim
Where giant movements tend;
Each man appears the same;
Friend vanishes from friend.

In the long path of lead
That changes place like light
No shape of hand or head
Means anything tonight.

Only the common will
For which explosion spoke
And stiff on field and hill
The dark blood of the folk.

YVOR WINTERS

From "THOU SHALT SURELY DIE . . ."

NO GHOST IS TRUE

No ghost is true,
But these at least are kind;
Comes night, they spaniel at the mind,
Or flicker on the blue
Impassive wall,
Riffed by the blind
Thumb, the dumb glans, the halt,
The imperfect heart: Old friends,
Performers, I remember your magical voices,
The liquid presence of your eyes.

O in the morning you were splendid,
Your delicate teeth, your loins,
Your aptitude at love — incredible!

In the evening you were still valid,
The fragrance of children trembled
In your bouquet under the ferns' arsenal.
In the evening you were still valid . . .

LESLIE A. FIEDLER

MOTIVE

The motive of all of it was loneliness,
All the panic encounters and despair
Were bred in fear of the lost night, apart,
Outlined by pain, alone. Promiscuous
As mercy. Fear-led and led again to fear
At evening toward the cave where part fire, part
Pity lived in that voluptuousness
To end one and begin another loneliness.

This is the most intolerable motive: this
Must be given back to life again,
Made superhuman, made human, out of pain
Turned to the personal, the pure release:
The rings of Plato and Homer's golden chain
Or Lenin with his cry of Dare We Win.

MURIEL RUKEYSER

THE BROKEN BOWL

To say it once held daisies and bluebells
    Ignores, if nothing else,
Its diehard brilliance where crashed on the floor
The wide bowl lies that seemed to cup the sun,
Its green leaves curled, its constant blaze undone,
Spilled all its glass integrity everywhere;
    Spectrums, released, will speak
Of colder flowerings where cold crystal broke.

Glass fragments dropped from wholeness to hodgepodge
    Yet fasten to each edge
The opal signature of imperfection
Whose rays, though disarrayed, will postulate
More than a network of cross-angled light
When through the dusk they point unbruised directions
    And chart upon the room
Capacities of fire it must assume.

259

The splendid curvings of glass artifice
    Informed its flawlessness
With lucid unities. Freed from these now,
Like love it triumphs through inconsequence
And builds its harmony from dissonance
And lies somehow within us, broken, as though
    Time were a broken bowl
And our last joy knowing it shall not heal.

The splinters rainbowing ruin on the floor
    Cut structures in the air,
Mark off, like eyes or compasses, a space
Of mathematic fixity, spotlight
Within whose circumscription we may set
All solitudes of love, room for love's face,
    Love's projects green with leaves,
Love's monuments like tombstones on our lives.

JAMES MERRILL

NEAR THE BORDER OF INSANITIES

We who also linger near the border of insanities
who eat daily like you, the spilt sun,
take repeatedly the other dreaming voyage
to the less personal city, where the daffodils
fly from the april ground like startled canaries
and paint gaily the imaginative sky.

And we who so dare to dance
under the shadow of the delicious domes
of possibility, who have seen our skin, iridescent
in the light divided, that filters
through the misty prism of our dreams,
have been irritated by the trek home,
have been afraid of the bell that is long
with doom and days.

For here now, lies only the rubble of history,
here now we wait as broken cities
under a grazing flock of stars,
here and here now, our brilliant tears
have dropped to splash brave oil-pools
that are lost in a darkening world.

Yet we who have music in our finger prints,
who have colors weeping behind our eyes,
will weave, must weave, the minute forever
where the sad journey home is no journey,
but a reawakening still yet in dream.

DANNIE ABSE

THE GROTTO

The sea still plunges where as naked boys
We dared the currents and the racing tides
That stamped red weals of fury on our thighs,
Yet did not know our first love was the sea
That rolled like colts between our shining knees
While under us the sands in golden curls
Coiled round our bodies like the plaits of girls.

We came oblique to passion on that shore
Identified with our blind will to danger,
As when we explored the slipping walls of caves
Booming with dark more fearful than the wave,
Whose silence magnified the heart's deep roar
Till senses beat that were asleep before
And in ourselves we recognized a stranger.

Or when we scaled by Frenchman's Bay the cliff
No man has dared (though boys there in the night
Still prove their manhood on its hostile side)
That was our climb from innocence to life;

And yet, if I could be there once again
My love, I'd pause amazed among the gulls
Afraid of both the triumphs and the falls.

In sea and grotto where we found our hearts
Our youth remained, and all our days return
In dream and vision to the mocking sea
Where womanhood and manhood proudly stirred
Within our silence like a singing bird,
And never a dawning day will break as pure
As our grave adoration, immature.

FRANCIS SCARFE

NIAGARA FALLS

We saw it all. We saw the souvenir shops, and sitting
on the mist above the falls, the brilliant signs
saying hotels to love in, cigarettes to smoke,
souvenirs for proof; we give you anything you want,
even towels. Our disgust was as stylized as billboards,
and we suggested to ourselves that even our sympathy
for the ugly people of the off-season was outworn.
But here it was, nevertheless, the ferocious, spastic
enjoyment, the hotels like freight-yards or packing crates,
the lights that murder sight, and the community snicker.
The falls, of course, continued with great dignity.

ALAN DUGAN

SCHOOLYARD IN APRIL

Little girls smearing
the stolen lipstick
of overheard grown-up talk
into their conversation,
unconscious of the beauty
of their movements

like milkweed in the wind,
are beginning to drift
over by the drinking fountain
where they will skip rope

They speak in whispers
about the omnipotent teachers
while the little boys
scoff over their ball-mitts

The teachers themselves
stare out of windows,
remembering April.

KENNETH KOCH

"DREAMS ARE THE ROYAL ROAD
TO THE UNCONSCIOUS"

— Freud

The King's Highway to the Dare-Not-Know
— but I beg my rides and oh I know
these boring roads where hundreds and hundreds
of cars fade by in hundred-hundreds
of flashing windows too bright too fast
to see my face. I am steadfast
long hours o' the morning, I am so sad.
An old-time trap, an ancient sad
horse and his farmer stop by the way,
they'll take me one mile on my way
— out of my way — is this the Way?
I used to think I used to be happy,
but is it possible to be happy?
What is it like? — like Plato oh
we'll copy it at large and oh
plan a city where all the distances
(where? where?) are walking distances.

PAUL GOODMAN

THE DIRTY WORD

The dirty word hops in the cage of the mind like the Pondicherry vulture, stomping with its heavy left claw on the sweet meat of the brain and tearing it with its vicious beak, ripping and chopping the flesh. Terrified, the small boy bears the big bird of the dirty word into the house, and grunting, puffing, carries it up the stairs to his own room in the skull. Bits of black feather cling to his clothes and his hair as he locks the staring creature in the dark closet.

All day the small boy returns to the closet to examine and feed the bird, to caress and kick the bird, that now snaps and flaps its wings savagely whenever the door is opened. How the boy trembles and delights at the sight of the white excrement of the bird! How the bird leaps and rushes against the walls of the skull, trying to escape from the zoo of the vocabulary! How wildly snaps the sweet meat of the brain in its rage.

And the bird outlives the man, being freed at the man's death-funeral by a word from the rabbi.

But I one morning went upstairs and opened the door and entered the closet and found in the cage of my mind the great bird dead. Softly I wept it and softly removed it and softly buried the body of the bird in the hollyhock garden of the house I lived in twenty years before. And out of the worn black feathers of the wing have I made these pens to write these elegies, for I have outlived the bird, and I have murdered it in my early manhood.

KARL SHAPIRO

THE FAT MAN IN THE MIRROR

What's filling up the mirror? O, it is not I;
Hair-belly like a beaver's house? An old dog's eye?

The forenoon was blue
In the mad King's zoo
Nurse was swinging me so high, so high!

The bullies wrestled on the royal bowling green;
Hammers and sickles on their hoods of black sateen . . .
Smoking on my swing,
The yellow-fingered King
Sliced apples with a pen-knife for his Queen.

This *I*, who used to mouse about the parafinned preserves,
And jammed a finger in the coffee-grinder, serves
Time before the mirror.
But this flabby terror . . .
Nurse, it is a person! It is nerves.

O where is Mother waltzing like a top to staunch
The blood of Rudolf, King of Faerie? Hip and haunch
Lard the royal grotto;
Straddling Rudolf's motto,
Time, the Turk, its sickle on its paunch . . .

Nurse, nurse, it rises on me . . . O, it starts to roll,
My apples, O, are charcoal in the meerschaum bowl . . .
If you'd only come,
If you'd only come,
Darling, if . . . The apples that I stole,

When nurse and I were swinging in the Old One's eye . . .
Only a fat man with his beaver on his eye,
Only a fat man,
Only a fat man
Breaks the mirror, O, it is not I!

ROBERT LOWELL

if(touched by love's own secret)we,like homing
through welcoming sweet miracles of air
(and joyfully all truths of wing resuming)
selves,into infinite tomorrow steer

— souls under whom flow(mountain valley forest)
a million wheres which never may become
one(wholly strange; familiar wholly)dearest
more than reality of more than dream —

how should contented fools of fact envision
the mystery of freedom?yet,among
their loud exactitudes of imprecision,
you'll(silently alighting)and i'll sing

while at us very deafly a most stares
colossal hoax of clocks and calendars

E. E. CUMMINGS

THE PARTY

The standing guests, a grotesque glade
Dispensing microcosmic gloom,
Make artifice of light and shade
In an eternal drawingroom.

Each tubrous tree within this grove
Thinks itself other than a tree,
Impressed, from "somewhere else," to prove
A social personality.

So is some vanity appeased
Some bravoure made articulate,
Each in his anecdotage pleased
To find himself sophisticate.

80-watt stars in crystal cups
Keep all perspectives squat and square.
No alien unthought breath corrupts
This decorously airless air.

MARGARET AVISON

THE ULTIMATE POEM IS ABSTRACT

This day writhes with what? The lecturer
On This Beautiful World Of Ours composes himself
And hems the planet rose and haws it ripe,

And red, and right. The particular question — here
The particular answer to the particular question
Is not in point — the question is in point.

If the day writhes, it is not with revelations.
One goes on asking questions. That, then, is one
Of the categories. So said, this placid space

Is changed. It is not so blue as we thought. To be blue,
There must be no questions. It is an intellect
Of windings round and dodges to and fro,

Writhings in wrong obliques and distances,
Not an intellect in which we are fleet: present
Everywhere in space at once, cloud-pole

Of communication. It would be enough
If we were ever, just once, at the middle, fixed
In This Beautiful World Of Ours and not as now,

Helplessly at the edge, enough to be
Complete, because at the middle, if only in sense,
And in that enormous sense, merely enjoy.

WALLACE STEVENS

SMALL PRAYER

Change, move, dead clock, that this fresh day
May break with dazzling light to these sick eyes.
Burn, glare, old sun, so long unseen,
That time may find its sound again, and cleanse
Whatever it is that a wound remembers
After the healing ends.

WELDON KEES

RETURN OF THE GODDESS ARTEMIS

Under your Milky Way
  And slow-revolving Bear,
Frogs from the alder thicket pray
In terror of your judgment day,
  Loud with repentance there.

The log they crowned as king
  Grew sodden, lurched and sank:
An owl floats by on silent wing,
Dark water bubbles from the spring;
  They invoke you from each bank.

At dawn you shall appear,
  A gaunt red-leggèd crane,
You whom they know too well for fear,
Lunging your beak down like a spear
  To fetch them home again.

ROBERT GRAVES

THE DEATH OF A TOAD

A toad the power mower caught,
Chewed and clipped of a leg, with a hobbling hop has got
To the garden verge, and sanctuaried him

Under the cineraria leaves, in the shade
  Of the ashen heartshaped leaves, in a dim,
  Low, and a final glade.

The rare original heartsblood goes,
Spends on the earthen hide, in the folds and wizenings, flows
  In the gutters of the banked and staring eyes. He lies
As still as if he would return to stone,
  And soundlessly attending, dies
    Toward some deep monotone,

  Toward misted and ebullient seas
And cooling shores, toward lost Amphibia's emperies.
  Day dwindles, drowning, and at length is gone
  In the wide and antique eyes, which still appear
    To watch, across the castrate lawn,
      The haggard daylight steer.

RICHARD WILBUR

VARIATION ON THE GOTHIC SPIRAL

Now especially, each flower moves
Me until I am distraught with a desire
To look upon
The flowering virgins, who think on their loves

While naked in the secluded pool,
Splashing their bodies with the private water.
Half of my spring
Is desire: I am a dream wound on a spool

For safer keeping. There is multiple need
For unreeling and shimmering in the sun
Like a cobweb,
For gazing at girls while I uncurl like greed.

W. S. MERWIN

THE TRAVELER

They pointed me out on the highway, and they said
"That man has a curious way of holding his head."

They pointed me out on the beach; they said "That man
Will never become as we are, try as he can."

They pointed me out at the station, and the guard
Looked at me twice, thrice, thoughtfully & hard.

I took the same train that the others took,
To the same place. Were it not for that look
And those words, we were all of us the same.
I studied merely maps. I tried to name
The effects of motion on the travelers,
I watched the couple I could see, the curse
And blessings of that couple, their destination,
The deception practised on them at the station,
Their courage. When the train stopped and they knew
The end of their journey, I descended too.

JOHN BERRYMAN

LEAR

When the world takes over for us
and the storm in the trees
replaces our brittle consciences
(like ships, female to all seas)
when the few last yellow leaves
stand out like flags on tossed ships
at anchor — our minds are rested

Yesterday we sweated and dreamed
or sweated in our dreams walking
at a loss through the bulk of figures
that appeared solid, men or women,

but as we approached down the paved
corridor melted — Was it I? — like
smoke from bonfires blowing away

Today the storm, inescapable, has
taken the scene and we return
our hearts to it, however made, made
wives by it and though we secure
ourselves for a dry skin from the drench
of its passionate approaches we
yield and are made quiet by its fury

Pitiful Lear, not even you could
out-shout the storm — to make a fool
cry! Wife to its power might you not
better have yielded earlier? as on ships
facing the seas were carried once
the figures of women at repose to
signify the strength of the waves' lash.

WILLIAM CARLOS WILLIAMS

UPON THIS ROCK

(For Helen Phillips)

By pain of stone and wearing down of bronze,
By plaster scrambled with excelsior,
Things come out which were not things before,
And bodies letch with all the grace of swans;

So thus, the strong wings that Leda knew
Holding her steady, while the beak applied its kiss
And she experienced that unsuspected bliss,
·Show how they became one symbol, never two;

And the twin-backed beast is common here,
The single symbol seems to search
For another one on which to perch
To make its abundant motives clear:

In excellent amity these forms combine
Whose easy couplings show that sex
Should not be feared, and should not vex
The wife, the harlot or the concubine.

Here Leda and the Centaurs speak
Of love and parentage unknown
To those whose lechery was thrown
At such who did not understand, whose weak

Longing petered out, who lived alone
And did not like it. Teach them, O plaster,
Bronze, that their disaster
Lay in their fear of attitudes of stone.

RUTHVEN TODD

THE SLEEPING BEAUTY: VARIATION
OF THE PRINCE

After the thorns I came to the first page.
He lay there grey in his fur of dust:
As I bent to open an eye, I sneezed.
But the ball looked by me, blue
As the sky it stared into . . .
And the sentry's cuirass is red with rust.

Children play inside: the dirty hand
Of the little mother, an inch from the child
That has worn out, burst, and blown away,
Uncurling to it — does not uncurl . . .
The bloom on the nap of their world
Is set with thousands of dawns of dew.

But at last, at the center of all the webs
Of the realm established in your blood,
I find you; and — look! — the drop of blood
Is there still, under the dust of your finger:

I force it, slowly, down from your finger —
And it falls and rolls away, as it should.

And I bend to touch — just under the dust
That was roses once — the steady lips
Parted between a breath and a breath
In love, for the kiss of the hunter, Death. . . .
Then I stretch myself beside you, lay
Between us, there in the dust, His sword.

When the world ends — it will never end —
The dust at last will fall from your eyes
In judgment, and I shall whisper:
"For hundreds of thousands of years I have slept
Beside you, here in the last long world
That you had found — that I have kept."

When they come for us — no one will ever come —
I shall stir from my long light sleep,
I shall whisper, "Wait, wait! . . . She is asleep."
I shall whisper, gazing, up to the gaze of the hunter,
Death, and close with the tips of the dust of my hand
The lids of the steady —
                    Look, He is fast asleep!

RANDALL JARRELL

THE LOOK

Now the narrowing track
Steepens, now the soul
Pauses, looking back,

Sees her path of toil
Gathered, coil on coil
Like a fallen scroll,

Scans the page outspread
Of the plain, a full
Tale till now unread;

Small green villages,
Pictures on the thread
Of the road she sees,

Smaller, smaller, till,
Merged, they meet the high
Earth-edge, whence their rill

Flowed as from a lake —
Sees she then the sky,
Where's no tale, no track,
But a flash, a sigh.

ELIZABETH DARYUSH

MARSH LEAF

The swamp reeds murmur the song.
The voices and tongues are brown.
Cold water-mouths move and sing,
And grey mist huddles down.
I look for a hopeful thing,
But the mud and reeds have been troubled long.

Inside of a low-roof house
The wavering walls are white.
I look for a natural truce,
But leaves are light;
And over the rolling marsh
Brown reeds are always blowing and loose.

A coward may run from grief
Or hide old pain from his eyes,
But the sight of a russet leaf

Reechoes the dry-lipped cries:
One leaf lying underfoot
Speaks, though dead and fallen and deaf.

DAVID R. WAGONER

STANZAS

I thought I woke: the midnight sun
flooded the street among the trees;
the people floated at their ease
to right and left, I moved alone.

The savage drone, the thrilling air
of bagpipes poured around the bend,
the valley echoed end to end;
I hastened to behold him there.

The meaning of dreams in this magic day
was clear as they befell, without
the need or use to think it out;
and where the shadows fell, they lay.

PAUL GOODMAN

THE CHILDREN OF THE POOR

I

People who have no children can be hard:
Attain a mail of ice and insolence:
Need not pause in the fire, and in no sense
Hesitate in the hurricane to guard.
And when wide world is bitten and bewarred
They perish purely, waving their spirits hence
Without a trace of grace or of offense
To laugh or fail, diffident, wonder-starred.
While through a throttling dark we others hear

The little lifting helplessness, the queer
Whimper-whine; whose unridiculous
Lost softness softly makes a trap for us.
And makes a curse. And makes a sugar of
The malocclusions, the inconditions of love.

2

What shall I give my children? who are poor,
Who are adjudged the leastwise of the land,
Who are my sweetest lepers, who demand
No velvet and no velvety velour;
But who have begged me for a brisk contour,
Crying that they are quasi, contraband
Because unfinished, graven by a hand
Less than angelic, admirable or sure.
My hand is stuffed with mode, design, device.
But I lack access to my proper stone.
And plenitude of plan shall not suffice
Nor grief nor love shall be enough alone
To ratify my little halves who bear
Across an autumn freezing everywhere.

3

And shall I prime my children, pray, to pray?
Mites, come invade most frugal vestibules
Spectered with crusts of penitents' renewals
And all hysterics arrogant for a day.
Instruct yourselves here is no devil to pay.
Children, confine your lights in jellied rules;
Resemble graves; be metaphysical mules.
Learn Lord will not distort nor leave the fray.
Behind the scurryings of your neat motif
I shall wait, if you wish: revise the psalm
If that should frighten you: sew up belief
If that should tear: turn, singularly calm
At forehead and at fingers rather wise,
Holding the bandage ready for your eyes.

GWENDOLYN BROOKS

THE SUICIDE

Shocked that she missed the footbridge! She cried out,
But no later than the water she fell in and drowned in;
God help me, they tell us she shouted, but she had
              no sovereign —
No one at all to order her out of that water.

Now the animals have charted the land for their
              reasonable holiday;
All have appointed this time to be there to see them.
Photographers capture each other — the carnival quickens!
The spectres, the hawkers, the talkers, the damned are
              all there.

V. R. LANG

ODE AGAINST ST. CECILIA'S DAY

Rise, underground sleepers, rise from the grave
    Under a broken hearted sky
And hear the swansinging nightmare grieve
    For this deserted anniversary
Where horned a hope sobs in the wilderness
    By the thunderbolt of the day.

Footfall echoing down the long ruin of midnight
    Knock like a heart in a box
Through the aural house and the sybilline cave
    Where once Cecilia shook her singing veils,
Echo and mourn. Footstepping word, attend her
    Here, where, bird of answer, she prevails.

Sleep, wormeaten weepers. Silence is her altar.
    To the drum of the skull, muffled
In a black time, the sigh is a hecatomb.
    Tender Cecilia silence. Silence is tender
    As never a word was. Now, dumb-
Struck she mourns in the catacombs of her grandeur.

277

O stop the calling killer in the skull
    Like beasts we turn towards!
For was the night-riding siren beautiful
Caterwauling war until her bed was full
    Of the uxorious dead?
Let the great moaners of the Seven Seas
    And only heaven mourn
With the shipwracked harp of creation on their knees
    Till Cecilia turns to a stone.

GEORGE BARKER

CIRCE

    Then lay I lax,
Halfway so hung, in measure, amidst my ends,
    As did excite her envious tongue
      In whose elixir
    I grew, a monster in her hands,

    Fatling thus fed
Slid to her lovely rack of arms that wooingly
    Drew me out, and in, till I broke
      Amuck at her bid
    Upon her, rollicked in my undoing

    Bruiting my snout
Into her cloisters where, in a stutter of hocks,
    We hanged devoutly,
    She on mine, I on her godless crucifix,
      Pig in that pyx.

    Now lying dull
Amidst my ends, since she, my disfigurement done,
    Detruded me from her stoup of swill
      In measure a man
    Halfway becalmed in a household lie

Of wise indemnity,
Ungolden mean, I mourn the incontinent sun
Whose alchemic eye
Informed our muds in a bright extremity,
Gods in that sty

WILLIAM GIBSON

From THINGS OF AUGUST

I

These locusts by day, these crickets by night
Are the instruments on which to play
Of an old and disused ambit of the soul
Or of a new aspect, bright in discovery —

A disused ambit of the spirit's way,
The sort of thing that August crooners sing,
By a pure fountain, that was a ghost, and is,
Under the sun-slides of a sloping mountain;

Or else a new aspect, say the spirit's sex,
Its attitudes, its answers to attitudes
And the sex of its voices, as the voice of one
Meets nakedly another's naked voice.

Nothing is lost, loud locusts. No note fails.
These sounds are long in the living of the ear.
The honky-tonk out of the somnolent grasses
Is a memorizing, a trying out, to keep.

3

High poetry and low:
Experience in perihelion
Or in the penumbra of summer night —

The solemn sentences,
Like interior intonations,
The speech of truth in its true solitude,
A nature that is created in what it says,
The peace of the last intelligence;

Or the same thing without desire,
He that in this intelligence
Mistakes it for a world of objects,
Which, being green and blue, appease him,
By chance, or happy chance, or happiness,
According to his thought, in the Mediterranean
Of the quiet of the middle of the night,
With the broken statues standing on the shore.

8

When was it that the particles became
The whole man that tempers and beliefs became
Temper and belief and that differences lost
Difference and were one? It had to be
In the presence of a solitude of the self,
An expanse and the abstraction of an expanse,
A zone of time without the ticking of clocks,
A color that moved us with forgetfulness.
When was it that we heard the voice of union?

Was it as we sat in the park and the archaic form
Of a woman with a cloud on her shoulder, rose
Against the trees and then against the sky
And the sense of the archaic touched us at once
In a movement of the outlines of similarity?

We resembled one another at the sight.
The forgetful color of the autumn day
Was full of these archaic forms, giants
Of sense, evoking one thing in many men,
Evoking an archaic space, vanishing
In the space, leaving an outline of the size

Of the impersonal person, the wanderer,
The father, the ancestor, the bearded peer,
The total of human shadows bright as glass.

WALLACE STEVENS

PROVINCETOWN, MASS.

The glazed day crumbles to its fall
Upon the tiny rout of fishing
Boats. Gulls convey it down,
Lengthening their cries that soon
Will rake the evening air; while some,
Silhouetted on a strand
In a jumbled line of target ducks,
Watch as ebb tide drains the bay.

From a rotted log upon
The shore, like the other beached
Mutations, shell and weed, I wait
For Highland Light to cast its eye.

July unhives its heaven in
A swarm of stars above my head.
And at my feet, flat to the water
That it rides, the lighthouse beam,
A broken spar, breaks its pulse.

"What have I learned of word or line?"
Ticks on, ticks off; ticks on, ticks off.
The bay, that was a clotted eye,
Is turned to water by the dark.
Only my summer breaks upon
The sea, the gulls, the narrow land.

HARVEY SHAPIRO

THE CAGE

And the Americans put Pound in a cage
In the Italian summer coverless
On a hillside up from Pisa in his age
Roofless the old man with a blanket yes

On the ground. *Shih* in his pocket luck jammed there
When the partigiani with a tommy-gun
Broke in the villa door. Great authors fare
Well; for they fed him, the Americans

And after four weeks were afraid he'd die
So the Americans took him out of the cage
And tented him like others. He lay wry
To make the Pisan cantos with his courage

Sorrow and memory in a slowing drive
(And after five months they told Dorothy
Where Ezra was, and what, — i.e., alive)
Until from fingers such something twitcht free

. . . O years go bare, a madman lingered through
The hall-end where we talked and felt my book
Till he was waved away; Pound tapped his shoe
And pointed and digressed with an impatient look

"Bankers" and "Yids" and "a conspiracy"
And of himself no word, the second worst,
And "Who is seeryus now?" and then "J. C.
Thought he'd got something, yes, but Ari was first"

His body bettered. And the empty cage
Sings in the wringing winds where winds blow
Backward and forward one door in its age
And the great cage suffers nothing whatever no

JOHN BERRYMAN

THE SELF UNSATISFIED RUNS EVERYWHERE

Sunday and sunlight ashen on the Square,
Hard wind, high blue, and clouded pennant sky,
Fifth Avenue empty in the autumn air,
As if a clear photograph of a dead day,
It was the Lord's day once, solemn and full
— Now I in an aftermath, desire spent,
Move with a will appeased and see a gull,
Then gulls drop from an arch — scythes of descent! —
Having (I guess) no wish beyond the foam
Toppling to them at each fresh exercise,
Knowing success like fountains, perhaps more wise
Than one who hesitantly writes a poem
— But who, being human, wishes to be a gull,
Knows nothing much, though birds are beautiful.

DELMORE SCHWARTZ

THE HEART FLIES UP, ERRATIC AS A KITE

Whistles like light in leaves, O light
And starlight on the heights, the reach of speech,
"I like you very much, but not tonight,"
And other true truths which no one can teach.
Emotion overthrown, a Christmas tree,
Blazing and glaring after the holiday,
Quickly rushing to darkness, falling away,
Hissing like flakes, though sparkling brilliantly.
Evergreen, heart forever! The head afire
Flowing and flowering in a fountain's death
Declares all turns and burns and yet returns,
The breast arises from the bobs of breath,
After the burst and lapsing of desire,
Light! Light like the deathless past remains.

DELMORE SCHWARTZ

THE POEM

The painter of Dante's awful ferry-ride
Declared the world only a dictionary,
Words, words, whose separate meanings must go wide
Unless the visionary
Compose them, so his eyes are satisfied.

The saint from Africa called every thing
A word, the world being a poem by God,
Each evil tuned to make a splendor sing,
Ordered by God
With opposites that praise His fingering.

Was Delacroix a fool? Was Augustine?
The dictionary seems a poor appliance,
With venerable terms become obscene,
Too fertile science.
We try the poem, but what does it mean?

The rhymes are slant, of course, the rhythms free
Or sprung, the figures moving through the mind
Close as a caravan across country
Often unkind.
It is magnificent in its privacy.

And yet the words are there: fire, earth, ocean,
Sound, silence, odor, shape and shadow, fear,
Delight, animal, mineral, time, space, motion,
Lovely and queer,
The crystal's patience, the baboon's devotion.

The words are there; according to his powers,
The saint, the painter, gave the work a gloss,
Loving it. Anguish, as it scours, devours,
Discovering loss.
The logic of the poem is not ours.

BABETTE DEUTSCH

LITTLE ODE

What beasts and angels practice I ignore,
but the best of human use is careless love,
    and surely bravery and cunning merit
    the prize, they are the method of success.

Then crown us, friends, as on we speed
and play us music when the train arrives,
    for we, outwitting the obstacular world
    and forcing one another beyond fear,

to careless lust have won our way. Oh here
it is quiet — Friends! do you remember?
    Spinoza said, "Happiness, not only the reward
    of virtue, is itself the virtue" — is

effective, and we spread our satisfaction
whence there is much, disarming envy;
    the hours are not boring, they stand still;
    we deviate straight forward to immortal death.

PAUL GOODMAN

"A WORLD WITHOUT OBJECTS IS A SENSIBLE EMPTINESS"

The tall camels of the spirit
Steer for their deserts, passing the last groves loud
With the sawmill shrill of the locust, to the whole honey of
    the arid
Sun. They are slow, proud,

And move with a stilted stride
To the land of sheer horizon, hunting Traherne's
Sensible emptiness, there where the brain's lantern-slide
    Revels in vast returns.

O connoisseurs of thirst,
Beasts of my soul who long to learn to drink
Of pure mirage, those prosperous islands are accurst
    That shimmer on the brink

Of absence; auras, lustres,
And all shinings need to be shaped and borne.
Think of those painted saints, capped by the early masters
    With bright, jauntily-worn

Aureate plates, or even
Merry-go-round rings. Turn, O turn
From the fine sleights of the sand, from the long empty oven
    Where flames in flamings burn,

Back to the trees arrayed
In bursts of glare, to the halo-dialling run
Of the country creeks, and the hills' bracken tiaras made
    Gold in the sunken sun,

Wisely watch for the sight
Of the supernova burgeoning over the barn,
Lampshine blurred in the steam of beasts, the spirit's right
    Oasis, light incarnate.

RICHARD WILBUR

ALCESTE IN THE WILDERNESS

(In Le Misanthrope *Alceste, having become disgusted with all
forms and manners of society, goes off into exile, leaving behind
Philinte, who shall now become his rival in love.)*

Evening is clogged with gnats as the light fails,
And branches bloom with gold and copper screams
Of birds with fancy prices on their tails
To plume a lady's gear; the motet wails
Through Africa upon dissimilar themes.

A little snuff-box whereon Daphnis sings
In pale enamels, touching love's defeat,
Calls up the color of her underthings
And plays upon the taut memorial strings,
Trailing her laces down into this heat.

One day he found, topped with a smutty grin,
The small corpse of a monkey, partly eaten.
Force of the sun had split the bluish skin,
Which, by their questioning and entering in,
A swarm of bees had been concerned to sweeten.

He could distill no essence out of this.
That yellow majesty and molten light
Should bless this carcass with a sticky kiss
Argued a brute and filthy emphasis.
The half-moons of the finger-nails were white,

And where the nostrils opened on the skies,
Issuing to the sinus, where the ant
Crawled swiftly down to undermine the eyes
Of cloudy aspic, nothing could diguise
How terribly the thing looked like Philinte.

Will-o'-the-wisp, on the scum laden water,
Burns in the night, a gaseous deceiver,
In the pale shade of France's foremost daughter.
Heat gives his thinking cavity no quarter,
For he is burning with the monkey's fever.

Before the bees have diagrammed their comb
Within the skull, before summer has cracked
The back of Daphnis, naked, polychrome,
Paris shall see the tempered exile home,
Peruked and stately for the final act.

ANTHONY HECHT

PART V

1950–1960
(Volumes 77–96)

THE MONSTER

Through a wild midnight all my mountainous past
Labored and heaved with all I had forgotten
Until a poem no bigger than a mouse
Came forth. And with the darkness finally passed
We faced each other, begetter and begotten:
"Monster!" I cried. And "Monster!" cried the mouse

HENRY RAGO

THE BEAUTY OF THINGS

To feel and speak the astonishing beauty of things — earth,
    stone and water,
Beast, man and woman, sun, moon and stars —
The blood-shot beauty of human nature, its thoughts, frenzies
    and passions,
And unhuman nature its towering reality —
For man's half dream; man, you might say, is nature
    dreaming, but rock
And water and sky are constant — to feel
Greatly, and understand greatly, and express greatly, the
    natural
Beauty, is the sole business of poetry.
The rest's diversion: those holy or noble sentiments, the
    intricate ideas,
The love, lust, longing: reasons, but not the reason.

ROBINSON JEFFERS

ON A PICTURE BY MICHELE DA VERONA, OF ARION AS A BOY RIDING UPON A DOLPHIN

Here is the foreign cliff and the fabled sea,
But where is the wealthy youth we read of,
Whose music charmed the dolphins, that they bore him
Out of the reach of murderous men
To Taenarus (green-marbled Matapan)?

When he played, surely the waves he filled
With music froze, and common time was stilled
As at the intricate measure of Orpheus' song,
Past in a flash and yet a lifetime long.

But here is no frozen trance: a naked urchin
Shouting dissolves the world in waves of sound;
The cavern of the winds is in his throat,
And all comes pouring out of that primal cave
In notes that harden into hills or seas.

Out of one source, brown billows and brown land;
The gondola darts like a fish, the spiny men
Are vertebrates of sea or shore, and the castle
Caught on the cliff-top like an ark is stranded.

Astride upon a winking dolphin's neck
Arion shouts and sings, his yellow cloak
Fills with the wind;
His viol is carved with the head of a rakish cat;
He is a little noisy brat;
Also, he has the world at his command.

ANNE RIDLER

CONCLUSION
Cio che per l'universo si squaderna

If what began (look far and wide) will end:
This lava globe huddle and freeze, its core

Brittle with cold, or pulled too near its friend
Pop once like one gun in a long-drawn war,
And the stars sputter one by one, the night
So empty judging *empty's* out of date
(Space and time gone), then only height on height
Mind that impelled those currents and that freight
Mind that after five days (see those days!
Regions all tropic one day, one all ice!)
Whistled man from the sea-moss, saw him raise
The blundering forepaw, blink from shaggy eyes —
If image, likeness in the ox-yoke brows
Long out of focus, focused mind to Mind —
Ah what inconceivable two-and-two allows
That silence huddle and all eyes go blind?
Our ups and downs — there! that remembered makes
Memory which is the single mind. How sweet
Molten stars of the maple fumed in rakes
At 1350 such and such a street.
A thing to keep in mind. Yes and keep yet
When the vile essence violescence lies.
Once near seven by the violet sill
Very quiet, the fireplace tiny in our eyes —
I mention this; there's more. The Almighty will
Aeons late stumble on it with surprise.

JOHN FREDERICK NIMS

VITTORIA COLONNA

I saw her die and did not kiss her brow

So from this life, male in its first motion,
Yearning ever for male, the motion goes,
And men who die more frequently than women
Never learning to die with a woman's ease.

You drop, a willing city, below the horizon,
Gable remembered, naive bell-tower dissolving;
Men fight covers, grasp nephews, curse the physician.
They bungle, inept in all, dying and living.

Before and after birth men lose before women,
And life, choosing the male, ever the loser.
You who spoke well and above the birds of omen,
Now pillowed on adders tell the adders your pleasure,
Now rimmed on the wheel, tell the rounds of pain
You marked in transit, under the eyes of men.

I, who sent this fur blanket because you sniffled,
Work in the cold chapel, the fingers swell double,
I groin them, blow on them, rap them on the scaffold.

I do not elect like you to love turning marble
Though marble I turn, and I turn finally now
From marble I never turned and shall outlast.
I saw you die and did not kiss your brow,
I was jealous of the chaste skill of your frost
And feared you most perfecting beyond my hand
A form small for me, brief, and somewhat common.

David is lost, standing the rain and wind,
Empty of beauty to bend like a limp woman.
I go to my several deaths among my cold lives.
Look for my fist in the burst of your bright leaves.

ROY MARZ

HOTEL DE L'UNIVERS ET PORTUGAL

The strange bed, whose recurrent dream we are,
Basin, and shutters guarding with their latch
The hour of arrivals, the reputed untouched Square.
Bleakly with ever fewer belongings we watch
And have never, it each time seems, so coldly before

Steeped the infant membrane of our clinging
In a strange city's clear grave acids;
Or thought how like a pledge the iron key-ring
Slid overboard, one weighty calm at Rhodes,
Down to the vats of its eventual rusting.

And letters moulting out of memory, lost
Seasons of the breast of a snowbird . . .
One morning on the pillow shall at last
Lie strands of age, and many a crease converge
Where the ambitious dreaming head has tossed

The world away and turned, and taken dwelling
Within the pillow's dense white dark, has heard
The lover's speech from cool walls peeling
To the white bed, whose dream they were.
Bare room, forever feeling and annulling,

Bare room, bleak problem set for space,
Fold us ever and over in less identity
Than six walls hold, the oval mirror face
Showing us vacantly how to become only
Bare room, mere air, no hour and no place,

Lodging of chance, and bleak as all beginning.
We had begun perhaps to lack a starlit Square.
But now our very poverties are dissolving,
Are swallowed up, strong powders to ensure
Sleep, by a strange bed in the dark of dreaming.

JAMES MERRILL

THE FOREBODING

Looking by chance in at the open window
   I saw my own self seated in his chair
With gaze abstracted, furrowed forehead,
   Unkempt hair.

I thought that I had suddenly come to die,
   That to a cold corpse this was my farewell,
Until the pen moved slowly on the paper
   And tears fell.

He had written a name, yours, in printed letters
   One word on which bemusedly to pore:
No protest, no desire, your naked name,
   Nothing more.

Would it be tomorrow, would it be next year?
   But the vision was not false, this much I knew;
And I turned angrily from the open window
   Aghast at you.

Why never a warning, either by speech or look,
   That the love you cruelly gave me could not last?
Already it was too late: the bait swallowed,
   The hook fast.

ROBERT GRAVES

THE PLACE AT ALERT BAY

Standing high on the shoulders of all things, all things.
Creation pole reaching over my teeming island
That plays me at last a fountain of images.
Away from the road, life rising from all of us,
The grove of animals and our souls built in towers.
A music to be resumed in God.

Our branched belief, the power-winged tree.
Tree of meanings where the first mothers pour
Their totems, their images, up among the sun.
We build our gifts : language of process offers
Life above life moving, a ladder of lives
Reaching to time that is resumed in God.

Did the thunderbird give you yourself? The man mourning?
The cedar forest between the cryings of ravens?
Everfound mother, streaming of dolphins, whale-white noon.
Father of salmon–clouded seas, your face.
Water. Weatherbeaten image of us all.
All forms to be resumed in God.

For here, all energy is form : the dead, the unborn,
All supported on the shoulders of us all,
And all forever reaching from the source of all things.
Pillars of process, the growing of the soul,
Form that is energy from these seas risen,
Identified. Resumed in God.

MURIEL RUKEYSER

SUICIDE POND*

It lay, dark in the corner of the field,
Deep and unclouded, like a devil's well,
The dark fern gathered round it in great clumps;
All the wild air was heavy with the smell
Of tansy; and it had the awful look
Of hidden and forbidden water. When
The seasons changed and winter dropped its cloud,
It did not dream in silver, but this fen
Remained a black hole gaping in the snow.
No stream led out of it, no stream led in;
No stars reflected in it; rumor said
Men plunged into its cold and took their sin,
Downing it with clenched hands and blinded eyes,
Far down the pitted water; and, alone
And trembling, we, when young, looked down and saw
Grim suicides in bottom-rock and stone.

KATHY MCLAUGHLIN

* This verse was written [at the University of Washington Workshop]
as part of an examination, within the three-hour [class] period. Eight
nouns, eight verbs, and eight adjectives were given. It was necessary
to use five from each list. — Ed. [Karl Shapiro]

THE INSTRUMENT

Death, and it is broken,
The delicate apparatus of the mind,
Tactile, sensitive to light, responsive to sound,
The soul's instrument, tuned to earth's music,
Vibrant to all the waves that break on the shores of the
    world.

Perhaps the soul only puts out a hand,
Antennae or pseudopodium, an extended touch
To receive the spectrum of colour, and the lower octave of
    pain,
Reaches down into the waves of nature
As a child dips an arm into the sea,
And death is a withdrawal of attention
That has discovered all it needs to know,
Or, if not all, enough for now,
If not enough, something to bear in mind.

And it may be that soul extends
Organs of sense
Tuned to waves here scarcely heard, or only
Heard distantly, in dreams,
Worlds other otherwise than as stars,
Asteroids, and suns are distant in natural space.
The supersonic voices of angels reach us
Even now, and we touch one another
Sometimes, in love, with hands that are not hands,
With immaterial substance, with a body
Of interfusing thought, a living eye,
Spirit that passes unhindered through walls of stone
And walks upon those waves that we call ocean.

KATHLEEN RAINE

NIJINSKY

298   The dive could come who was its fledgling first
Of wings that feathered ankles and stood up

And leapt and wide in the deep air immersed
The body that came down as soul went up
And taught the throat the foremost wind: and back
The living blood curved in the fluid hand
Whose fingers paused, and poised: the deadened slack
Was time's who stopped to see a dancer stand
Where sky was . . . There was God, where man was not
And heat in the heaving heart that moved alone
And left like a lover the still, praying spot
To surge where there were only air and bone
But once, as a mere odor comes and goes,
Dream: and the great anthropomorphic rose.

PARKER TYLER

ON THE APPARITION OF ONESELF

He carries shadows in his face like caves,
Where we confront the dragon never vanquished,
The hero never chaste. Gold hair and fiery
Breath are there in the dark entangled,
And which is burning and which is burned
We cannot tell. There opens the old suspicion
Of a grin in back of the brain —

But seen here walking, we flee it;
Or suddenly turned, stand stricken
To that moment fatal in our lives,
And cannot move nor cry nor try to
Smile the ravaged face away. We wait
For it to pass, as though not having recognized
Our brother, friend, or a creature even of this flesh.

WILLIAM BURFORD

THE SHIELD OF ACHILLES

She looked over his shoulder
For vines and olive trees,
Marble, well-governed cities
And ships upon wine-dark seas;

299

But there on the shining metal
   His hands had put instead
An artificial wilderness
   And a sky like lead.

A plain without a feature, bare and brown,
  No blade of grass, no sign of neighborhood,
Nothing to eat and nowhere to sit down;
   Yet, congregated on that blankness, stood
   An unintelligible multitude,
A million eyes, a million boots, in line,
Without expression, waiting for a sign.

Out of the air a voice without a face
  Proved by statistics that some cause was just
In tones as dry and level as the place;
   No one was cheered and nothing was discussed,
   Column by column, in a cloud of dust,
They marched away, enduring a belief
Whose logic brought them, somewhere else, to grief.

She looked over his shoulder
   For ritual pieties,
White flower-garlanded heifers,
   Libation and sacrifice:
But there on the shining metal
   Where the altar should have been
She saw by his flickering forge-light
   Quite another scene.

Barbed wire enclosed an arbitrary spot
  Where bored officials lounged (one cracked a joke)
And sentries sweated for the day was hot;
   A crowd of ordinary decent folk
   Watched from outside and neither moved nor spoke
As three pale figures were led forth and bound
To three posts driven upright in the ground.

The mass and majesty of this world, all
   That carries weight and always weighs the same,

Lay in the hands of others; they were small
  And could not hope for help, and no help came;
  What their foes liked to do was done; their shame
Was all the worst could wish: they lost their pride
And died as men before their bodies died.

    She looked over his shoulder
      For athletes at their games,
    Men and women in a dance
      Moving their sweet limbs,
    Quick, quick, to music;
      But there on the shining shield
    His hands had set no dancing-floor
      But a weed-choked field.

A ragged urchin, aimless and alone,
  Loitered about that vacancy; a bird
Flew up to safety from his well-aimed stone:
  That girls are raped, that two boys knife a third,
  Were axioms to him, who'd never heard
Of any world where promises were kept
Or one could weep because another wept.

    The thin-lipped armorer
      Hephaestos hobbled away;
    Thetis of the shining breasts
      Cried out in dismay
    At what the God had wrought
      To please her son, the strong
    Iron-hearted man-slaying Achilles
      Who would not live long.

           W. H. AUDEN

AFTER THE PERSIAN

I

I have wept with the spring storm;
Burned with the brutal summer.

Now, hearing the wind and the twanging bow-strings
I know what winter brings.

The hunt sweeps out upon the plain
And the garden darkens.
They will bring the trophies home
To bleed and perish
Beside the trellis and the lattices,
Beside the fountain, still flinging diamond water,
Beside the pool
(Which is eight-sided, like my heart).

2

All has been translated into treasure:
Weightless as amber,
Translucent as the currant on the branch,
Dark as the rose's thorn.

Where is the shimmer of evil?
This is the shell's iridescence
And the wild bird's wing.

3

Ignorant, I took up my burden in the wilderness.
Wise with great wisdom, I shall lay it down upon flowers.

4

Goodbye, goodbye!
There was so much to love, I could not love it all;
I could not love it enough.

Some things I overlooked, and some I could not find.
Let the crystal clasp them
When you drink your wine, in autumn.

LOUISE BOGAN

THEN THE ERMINE:

"Rather dead than spotted"; and believe it
    despite reason to think not,
I saw a bat by daylight;
hard to credit

But I know that I am right. It charmed me —
    wavering like a jack o' the green,
weaving about above me
insecurely.

Instead of hammerhanded bravado
    adopting force for fashion,
momentum with a motto:
non timeo

vel mutare — I don't change or frighten;
    though all it means is really,
am I craven?
Nothing's certain.

Fail, and Lavater's physiography
    has another admirer
of skill that axiomatically
flowers obscurely.

Both paler and purpler than azure, note marine
    uncompliance — bewarer
of the weak analogy — between
waves in motion.

Change? Of course, if the palisandre settee can express
    for us, "ebony violet" —
Master Corbo in full dress
and shepherdess

at once — exhilarating hoarse crownote
    and dignity with intimacy.

Our foiled explosiveness is yet
a kind of prophet,

a perfecter, and so a concealer —
        with the power of implosion —
like violets by Dürer;
even darker.

MARIANNE MOORE

EPIGRAM

And what is love? Misunderstanding, pain,
Delusion, or retreat? It is in truth
Like an old brandy after a long rain,
Distinguished, and familiar, and aloof.

J. V. CUNNINGHAM

SESTINA IN TIME OF WINTER

Walking towards the house, the terraces
where lords and ladies, feathers in their hands,
questioned the wind, I see the naked urns
silent and filled with snow like milky bells
rising abandoned, and deformed by ice
the marble cupids tightening in the ponds.

There are no deer, nor ducks upon the ponds
where the black reeds against the terraces
clack with their beaks and mandibles of ice,
nor do the wicked footmen, holding hands,
skate in the winter mornings blue as bells
and drink the whiskey hidden in the urns.

But, always, as I walk amongst the urns
or through the formal gardens to the ponds

in the white landscape where the jangling bells
of sleighs do not approach the terraces,
some dedication rustles in the hands
with which I pluck myself a rose of ice,

and through the tones of twilight and of ice
I feel my blood brocade me till, by urns
pacing and grave, the graces of my hands
dismiss the yew green vistas to the ponds,
conduct the silence of the terraces
and then at solemn doors knock and ring bells.

Deep in the house are dusty waves of bells
but no one answers and I break through ice
into those rooms behind the terraces
where mirrors darken like the reeded ponds
no birds alight on, chandeliers and urns
glitter obscurely at the clock's stopped hands.

But in the absence of all smiles and hands
I feel my heart flow back into that bell
whose voice still waits within the fluted urns:
then in the lovely negative of ice
pleasures alight in flocks upon the ponds,
peacocks and lovers crowd the terraces —
summer and winter strolling hand in hand
and chateau childhoods prisoned in the bell
of dark, held back excited by the urns.

PATRICK ANDERSON

NIGHTWOOD

Seeking in squalor lean, elusive youth,
The pale quean haunts the bars, the murky streets,
Moving from love to love to love to love,
And loving but the self that Love defeats:

And loving but the robin and the wren
That hop from stone to stone on splintered legs,
And do not touch the hearts of buried men;
While clothed in soft, white light, the dark wolf digs.

WILLIAM JAY SMITH

FROM THE EMBASSY

I am Ambassador of Otherwhere
To the unfederated states of Here and There,
Enjoy (as the phrase is)
Extra-territorial privileges.
With heres and theres I seldom come to blows
Or need, as once, to sandbag all my windows.
Then, though the Otherwhereish currency
Cannot be quoted yet officially,
I meet less hindrance now with the exchange,
Nor is my garb, even, considered strange,
And shy enquiries for literature
Come in by every post, and the side door.

ROBERT GRAVES

LOBOTOMY

The cells hold mock convention in the brain,
tossing red pennants through the corridors
where smoke-filled doubts and dusty stores
of worn-out mottoes vote to go insane.
The chair is hesitant to rule: this memory
or that unwished-for wish calls "Question!"
and the insurgent hairy palms of ape agree
to overrule the men in ragged vestment
who lift their ho-hum freckled hands, but snore.
Then earthquake shakes the landscape:

delicate forceps snip off votes, and ape
stalks, rioting; but cannot now restore
what I, one rebel cell disguised, sees lost:
the waking truth in dying eyes, like frost.

KENNETH PITCHFORD

PRISON SONG

The skin ripples over my body like moon-wooed water,
rearing to escape me. Where could it find another
animal as naked as the one it hates to cover?
Once it told me what was happening outside,
who was attacking, who caressing, and what the air
was doing to feed or freeze me. Now I wake up
dark at night, in a textureless ocean of ignorance,
or fruit bites back and water bruises like a stone.
It's jealousy, because I look for other tools to know
with, and other armor, better girded to my wish.
So let it lie, turn off the clues or try to leave:
sewn on me seamless like those painful shirts
the body-hating saints wore, the sheath of hell
is pierced to my darkness nonetheless: what traitors
labor in my face, what hints they smuggle through
its arching guard! But even in the night it jails,
with nothing but its lies and silences to feed upon,
the jail itself can make a scenery, sing prison songs,
and set off fireworks to praise a homemade day.

ALAN DUGAN

From SONNETS OF THE TRIPLE-HEADED MANICHEE

II

Keelhauled across the star-wrecked death of God
How loud I cry that corpse is truly shattered
Showing the vascular burning ship and vessel
On which the howling Nietzsche has been martyred.

O lacerations multiply! O hundred tongues
Affirm in the despairing hymns of blood
That like a right rolling among its wrongs
My God is dead, but his bone can wrestle.
What liberty we know among the stars
No, is not liberty but a pillar to post
Mopping and mowing of a cause that's lost
Its way and will boxing the compassed stars
That swing at a half-mast head over the vast
Dead sea of the dead god of the dead stars.

GEORGE BARKER

THE WORD OF WATER

The word of water spoke a wavy line
To the Egyptians; we can also hear
Variations from the strict linear
In fall and faucet, pail and ice-pitcher.
Whether in fountain or in porcelain
It speaks a speech so crystal in its chime
We never think to question this cold
Transparent wanderer from the underworld
About the dead, — whose resurrection fills
More than half the earth uttering a word
That no man living has interpreted.

E. L. MAYO

MARGINALIA

Things concentrate at the edges; the pond-surface
Is bourne to fish and man and it is spread
In textile scum and damask light, on which
The lily-pads are set; and there are also
        Inlaid ruddy twigs, becalmed pine-leaves,
        Air-baubles, and the chain mail of froth.

Descending into sleep (as when the night-lift
Falls past a brilliant floor) we glimpse a sublime
Décor and hear, perhaps, a complete music,
But this evades us, as in the night meadows
      The crickets' million roundsong dies away
      From all advances, rising in every distance.

Our riches are centrifugal; men compose
Daily, unwittingly, their final dreams,
And those are our own voices whose remote
Consummate chorus rides on the whirlpool's rim,
      Past which we flog our sails, toward which we drift,
      Plying our trades, in hopes of a good drowning.

RICHARD WILBUR

THE ALPHABET

The letters of the Jews as strict as flames
Or little terrible flowers lean
Stubbornly upwards through the perfect ages,
Singing through solid stone the sacred names.
The letters of the Jews are black and clean
And lie in chain-line over Christian pages.
The chosen letters bristle like barbed wire
That hedge the flesh of man,
Twisting and tightening the book that warns.
These words, this burning bush, this flickering pyre
Unsacrifices the bled son of man
Yet plaits his crown of thorns.

Where go the tipsy idols of the Roman
Past synagogues of patient time,
Where go the sisters of the gothic rose,
Where go the blue eyes of the Polish women
Past the almost natural crime,
Past the still speaking embers of ghettoes,
There rise the tinder flowers of the Jews.

The letters of the Jews are dancing knives
That carve the heart of darkness seven ways.
These are the letters that all men refuse
And will refuse until the king arrives
And will refuse until the death of time
And all is rolled back in the book of days.

KARL SHAPIRO

A ROMANCE

He rode forth armed: breast-plate and crest
And science; he rode forth dressed
To kill, but death was in his eye,
Death in his heart; under the family crest
Hemmed in, unwilling to escape, was death;
And when he thought, he knew he was to die.

He rode forth armed: sense, experience,
Self-interest, and impatience
For a quick wooing, hid his thirst
For love; and, wanting that experience,
He charged upon his enemy with love.
He loved, he died. No one knows which came first.

CHESTER KALLMAN

HORATIAN ODE

Let the pines rock in torment of the storm
Of pressured weathers in the clouds contending
And the sheer slopes about us plunge headlong
Down to the waters' frantic rush and spending.

Our timbers morticed solid in the rock
And floor tiles in cement as firmly set
As if in molten lava petrified,
We keep the moveless center and can mock

At bedlam on the loose. Even the fire
In the chimney is menace broken to our will.
We are well at ease in our tight citadel.
Only if lightning strike or the earth yawn

Do we risk disruption . . . or even, say, extinction!
And how should accidents beyond control
Of mortal engineering now subvert
Our state with fears that do not touch the soul?

JOSEPH WARREN BEACH

DIDACTIC SONNET

Love the unholy, that frost which quickens summer,
And crispens the thighs like a thorn or a rose
As you lie sleeping; clasp to your belly
The lizard of the great sun, and love him, too.
Admit that you are breathless, like a harried runner,
But do not trade your scepter for fanciful clothes;
Instead of Pegasus, ride on the back of a saddle-green filly
To the moon's other window, and using this platform, screw
Yourself up to the summit of stars. The setting hen
Who hatches shooting stars will love you then,
Even though you steal her eggs for your mother's ocean.
But you must take care, for the sparkling motion
Of star-eggs falling into water causes fog. Fear fog,
For he shall eat your sweetbreads, like a dog.

MELVIN WALKER LA FOLLETTE

THE SAPPHIRE

After a dream in which your love's fullness
Was heaven and earth, I stood on nothing in darkness,
Neither finding nor falling, without hope nor dread,
Not knowing pleasure nor discontented.
In time, like the first beam arriving from

311

The first star, a ray from a seed of light came,
Whose source, coming nearer (I could not say whether
It rose or descended, for there was no higher nor lower),
To a trumpet's thin sweet highest note
Which grew to the pitch of pain, showed how its white
Light proceeded all from a blue crystal stone
Large as a child's skull, shaped so, lucent as when
Daylight strikes sideways through a cat's eyes;
Blue not blinding, its light did not shine but was;
And came, as the trumpet pierced through into silence,
To hover so close before my hands
That I might have held it, but that one does not handle
What one accepts as a miracle.
A great sapphire it was whose light and cradle
Held all things: there were the delights of skies, though
Its cloudness blue was different; of sea and meadow,
But their shapes not seen. The stone unheld was mine,
But yours the sense by which, without further sign
I recognized its visionary presence
By its clarity, its changeless patience,
And the unuttered joy that it was,
As the world's love before the world was.

W. S. MERWIN

COLD

Cold and the colors of cold: mineral, shell,
And burning blue. The sky is on fire with blue
And wind keeps ringing, ringing the fire bell.

I am caught up into a chill as high
As creaking glaciers and powder-plumed peaks
And the absolutes of interstellar sky.

Abstract, impersonal, metaphysical, pure,
This dazzling art derides me. How should warm breath
Dare to exist — exist, exult, endure?

Hums in my ear the old Ur-father of freeze
And burn, that pre–post–Christian Fellow before
And after all myths and demonologies.

Under the glaring and sardonic sun,
Behind the icicles and double glass
I huddle, hoard, hold out, hold on, hold on.

ROBERT FRANCIS

AGING

I wake, but before I know it it is done,
The day, I sleep . . . And of days like these the years,
A life are made. I nod, consenting to my life.
— But who can live in these quick-passing hours?
I need to find again, to make a life,
A child's Sunday afternoon, the Pleasure Drive
Where everything went by but time — the Study Hour
Spent at a desk with folded hands, in waiting.
In those I could make. Did I not make in them
Myself? the Grown One whose time shortens,
Breath quickens, heart beats faster, till at last
It catches, skips? Yet those hours that seemed, were endless
Were still not long enough to have remade
My childish heart: the heart that must have, always,
To make anything of anything, not time,
Not time but —
                        but, alas! eternity.

RANDALL JARRELL

CHEZ JANE

The white chocolate jar full of petals
swills odds and ends around in a dizzying eye
of four o'clocks now and to come. The tiger,
marvellously striped and irritable, leaps

on the table and without disturbing a hair
of the flowers' breathless attention, pisses
into the pot, right down its delicate spout.
A whisper of steam goes up from that porcelain
eurythra. "Saint-Saëns!" it seems to be whispering,
curling unerringly around the furry nuts
of the terrible puss, who is mentally flexing.
Ah be with me always, spirit of noisy
contemplation in the studio, the Garden
of Zoos, the eternally fixed afternoons!
There, while music scratches its scrofulous
stomach, the brute beast emerges and stands,
clear and careful, knowing always the exact peril
at this moment caressing his fangs with
a tongue given wholly to luxurious usages;
which only a moment before dropped aspirin
in this sunset of roses, and now throws a chair
in the air to aggravate the truly menacing.

FRANK O'HARA

THE ISLAND IN THE EVENING

At the gathered ends of rooty paths
The wharf attracts the playing children
Voices call across the water
Beginning games on a summer evening
A gull who drops on another island
Calls down the day below the sky

As the light rises into the sky
Softness comes to mossy paths
A breeze slides off the island
Against the faces of the children
Using the withering light of the evening
Reflected from the shadowless water

The games are new on the permanent water
And children under the yellow sky

Have no fear of the friendly evening
Who feel their way on darkening paths
Over roots that previous children
Knew as the shape of the sheltering island

Shadowed forests on the island
And beaches worn by tidal water
Keep some strangeness from the children
Under the candid giant sky
And all familiar forest paths
Are edged with strangeness in the evening

Yellow primroses of the evening
In bushy clearings on the island
And yellow mullein beside the paths
In rocky meadows with little water
Focus all the covering sky
In single blossoms for the children

Games invented by the children
Hold the light of the delicate evening
Before it is lost in the permanent sky
Starting again the life of the island
Eroded by the moving water
And running feet on rocky paths

Worn paths bring home the children
From tidal water on a summer evening
Across the island below the sky

FAIRFIELD PORTER

O NOW THE DRENCHED LAND WAKES

O now the drenched land wakes;
Birds from their sleep call
Fitfully, and are still.
Clouds like milky wounds
Float across the moon.

O love, none may
Turn away long
From this white grove
Where all nouns grieve.

KENNETH PATCHEN

BEACH TALK

Put off the deference that this sea compels
And from the scroll of cloud look proud and make
A marriage of my other look that tells
Why dynasties died down and for what sake.

The sand remarks you in the heedless air
That trembles in from islands that are you.
I take that trembling and make everywhere
The flinching wave, the slow surrounding blue.

And being of everywhere, I hold you in
With a transcending hand. I stare at it,
Looking to see an actual shore begin
On which this other one could lie and fit.

Then every history could happen here.
The sand a Golden, cloud a Silver Age
Would civilise one moment and with their
Enormous deaths enlarge us stage by stage.

Until as ordinary as events we'd lie
Needing no proclamation to be us.
Hide from the blandishing summer. Do not cry
Because its light fails to be obvious.

NORMAN MACCAIG

HIGH FIDELITY

I play your furies back to me at night,
The needle dances in the grooves they made,
For fury is passion like love, and fury's bite,
These grooves, no sooner than a love-mark fade;
Then all swings round to nightmare: from the rim,
To prove the guilt I don't admit by day,
I duck love as a witch to sink or swim
Till in the ringed and level I survey
The tuneless circles that succeed a voice.
They run, without distinction, passion, rage,
Around a soloist's merely printed name
That still turns, from the impetus not choice,
Surrounded in that played-out pose of age
By notes he was, but cannot be again.

THOM GUNN

CHRONOLOGY

The circling shadow on the measured dial,
The calibrated falling of the weight,
Are both time's gauge and time's discreet denial.

No captive shade, returning at its date
Unchanged, no loud imprisoned pendulum
Through changeless gravity can calculate

The unimagined change — the swift and dumb
Deforming of the days that countermands
Pursuit of time as a continuum.

Go rather to the random falling sands,
That funnel quicker with decreasing mass;
Go to a lens, that blurs what it expands;
To candles crumbling as their lusters pass;

To cold quicksilver backing mounted glass.

317

TURNER CASSITY

ELEGY FOR DYLAN THOMAS

Black Venus of the Dead, what Sun of Night
Lies twined in your embrace, cold as the vine?
O heart, great Sun of Darkness, do you shine

For her, to whom alone
All men are faithful — faithless as the wave
To all but her to whom they come after their long
wandering —

Black giantess who is calm as palm-trees, vast
As Africa! In the shade of the giantess
He lies in that eternal faithfulness.

He, made of the pith and sap of the singing world —
Green kernal of a forgotten paradise
Where grass-hued, grass-soft suns brought the first spring
(Green fervours, singing, saps, fertilities)
And heat and moist lay on unseeing eyes
Till shapeless lumps of clay grew into men, now lies

Far from the Babel-clamour. In his rest,
He holds the rays of the universe to his stilled breast.

Before our Death in Birth, and Birth in Death,
Teaching us holy living, holy dying, we who cry
At the first light and the first dark, must learn
The oneness of the world, and know all change
Through the plant, the kingly worm (within whose shape all
        Kings begin,
To whom all Kings must come) through beast to Man.

The fraternal world of beast and plant lies on his eyes:
The beast that holds all elements in itself —
The earth, the plant, the solar system: for each beast
Is an infinity of plants, a planet, or a moon,
A flower in the green dark, freed from its stem in earth.

Shrouded with black veils like the mourning Spring
Under the vines of Grief (the first plantation since the Flood)
The mourners weep for the solary iris that God showed to
    Noah —

Our hope in this universe of tears. But he is gone —
He sleeps, a buried sun
That sank into the underworld to spread
A gold mask on the faces of the Dead, —

Young country god, red as the laughing grapes
When Sirius parches country skins to gold and fire.

And he who compressed the honey-red fire in holy shapes,
Stole frozen fire from gilded Parnassian hives,

Was Abraham-haired as the fleeces of wild stars
That all night rage like foxes in the festival
Of wheat, with fire-brands tied to their tails under the wheat-
    ears
To avert the wrath of the Sun gold as those fleeces
Of honey-red foxes. Now he is one with Adam, the first
    gardener. He sang

Of the beginning of created things, the secret
Rays of the universe, and sang green hymns
Of the great waters to the tearless deserts. Under
The fertilisation of his singing breath
Even the greyness and the dust of Death
Seemed the grey pollen of the long September heat

On earth where Kings lie wearing the whole earth as their
    crown,
Where all are equal in the innocent sleep
That lulls the lion like a child, and is the clime
Of our forgiveness. Death, like the holy Night
Makes all men brothers. There, in the maternal
Earth, the wise and humbling Dark, he lies —

The emigrant from a forgotten paradise —
The somnambulist
Who held rough Ape-dust and a planet in his fist —

Far from the empires of the human filth
Where the Gorgons suckle us with maternal milk
Black as the Furies', and the human breast
Can yield not even the waters of the Styx. But rest

For these he brought, and to the Minotaur in the city office
And the young Theseus who will never find
A gold thread leading from the Labyrinth

He brought a memory of their other lives —
Crying to the dunghill in the soul "See, it is morn!"

And seeing all glory hidden in small forms,
The planetary system in the atom, the great suns
Hid in a speck of dust.
                    So, for his sake,

More proudly will that Sisyphus the heart of Man
Roll the Sun up the steep of heaven, and in the street
Two old blind men seem Homer and Galileo — blind
Old men that tap their way through worlds of dust
To find Man's path near the Sun.

EDITH SITWELL

AUTHOR'S NOTES

Verse 7 contains references to Lorenz Oken's *Elements of Physiophilosophy*.
Verse 8, line 3, "the solary iris that God showed to Noah," Sir Thomas Browne.

THE WALL

We don't know the ins and outs
        how should we? how could we?
It's not for the likes of you and me to cogitate
high policy or to guess the inscrutable economy of
the pontifex

from the circuit of the agger
      from the travers e of the wall.
But you see a thing or two
      in our walk of life
      walking the compass of the vallum
walking for twenty years of nights
      round and round and back & fro
on the walls that contain the world.

You see a thing or two, you think a thing or two,
in our walk of life, walking for twenty years, by day,
by night, doing the rounds on the walls that maintain
the world

            on the hard tread of the silex
            on the heavy tread of the mound
up in the traversed out-work, stepping it at the
alert, down on the *via quintana* stepping it double-
quick by numbers to break y'r trio-heart . . .
            dug in wrong side the *limes*
or walled in back at depot?
                        it's evens, more or less
as far as jumping to it goes.

      But what about The Omphalos
there's the place for the proud walkers
            where the terminal gate
            arcs for the sections in column
stepping their extra fancy step
            behind the swag an' spolia
o' the universal world

      . . . out from The Camp
in through the dexter arch of double-wayed Carmenta
by where Aventine flanks The Circus
                  (from Arx the birds deploy?)
to where the totem mother
                  imported
                  Ionian
                  of bronze

brights Capitoline for ever
                    (from the Faunine slope
of creviced Palatine does the grey wraith erect her
throat to welcome the lupine gens?)

Erect, crested with the open fist that turns the
evil spell, lifting the flat palm that disciplines
the world, the signa lift in disciplined
acknowledgement, the eagles stand erect for Ilia
                    O Roma
                    O Ilia
                    Io Triumphe, Io, Io . . .
                    the shopkeepers presume to
                    make
the lupine cry their own
                            the magnates of the Boarium
leave their nice manipulations. You may call the day
ferial, rub shoulders with the plebs. All should
turn out to see how those appointed to die take the
Roman medicine. They crane their civvy necks half
out their civvy suits to bait the maimed king in his
tinctured vesture, the dying *tegérnos* of the wasted
landa well webbed in our marbled parlour, bitched and
bewildered and far from his dappled patria far side
the misted Fretum.
                    You can think a thing or two
on *that* parade:

                    Do the celestial forechoosings
                    and the hard journeyings
come to this?
                    Did the empyreal fires
hallow the chosen womb
                    to tabernacle founders of
                    emporia?
Were the august conjoinings
                    was the troia'd wandering
                    achieved

did the sallow ducts of Luperca

nourish the lily white boys
was Electra chose
from the seven stars in the sky
did Ilia bear fruit to the Strider
was she found the handmaid of the Lar
did the augurs inaugurate, did the Clarissimi steady
the transverse rods, did they align the plummets
carefully, did they check the bearing attentively,
was the templum dead true at the median intersection
did the white unequal pair
labour the yoke, tread the holy circuit
did they, so early
in the marls of Cispadana
show forth, foretoken
the rudiments of our order
when the precursors at the
valley-sites made survey of the loam
plotted the trapezoids on the sodden piles
digged the sacred pits before the beginning . . .
did they square the hill-sites
for the hut-circles, did the hill-groups look to each
other, were the hostile strong-points, one by one,
made co-ordinate
did Quirinal with Viminal
call to the Quadrata, did the fence of Tullius
embrace the mixed kindreds
did the magic wall
(that keeps the walls)
describe the orbit
did that wall contain a world
from the beginning
did they project the rectilineal plane upwards
to the floor of heaven
had all
within that reaching prism
one patria:
rooted clod or drifted star
dog or dryad or
man born of woman

did the sacred equation square the mundane site
was truth with fact conjoined
                    did the earth-mother
blossom the stone lintels
                    did *urvus* become *urbs*
did the bright share
                    turn the dun clod
to the star plan
                    did they parcel out
per scamna et strigas
                    the *civitas* of God
that we should sprawl
                    from Septimontium
a megalopolis that wills death?

Does the pontifex, do our lifted trumpets, speak
to the city and the world to call the tribes to
Saturnalia, to set misrule in the curule chair,
to bind the rejected fillet on the King of the Bean?
                    It's hard to trapes these things
from the circuit of the agger, from the traverse of
the wall, waiting for the middle watch to pass,
wanting the guard-house fug, where the companions
        nod,
where the sooted billikin brews the night broth
                    so cold it is, so numb the
intelligence, so chancy the intuition, so alert the
apprehension, for us who walk in darkness in the
shadow of the *onager*, in the shadow of the labyrinth
of the wall, of the world, of the robber walls of the
world city, trapesing the macrocosmic night.
Or, trapesing the night within, walking the inner
labyrinth where also the night is, under the tortoise
of the skull for every man walking? Under the
legionary's iron knob, under the tribune's field crest,
under the very distinguished gilt *cassis* of the
Legatus himself?
                    We don't know the ins and outs
how can we? how shall we?

What did our mothers tell us? What did their mothers
tell to them? What the earth-mother told to them?
But what did the queen of heaven tell *her?*

What was it happened by the fire flame, eating the
griddle-cake . . . or by the white porch where our sister
sang the Sabine dirge.

        . . . they used to say
we marched for Dea Roma, behind the wolf-sign, to
eat up the world, they used to say we marched for
the Strider
       the common father of the Roman people,
the father of all in our walk of life, by whose
very name you're called . . . but now they say the
Quirinal Mars turns out to be no god of war but of
armed peace. Now they say we march for kind Irene,
  who crooks her rounded elbow for little Plutus,
  the gold-getter — they say that sacred brat has a
future . . . now all can face the dying god, the
dying Gaul, without regret. But you and me,
    comrade,
the Darlings of Ares, who've helped a lot of Gauls
    and
gods to die, we shall continue to march and to bear
in our bodies the marks of The Marcher, by whatever
name they call him — we shall continue to march

      round and round the cornucopia:

that's the new fatigue.

DAVID JONES

AUTHOR'S NOTES

1. This fragment, called, provisionally, "The Wall," is a draft, under revision,
of some passages of an uncompleted work begun some years back. The few
pages given here are a small part of a lengthy soliloquy which in places becomes
a colloquy between two soldiers of a Roman unit doing guard duty on the walls
of a city in the Near East under the Early Empire.

2. On the third page of the poem, I use the words *tegérnos* and *landa*. The first is said to mean something like "lord" and the second means "land." Present-day derivatives are found in the Welsh words *teyrn,* "monarch," and *llan* "enclosure." The context of a Roman triumph will indicate why I chose forms from the Common Celtic language current in the Europe of Vercingetorix or Caratacus. I have (in my text) accented the penultimate syllable in *tegernos* in order to make certain the stress on that syllable.

OUT OF A WAR OF WITS

Poem "Ten" in Notebook "Started February, 1, 1933"; dated February 22, 1933

Out of a war of wits, when folly of words
Was the world's to me, and syllables
Fell hard as whips on an old wound,
My brain came crying into the fresh light,
Called for confessor there was none
To purge after the wit's fight,
And I was struck dumb by the sun.
Praise that my body be whole, I've limbs,
Not stumps, after the hour of battle,
For the body's brittle and the skin's white.
Praise that only the wits are hurt after the wit's fight.

Overwhelmed by the sun, with a torn brain
I stand beneath the cloud's confessional,
But the hot beams rob me of speech,
After the perils of friends' talk
Reach asking arms up to the milky sky,
After a volley of questions and replies
Light wit-hurt head for sun to sympathise,
And the sun heals, closing sore eyes.
It is good that the sun shine,
And, after it has sun, the same moon,
For out of a house of matchboard and stone
Where men would argue till the stars be green,
It is good to step onto the earth, alone,
And be struck dumb, if only for a time.

DYLAN THOMAS

GRAND ABACUS

Perhaps this valley too leads into the head of long-ago days.

What, if not its commercial and etiolated visage, could break
through the meadow wires?

It placed a chair in the meadow and then went far away.

People come to visit in summer, they do not think about the
head.

Soldiers come down to see the head. The stick hides from
them.

The heavens say, "Here I am, boys and girls!"

The stick tries to hide in the noise. The leaves, happy, drift
over the dusty meadow.

"I'd like to see it," someone said about the head, which has
stopped pretending to be a town.

Look! A ghastly change has come over it. The ears fall off —
they are laughing people.

The skin is perhaps children, they say, "We children," and are
vague near the sea. The eyes —

Wait! What large raindrops! The eyes —

Wait, can't you see them pattering, in the meadow, like a dog?

The eyes are all glorious! And now the river comes to sweep
away the last of us.

Who knew it, at the beginning of the day?

It is best to travel like a comet, with the others, though one
does not see them.

How far that bridle flashed! "Hurry up, children!"

The birds fly back, they say, "We were lying,

We do not want to fly away." But it is already too late. The
children have vanished.

JOHN ASHBERY

LANDED: A VALENTINE

See how the brown kelp withers in air
    Gasping to its death
Upon the salty ice. A moment
    Only was enough

To banish the loveliness that made
    Of a few rather
Inexpressive weeds under water
    A lover's emblem
Of success — easy-moving, soft and
    In the heart's color.

Can simple air become so foul? Now
    After a short time
Parted from warm company we kept
    Together, I share
That condition, a gradual rot
    So far from the sea:
Absence of the proper element
    Will take effect, take
Soon the mouth out of my very words.

RICHARD HOWARD

GOOSE POND

Goose Pond's imaginable snows,
The fall of twenty years at once,
Like subtler moons reflect the rose
Decompositions of the sun.

A feather tumbling from a cloud
Scrolls thunders of the natural law;
The cat-tails rattle; cinnamon-fern
Raises rag banners towards the thaw,

And early-footed ghost-flowers scour
Through willow-dapplings to a cave
Where secrecy grows fur. Self burns
At the pulpits where Jack-preachers rave!

Now a sulky weather dogs the heart,
There is no bottom to the day,

The water-lily's Chinese stalk
Drags heavy, as the white-lipped boy

Climbs from detritus of his birth,
The rusted hoop, the broken wheels,
The sunken boat of little worth,
Past balconies of limber eels

Until, along that marshy brink,
The springy trails devoid of plan,
He meets his childhood beating back
To find what furies made him man.

STANLEY KUNITZ

RADIO

Why do you play such dreary music
on Saturday afternoon, when tired
mortally tired I long for a little
reminder of immortal energy?
                              All
week long while I trudge fatiguingly
from desk to desk in the museum
you spill your miracles of Grieg
and Honegger on shut-ins.
                        Am I not
shut in too, and after a week
of work don't I deserve Prokofieff?

Well, I have my beautiful de Kooning
to aspire to. I think it has an orange
bed in it, more than the ear can hold.

FRANK O'HARA

BRAEMAR

One night from the stern I thought, as I watched
The gulls wheeling through the dark air, their
White bodies nervously adrift aloft
In the night, How long in darkness, now
The sea has stretched us shoreless, may we hold
Senseless their flight? Once meeting you in darkness,
I blew a flame on my hand, and touched you;
Then blew the flame out, but let its light
Abide in your face; and turned myself away,
Myself blown out. You, you do not think
Of that night, of course. And yet it was
Such a night as from the stern I saw,
Quivering, huddled in the sky astern, these
Pale bodies the sea's farness from their shore.

GALWAY KINNELL

COKKILS

Doun throu the sea
    Continuallie
A rain of cokkils, shells
    Rains doun
Frae the ceaseless on–ding   assault
O' the reefs abune   above
    Continuallie.

Slawlie throu nillenia
Biggan on the ocean bed
Their ain subaqueous Him-
    alaya
Wi a fine white rain o
    shells
Faa'an continuallie   falling
    Wi nae devall.   respite

Sae, in my heid as birdsang
falls Faas throu simmer treen summer trees
Is the thocht o my luve
Like the continual rain
O' cokkils throu the middle
 seas
  Wi nae devall —
The thocht o my true-luve
 Continuallie.

SYDNEY GOODSIR SMITH

PERMANENTLY

One day the Nouns were clustered in the street.
An Adjective walked by, with her dark beauty.
The Nouns were struck, moved, changed.
The next day a Verb drove up, and created the Sentence.

Each Sentence says one thing — for example, "Although it was
 a dark rainy day when the Adjective walked by, I shall
 remember the pure and sweet expression on her face until
 the day I perish from the green, effective earth."
Or, "Will you please close the window, Andrew?"
Or, for example, "Thank you, the pink pot of flowers on the
 window sill has changed color recently to a light yellow,
 due to the heat from the boiler factory which exists
 nearby."

In the springtime the Sentences and the Nouns lay silently on
 the grass.
A lonely Conjunction here and there would call, "And! But!"
But the Adjective did not emerge.

As the adjective is lost in the sentence,
So I am lost in your eyes, ears, nose, and throat —
You have enchanted me with a single kiss
Which can never be undone
Until the destruction of language.

331

KENNETH KOCH

BIRTH OF VENUS

What day was it she slid
Up from the innocent sea
Unstirred by tug of tide?
Under her feet the sand

Shifted. The waiting land
Enclosed her like a shell.
The stallions in the foam
Remarked her and were tame;

The chariot of flame
Stood still to see her come.
All nature felt the weight
Of her first faltering steps.

Time shifted, and the shapes
Of ordinary things
Altered beneath her touch;
There was no way to turn

Back. She must stay and learn
The role they had assigned:
To be their goddess, serve
The movable feasts of love.

CONSTANCE URDANG

PRIVATE PANTOMIME

I will reach into the grab-bag of unconscious things
And pull forth what? Here, a featherless bird
Supine in the palm of my hand with bony wings
Folded inert, beak agape. What sort of raw word
Explains pinfeathered skin and the certain death
That rides in the quivering flesh? I turn it out.
It falls with a weighted thud. Blood and the sight

Of such weak eyes waiting, puts my humor about;
And I thrust both my hands into a pair of gloves, tight.

RUTH STONE

METAMORPHOSIS

Haunched like a faun, he hooed
from grove of moon-glint and fen-frost
until all owls in the twigged forest
flapped black to look and brood
on the call this man made.

No sound but a drunken coot
lurching home along river bank;
stars hung water-sunk, so a rank
of double star-eyes lit
boughs where those owls sat.

An arena of yellow eyes
watched the changing shape he cut,
saw hoof harden from foot, saw sprout
goat-horns; marked how god rose
and galloped woodward in that guise.

SYLVIA PLATH

From INSCRIPTIONS ON CHINESE PAINTINGS

I

LINES TO DO WITH YOUTH

I

Willow-tassels grow in tremors of the spring wind
On this Festival of Peace in the Fourth Month,

1957

And swallows guide their young close to the Women's
    Quarters
For a fluttering trial of new wings.

2

After I had brushed the floor, burned incense, shut myself in
    and slept,
The pattern of the mat looked like water and the gnats like a
    mist:
I had been waked as by winter and did not know where I
    was,
Till I opened the western window and saw mountains surging
    into heaven.

3

Though grass grow lowlier than the flowers
And be hidden by their laden stems,
Only happiness exists
For a handmaiden of the Ch'êngs.

4

Having passed his government examinations,
He rides back home
Through ten miles radiant with almond blossoms
On a horse of air.

5

Past the water-crystal casement of her chamber
Butterflies fluttered under the eaves;
But the cats have wakened her from blissful dreaming
And her lover fades away.

6

Nothing is pleasanter than a cup of wine in the hand
And it is a surer thing than twelve moonrises.

7

Cockcrow in the moonlight, the roof of an inn,
A footprint in the frost on a wooden bridge.

8

Mountain-streams everywhere but no path,
Till under the dark willows blooms a village.

WITTER BYNNER

From THE ARK

ARK TO NOAH

I wait, with those that rest
In darkness till you come,
Though they are murmuring flesh
And I a block and dumb.

Yet when you come, be pleased
To shine here, be shown
Inward as all the creatures
Drawn through my bone.

ARK ARTICULATE

Shaped new to your measure
From a mourning grove,
I am your sensing creature
And may speak for love.

If you repent again
And turn and unmake me,
How shall I rock my pain
In the arms of a tree?

ARK ASTONISHED

Why did your spirit
Strive so long with me?
Will you wring love from deserts,
Comfort from the sea?

Your dove and raven speed,
The carrion and the kind.
Man, I know your need,
But not your mind.

JAY MACPHERSON

METAPHYSICAL

In festo Christi Regis

The level slope of colored sea
Rises degree upon degree
To hide the brazen ball of sun.
Ponderous is the planet side,
And nothing here but heart can slide,
And nothing but the day is done.

Glory the heavens here declare
Heavens in gloom deny elsewhere.
The jackal and the gaping shark
Possess the shambles of the night.
As upward eyries take the light
The downward longitudes are dark.

Eyes on the telluric rim
In tangent angles peering dim
Find shape and hour dark or down.
But centered lordship knows the art
Of bearing so toward every part
The studded sphere becomes his crown.

Rays of his mercy are besought
To magnetize my speck of thought.
Elated let the evening fall,
Abysmal be the golden day;
The ravaged carcass far away
Be supple in the life of all.

ROBERT FITZGERALD

THE REAL MUSE

No for you, my queyn, will I prepare — girl
Some jewelled mansion in supernal air,
clothe — Nor cled ye in a queen's imperial goun,
And get ye constellations for a croun:
But I sall mak a hame here in my briest
early — Whaur aer or late, ye'll find some peace and rest,
And real love sall be your wearless dress,
calm — A lown licht set aff ilk yellow tress.

Frae ilka thing that's real I sall draw out
Some essence to wap in your ilka clout: — weave
salt — The tang of saut oil in the harbour air,
stench — And reek of stale ammonia on the stair;
bulk — Yon hillock's bouk upreared abuin the toun,
The broken twigs the burn in spate brings doun: — flood
Something frae the tenements and the streets,
And something frae the bothies and the peats. — huts and peat-hags.

gossiping — The wails of clekkand gulls in public parks,
drenched — Lamp-posts droukt by ilka breed that barks
Sall all be made to yield some tribute til ye —
And you will no be blate to tak them, will ye? — afraid
The morning cups of tea, the hauf-croun lunches
mingle — Mell with your swift thochts and faddomed hunches, — fathomed
And bairns in the street sall mime for you
The ritual sacrifie wes ance your due.

The typewriter, the loud conveyor belt,
The smeltand furnace and the airn smelt: —   iron
the donkey-engines chatterand in sumps
And diesel anes drivand the pechand pumps: —   hard-
Sall bring some bit of girst intil your mill,   breathing
And yet the singing-tree be singand still;
The burn aye bear the trout, the trout the spawn,
And owre the tarn's mirk water smool the swan.   dark, glide

suchlike   Frae siccan things, my love, I'll mak your goun,
Leavand hevin and hell for the real toun,
voyaging   And hame frae vaiging in the skies and seas,
Frae earth mak you immortal images.

TOM SCOTT

TO REDOUTÉ

To true roses uplifted on the bilious tide of evening
To morning-glories dotting the crescent day
The oval shape responds:
My first is a haunting face
In the hanging-down hair.
My second is wine:
I am a sieve.

My only new thing:
The penalty of light forever
Over the heads of those who were there
And back into the night, the cough of the finishing petal.

Once approved the magentas must continue,
But the bark island sees
Into the light.
It grieves for what it gives:
Tears that streak the dusty firmament.

JOHN ASHBERY

THE HIGHWAY

It seems too enormous just for a man to be
Walking on. As if it and the empty day
Were all there is. And a little dog trotting
In time with the heat waves, away down
Near the horizon, seeming never to get
Any further. The sun and everything
Are struck in the same places, and the ditch
Is the same all the time, full of every kind
Of bone, while the empty air keeps humming
That sound it has memorized of things going
Past. And the signs with huge heads and starved
Bodies, dancing suggestive dances in
The heat without moving from where they stand,
And the others big as houses, all promise
But with nothing inside and only one wall,
Tell of other places where you can eat
And drink and get a bath and lie on a bed
Listening to music, and be safe. If you
Look around you see it is just the same
The other way, going back. Maybe hope
Was never anything but feet, and wherever
It heads for it must get there burning.

W. S. MERWIN

THE APPROACH TO THEBES

In the zero of the night, in the lipping hour,
Skin-time, knocking-time, when the heart is pearled
And the moon squanders its uranian gold,
She taunted me, who was all music's tongue,
Philosophy's and wilderness's breed,
Of shifting shape, half jungle-cat, half-dancer,
Night's woman-petaled, lion-scented rose,
To whom I gave, out of a hero's need,
The dolor of my thrust, my riddling answer,

Whose force no lesser mortal knows. Dangerous?
 Yes, as nervous oracles foretold
Who could not guess the secret taste of her:
Impossible wine! I came into the world
To fill a fate; am punished by my youth
No more. What if dog-faced logic howls,
Was it art or magic multiplied my joy?
Nature has reasons beyond true or false.
We played like metaphysic animals
Whose freedom made our knowledge bold
Before the tragic curtain of the day:
I can bear the dishonor now of growing old.
Blinded and old, exiled, diseased, and scorned —
The verdict's bitten on the brazen gates,
For the gods grant each of us his lot, his term.
Hail to the King of Thebes! — my self, ordained
To satisfy the impulse of the worm,
Bemummied in those famous incestuous sheets,
The bloodiest flags of nations of the curse,
To be hung from the balcony outside the room
Where I encounter my most flagrant source.
Children, grandchildren, my long posterity,
To whom I bequeath the spiders of my dust,
Believe me, whatever sordid tales you hear,
Told by physicians or mendacious scribes,
Of beardless folly, consanguineous lust,
Fomenting pestilence, rebellion, war,
I come prepared, unwanting what I see,
But tied to life. On the royal road to Thebes
I had my luck, I met a lovely monster,
And the story's this: I made the monster me.

STANLEY KUNITZ

THE UNSETTLED MOTORCYCLIST'S
VISION OF HIS DEATH

Across the open countryside,
Into the walls of rain I ride.

It beats my cheek, drenches my knees,
But I am being what I please.

The firm heath stops, and marsh begins.
Now we're at war: whichever wins
My human will cannot submit
To nature, though brought out of it.
The wheels sink deep; the clear sound blurs:
Still, bent on the handle-bars,
I urge my chosen instrument
Against the mere embodiment.
The front wheel wedges fast between
Two shrubs of glazed insensate green
— Gigantic order in the rim
Of each flat leaf. Black eddies brim
Around my heel which, pressing deep,
Accelerates the waiting sleep.

I used to live in sound, and lacked
Knowledge of still or creeping fact,
But now the stagnant strips my breath,
Leant on my cheek in weight of death.
Though so oppressed I find I may
Through substance move. I pick my way,
Where death and life in one combine,
Through the dark earth that is not mine,
Crowded with fragments, blunt, unformed;
While past my ear where noises swarmed
The marsh plant's white extremities,
Slow without patience, spread at ease
Invulnerable and soft, extend
With a quiet grasping toward their end.

And though the tubers, once I rot,
Reflesh my bones with pallid knot,
Till swelling out my clothes they feign
This dummy is a man again,
It is as servants they insist,
Without volition that they twist;

And habit does not leave them tired,
By men laboriously acquired.
Cell after cell the plants convert
My special richness in the dirt:
All that they get, they get by chance.

And multiply in ignorance.

THOM GUNN

From KING MIDAS

THE KING'S SPEECH

The palace clocks are stiff as coats of mail.
Time stopped; I flicked it with my fingernail.
My taste is shattered on these works of art
It fathers by a touch: My bread's too rich,
My butter much too golden, and my meat
A nugget on my plate as cold as ice;
Fresh water in my throat turns precious there,
Where every drop becomes a millionaire.

I rather would be blind than see this world
All affluent in yellow, bought and sold
By Kings that hammer roses into gold:
I did not know I loved their warring thorns
Until they flowered into spikes so hard
My blood made obdurate the rose's stem.
My God was generous. O much too much!
The nearest rose is now beyond my reach.

My furry cat is sculpture, my dog dead;
They stare at me with four wild sparkling eyes
That used to sparkle with dry wit; instead,
Having no wit that they can profit by,
They are pure profit, and their silences
Might make a King go mad, for it was I
Who made their lively muscles stiffly pose —
This jaundice is relentless, and it grows.

Princess, come no closer; my rigid kiss,
Though it is royal still, will make you this
Or that kind of a statue. And my Queen,
Be armed against this gold paralysis,
Or you will starve and thinly bed alone,
And when you dream, a gold mine in your brain
Will have both eyes release their golden ore
And cry for tears they could not cry before.

I would be nothing but the dirt made loud,
A ripeness of the weeds, a timid sun,
Or oppositely be entirely cloud,
Absolved of matter, dissolving in the rain,
Or any small, anonymous live thing
Than be the reigning King of this dominion
Where gold makes poor the richness of decay.
O Dionysus, change me back to clay!

HOWARD MOSS

WREATHS

I

Each day the tide withdraws; chills us; pastes
The sand with dead gulls, oranges, dead men . . .
Uttering love, that outlasts or outwastes
Time's attrition, exiles appear again,
But faintly altered in eyes and skin. . . .

II

Into what understanding all have grown!
(Setting aside a few things, the still faces,
Climbing the phosphorus tide, that none will own)
What paradises and watering-places!
What hurts appeased by the sea's handsomeness!

GEOFFREY HILL

343

A MORNING LETTER

The various members of the hierarchy move,
early morning awakening of the world.
They are like the shuffling of doors,
eager and reluctant, two-faced, I suppose.
Eight o'clock carillons seem universal magic.

Now after hoping for magic,
I was an ordinary messenger to arrive.
Wake up, you are yourself the God of Love
asleep. Whom did you expect? you lay
eyes closed as if afloat.
Proud boy,
whom did you expect who did not wear
only your lesser face? someone from up there?
someone just stepped down from a throne,
smelling of majesty?
Poetry has gone straight to your head.
Your mind wanders.
There are no empty thrones in heaven.
This is early morning in a world without kings.
A small-time Don Juan knocks at your door.
I put on all my pride to climb the stairs.

I was only messenger of myself
to tell you you are yourself Love.
How do you arrange the young men in your dreams?
arranging and re-arranging youth's hierarchies.
Don't you hear the bells ringing,
starting the day out with common tunes?
Ta-ra-ra-boom-de-ay and *Auld Lang Syne*.
Waking up from your Imperial World,
you, for a moment, not I,
are Emperor of my world.
The hierarchies of powers move like doors
— this is a good dream figure.
I am not dreaming.

I came to praise Love, not you.
And the poor writhe.
Bringing spiteful wreathes to celebrate. . . .
I, being poor, brought my pride.
Wake up from your Empire. I am still dreaming.
This is early morning in a world of kings.

ROBERT DUNCAN

HOLDING THE MIRROR UP TO NATURE

Some shapes cannot be seen in a glass,
those are the ones the heart breaks at.
They will never become valentines
or crucifixes, never. Night clouds
go on insanely as themselves
though metaphors would be prettier;
and when I see them massed at the edge
of the globe, neither weasel nor whale,
as though this world were, after all,
non-representational, I know
a truth that cannot be told although
I try to tell you, "We are alone,
we know nothing, nothing, we shall die
frightened in our freedom, the one
who survives will change his name
to evade the vengeance for love . . ."
Meanwhile the clouds go on clowning
over our heads in the floodlight of
a moon who is known to be Artemis
and Cynthia but sails away anyhow
beyond the serious poets with their
crazy ladies and cloudy histories,
their heroes in whose idiot dreams
the buzzard circles like a clock.

HOWARD NEMEROV

ART OF THE SONNET: LVI

Night comes. Day runs for its life into my eyes.
A sound dropped from a tower banishes my throat.
Something always is proving us, thus to assure
us we can let it go, even the last of the light.
But I'm not so sure. I connect my own
hands, not to wring out the bone, but to know
I can withdraw with lavish reluctance and loom
upon myself, keeping days through nights for mornings.
Day comes. Night runs for its life into my eyes,
seeking sound advices. But I will not hang
the dark in a tower, to be shown in all
its hiddenness, though I am promised I can tell
all about it. We haven't thought of ourselves
enough as shelters, and I am practicing.

GIL ORLOVITZ

IN TIME OF GOLD

Now there are gold reflections on the water,
how old am I and how have the years passed?

I do not know your age nor mine, nor when you died;
I only know your stark, hypnotic eyes

are different and other eyes meet mine, amber and fire,
in the changed content of the gazing-glass.

Oh, I am old, old, old and my cold hand
clutches the shawl about my shivering shoulders,

I have no power against this bitter cold,
this weakness and this trembling, I am old;

who am I, why do I wait here, what have I lost?
nothing or everything but I gain this,

an image in the sacred lotus pool,
a hand that hesitates to break

the lily from the lily-stalk and spoil
what may be vision of a Pharaoh's face.

H. D.

STRAY DOG, NEAR ECULLY

Commune du Rhône

The dog called Sesamë slewed out
  Under the Norman arch, open
For the gardener's walked bicycle. No doubt
  On some wild leash still, in three-leggèd loping

He circles the gray stone and barley fringe
  Of the Roman amphitheatre, canting
To quit the guide, the stopped sun, the mélange
  Of Rome's new coin-conducted legion. Panting

He sloughs all touring finally in the shade
  Of a wild apricot-tree, not glancing up.
Fire-points in his sad eyes fix on the fading
  Campagna ghost. A Rouault hoop

The limited landscape wobbles down
  Its sandy track of planetary time.
Back in the courtyard, through the hills around
  Deployed, they search, shouting "Sey-sahm, Sey-sahm."

MARGARET AVISON

SHEPHERD

According to the silence, winter has arrived —
a special kind of winter. I, its inventor,
watch it freeze in calendars and stare
out of clocks. I do not feel its cold.

347

Across a certain farm evening crows go flying,
intervals of sky that I have seen before,
the bearing of a river: I advance, a wanderer
out of thought country, that serious, quiet place,

Till according to the silence all the light is gone
and according to the dark all wanderers are home.

WILLIAM STAFFORD

DEMANDS OF THE MUSE

I call up words that he may write them down.
My falling into labour gives him birth.
My sorrows are not sorrows till he weeps.
I learn from him as much as he from me
Who is my chosen and my tool in time.

I am dumb: my burden is not like another.
My lineaments are hid from him who knows me.
Great is my Earth with undelivered words.
It is my dead, my dead, that sing to him
This ancient moment; and their voice is he.

Born into time of love's perceptions, he
Is not of time. The acts of time to him
Are marginal. From the first hour he knows me
Until the last, he shall divine my words.
In his own solitude he hears another.

I make demands of him more than another.
He sets himself a labour built of words
Which, through my lips, brings sudden joy to him.
He has the illusion that at last he knows me.
When the toil ends, my confidant is he.

Vision makes wise at once. Why then must he
Wait through so many years before he knows me?

The bit is tempered to restrain his words
And make laborious all that's dear to him.
So he remains himself and not another.

Why is he slow to praise me when another
Falls at my feet? What conscience moves in him
To make a stubborn stand before he knows me?
It is reluctance that resolves his words.
I have been cursed, indeed, by such as he.

Yet, though a school invoke me, it is he
I choose, for opposition gives those words
Their strength; and there is none more near to him
In thought. It is by conflict that he knows me
And serves me in my way and not another.

VERNON WATKINS

T. R.

Granted that what we summon is absurd:
Moustaches and the stick, the New York fake
In cowboy costume grinning for the sake
Of cameras which always just occurred;
Granted that his Rough Riders fought a third-
Rate army badly run, and had to make
Headlines to fatten Hearst; that one can take
Trust-busting not precisely at its word;

Robinson, who was drunken and unread,
Received a letter with a White House frank.
To court the Muse, T. R. might well have killed her,
And had her stuffed, yet here this mountebank
Chose to belaurel Robinson instead
Of famous men like Richard Watson Gilder.

DONALD HALL

TO THE SNAKE

Green Snake, when I hung you round my neck
and stroked your cold, pulsing throat
    as you hissed to me, glinting
arrowy gold scales, and I felt
    the weight of you on my shoulders,
and the whispering silver of your dryness
    sounded close at my ears —

Green Snake — I swore to my companions that certainly
    you were harmless! But truly
I had no certainty, and no hope, only desiring
    to hold you, for that joy,
                   which left
a long wake of pleasure, as the leaves moved
and you faded into the pattern
of grass and shadows, and I returned
smiling and haunted, to a dark morning.

DENISE LEVERTOV

THE CONSTRUCTED SPACE

Meanwhile surely there must be something to say,
Maybe not suitable but at least happy
In a sense here between us two whoever
We are. Anyhow here we are and never
Before have we two faced each other who face
Each other now across this abstract scene
Stretching between us. This is a public place
Achieved against subjective odds and then
Mainly an obstacle to what I mean.

It is like that, remember. It is like that
Very often at the beginning till we are met
By some intention risen up out of nothing.
And even then we know what we are saying

Only when it is said and fixed and dead.
Or maybe, surely, of course we never know
What we have said, what lonely meanings are read
Into the space we make. And yet I say
This silence here for in it I might hear you.

I say this silence or, better, construct this space
So that somehow something may move across
The caught habits of language to you and me.
From where we are it is not us we see
And times are hastening yet, disguise is mortal.
The times continually disclose our home.
Here in the present tense disguise is mortal.
The trying times are hastening. Yet here I am
More truly now this abstract act become.

W. S. GRAHAM

AUBADE: THE DESERT

Dunes are graying that were blackest;
Truckers catching a quick breakfast
Where the all-night pinks the cactus
    Think the morning looks okay;
But these couples who awaken
Perched above their eggs and bacon
Eye with arid eyes the sacred
    Languors of beginning day.

Now their linking turns astringent;
Though a kiss may seem convincing
And beholden to some clinching
    Moment of their happy play,
All their wooing of love's magic
Breaks like a mirage — so fragile
Is their nearest simulacrum,
    The black art of being gay.

Even whispers are too risky;
Through a desert streaked with mystic
Splendors of the dawn will whisk off
   Lovers with no more to say.
Yet what roadman but feels richer
As he stakes out wonder-stricken
Claims on sweetness through these kitchen
   Odors and the stink backway?

FREDERICK BOCK

SKYKOMISH RIVER RUNNING

Aware that summer baked the water clear
Today I came to see a fleet of trout
But as I wade the salmon limp away,
Their dorsal fins like gravestones in the air,
On their sides the red that kills the leaves.
Only sun can beat a stream this thin.
The river Sky is humming in my ear.

Where this river empties in the sea
Trout are waiting for September rain
To sting their thirst alive. If they speed
Upstream behind the kings and eat the eggs
The silvers lay, I'll pound the drum for rain.
But sunlight drums, the river is the same
Running like old water in my ear.

I will cultivate the trout, teach their fins
To wave in water like the legs of girls
Tormented black in pools. I will swim
A week to be a witness to the spawning,
Be a trout, eat the eggs of salmon —
Anything to live until the trout and rain
Are running in the river in my ear.

The river Sky is running in my hair.
I am floating past the troutless pools
Learning water is the easy way to go.

I will reach the sea before December
When the Sky is turning grey and wild
And rolling heavy from the east to say
Late autumn was an oriental child.

RICHARD F. HUGO

CLOSE-UP

Are all these stones
   yours
I said
and the mountain
pleased

but reluctant to
admit my praise could move it much

shook a little
and rained a windrow ring of stones
to show
that it was so

Stonefelled I got
up addled with dust

and shook
   myself
without much consequence

Obviously I said it doesn't pay
to get too
close up to
   greatness

and the mountain friendless wept
   and said
it couldn't help
itself

353

A. R. AMMONS

From THE KINGDOM OF POETRY

SWIFT

What shall Presto do for pretty prattle
To entertain his dears? Sunday: lightning fifty times!
This week to Flanders goes the Duke of Ormond!
Small hope of him, although he loves me well!

All of my hopes now possible,
None certain. As, my lampoon
Talked up all over, cried up to the sky
— You are an impudent slut to be so positive
Though all has gone just as you said it would!
Sirrah! write constantly! don't I write every day
And sometimes twice? Stella writes like an emperor.

Sirrah, I am surprised forever — by myself!
Or by the others — dee dee: an angel child
Stupid in me, stupid or innocent
Astonished by the gush of vanity
The stone and eyes of pride — yet equally
By the least straw or glitter of nobility!

— Faith, Madame Dingley, what think you of the
    world to come?
Patience! Patience is a gay thing — O saucy rogues,
Patience is better than luck: be gay till I return.

Mr. Harley speaks every kind thing to me.
Truly, I do believe, would serve me if I stayed
— Called at the coffee house, stayed there a while,
Coldly conversed with Mr. Addison:
All our friendship and dearness now are off
Is it not odd? I think he has used me ill:
I have as little pleasure as anyone
In all the world, although I am
In full favor with the entire ministry.
Nothing gives Presto any dream of happiness
But letters now and then from his deelest ones.

The pride of power, the pride and pleasure of place
   and power are Towers
And trivial toys which lure me grievously
Ravaging furiously in a lunation's infuriation. . . .
Bursting the Rome in my head, my empire!
Gulliver? gullible! The Caesars in my heart
Tell me how all infamy is possible,
And certain treacheries extremely probable!

I must take leave of deelest MD now. Prithee,
Be merry, patient girls and love your Presto.
I have read all the trash and I am weary:
Deelest lives, there is peace and quiet with thee
And thee alone. None have the leisure here for little
   things.
Farewell again, dear rogues; I am never happy
But when I think of thee MD. Sirrah,
I have had enough of courts and ministries.
I wish I were once more at Laracor:
Faith, do you know each syllable I write
I hold my lips exact for all the world
As if I talked the little language with MD.

Yesterday died the Duke of Ormond's daughter:
Poor dear, she was with child. She was
My favourite pet — save thee — I hardly knew
A being more valuable, more beautiful,
Of more nobility. I fear the certainty
That she was thrown away quite carelessly,
And merely lacked care. 'Tis clear, at any rate,
That she was very healthy naturally.

— Her Lord's a puppy, I'll no more of him,
Now that he's lost his only valuable . . .
— I hate life when I see it thus exposed
To accidents like these, so many thousands
Burthening the earth with their stupidity,
While such as she must die — abruptly — pointlessly —

Somebody is coming wants a little place.
My heart is set upon the cherry trees
By the river side. My saucy sluts
Farewell my deelest Nite poo dee MD. . . .

Y'see a Sea that's ten miles wide, a town
On t'other side, ships sailing in the Sea
Discharging great Canons at MDs and mee,
I see a great Sky, Moon and Stars, and ALL:
          I am a Fool.

                    DELMORE SCHWARTZ

DREAM

I see you displaced, condensed, within my dream,
Yet here before me in your daily shape.
And think, can my dream touch you any way
Or move you as in it you otherwise moved?

I prosper in the dream, yet may it not
Touch you in any way or make you move.
It is the splendour of the possible
Not to appear in actual shape and form.

It is the splendour of the actual
So to be still and still be satisfied,
That any else or more becomes a dream,
Displaced, condensed, as by my dreamed regard.

                    JOSEPHINE MILES

THE FIRE AT ALEXANDRIA

Imagine it, a Sophocles complete,
the lost epic of Homer, including no doubt

his notes, his journals, and his observations
on blindness. But what occupies me most,
with the greatest hurt of grandeur, are those
magnificent authors, kept in scholarly rows,
whose names we have no passing record of:
scrolls unrolling Aphrodite like Cleopatra
bundled in a rug, the spoils of love.

Crates of volumes on the wharves,
and never opened, somehow started first.
And then, as though by imitation, the library
took. One book seemed to inspire another,
to remind it of the flame enclosed
within its papyrus like a drowsy torch.
The fire, roused perhaps by what it read,
its reedy song, raged Dionysian, a band
of Corybantes, down the halls now headlong.

For all their tears the scribes,
unable to douse the witty conflagration —
spicy too as Sappho, coiling, melted
with her girls: the Nile no less, reflecting,
burned — saw splendor fled, a day consummate
in sunset ardencies. Troy at its climax
(towers finally topless) could not have been
more awesome, not though the aromatic house
of Priam mortised the passionate moment.

For here inside the holocaust
like a flock of phoenixes the luminaries
hand in hand composed a frantic dance.

Now whenever I look into a flame
I try to catch a single countenance:
Cleopatra, winking out from every joint;
Tiresias eye to eye; a magnitude, long lost,
restored to the sky and the stars he once
struck unsuspected parts of into words.

Fire, and I see them resurrected,
madly crackling perfect birds, the world
lit up as by a golden school, the flashings
of the fathoms of set eyes.

T. WEISS

LINES FOR A YOUNG WANDERER IN MEXICO

This lonely following in the old town
At dark, which hides the old blood drawn up
From the Latin bricks your feet form on
In the light rain, after many dead
Women and men, after the small child
Who burns in the big, Mexican sun
And cries with you in these late night times —
But laughs when you do not — this wander-
ing, I say, is a dancing. Young man
You come before these live and dead and
Dance. Light clothed and lithe, intent, you dance
Before them all, without any songs.
The supple changings of your limbs pass,
Movement to movement, in all the grace
Of youth, of distance from the long dead
In the audience of wanderers.
You hold the agony both of young
And old in the cloak of your turning
Body, which quickens to a spider,
Wheeling, fragile, and quickens to a
Star. I desire to shout words of praise,
Shout arrogantly over the heads
Of the people: See, see, his dancing
Is not the dancing of the harlot.
It goes up from the midst of us all
Sudden and male and sweet, until it
Falls back on this rain wet, brick real street.

JOHN LOGAN

TEACHING SWIFT TO YOUNG LADIES

Garments of inattention, oh mere items,
Wagging your countenances here and there,
You blunt obstructions to my thoroughfare,
Who plucked you from your white paternal stems
And told you, go to school? Quotidians
With Dresden crockery faces, pastry hair,
You with the *balcon,* you with the *derrière,*
You with the eyes like idiot apothegms . . .

Well, do the crossword puzzle, go to sleep,
Mouth open, hands laid vulnerable in your lap.
Reason and I will rage at your dumb nap
As we always rage, and you, I guess, will keep
Some infantile kind of chastity as you go,
Safe in a world you do not need to know.

WILLIAM DICKEY

THE LANDFALL

Blue water; upon it two possible movements.
For hours I put them together.
My shoulders shut and were opened,
And the land fell out of the world.
In my parallel hands I turned
The huge sea over and over,
And looked in her eyes as I rowed,
Seeing there no promise of landfall,
But only my head set its jaw,

Burn out in her mind, and come back,
And I turned in my ribs, and beheld,
Far back in the whaling glitter,
A place in the sun, a bar
Of sand, a province of shadowless trembling.

We rowed round it, bringing our presence.
In sand we drew a circle for a bed.
Beside it we posted an oar,
And felt, as it rooted in burning,

All fish struck around us down
To the floor of the sea by the sun.
Our garments fell from us like grave-cloths.
Her hair shone on me and hurt me.
I entered her man-killing image;
The oar-stock burst into leaves.
My shoulder-blades hovered above me
Like wings, as we moved with each other.
In her eyes I flew like a gull

On the strength of two possible movements.
And yet, at the height of that motion,
We could not shade one another
In any position we measured.
Pain stitched my white back to the sun.
Her face changed color beneath me.
I dragged the boat onto the bar,
Overturned it, and we crept under.
Each fought to give breath to the other,

As the boards sprained apart in the heat,
And one fiery crack pursued us
Down the hull, where it died on her breast.
A wind reached the air. Another
Thing shone. In the cool-bodied water we knelt,
And righted the boat, and embarked.
We stepped through the moonlight for hours
On wood I waved thinly through water.
At midnight I turned from the ocean,

Up a still, mossed canal between roadways,
With trees broad as lawns leaning over
Our crusted, salt-glittering heads,
And lights going out within houses

As the wind turned around,
And we rose up at last in the boat
By two banks of land balanced strongly,
And touched one another,
Come back from the unrelieved kingdom

To kiss with black lips in the city,
To dream of mild sleep in a bed
Swept clean with a broom of its sand-grains,
Where the frame of a window upon us
Would hold, first a tree, and then features
Emerging from dark into presence
Above the bed's bearable glow, wherefrom
That child, never touched by the rays of the sun,
Might rise, because of love.

JAMES DICKEY

THE DEATH OF MYTH-MAKING

Two virtues ride, by stallion, by nag,
    To grind our knives and scissors:
Lantern-jawed Reason, squat Common Sense,
One courting doctors of all sorts,
    One, housewives and shopkeepers.

The trees are lopped, the poodles trim,
    The laborer's nails pared level
Since those two civil servants set
Their whetstone to the blunted edge
    And minced the muddling devil

Whose owl-eyes in the scraggly wood
    Scared mothers to miscarry,
Drove the dogs to cringe and whine,
And turned the farmboy's temper wolfish,
    The housewife's, desultory.

SYLVIA PLATH   361

From THE BEAN EATERS

WE REAL COOL

The pool players.
Seven at the Golden Shovel.

We real cool. We
Left school. We

Lurk late. We
Strike straight. We

Sing sin. We
Thin gin. We

Jazz June. We
Die soon.

GWENDOLYN BROOKS

THE SPIDER

I

The spider expects the cold of winter.
When the shadows fall in long Autumn
He congeals in a nest of paper, prepares
The least and minimal existence,
Obedient to nature. No other course
Is his; no other availed him when
In high summer he spun and furled
The gaudy catches. I am that spider,
Caught in nature, summer and winter.
You are the symbol of the seasons too.

II

Now to expatiate and temporize
This artful brag. I never saw so quieting

A sight as the dawn, dew-clenched foot-
Wide web hung on summer barn-eaves, spangled.
It moves to zephyrs that is tough as steel.
I never saw so finely-legged a creature
Walk so accurate a stretch as he,
Proud, capable, patient, confident.
To the eye he gave close penetration
Into real myth, the myth of you and me.

III

Yet, by moving eyesight off from this
There is another dimension. Near the barn,
Down meadow to shingle, no place for spiders,
The sea in large blue breathes in brainstorm tides,
Pirates itself away to ancient Spain,
Pirouettes past Purgatory to Paradise.
Do I feed deeper on a spider,
A close-hauled view upon windless meaning,
Or deeper a day or dance or doom bestride
On ocean's long reach, on parables of God?

RICHARD EBERHART

RETURNING TO ROOTS OF FIRST FEELING

Feld, groes or *goers, hus, doeg, dung,*
in field, grass, house, day and dung we share
with those that in the forests went
    singers and dancers out of the dream;
for cradles, goods and hallows came
    long before Christendom,
wars and warblers-of-the-word where

me bifel a ferly, a fairy me thoughte:
and those early and those late saw
some of them poets
a faire felde ful of folke fonde I there bitwene,
for the vain and the humble go into one Man
and as best we can we make his song,

363

a simple like making of night and day
encumbered by vestiges and forebodings
in words of need and hope striving
to awaken the old keeper of the living
and restore lasting melodies of his desire.

ROBERT DUNCAN

ALICE CORBIN IS GONE

Alice Corbin is gone
and the Indians tell us where.
　　She trusted the Indians
　　and they kept a trust in her
She took a four-line Indian song
　　and put it into English.
You can sing it over and over and
　　no harm done:

The wind is carrying me round the sky;
The wind is carrying me round the sky.
　　My body is here in the valley —
The wind is carrying me round the sky.

CARL SANDBURG

NUDE DESCENDING A STAIRCASE

Toe after toe, a snowing flesh,
a gold of lemon, root and rind,
she sifts in sunlight down the stairs
with nothing on. Nor on her mind.

We spy beneath the banister
a constant thresh of thigh on thigh;
her lips imprint the swinging air
that parts to let her parts go by.

364

One-woman waterfall, she wears
her slow descent like any drape
and pausing on the final stair,
collects her motions into shape.

X. J. KENNEDY

SONG

What I took in my hand
grew in weight. You must
understand it
was not obscene.

Night comes. We sleep.
Then if you know what
say it.
Don't pretend.

Guises are
what enemies wear. You
and I live
in a prayer.

Helpless. Helpless,
should I speak.
Would you.
What do you think of me.

No woman ever was,
was wiser
than you. None is
more true.

But fate, love, fate
scares me. What
I took in my hand
grows in weight.

ROBERT CREELEY

IN FAVOR OF ONE'S TIME

The spent purpose of a perfectly marvellous
life suddenly glimmers and leaps into flame
it's more difficult than you think to make charcoal
it's also pretty hard to remember life's marvellous
but there it is guttering choking then soaring
in the mirrored room of this consciousness
it's practically a blaze of pure sensibility
and however exaggerated at least something's going on
and the quick oxygen in the air will not go neglected
will not sulk or fall into blackness and peat

an angel flying slowly, curiously singes its wings
and you diminish for a moment out of respect
for beauty then flare up after all that's the angel
that wrestled with Jacob and loves conflict
as an athlete loves the tape, and we're off into
an immortal contest of actuality and pride
which is love assuming the consciousness of itself
as sky over all, medium of finding and founding
not just resemblance but the magnetic otherness
that that that stands erect in the spirit's glare
and waits for the joining of an opposite force's breath

so come the winds into our lives and last
longer than despair's sharp snake, crushed before it conquered
so marvellous is not just a poet's greenish namesake
and we live outside his garden in pure tempestuous rights

FRANK O'HARA

ANGEL

Above my desk, whirring and self-important
(Though not much larger than a hummingbird)
In finely woven robes, school of Van Eyck,

Hovers an evidently angelic visitor.
He points one index finger out the window
At winter snatching to its heart,
To crystal vacancy, the misty
Exhalations of houses and of people running home
From the cold sun pounding on the sea;
While with the other hand
He indicates the piano
Where the Sarabande No. 1 lies open
At a passage I shall never master
But which has already, and effortlessly, mastered me.
He drops his jaw as if to say, or sing,
"Between the world God made
And this music of Satie,
Each glimpsed through veils, but whole,
Radiant and willed,
Demanding praise, demanding surrender,
How can you sit there with your notebook?
What do you think you are doing?"
However he says nothing — wisely: I could mention
Flaws in God's world, or Satie's; and for that matter
How did he come by *his* taste for Satie?
Half to tease him, I turn back to my page,
Its phrases thus far clotted, unconnected.
The tiny angel shakes his head.
There is no smile on his round, hairless face.
He does not want even these few lines written.

JAMES MERRILL

AFTER PLOTINUS

When a statue turns its real gaze
dust regains its honest place.
The scene goes thin, except the things
that should be where they are: nature
under that still gaze turns real.

Have you felt a statue's fear? It sees
no truth but creatures from its place,
with skulls that mould the statue's world.
Poor stone! We give it all we have to give —
mortality. And it makes our world stone.

WILLIAM STAFFORD

PART VI

1960–1970
(Volumes 97–116)

POPULATION

Like a flat sea,
Here is where we are, the empty reaches
Empty of ourselves

Where dark, light, sound
Shatter the mind born
Alone to ocean

Save we are
A crowd, a population, those
Born, those not yet dead, the moment's

Populace, sea-borne and violent, finding
Incredibly under the sense the rough deck
Inhabited, and what it always was.

GEORGE OPPEN

GRAVELLY RUN

I don't know somehow it seems sufficient
to see and hear whatever coming and going is,
losing the self to the victory
   of stones and trees,
of bending, sandpit lakes, crescent

round groves of dwarf pine;
for it is not so much to know the self
as to know it as it is known
   by galaxy and cedar cone,
as if birth had never found it

and death could never end it:
the swamp's slow water comes
down Gravelly Run fanning the long,
   stone-held algal
hair and narrowing roils between

the shoulders of the highway bridge:
holly grows on the banks in the woods there,
and the cedars' gothic-clustered
   spires could make
green religion in winter bones: so I

look and reflect, but the air's glass
jail seals each thing in its entity: no
use to make any philosophies here:
   I see no
god in the holly, hear no song from

the snowbroken weeds: Hegel is not the winter
yellow in the pines: the sunlight has never
heard of trees: surrendered self among
   unwelcoming forms: stranger,
hoist your burdens, get on down the road

A. R. AMMONS

INSIDE THE RIVER

Dark, deeply. A red.
All levels moving
A given surface.
Break this. Step down.
Follow your right
Foot nakedly in
To another body.
Put on the river
Like a fleeing coat,
A garment of motion,
Tremendous, immortal.
Find a still root

To hold you in it.
Let flowing create
A new, inner being:
As the source in the mountain
Gives water in pulses,
These can be felt at
The heart of the current.
And here it is only
One wandering step
Forth, to the sea.
Your freed hair floating
Out of your brain,

Wait for a coming
And swimming idea.
Live like the dead
In their flying feeling.
Loom as a ghost
When life pours through it.
Crouch in the secret
Released underground
With the earth of the fields
All around you, gone
Into purposeful grains
That stream like dust

In a holy hallway.
Weight more changed
Than that of one
Now being born.
Let go the root.
Move with the world
As the deep dead move,
Opposed to nothing.
Release. Enter the sea
Like a winding wind.
No. Rise. Draw breath.
Sing. See no one.

JAMES DICKEY

From SIERRA KID

HE FACES THE SECOND WINTER

A hard brown bug, maybe a beetle,
Packing a ball of sparrow dung.
    What shall I call you?
Shit beetle? Why're you pushing here
At this great height in the thin air
    With your ridiculous waddle

Up the hard side of Hard Luck Hill?
And the furred thing that frightened me
    Bobcat, coyote, wild dog —
Flat eyes in winter bush, stiff tail,
Holding his ground, a rotten log.
    Grass snakes that wouldn't die,

And night hawks hanging on the rim
Of what was mine. I know them now;
    The have absorbed the mind
Which must endure the freezing snow
They endure and, freezing, find
    A clear sustaining stream.

                  PHILIP LEVINE

TO A VISITING POET IN A COLLEGE DORMITIORY

Here tame boys fly down the long light of halls
In this late nightmare of your fourth decade:
Medley of shoe-thuds, towel-slaps and horseplay,
Clamorous radios, counterpoint of squalling
Bed-springs and shower pipes across your ceiling.

Nocturnal soundings turn you back always
To a broken fountain, faces damp as leaves

Stuck to the fountain's lip in autumn, draining
From an era swamped in war's impersonal seas.
Do you sleep empty and long, or cannonading

Through these nautical chambers, having gathered all
Your strength into one battered bowling ball,
Asleep, ramp up and down these corridors of boys,
Barely knocking at doors, but bursting into
Identical rooms, like icicles ablaze?

Now, as I hope you sleep, I turn these pages
Of your committed life — rather the notations
Of sensation coaxed and cheated into poems.
Loves are interred three deep, or rise like drowned
Ruined choristers, to flaunt your praises.

Fisher of bodies, when the lure is failing,
Still you proffer the old nibble of boy-bait
Though nothing comes now: arias or kingdoms.
You may not deny death, nor contrive it soon.
Only escape, your orphanhood outrun,

Run from the glisten of those refracting egos
Where you could love and loathe yourself on sight,
To the worst priesthood, or test-tube remedy
For fratricidal passion. Run from the children!
To father men and poems in your mind.

CAROLYN KIZER

how many moments must(amazing each
how many centuries)these more than eyes
restroll and stroll some never deepening beach

locked in foreverish time's tide at poise,

love alone understands:only for whom
i'll keep my tryst until that tide shall turn;

and from all selfsubtracting hugely doom
treasures of reeking innocence are born.

Then, with not credible the anywhere
eclipsing of a spirit's ignorance
by every wisdom knowledge fears to dare,

how the(myself's own self who's)child will dance!

and when he's plucked such mysteries as men
do not conceive — let ocean grow again

E. E. CUMMINGS

THE ILLUSTRATION — A FOOTNOTE

Months after the Muse
had come and gone across the lake of vision,
arose out of childhood the long-familiar
briefly-forgotten presaging of her image —

"The Light of Truth" — frontispiece
to "Parables from Nature", 1894 — a picture
intending another meaning than that which it gave
(for I never read the story until now)

intending to represent folly
sinking into a black bog, but for me having meant
a mystery, of darkness, of beauty, of serious
dreaming pause and intensity

where not a will o' the wisp but
a star come to earth burned before the
closed all-seeing eyes
of that figure later seen as the Muse.

By which I learn to affirm
Truth's light at strange turns of the mind's road,
wrong turns that lead
over the border into wonder,

mistaken directions, forgotten signs
all bringing the soul's travels to a place
of origin, a well
under the lake where the Muse moves.

DENISE LEVERTOV

ON A CELTIC MASK BY HENRY MOORE

The burnished silver mask hangs in white air,
The eyes struck out, the lips raised in a smile:
Where eyes had been, the hawk-winged Hebrides,
Tall, weeping waves against their friendless shores,

Rain in small knives that cut the flesh away,
And Sun the sword that flashes from the sky:
Sea-lion-headed creatures stalk these islands,
And breed their young to stand before their graves.

A crying Magdalen sings from her grotto,
Precarious life-in-death between the waters —
None see her breasts, flushed limbs and winding hair —
The women hear her in the new moon's madness.

HORACE GREGORY

REMORSE

The snake tooth pinches his own mail.
The rabid dog fox bites his foot.
Cancerous claw and scorpion tail
turn inward and self-rend. Brute

crab in the box eats the lung.
He tears the fact, unmakes the made.
The pelican who feeds his young
on his own flesh by flesh betrayed

reverses beak to split the wound,
bites on the sack and pulls it through,
throws heart and vitals on the ground
to prove that heart, at least, was true.

RICHMOND LATTIMORE

VETUS FLAMMA

That love which once was nearest to my heart
And pressed against my arm and forehead too,
Is gone and you went with it. We are two.
You have your legends, I, an empty heart;
And in the quieted pounding of that heart,
I hear what future I awaken to.
Night falls each dawn and stays a week or two,
And all there is to eat is my own heart.

I nurse a broken love, your broken word,
And cannot even recollect your name,
But keep the smallest remnant of your word
To ornament my door with what I lost.
Unaging ghost, you never said your name —
You only came to wrestle, and I lost.

ROBERT MEZEY

FOR THE PASSING OF GROUCHO'S PURSUER

PLAYED ALWAYS BY MARGARET DUMONT

*"Someone oughta tear you down and put
up a new building"* — Groucho Marx

Now that high, oft affronted bosom heaves
A final sigh, crushed by the wrecker's ball;
Like a definitive mansard, it leaves
Our view an empty lot. Before the fall
The game was to make sex grotesque, but when

Was anything more grave? For us, our grace
Was being the yoohooed-at, naughty men
Whose eyes would lower, finally, from that face.
Death, be not bowed by that solidity
But bear her ever upward, cloud by cloud,
To where she sits with vast solemnity
Enthroned; and may we, some day, be allowed
    If not a life of constant flight there, than a
    Glimpse of that fierce green land of mink and henna.

JOHN HOLLANDER

NOTES FOR A HISTORY OF POETRY

When Memory's Fabled Daughter
Descended to the Word,
The lapping sound of water
Was profitably heard.
Through language set in motion
By river, stream, or ocean
Men acted their devotion,
Both tragic and absurd.

Absurdity was troubling:
See now the poet's task:
Leave histrionic doubling
To don a simpler mask.
Winds of the world were nipping;
The bardic robe was slipping:
The poet wanders, sipping
The sad, hypnotic flask.

Now tipsy with suggestion
He staggers all alone,
Resolving every question
To solipsistic moan.
The voice was human; therefore
We credited its flaws:
Now it's the blanks we care for,
And listen for the pause.

379

Then crossed with this deflation
Came ironies of style,
Importing conversation,
The squint sardonic smile.
Then "Sir" declines to "Mister",
And "Mister" falls to "Bud";
The hail becomes a whisper,
The rocks dissolve to mud,
Which purify to water
In critical amend,
And memory's fabled daughter
Is Silence in the end.

DAVID DAICHES

POEM

Time and the weather wear away
The houses that our fathers built.
A ghostly furniture remains:
All the sad sofas we have stained
With tears of boredom and of guilt,

The fraying mottoes, the stopped clocks . . .
And still sometimes these monstrous shapes
Haunt the damp parlors of the heart.
What Sunday prisons they recall!
And what miraculous escapes!

DONALD JUSTICE

THE DRAGONFLY

Under the pond, among rocks
Or in the bramble of the water-wood,
He is at home, and feeds the small
Remorseless craving of his dream,

His cruel delight; until in May
The dream transforms him with itself
And from his depths he rises out,
An exile from the brutal night.

He rises out, the aged one
Imprisoned in the dying child,
And spreads his wings to the new sun:
Climbing, he withers into light.

HOWARD NEMEROV

THE ASTRONOMERS OF MONT BLANC

Who are you there that from your icy tower
Inspect the colder distances, the far
Escape of your whole universe to night;
That watch the moon's blue craters, shadowy crust,
And blunted mountains mildly drift and glare,
Ballooned in ghostly earnest on your sight;
Who are you, and what hope persuades your trust?

It is your hope that you will know the end
And compass of our ignorant restraint
In that lost time where what was done is done
Forever as a havoc overhead.
Aging, you search to master in the faint
Persistent fortune which you gaze upon
The perfect order trusted to the dead.

EDGAR BOWERS

AFTER THE NIGHT HUNT

Along the dark bank of the river
The moon through the laurel strikes
With the best inner parts of itself.
Where the ground is bright, it is water.

Part of the moon is its blackness.
It is still, that the river may flow.
I look for the light at its darkest
And step there mile after mile
    And do not fall away.

Snakes slip wholly into the moon
As into the source of their lives;
Bent fish leap out of it quickly
And shine before they return,
And birds hold branches as though
Borne somewhere safely by sleep
As the river would bear them,
Small shadows, tottering hugely,
    And not to fall away.

    At last the lake opens my eyes
As it opens the moon from the forest
Like a great, shining book on its table.
I stand by my dew-heavy blanket
Looking over the vast, trembling script
And joy slides out of my breast
Winding back in a curve through the woods
Where I walked in the dark steps of moonlight
    And did not fall away.

I stand in my own coming sleep,
A tall spirit ready to wind
Like a ball of bright thread the wild river
All night around the still form
That shall lie exposed in the open,
Sustained at the heart of the danger
I have passed in the thickets this night
Which shall keep me safe till I wake
    And rise, and fall away.

JAMES DICKEY

TECHNIQUE ON THE FIRING LINE

The target shudders in the layered heat,
And every aim is hazard. Schooled or not,
Secure and dry, or slick with its own sweat,
The hand alone cannot perfect the shot.

Distance and windage, or the quirks of use,
The sights will compensate. Will they restore,
Where each concentric circle grows diffuse,
An aim whose center can be seen no more?

TURNER CASSITY

STARS OVER THE DORDOGNE

Stars are dropping thick as stones into the twiggy
Picket of trees whose silhouette is darker
Than the dark of the sky because it is quite starless.
The woods are a well. The stars drop silently.
They seem large, yet they drop, and no gap is visible.
Nor do they send up fires where they fall
Or any signal of distress or anxiousness.
They are eaten immediately by the pines.

Where I am at home, only the sparsest stars
Arrive at twilight, and then after some effort.
And they are wan, dulled by much traveling.
The smaller and more timid never arrive at all
But stay, sitting far out, in their own dust.
They are orphans. I cannot see them. They are lost.
But tonight they have discovered this river with no trouble;
They are scrubbed and self-assured as the great planets.

The Big Dipper is my only familiar.
I miss Orion and Cassiopeia's Chair. Maybe they are
Hanging shyly under the studded horizon
Like a child's too-simple mathematical problem.

Infinite number seems to be the issue up there.
Or else they are present, and their disguise so bright
I am overlooking them by looking too hard.
Perhaps it is the season that is not right.

And what if the sky here is no different,
And it is my eyes that have been sharpening themselves?
Such a luxury of stars would embarrass me.
The few I am used to are plain and durable;
I think they would not wish for this dressy backcloth
Or much company, or the mildness of the south.
They are too puritan and solitary for that —
When one of them falls it leaves a space,

A sense of absence in its old shining place.
And where I lie now, back to my own dark star,
I see those constellations in my head,
Unwarmed by the sweet air of this peach orchard.
There is too much ease here; these stars treat me too well.
On this hill, with its view of lit castles, each swung bell
Is accounting for its cow. I shut my eyes
And drink the small night chill like news of home.

SYLVIA PLATH

THE REPLY

I stand in the late sun
With nothing I can name,
Recalling we were one
Before an act became
More than an act should be.
The earth, the darkened tree
Of winter, and the sky
Motionless and thin
Shuddered with your reply:
The emptiness within.

What was I to do?
I did the best I could:
Alone, despising you,
I dug the silent wood
For root and muscle weed.
My hunger and my greed
Thrived on what was small,
Dead seed and crusted thorn.
I lived — and that was all —
Where nothing could be born.

Light fails, and I absorb
A heaviness of air.
Nothing can disturb
Your coming everywhere:
It takes what it denies.
Your eyes within my eyes
Return at last, and I
Am given to the hand
Which bears eternity
To the last command.

PHILIP LEVINE

THE BLACK ART

A woman who writes feels too much,
those trances and portents!
As if cycles and children and islands
weren't enough; as if mourners and gossips
and vegetables were never enough.
She thinks she can warn the stars.
A writer is essentially a spy.
Dear love, I am that girl.

A man who writes knows too much,
such spells and fetiches!
As if erections and congresses and products

385

weren't enough; as if machines and galleons
and wars were never enough.
With used furniture he makes a tree.
A writer is essentially a crook.
Dear love, you are that man.

Never loving ourselves,
hating even our shoes and our hats,
we love each other, *precious*, *precious*.
Our hands are light blue and gentle.
Our eyes are full of terrible confessions.
But when we marry,
the children leave in disgust.
There is too much food and no one left over
to eat up all the weird abundance.

ANNE SEXTON

DEATH'S THE CLASSIC LOOK

Death's the classic look. It goes
down stoneworks carved with Latin Prose
and Poetry. And scholar's Greek
that no one now can really speak,
though it's all guessed at. The long view
contains bits of Etruscan, too,
(as guessed at as the Greek is, but
no one yet has figured out
more than a first few words, and those
the names for fish, bird, water, rose
painted beside the painting of
what a dead man kept to love
inside his tomb). In back of that
the view runs desert-rimmed and flat
past writings that were things, not words:
roses, water, fish, and birds.
The thing before the letters came,
the name before there was a name.

And back of things themselves? Who knows?
Jungle spells it as it grows
where the damp among the shoots
waterlogs the classic roots,
and the skulls and bones of things
last half as long as a bird sings,
as a fish swims, as a rose fills,
opens, lets out its breath, and spills
into the sockets where things crawl,
and death looks like no look at all.

JOHN CIARDI

FROM HERACLITUS

Matter is palsy: the land heaving, water
breaking against it, the planet whirling
days in night. Even at the still point
of night I hear the jockeying for place
and each thing wrestling with itself
to be a wrestler. Is the stress that holds
them, whirling in themselves, an ache?
If so strained to shape and aching for release,
explode to peace! But I am here poised
within this eddy, sentenced to a shape,
and have to wrestle through a gust of violence
before I sleep; so may I make or augment
all these lights at night, so as to give out
all the temporary ornaments I can to peace.

ALAN DUGAN

AFTER A PASSAGE IN BAUDELAIRE

Ship, leaving or arriving,
my soul, leaving or coming into this harbor,
among your lights and shadows shelterd,
at home in your bulk, the cunning

387

regularity and symmetry throughout
of love's design, of will, of your
attractive cells and chambers.

Riding forward, darkest of shades
over the shadowd waters;
into the light, neat, symmetrically
arranged above your watery reflections;
disturbing your own image, moving as you are

    What passenger, what sailor,
looks out into the swirling currents round you,
as if into those depths into a mirror?

What lights in what port-holes
raise in my mind again hunger and impatience?
To make my bed down again, there, beyond me,
as if this room too, my bedroom, my lamp at my side,
were among those lights, sailing out,
    away from me?

We too, among the others, passengers
in that *charme infini et mystérieux*,
in that suitable symmetry, that precision
everywhere, the shining fittings, the fit
of lights and polishd surfaces to the dark,
to the flickering shadows of them,
we too, unfaithful to me, sailing away,
    leaving me.

L'idée poétique, the idea of a poetry,
that rises from the movement, from the
outswirling curves and imaginary figures
round this ship, this fate, this sure thing,

est l'hypothèse d'une être vaste, immense,

compliqué, mais eurythmique

ROBERT DUNCAN

IAMBIC FEET CONSIDERED AS HONORABLE SCARS

You see these little scars? That's where my wife
— The principle of order everywhere —
Grazes me, shooting at the sloppy bear
That lurches from the urinals of life.
He is the principle of god knows what;
He wants things to be shapeless and all hair.
Only a fool would want to fight him fair,
Only a woman would think he could be shot.

WILLIAM MEREDITH

THE MAD SCENE

Again last night I dreamed the dream called Laundry.
In it, the sheets and towels of a life we were going to share,
The milk-stiff bibs, the shroud, each rag to be ever
Trampled or soiled, bled on or groped for blindly,
Came swooning out of an enormous willow hamper
Onto moon-marbly boards. We had just met. I watched
From outer darkness. I had dressed myself in clothes
Of a new fiber that never stains or wrinkles, never
Wears thin. The opera house sparkled with tiers
And tiers of eyes, like mine enlarged by belladonna,
Trained inward. There I saw the cloud-clot, gust by gust,
Form, and the lightning bite, and the roan mane unloosen.
Fingers were running in panic over the flute's nine gates.
Why did I flinch? I loved you. And in the downpour laughed
To see us wrung white, gnarled together, one
Topmost mordent of wisteria,
As the lean tree burst into grief.

JAMES MERRILL

IF THE BIRDS KNEW

It is better this year.
And the clothes they wear
In the gray unweeded sky of our earth
There is no possibility of change
Because all of the true fragments are here.
So I was glad of the fog's
Taking me to you
Undetermined summer thing eaten
Of grief and passage — where you stay.
The wheel is ready to turn again.
When you have gone it will light up,
The shadow of the spokes to drown
Your departure where the summer knells
Speak to grown dawn.
There is after all a kind of promise
To the affair of the waiting weather.
We have learned not to be tired
Among the lanterns of this year of sleep
But someone pays — no transparency
Has ever hardened us before
To long piers of silence, and hedges
Of understanding, difficult passing
From one lesson to the next and the coldness
Of the consistency of our lives'
Devotion to immaculate danger.
A leaf would have settled the disturbance
Of the atmosphere, but at that high
Valley's point disbanded
Clouds that rocks smote newly
The person or persons involved
Parading slowly through the sunlit fields
Not only as though the danger did not exist
But as though the birds were in on the secret.

JOHN ASHBERY

AUTUMN IMAGINED

The shuffle and shudder of Autumn
Are in our love.
Those last thin garments, come
Let's have them off!

Drop them about your knees.
The beech-tree rains its gold.
We are deciduous trees,
And our year grows old.

We cannot procrastinate.
Although we seem to delay
By having children late,
Our Autumn is today.

Indeed, give my body its due,
It read the signs aright
When it trembled at Autumn's hue
On our wedding night.

DONALD DAVIE

From NINE DREAM SONGS

SNOW LINE

It was wet & white & swift and where I am
I don't know. It was dark and then
it isn't.
I wish the barker would come. There seems to be to eat
nothing. I am unusually tired.
I'm alone too.

If only the strange one with so few legs would come,
I'd say my prayers out of my mouth, as usual.
Where are his notes I loved?

There may be horribles; it's hard to tell.
The barker nips me but somehow I feel
he too is on my side.

I'm too alone. I see no end. If we could all
run, even that would be better. I am hungry.
The sun is not hot.
It's not a good position I am in.
If I had to do the whole thing over again
I wouldn't.

JOHN BERRYMAN

MIRAMAR BEACH

The night is still. The unfailing surf
In passion and subsidence moves
As at a distance. The glass walls,
And redwood, are my utmost being.
And is there there in the last shadow,
There in the final privacies
Of unaccosted grace, — is there,
Gracing the tedium to death,
An intimation? something much
Like love, like loneliness adrowse
In states more primitive than peace,
In the warm wonder of winter sun.

J. V. CUNNINGHAM

AFTER LORCA

The clock says "When will it be morning?"
The sun says "Noon hurt me."
The river cries with its mouthful of mud
And the sea moves every way without moving.

Out of my ear grew a reed
Never touched by mouth.
Paper yellows, even without flame,
But in words carbon has already become diamond.

A supple river of mirrors I run on
Where great shadows rise to the glance,
Flowing all forward and bringing
The world through my reflection.

A voice like a ghost that is not
Rustle the dead in passage
Leaving the living chilled,
Wipe clear the pure glass of stone.

Wipe clear the pure stone of flesh.
A song tickling God's ear
Till he laughs and catches it with his hand.
A song with a man's face
That God holds up in his fingers.

TED HUGHES

THE WORDS

Wind, bird, and tree,
Water, grass, and light:
In half of what I write
Roughly or smoothly
Year by impatient year,
The same six words recur.

I have as many floors
As meadows or rivers,
As much still air as wind
And as many cats in mind
As nests in the branches
To put an end to these.

Instead, I take what is:
The light beats on the stones,
And wind over water shines
Like long grass through the trees,
As I set loose, like birds
In a landscape, the old words.

DAVID WAGONER

IN MEMORY OF V. R. LANG

(1924–1956)

I wore this very dress
The night that Virgil died.

I was there and I remember the brown brocade
With pearls like tears gleaming on the bodice.
We lounged at court, at ease, on lavender cushions,
Toating Augustus, when Maecenas brought the news.
I remember you held his wrinkled ringless hands,
Gazing deep for comfort in his ancient eyes,
Avoiding relevant words. He looked like Death.
You rose to depart, draped like an autumn goddess,
The jewel I gave you burning at your throat,
And fainted. I caught you as you drifted down.
But, you were no friend to Virgil, wrote him no poems.
The hurt was deeper. Once we stood in the Forum
And stared at a pompous hearse. Your beautiful eyes,
Full of the tears of the ages, said everything dies.

MAC HAMMOND

SEEING AUDEN OFF

Ithaca last night, Syracuse at noon, Cedar Rapids tonight.
His face cracked like a dry salt flat, a line for every poem,
394   he tries two airport Gibsons, reserved (behind dark glasses)
for his flight. Sleet primes the runways, candlelight

preserves the bar. The jets suck air, burning their own feces.
Jakarta, Shannon, Idlewild, are everywhere the same.
Ithaca and Syracuse behind him, Iowa tonight.

He autographs deserted landing strips. In Iowa tonight
he'll sign five gins, whet his faults, and lust for limestone.
He has his autopilot on; who am I to name the pieces
into which a poet cracks? Fire and sleet and candlelight.
I gulp the beer he pays for, and see through his smeared
    glasses
the dark impossibility of home: we drink the price of being
    done
with Ithaca and Syracuse; I wave him off, toward Iowa,
    tonight.

PHILIP BOOTH

THE GARDENS OF PROSERPINE

1897, 1962

Iron queen of uncreations
   And of aborted birth,
Her pedestals new nations,
   Her form benchmarks the Earth.
    With all life disregarded,
    And greed no more rewarded,
    Her alias discarded,
She concedes Death his worth.

If life renews without her,
   And Death finds there new need,
Death was too long about her
   That she should now be freed.
    Lace mantle ordered rightly,
    The tiny crown set tightly,
    Her double chins unsightly,
She counts the alien seed.

TURNER CASSITY

HERE LIES . . .

Here lies a poet who would not write
His soul runs screaming through the night,
"Oh give me paper, give me pen,
And I will very soon begin."

Poor Soul, keep silent. In Death's clime
There's no pen, paper, notion — and no Time.

STEVIE SMITH

LIKE ROUSSEAU

She stands beside me, stands away,
the vague indifference
of her dreams. Dreaming, to go on,
and go on there, like animals fleeing
the rise of the earth. But standing
intangible, my lust a worked anger
a sweating close covering, for the crudely salty soul.

Then back off, and where you go? Box of words
and pictures. Steel balloons tied to our mouths.
The room fills up, and the house. Street tilts.
City slides, and buildings slide into the river.
What is there left, to destroy? That is not close,
or closer. Leaning away in the angle of language.
Pumping and pumping, all our eyes criss cross
and flash. It is the lovers pulling down empty structures.
They wait and touch and watch their dreams
eat the morning.

LEROI JONES

ABOUT MY POEMS

How fashionably sad my early poems are!
On their clipped lawns and hedges the snows fall;

Rains beat against the tarpaulins of their porches,
Where, Sunday mornings, the bored children sprawl,
Reading the comics, before the parents rise.
— The rhymes, the meters, how they paralyze!

Who walks out through their streets tonight? No one.
You know these small towns, how all traffic stops
At ten; the corner streetlamps gathering moths;
And the pale mannequins waiting in dark shops,
Undressed, and ready for the dreams of men.
— Now the long silence. Now the beginning again.

DONALD JUSTICE

METAPHYSIC OF SNOW

Tumbling, pausing, leaping, knocking together,
but always in ranks and serries, grimly in order,
herded by wind aslant the insentient trees,
the cold cattle of heaven come down, come down.

Now they are dancing, swinging in perfect figures,
in perfect time, with a thousand subtle kinds
of counter-point and turn and counter-turn;
stars trail from their horns, leap from their shoulders.

Arm in glittering arm, the galaxies
wheel like fat grandes-dames at the whim of air,
waltz after wheezing waltz, night after night,
or fling up their jewelled skirts and fall into bed.

The wind blows as he goes on his icy flute,
and numb, mindless, stumbling, willy nilly,
drunk on the stream of his music the cattle come,
reeling to left and right, and always, down.

DONALD FINKEL

From CONTRA MORTEM

Thirty spokes unite in one nave,
And because of the part where nothing is
We have the use of a wheel.

— Lao–tse

THE BEING

Wherever shadow falls wherever the drowning
of darkness in great light takes waking under
and still awake and still alldiscerning
reaching as if to enter
in anysoever passages or subsurfaces burning
like a dry film upon the inner attaining
of earth of leaf of water of stone
of blood There murmuring in the din
of a talontaken grievance There in a flood
seething or in the rattle
of dry snowseas There trembling for the mood
of hysterical winds deceitful thistles
meteors blooming There in the huge fire
that rusts every thing away the opening middle
where the world falls in forever There There.

THE LITTLE DEATH

Falling plummeting unexpectedly sickeningly
through the regions of gray cloud inhabited
by floating objects such as an eye
that grows on a stem a bed
hopping like a rabbit a glass finger a tray
of rings and minnows a wooden boy
a pistol descending through this
in rolling swoops backward helpless
filled with nausea until far far down
far in a distant night
the clouds open on a dark pool and then
a reflected star With a desolate

cry falling falling falling into the star
the candleflame the spark and through and out
in the noplace where all the nothings never are.

THE COMING OF SNOW

Along the denuded aisles a shadow walks
casting no body bending no branch nor cracking
one dry twig It sighs and talks
or maybe only the bracken
is mumbling in the wind nothing or no one takes
the time to care The snow comes a few flakes
unobserved then thicker softening
the raw air almost as in the spring
apple petals falling diffuse the sun
but cold and with a tang
of reality And though at first they seem to run
him through and vanish on his tongue
slowly he takes an outline and footprints show
the passage he has truly made among
the rubble graces brightening in the snow.

THE WATER

The brook had been frozen almost everywhere Mounds
of snow covered the ice voluptuously serene
and white as corpseflesh and quiet small sounds
came from the holes where the black skein
of water continued winding But now
only the scraps and tatters of the snow
are left on the banks and the water
seems purged of darkness brighter
than its winding immanence In the shallows
where pebbles excite the current
the brook is shaken like the quivering lightandshadow
of aspenleaves or like the cadence
of hundreds of migrant wings flashing in sunlight
against the flow forever far from their nests
and singing singing so pleasantly in their flight.

THE LEAVES

If the sky were green instead of blue its green
would be the aspenleaves which have the same
inlighted sweet intensity of tone
and are the first to come
in spring closefollowed by hickory ash persimmon
and the rest with butternut last Each has its own
conception of green some yellow some blue
some like the rockmaple reddish nor
is any leaf precisely like any other
Their tide assaults the mountain
by way of the gradual foothills Greening breakers
lunge and snap at the heights counting
the evenings forest by forest until the waves
splash on the far high summit announcing
the actual world in the heyday of the leaves.

THE WOMAN'S GENITALS

Oh this world and oh this dear worldbody
see how it has become become become
how it has flowered and how it has put on gaudy
appearances how it is a plum
in its ripening a rose in its reddening a berry
in its glittering a finch in its throbbing a cowry
in its extraordinary allusiveness a night
of midsummer in its fragrance a tide
in its deepsurging and a dark woodland spring
in its concealing sources
see how it is velvety how its innerness clings
and presses how nearly it repulses
how it then takes and cherishes how it is austere
how it is free how it reviles abuses
and how it is here and how it was always here.

HAYDEN CARRUTH

THE WEDDING NIGHT

There was this time in Boston
before spring was ready — a short celebration —
and then it was over.
I walked down Marlborough Street the day you left me
under branches as tedious as leather,
under branches as stiff as drivers' gloves.
I said, (but only because you were gone)
"Magnolia blossoms have rather a southern sound,
so unlike Boston anyhow,
and whatever it was that happened, all that pink,
and for so short a time,
was unbelievable, was pinned on."

The magnolias had sat once, each in a pink dress,
looking, of course, at the ceiling.
For weeks the buds had been as sure bodied
as the twelve year old flower girl I was
at Aunt Edna's wedding.
Will they bend, I had asked,
as I walked under them toward you,
bend two to a branch,
cheek, forehead, shoulder to the floor?
I could see that none were clumsy.
I could see that each was tight and firm.
Not one of them had trickled blood —
waiting as polished as gull beaks,
as closed as all that.

I stood under them for nights, hesitating,
and then drove away in my car.
Yet one night in the April night
someone (someone!) kicked each bud open —
to disprove, to mock, to puncture!
The next day they were all hot-colored,
moist, not flawed in fact.
Then they no longer huddled.
They forgot how to hide.

Tense as they had been
they were flags, gaudy, chafing in the wind.
There was such abandonment in all that!
Such entertainment
in their flaring up.

After that, well —
like faces in a parade,
I could not tell the difference between losing you
and losing them.
They dropped separately after the celebration,
handpicked,
one after the other like artichoke leaves.
After that I walked to my car awkwardly
over the painful bare remains on the brick sidewalk,
knowing that someone had, in one night,
passed roughly through,
and before it was time.

ANNE SEXTON

From THROUGH THE SMOKE HOLE

For Don Allen

I

There is another world above this one; or outside of this one;
the way to it is thru the smoke of this one, & the hole that
smoke goes through. The ladder is the way through the
smoke hole; the ladder holds up, some say, the world above;
it might have been a tree or pole; I think it is merely a way.

Fire is at the foot of the ladder. The fire is in the center. The
walls are round. There is also another world below or inside
this one. The way there is down thru smoke. It is not
necessary to think of a series.

Raven and Magpie do not need the ladder. They fly thru the smoke holes shrieking and stealing. Coyote falls thru; we recognize him only as a clumsy relative, a father in old clothes we don't wish to see with our friends.

It is possible to cultivate the fields of our own world without much thought for the others. When men emerge from below we see them as the masked dancers of our magic dreams. When men disappear down, we see them as plain men going somewhere else. When men disappear up we see them as great heroes shining through the smoke. When men come back from above they fall thru and tumble; we don't really know them; Coyote, as mentioned before.

GARY SNYDER

"THE WISH TO BE BELIEVED"

It is never enough to know what you want.
The brick in your hand, dampened but solid, crumbles,
and a boundary being built, in the midst of building,
stops. (Why shouldn't one say what it is like?
How would they ever know, otherwise?)

You find in your pocket a key, two keys,
one with a curlicued stem, heavy, absurd,
the other perfectly blank, anonymous.
Who knows what they open; you glance at keyholes.
It is like — you can't, after all, say exactly.

And the rooms, supposing you enter them calmly,
are different from your own; one is bare,
with a gilt-framed mirror facing the door.
Suppose you are tempted to insert your face —
you see a face, and the door closing.

And you go on past the half-built boundary,
clicking the keys together, entering.

And you reach, finally, a vivid, absolute place,
and stand in the center, saying to someone,
"Believe. Believe this is what I see."

MONA VAN DUYN

THE DOOR

Too little
has been said
of the door, its one
face turned to the night's
downpour and its other
to the shift and glisten of firelight.

Air, clasped
by this cover
into the room's book,
is filled by the turning
pages of dark and fire
as the wind shoulders the panels, or unsteadies that burning.

Not only
the storm's
breakwater, but the sudden
frontier to our concurrences, appearances
and as full of the offer of space
as the view through a cromlech is.

For doors
are both frame and monument
to our spent time,
and too little
has been said
of our coming through and leaving by them.

CHARLES TOMLINSON

OCTOBER

My wife sits reading in a garden chair
Pope's *Moral Essays* by the failing light,
As leaves turn epileptic in the air
And through the woods come poachers, and the night.

Pope's natural habitat: a bullet rips
The homespun silence and the volume slips,
But catching it she finds her place in time
And never drops the stitches of a rhyme.

Braving the season in the name of wit,
She holds each couplet in such close esteem
No maniac can put a hole in it.
The year's in tatters, but she makes a seam;

The house is civil, though the wood's insane,
And man's the missing link who lets the chain-
Of-being shake. It's hanging by a hair.
My wife sits reading in a garden chair.

BARRY SPACKS

SWAN AND SHADOW

```
                    Dusk
                  Above the
              water hang the
                      loud
                      flies
                      Here
                    O so
                    gray
                    then
              What             A pale signal will appear
              When        Soon before its shadow fades
              Where       Here in this pool of opened eye
              In us    No Upon us As at the very edges
               of where we take shape in the dark air
                this object bares its image awakening
                  ripples of recognition that will
                      brush darkness up into light
even after this bird this hour both drift by atop the perfect sad instant now
                       already passing out of sight
                    toward yet-untroubled reflection
                this image bears its object darkening
              into memorial shades Scattered bits of
              Light     No of water Or something across
              water        Breaking up No Being regathered
              Soon           Yet by then a swan will have
              gone              Yes Out of mind into what
                  vast
                  pale
                  hush
                   of a
                  place
                   past
              sudden dark as
                if a swan
                  sang
```

JOHN HOLLANDER

SECULAR GAMES

Levin, on his way to Kitty's love,
Saw children walking in a row to school,
Bluish doves flying down from the eaves
And little floury loaves thrust out
By an unseen hand. "It all happened at once,"
Tolstoy says: a boy ran suddenly
Toward a dove and glanced back, smiling,
At Levin. The dove flew up, wheeling,

And the snowflakes glittered in the sun.
From the windows came a smell of fresh bread
And the loaves were put out. Remember?
So much grace Tolstoy grants without God.

"It all happened at once," once at midnight
In that unseasonable fall of ours —
It seemed to me the universe slowed down
And lingered in a climate of its choice
As if without the Law. I had a sense
Of something ceded, something given over
In that bad autumn, when day after day
The city warmed, its summer smells restored
To a tempting lie. All our sparrows stayed
While even migratory birds confined
Their circulation, did not go, but hung
Upon the hindered weather like a curse.

I reached our crooked corner where the night
Unwinds. Like Levin, I was on my way.
Slowly the citizens moved past, so many
Allegories of choice, most of them gay
As bright October's wreck or brazenly
Concealing the winter to come. Over us loomed
The ladies' prison where The Girls called down
Inaccurate obscenities to us
Or to each other, inside out. Above
Our "rescued" Ruskin courthouse roof
The tower held its numb Gothic dial
Gold as a medal against the dim sky.

There I stood among The Boys, marvelling
While they murmured by me like a stream
Beneath the shouting girls, shorn Rapunzels
In their castle keep, and stared above
At the clock, at the unfeeling sky
Above even that, wondering what wind
Could carry off our grief, could save us

Or by leaving soothe? Was liberty
To leave enough? It was enough to stay,
To inhabit earth, where we do not stay
But unlike God in heaven, come and go.

RICHARD HOWARD

PRIEST LAKE

How rich we were, to know them, exiles
in our century! Quiet as a bobcat
I come again to their lake, witness
for the jigsaw it takes: one by
one the oak leaves part and establish
their house, dreamed empty today by the careless.

Easy, they said, we tame birds can find
the marsh, the richer grain lavished
where mild wanderers can glean. And they let
this lake maintain them, summers, as they would.
In winter, snow and psychiatry took over. Their
cabin had an arm of the bay for porch.

There they spun. The country seldom
startled as a moose encountered them. Ignored,
they liked it impersonal, spoke German in presence
of the mountains. Now all the Rorschach lakes
deny their shorelines in blizzards, but I come
back, far down these evenings, faithful, to glean.

WILLIAM STAFFORD

THE BEAST IN THE SPACE

Shut up. Shut up. There's nobody here.
If you think you hear somebody knocking
On the other side of the words, pay
No attention. It will be only

The great creature that thumps its tail
On silence on the other side.
If you do not even hear that
I'll give the beast a quick skelp
And through Art you'll hear it yelp.

The beast that lives on silence takes
Its bite out of either side.
It pads and sniffs between us. Now
It comes and laps my meaning up.
Call it over. Call it across
This curious, necessary space.
Get off, you terrible inhabiter
Of silence. I'll not have it. Get
Away to whoever it is will have you.

W. S. GRAHAM

FRAUDULENT DAYS

Fraudulent days, the surfaces collapse
When against them you press your finger
The beautiful brick suit
When you scrape it is only a tinsel clothing
The whole upper stories of the building
Touched, is a seagull's back, revealed

And when I press in on you with my shynesses,
An acceleratedly decreasing circle,
Your eyes look up as if to discourage
Departure. Your eyelids constantly falling
Under the lampshade, beneath this greenish light
In this wholly improvised conviction

MICHAEL BENEDIKT

HURRYING AWAY FROM THE EARTH

The poor, and the dazed, and the idiots
Are with us, they live in the casket of the sun
And the moon's coffin, as I walk out tonight
Seeing the night wheeling their dark wheelbarrow
All about the plains of heaven,
And the stars inexorable rising.
Dark moon! Sinister tears!
Shadow of slums and of the conquering dead!

Some men have pierced the chest with a long needle
To stop their heart from beating any more;
Another put blocks of ice in his bed
So he would die, women
Have washed their hair, and hung themselves
In the long braids, one climbed
A high tree above her house
And lawn and swallowed poisonous spiders —

The time for exhortation is past. I have heard
The iron chairs scraping in asylums,
As the cold bird hunches into the winter
In the windy nights of November.
The coal miners rise from their pits
Like a flash flood,
Like a rice field disintegrating.
Now men cry when they hear stories of someone
    rising from the dead.

ROBERT BLY

DIVINITIES

Having crowded once onto the threshold of mortality
And not been chosen
There is no freedom such as theirs
That have no beginning

The air itself is their memory
A domain they cannot inhabit
But from which they are never absent

What are you they say *that simply exist*
And the heavens and the earth bow to them
Looking up from their choices
Perishing

All day and all night
Everything that is mistaken worships them
Even the dead sing them an unending hymn

W. S. MERWIN

From WHITE-HAIRED LOVER

I swore to stab the sonnet with my pen
Squash the black widow in a grandstand play
By gunning down the sonnet form — and then
I heard you quote my schoolboy love Millay.
I went to find out what she used to say
About her tribulations and her men
And loved her poetry though I now am gray
And found out love of love poems once again.
Now I'm the one that's stabbed — son of a bitch! —
With my own poisoned ballpoint pen of love
And write in *sonnet* form to make my *pitch*,
Words I no longer know the meaning of.
If I could write one honest sentence now
I'd say I love you but I don't know how.

KARL SHAPIRO

USES OF POETRY

Love poems they read
Were work of an aging man
Alone and celibate

Who published them in joy
Of his craftsman's skill,
How they folded into each other.

Many a lust-starched boy
Read them aloud to his girl
Till her widening eyes darkened
Till her breath trembled thin
Till the boy threw down the book
And they folded into each other.

WINFIELD TOWNLEY SCOTT

SLOWLY, SLOWLY WISDOM GATHERS

Slowly, slowly wisdom gathers:
Golden dust in the afternoon,
Somewhere between the sun and me,
Sometimes so near that I can see,
Yet never settling, late or soon.

Would that it did, and a rug of gold
Spread west of me a mile or more:
Not large, but so that I might lie
Face up, between the earth and sky,
And know what none has known before.

Then I would tell as best I could
The secrets of that shining place:
The web of the world, how thick, how thin,
How firm, with all things folded in;
How ancient, and how full of grace.

MARK VAN DOREN

CWMRHYDYCEIRW ELEGIACS*

Go, swallow, and tell, now that the summer is dying,
Spirits who loved him in time, where in the earth he is laid.
Dumb secrets are here, hard as the elm-roots in winter;
We who are left here confront words of inscrutable calm.
Life cuts into stone this that on earth is remembered,
How for the needs of the dead loving provision was made.
Strong words remain true, under the hammer of Babel:
Sleeps in the heart of the rock all that a god would restore.

Never shall time be stilled in the quarry of Cwmrhydyceirw,
Not while the boulder recoils under the force of the fuse.
Tablets imprisoned by rock, inert in the sleeping arena,
Quake in the shudder of air, knowing the swallow has passed.
One grief is enough, one tongue, to transfigure the ages:
Let our tears for the dead earn the forgiveness of dust.

VERNON WATKINS

*In a letter to *Poetry* just a few months before his death the poet told us that the
Welsh name in the title is pronounced Coomrheedercyroo. "It means 'Valley
of the Giants,' and in this quarry I found the memorial stone for Dylan
Thomas, presented by Caedmon, which is in Cwmdonkin Park in Swansea."

THE CHANCES OF RHYME

The chances of rhyme are like the chances of meeting —
    In the finding fortuitous, but once found, binding:
They say, they signify and they succeed, where to succeed
    Means not success, but a way forward
If unmapped, a literal, not a royal succession;
    Though royal (it may be) is the adjective or region
That we, nature's royalty, are led into.
    Yes. We are led, though we seem to lead
Through a fair forest, an Arden (a rhyme
    For Eden) — breeding ground for beasts
Not bestial, but loyal and legendary, which is more
    Than nature's are. Yet why should we speak

413

Of art, of life, as if the one were all form
   And the other all Sturm-und-Drang? And I think
Too, we should confine to Crewe or to Mow
   Cop, all those who confuse the fortuitousness
Of art with something to be met with only
   At extremity's brink, reducing thus
Rhyme to a kind of rope's end, a glimpsed grass
   To be snatched at as we plunge past it —
Nostalgic, after all, for a hope deferred.
   To take chances, as to make rhymes
Is human, but between chance and impenitence
   (A half-rhyme) come dance, vigilance
And circumstance (meaning all that is there
   Besides you, when you are there). And between
Rest-in-peace and precipice,
   Inertia and perversion, come the varieties
Increase, lease, re-lease (in both
   Senses); and immersion, conversion — of inert
Mass, that is, into energies to combat confusion.
   Let rhyme be my conclusion.

                  CHARLES TOMLINSON

THE KING'S MEN

What is it, inside them and undeniable,
that mourns him? that drives them, searching
for the moon-shaped tracks of his horse,
a glint of armor within a maze of pines?

He'd know their barbarous need would never wane.
They will keep on to the next horizon,
where he waits. They will keep on, lowering
their barred visors against the setting sun.

                  WILLIAM HEYEN

THE DISTANCES

The accumulation of reefs
piling up one over the others
like thoughts of the sky increasing as the head rises
unto horizons of wet December days perforated
with idle motions of gulls . . . and our feelings.

I've been wondering about what you mean,
standing in the spray of shadows before an ocean
abandoned for winter, silent as a barque of blonde hair.

And the way the clouds are bending, the way they "react"
to your position, where your hands close over your breasts
like an eyelid approving the opening of "an evening's light."

Parasites attach themselves to the moss covering
your feet. Blind Cubans tossing fish across the jetty,
and the sound of blood fixes our eyes on the red waves.

                                    It is a shark!

And our love is that rusted bottle . . . pointing north,
the direction which we turn, conjuring up our silver knives
and spoons and erasing messages in the sand, where you wrote

"freezing in the arctic of our dreams," and I said
"yes" delaying the cold medium for a time
while you continued to "cultivate our possessions."

As the moon probably "continued" to cradle,
tan below the slant of all those wasted trees
while the scent carried us back to where we were:

dancing like the children of great diplomats
with our lean bodies draped in bedsheets and
leather flags while the orchestra made sounds

which we thought was the sky, but was only a series
of words, dying in the thick falsetto of mist.
For what can anyone create from all these things:

the fancied tilt of stars, sordid doves
burning in the hollow brick oven, oceans
which generalize tears. It is known to us

in immediate gestures, like candle drippings
on a silk floor. What are we going to do with anything?
beside pick it up gently and lay it on the breath

of still another morning, mornings which are
always remaining behind for one thing or another
shivering in our faces of pride and blooming attitude.

In the draught of winter air my horse is screaming.
You are welcoming the new day with your hair leaning
against the sand. Feet dive like otters into the frost,

and the sudden blue seems to abandon as you leap. O
to make everything summer! Soldiers move along lines
like wet motions in the violet shade's reappearance.

But what if your shadow no longer extended to my sleeping?
and your youth dissolves in my hand like a tongue, as
the squandered oceans and skies will dissolve into a single
        plane.

(So I'll move along that plane) unnoticed and gray
as a drift of skulls over the cool Atlantic, where I am
standing now, defining you in perhaps the only word I can,

as other words are appearing, so cunningly, on the lips
of the many strips of light. Like naked bodies
stretched out along the only beach that remained:
brown and perfect below the descending of tides.

                                        JIM CARROLL

THE MASOCHIST

My black-eyed lover broke my back,
that hinge I swung on in and out
and never once thought twice about,

expecting a lifetime guarantee.
He snapped that simple hinge for me.
My black-eyed lover broke my back.

All delicate with touch and praise
he one by one undid the screws
that held the pin inside its cup

and when I toppled like a door
— his bitch, his bountiful, his whore —
he did not stay to lift me up.

Beware of black-eyed lovers. Some
who tease to see you all undone,
who taste and take you in the game

will later trample on your spine
as if they never called you *mine,
mine, mine.*

MAXINE KUMIN

OPEN LETTER FROM A CONSTANT READER

To all who carve their love on a picnic table
or scratch it on smoked glass panes of a public toilet,
I send my thanks for each plain and perfect fable
of how the three pains of the body, surfeit,

hunger, and chill (or loneliness), create
a furniture and art of their own easing.
And I bless two public sites and, like Yeats,
two personal sites where the body receives its blessing.

417

Nothing is banal or lowly that tells us how well
the world, whose highways proffer table and toilet
as signs and occasions of comfort for belly and bowel,
can comfort the heart too, somewhere in secret.

Where so much constant news of good has been put,
both fleeting and lasting lines compel belief.
Not by talent or riches or beauty, but
by the world's grace, people have found relief

from the worst pain of the body, loneliness,
and say so with a simple heart as they sit
being relieved of one of the others. I bless
all knowledge of love, all ways of publishing it.

MONA VAN DUYN

VENOM

For William Haast

Forever, it comes from the head. *Where does it end?*
In life-blood. All over it, in fact, like thrown
Off and thrown-again light. There is little help
      For it, but there is some.

    The priest of poison: where is he? Who is
      His latest snake? How does he work?

He has taken it all, brother, and his body lies
    With its hand in ice, in a lung

Of iron
            but at last he rises, his heart changing
What the snake thought. Tooth-marks all over
    Him are chattering of life, not death, not
      What God gave them. He shimmers

With healing. He will lie down again
   With him the snake has entered.
   His blood will flow the length
Of the veins of both. They will clasp arms and double-dream

   Of the snake in the long low smothering
Sun. Look down! They stretch out giving
And taking. Clouds of family beat the windows
   Of doctors with their breath. Here lies

    The man made good by a hundred
   Bites. It is not God but a human
   Body they pray to: Turn the poison
  Round turn it back on itself O turn it
Good: better than life, they whisper:
   Turn it, they hammer whitely:
     Turn it, turn it,
     Brother.

JAMES DICKEY

THE SCHOOL OF NIGHT

What did I study in your School of Night?
When your mouth's first unfathomable yes
Opened your body to be my book I read
My answers there and learned the spell aright,
Yet, though I searched and searched, could never guess
What spirits it raised nor where their questions led.

Those others, familiar tenants of your sleep,
The whisperers, the grave somnambulists
Whose eyes turn in to scrutinize their woe,
The giant who broods above the nightmare steep,
That sleeping girl, shuddering, with clenched fists,
A vampire baby suckling at her toe,

They taught me most. The scholar held his pen
And watched his blood drip thickly on the page
To form a text in unknown characters
Which, as I scanned them changed and changed again:
The lines grew bars, the bars a Delphic cage
And I the captive of his magic verse.

But then I woke and naked in my bed
The words made flesh slept, head upon my breast;
The bed rode down the darkness like a stream;
Stars I had never seen danced overhead.
"A blind man's fingers read love's body best:
Read all of me!" you murmured in your dream.

"Read me, my darling, translate me to your tongue,
That strange Man-language which you know by heart;
Set my words to your music as they fall;
Soon, soon, my love! The night will not be long;
With dawn the images of sleep depart
And its dark wisdom fades beyond recall."

Here I stand groping about the shores of light
Too dazzled to read that fading palimpsest
Faint as whisper that archaic hand
Recalls some echo from your school of night
And dead sea scrolls that were my heart attest
How once I visited your holy land.

A. D. HOPE

AUBADE: DONNA ANNA TO JUAN,
STILL ASLEEP

The window pales, and by its paltry light
    I lose you. I want more.
Rousing (if I ever slept) I slither
    Out of bed, cautiously
Holding my breath, and my breasts in both hands,
    Until the straw subsides

And with no more than a frown you resume
Your peremptory snores.
We have made a hot night of it, one way
Or another, and now

The shutters open onto a darkness
Already not itself.
I'll close them, rescuing the universe,
And return in the same
Silence, breathless with anticipation,
To my place beside you,
Biding my time to take it, when I can,
By some becoming move.
I watch your body wake and make in each
Of its private partings

A circuitous gesture (I wonder
Why they call it coming)
Hardening fast into departure.
From memories of maps
You'd suppose it is the same avenue,
A coming-to that must
Be come to once again, but believe me,
It is a new journey,
On these slopes you will take another fall
Altogether, past old

Suspensions to the present standpoint for
That final balancing
Act of darkness, while in the sudden
Landscape, time — Juan, time dies.
Nothing here will ever happen twice, no
Two mouths drink from the same
Sluggish river, nor one flesh (which we are
Made) be the same giver.
We trust too much to words, repeating mere
Names that were meant for once.

I stare the melted waxworks of your sleep
Into countenance: up!

Odd what we take it onto our heads
    To urge, and stop our mouths
On a steep but merging syllable: O
    It is a gift of tongues
And lungs we lavish on your limbs, thirsting
    For the first occasion
To worship, in the articulate temple,
    The unspeakable god.

RICHARD HOWARD

THE GREEKS

Deep in the air the past appears
As unreal as air to the boy
Or the apple of the world
To a girl whose eyes are pale and mild
Her hair is probably not real gold
Only a very good imitation of the Greeks'
Like a map of that world of early days
Where woman lives on a scarlet cloud
While man in colorless blunt noon
Splashes up at the blue variables
That pass by on an airplane of words
Into the sky which distributes gifts of
Rain and light over our lives equally
Infinite gifts we are unable to behold

TOM CLARK

THE TABLE

To sit composing like a sunlit ghost
Beside the window, saying: if the lost
Wind quicken in the tree, the dancing heaven
Thicken to snowy furrows by evening,
I will have less to tell you. Blue by green,
The lake is where three terns are drifting; when

rth, circling the air, settles beside them,
tighten together on the wide surface

now have lifted. All the window shows
ked water and a green slope. Composing
the sun itself, making the light fall
Neatly on each thing, is to mark the balance
Within which we will find ourselves arranged,
Oddly, in one room, at a stranger's table.

MICHAEL HEFFERNAN

MISSION BAY

The man-made bay, its fat weeds
Hidden by brack water, which daily
Floats the picnic-papers out to sea;
Divided in two by a thin spit of sand
Drying its back in the hot sun.
Then the ocean recovers, and the bay
Becomes one flat pond concealing lives
That are just not interested in mine.
In the eyeless eyes of the fish
People from Arizona drive up in white cars,
Suspended like things in a test tube among
The blunt orange buildings lining the shore
Of this bay where I learned how to speak, to
And of myself, by merely repeating the words
With no more distance than the earth can bear.

JOHN KOETHE

FIRE ISLAND

The Milky Way above,
the milky waves beside,
when the sand is night

the sea is galaxy.
The unseparate stars
mark a twining coast

with phosphorescent surf
in the black sky's trough.
Perhaps we walk on black

star ash, and watch
the milks of light
foam forward, swish and spill

while other watchers, out
walking in their white,
great swerve, gather

our low spark,
our little Way the dark
glitter in their sight.

MAY SWENSON

INVOCATION

Silent, about-to-be-parted-from house.
Wood creaking, trying to sigh, impatient.
Clicking of squirrel-teeth in the attic.
Denuded beds, couches stripped of serapes.

Deep snow shall block all entrances
and oppress the roof and darken
the windows. O Lares,
don't leave.
The house yawns like a bear.
Guard its profound dreams for us,
that it return to us when we return.

DENISE LEVERTOV

HANDBOOK OF VERSIFICATION

One thought the recurring "image" in the poet's song an
  instance of consciousness,

Clear, clear day, in sun, one's majority upon one, it
  is seen to be simple obsession, and helpless,

The mind careening through the infinite spaces of itself
  snags on some plain word:

Through and between whose familiar letters the true
  true image of what happened: of the blank world.

GILBERT SORRENTINO

DEAD CENTER

No earthquake. Chapped, a lifting in this field.
Flesh. If indeed flesh, half boiled.
An emergence.
Our mid-winter event for the séance.

She expounds compromise. She. The imprecise
Smile fits the middle of the round face.
Taking. I'm never
More certain we've met before. Some before.

Before glass. After sand. A quality.
Molten? A lapsed work, shall we say?
Your health. Come in.
Between. Between. Between. Between. Between.

CHESTER KALLMAN

HOTEL IN PARIS

Night is a black swan wholly adrift
through liquid prisms of its own understanding.
It passes the moon and rivers; silos, trees,

425

gargoyles, grappling hooks, bicycles, torches,
mangoes, bidets, placentas, shepherds, silence.

It passes the emptiness of corridors and pits,
and approaches the gownlike whisper
of something sliding through alleys
to answer an old man in a dirty tunic
piping on a bamboo flute.

Night is a swan. We see its underbelly; we feel
its outer ripples: and the terrible strength
of each merciful, tucked wing.

DENNIS TRUDELL

TRANSACTION

I attended the burial of all my rosy feelings:
I performed the rites, simple and decisive:
the long box took the spilling of gray ground in
with little evidence of note: I traded slow

work for the usual grief: the services were private:
there was little cause for show, though no cause not
to show: it went indifferently, with an appropriate
gravity and lack of noise: the ceremonies of the self

seem always to occur at a distance from the ruins of men
where there is nothing really much to expect, no arms,
no embraces: the day was all right: certain occasions
outweigh the weather: the woods just to the left

were average woods: well, I turned around finally from
the process, the surface smoothed into a kind of seal,
and tried to notice what might be thought to remain:
everything was there, the sun, the breeze, the woods

(as I said), the little mound of troublesome tufts of
grass: but the trees were upright shadows, the breeze

was as against a shade, the woods stirred gray
as deep water: I looked around for what was left,

the tools, and took them up and went away, leaving
all my treasures where they might never again disturb
me, increase or craze: decision quietens:
shadows are bodiless shapes, yet they have a song.

A. R. AMMONS

COUNTERPARTS

There is no sky today. Echoes of birds
worry their way northward. They must have
everything repeated many times. You are here
and elsewhere, your face breeding like fear.
It is not for nothing that I keep my hands
raised for the fall. This is a country of smaller wars.

You have your office and ranch house, your foreign car
and family. You are still not necessary. I see
your face in a photograph from the war, surrounded
by soldiers convinced by their smiles. Later
there will be that look of faint surprise
as you meet the world and lie down to be counted.

The colors of blood are legion. Of necessity
your name must be also. Choose any direction
and it will lead to the heart. We call it a diamond.
Placed on the ground, we heap stones around it,
logs over it. What loss to a two car family?
We bring flowers. In error, people will call it a funeral.

Days pass, fires to be tended — their flames
like small fingers looking for your eyes. You have
already torn them from you. All things desire
to be surrounded by stone. There is rain on my hands.
There is the steady thud of birds falling into hills
sloping with sheep. We memorize the art of decay.

427

A swift and pervading grey slips through my fingers,
cloud covered and accustomed to war. A bone
is my weapon. It may not have been mine. Each end
is sharpened and carefully aimed. The ground
and pine boughs hiss a warning. There are rumours
of summer. There are seasons no longer acceptable.

STEPHEN DOBYNS

UNTITLED

Words do not grow on the landscape
But night and day fall there,
The sun and moon sink, and there
The wind brushes the face of the earth
And its outstretched trees.

Then let us sit in silence on the hillside
By the bending grasses, and the restless wind;
There is the lesson that there is no peace.
Alone, each on his own far hillside,
Let us sit and not break the silence.

JEAN MALLEY

THE MUSIC OF THE SPHERES

Hard knowledge to come by. Finally,
the greatest satisfaction is to survive
not as knowledge or music
but on *this* sphere as old magic.
The black highlights take away parents
and friends in old story, style of mystery.

Who goes there? — among gravestones
could crush you, ground give way under,
and all the time the dead
reacting like fiber in an earth of bed.

Hard to see your way, that doesn't help
to *see* help or know old love buried.

Still, these were something to stand on,
bodies we held to, and hold to,
to whom we were told to
promise small favors, and we didn't.
They gave us guilt and the past,
and we sing what we know best.

MARVIN BELL

THE MESSENGER

Is this man turning angel as he stares
At one red flower whose name he does not know,
   The velvet face, the black-tipped hairs?

His eyes dilated like a cat's at night,
His lips move somewhat but he does not speak
     Of what completes him through his sight.

His body makes to imitate the flower,
Kneeling, with splayed toes pushing at the soil,
     The source, crude, granular, and sour.

His stillness answers like a looking glass
The flower's, it is repose of unblown flame
     That nests within the glow of grass.

Later the news, to branch from sense and sense,
Bringing their versions of the flower in small
     Outward into intelligence.

But meanwhile, quiet and reaching as a flame,
He bends, gazing not at but into it,
     Tough stalk, and face without a name.

429

THOM GUNN

ISLANDERS, INLANDERS

For John and Catherine Howett

Welcomed to islands over the long water,
they jibe about our bow, inconstant kingdoms,
rock bluffs, the sea mews, under spells of water.
And afterwards in cottages with tiny gardens
remembered days at sea, the wind in wheatfields
runs tides up to our shores, our easy exile
ground on the pebbles, beached but always waiting.

Far into continents, at night the freight trains
wail over prairies. Land by long extension
brings us no homestead. Out from glowing cities
on roads we count the poles, deep into darkness,
place after place we touch no more than going.

MICHAEL MOTT

SUNSET AFTER RAIN

Old cloud passes mourning her daughter
can't hear what anyone tells her
every minute is one of the doors that never opened

Little cold stream wherever I go
you touch the heart
night follows

The darkness is cold
because the stars do not believe in each other

W. S. MERWIN

SEPTEMBER 2

In the evening there were flocks of nighthawks
passing southward over the valley. The tall
sunflowers stood, burning on their stalks

to cold seed, by the still river. And high
up the birds rose into sight against the darkening
clouds. They tossed themselves among the fading
landscapes of the sky like rags, as in
abandonment to the summons their blood knew.
And in my mind, where had stood a garden
straining to the light, there grew
an acceptance of decline. Having worked,
I would sleep, my leaves all dissolved in flight.

WENDELL BERRY

TOO DARK

The boy was lying upside-down from me
and said, twisting a spray of twigs, "Hello."
"And you," I said, holding on to branches,
forgetting I had never seen him.
Then he said, "Where do you live?" —
but I was moving on still and answered,
"The grey house" (not "below the woods"
and not how close it was) and smiled back.
He had gone to shaking leaves again,
and I remembered only he was there
and wanted me to ask where he would go.
Inside, the high woods behind the house
closing like a stage, it is too dark
to prove that I have ever seen him.

MARK MC CLOSKEY

HOMOSEXUALITY

So we are taking off our masks, are we, and keeping
our mouths shut? as if we'd been pierced by a glance!

The song of an old cow is not more full of judgment
than the vapors which escape one's soul when one is sick;

so I pull the shadows around me like a puff
and crinkle my eyes as if at the most exquisite moment

of a very long opera, and then we are off!
without reproach and without hope that our delicate feet

will touch the earth again, let alone "very soon."
It is the law of my own voice I shall investigate.

I start like ice, my finger to my ear, my ear
to my heart, that proud cur at the garbage can

in the rain. It's wonderful to admire oneself
with complete candor, tallying up the merits of each

of the latrines. 14th Street is drunken and credulous,
53rd tries to tremble but is too at rest. The good

love a park and the inept a railway station,
and there are the divine ones who drag themselves up

and down the lengthening shadow of an Aybyssinian head
in the dust, trailing their long elegant heels of hot air

crying to confuse the brave "It's a summer day,
and I want to be wanted more than anything else in the
    world."

FRANK O'HARA

GABRIEL'S BLUES

Everyone's going to ride tomorrow
Though poor sons lie, steal; I know
The air of Jesus: whirling strongly

Becoming a wall. Come to my comfort
Child and hear the horses in my head.
On the road read their direction; one

Ear lies unwounded: listen to the hoofs
From the other side of the world explode.
I know days when altars open like a mouth

Stretching out for air and sounds breaking
Become a shield bright below me while his
Dust and dirt blow into my trailing face.

CALVIN FORBES

HOPE

On the avenue the faces change each day,
    washed like white pebbles on the sand.
  The undertow rolls them. Some must swim away

to form new coral islands. Some swarm, like bees,
    around a silver monarch building an empire
from the mouth of the Amazon to the Hebrides.

But most, like friends, are turned by the water's care
    into smooth round stones that harden as they grow old,
  etched with error and excessive wear.

They bear their burdens sadly, for they bear them long.
    They barter scars of tragedies for fears
although, like old religions, all prove wrong.

From this coarse commerce a lover picks by day
    what he can. His hand in his pocket smiles that one
warm stone remains when the rest are washed away.

F. D. REEVE

BLACK MAPS

Not the attendance of stones,
nor the applauding wind,
shall let you know
you have arrived,

nor the sea that celebrates
only departures,
nor the mountains,
nor the dying cities.

Nothing will tell you
where you are.
Each moment is a place
you've never been.

You can walk
believing you cast
a light around you.
But how will you know?

The present is always dark.
Its maps are black,
rising from nothing,
describing,

in their slow ascent
into themselves,
their own voyage,
its emptiness,

the bleak, temperate
necessity of its completion.
As they rise into being
they are like breath.

And if they are studied at all
it is only to find,
too late, what you thought
were concerns of yours

do not exist.
Your house is not marked
on any of them,
nor are your friends,

waiting for you to appear,
nor are your enemies,
listing your faults.
Only you are there,

saying hello
to what you will be,
and the black grass
is holding up the black stars.

MARK STRAND

NIGHTLETTER

The night is a furrow, a queasy, insistent wound. Heavy the
flies hang, slow wheel the lingering birds. And the needle
between the fingers, stitching, stitching? Sutures, it wants to
say, O, sutures, but finds no edge.

When they fold your skin for a boutonniere, will it flower?
When they give your tongue to the flames, will the ashes
speak for themselves? The thing that is not left out always
is what is missing. Everything's certain.

CHARLES WRIGHT

PART VII

1970–1977
(Volumes 117–131)

PLAY

Nothing's going to become of anyone
except death:
   therefore: it's okay
to yearn
too high:
the grave accommodates
swell rambunctiousness &

ruin's not
compromised by magnificence:

the cut-off point
liberates us to the
common disaster: so
   pick a perch —
apple bough for example in bloom —
tune up
and if you like

drill imagination right through necessity:
it's all right:
it's been taken care of:

is allowed, considering

A. R. AMMONS

FOR DAVID SHAPIRO

Listen! The garbage pouring down the chutes
And the skies are wrong. The thunder tells you.

You believe them. We call them
Poets, who extinguish the light
of the morning, gather on the corner
every morning, and decide upon your sky.

What colors? Will it sleep? Or a cold
you're coming down with . . . sniffles . . . penalties.
The neighbors are all asleep. But next door a kid
is dark and his mother on the bed
watches. The windowshades lean heavy
seem to attack: his head is large. Another
morning, gathered in the corner
of the sky, collected prayers — what you once believed.

DAVID LEHMAN

ODE ON ZERO

A hoop, a rolling O, oh those have power
To hold within their hungry void the gist
Of all things; is not the whole universe
One long continuous band with a half twist?
So seasons run their courses, drawn in turn
By rotating moon, and globe whose very round
Revolves in all suns' orbit; once knowing
The inside, one must ask what lies beyond
The mobile limit; ask, and ask again!
For who can say what absolute nothing is?
All bodies lie within; there cannot be
Another body other than nothingness
Outside; and if that's so, then inward too
(All points made positive on the center organ)
The YES, together with the outward NO,
Must both, in total, be THE GREAT ZERO.

PHOEBE PETTINGELL

CIRCUMAMBULATION OF MT. TAMALPAIS

Those paths on the mountainside which neither ascend nor descend
but proceed at a level, are overgrown from disuse
by human beings if ever they went
along these routes.

Animals and other spirits who do not disturb the foliage overhead
walk through the foothills, past the mountain,
without observing its heights or
the surrounding depths.

Because, while in the vicinity, they are among the moving parts
of the mountain, excepted from the prospect of its apex
and its perspective from a distance
by circumambulation.

These creatures know their locale, make minute observations
of the mountain, recount the pebbles in its paths,
record the fall of leaves, see each other,
watch us climb up, run down.

ANDREW HOYEM

REASONS

For our own private reasons
We live in each other for an hour.
Stranger, I take your body and its seasons,
Aware the moon has gone a little sour

For us. The moon hangs up there like a stone
Shaken out of its proper setting.
We lie down in each other. We lie down alone
And watch the moon's flawed marble getting

Out of hand. What are the dead doing tonight?
The padlocks of their tongues embrace the black,
Each syllable locked in place, tucked out of sight
Even this moon could never pull them back,

Even if it held them in its arms
And weighed them down with stones,
Took them entirely on their own terms
And piled the orchard's blossom on their bones.

I am aware of your body and its dangers.
I spread my cloak for you in leafy weather
Where other fugitives and other strangers
Will put their mouths together.

THOMAS JAMES

IN SEPIA

Often you walked at night, houselights made
   nets of their lawns, your shadow
briefly over them. You had been talking about
   Death, over & over. Often
you felt dishonest, though certainly some figure
   moved in the dark yards, a parallel
circumstance, keeping pace. By Death, you meant
   a change of character: He is
a step ahead, interlocutor, by whose whisper
   the future parts like water,

allowing entrance. That was a way of facing it
   & circumventing it: Death
was the person into whom you stepped. Life, then,
   was a series of static events;
as: here the child, in sepia, climbs the front steps
   dressed for winter. Even the snow
is brown, &, no, he will never enter that house
   because each passage, as into
a new life, requires his forgetfulness. Often you
   would explore these photographs,

these memories, in sepia, of another life.
   Their use was tragic,
evoking a circumstance, the particular fragments
   of an always shattered past.
Death was process then, a release of nostalgia
   leaving you free to change.
Perhaps you were wrong; but walking at night
   each house got personal. Each
had a father. He was reading a story so hopeless,
   so starless, we all belonged.

JON ANDERSON

THE BLACK MESA

So much is parchment where I gloom,
Character still sharp enough to prick
Into the hide my igneous
Old spells and canticles of doom.
The things that shape a person! Peace.
Depth therapy in early stages crowned
One fuming anchorite with river stones.

Remember, though, how in *Thaïs*
The desert father falls for the land's lie —
That "grande horizontale" (blown shawls
Shining and raveling to this day
Above erosions in her pot of rouge)
Whom any crossing cloud turns dim,
Ascetic, otherworldly, lost to him.

By way of you a thousand human
Frailties found in me their last refuge.
The turquoise lodged for good one night
In a crevice where the young blood drummed.
Discharge, salvo, sulfur ringed me round
Below the waist. I knew thirst. Dawns,
The viceroy's eagle glittered like a gnat.

443

Sieges like that come late and end
Soon. And we are friends now? Funny friends.
Glaringly over years you knit
A wild green lap robe I shake off in tears.
I steal past him who next reclaims you, keep
Our hushed appointments, grain by grain . . .
Dust of my dust, when will it all be plain?

JAMES MERRILL

AFTER LONG BUSYNESS

I start out for a walk at last after weeks at the desk.
Moon gone, plowing underfoot, no stars, not a trace of light!
Suppose a horse were galloping toward me in this open field?
Every day I did not spend in solitude was wasted.

ROBERT BLY

THE MAGI

Toward world's end, through the bare
Beginnings of winter, they are traveling again.
How many winters have we seen it happen,
Watched the same sign come forward as they pass
Cities sprung around this route their gold
Engraved on the desert, and yet
Held our peace, these
Being the Wise, come to see at the accustomed hour
Nothing changed: roofs, the barn
Blazing in darkness, all they wish to see.

LOUISE GLÜCK

BAUCIS AND PHILEMON

Like a pair of companionable porcupines
Ambling up the mountain path,
Their chat is low and unintelligible.
Their subject soups and soaps and pennies off,
They push their sparsely laden cart
Along the strait paths of the First National.
Never a Super, the market has declined
To match its patrons' gentle poverty.
They never Super, either — but once had hopes
And children, good luck and bad, and youth.

They're grizzled now — two stooped and frail and grizzled
Children, they play store, play house.
Seldom quarrel, but turn impatient sometimes.
Why does he act so old and slow?
Why don't she look pretty any more?
Then recollect that both are old
And are each other's sole support and friend.

The God delays his promised change
To valiant oak, to curative linden.
Yet their small evening selves
Stretch shadows long and straight and spare
As of young trees, new-leaved.

KATHERINE HOSKINS

INDOORS

Says the window
what heart
in this weather?

Says the blizzard
outdoors.

Says the pond
　slow blood
　deep down
　in hard mud.

Says the world
　no peace
　no shelter.

Says music
　the life.

Says the evening
　　shut.

Says the stove
　hot iron
　hot breath
　in the pipe.

Good night.

GEORGE JOHNSTON

FOR CORA LIGHTBODY, R.N.

You are a landscape in the Tale of Terror,
　Ca. 1910. Your bibful of breasts secrete
　Those dreamy fields, fens, fells, that sinister street
Of the Georgian nightmare I must love forever,
Where up in the attic, or crouched behind a mirror,
　Now in a cloud, now in a winding-sheet,
　The Thing is lurking; cling your ineffably sweet
Lips to mine, softly as all that sugary horror.

And your one hour is the evening of the ending
　　When under a sky like the breast of a dove
　　　　The dénouement climbs the creaking staircase — *Blood!*
Shots, screams, italics! In a spasm like my spending
　　The Foul Thing drops . . . In you, my hospital Love,
　　　　I sink my shaft as in auriferous mud.

　　　　　　　　　　　　　　　　JOHN GLASSCO

CLIMBING YOU

　　　　I want to understand the steep thing
　　　　That climbs ladders in your throat.
　　　　I can't make sense of you.
　　　　Everywhere I look you're there —
　　　　a vast landmark, a volcano
　　　　poking its head through the clouds,
　　　　Gulliver sprawled across Lilliput.

　　　　I climb into your eyes, looking.
　　　　The pupils are black painted stage flats.
　　　　They can be pulled down like window shades.
　　　　I switch on a light in your iris.
　　　　Your brain ticks like a bomb.

　　　　In your offhand, mocking way
　　　　you've invited me into your chest.
　　　　Inside: the blur that poses as your heart.
　　　　I'm supposed to go in with a torch
　　　　or maybe hot-water bottles
　　　　& defrost it by hand
　　　　as one defrosts an old refrigerator.
　　　　It will shudder & sigh
　　　　(the icebox to the insomniac).

　　　　Oh there's nothing like love between us.
　　　　You're the mountain, I am climbing you.

If I fall, you won't be all to blame,
but you'll wait years maybe
for the next doomed expedition.

ERICA JONG

LOST

Stand still. The trees ahead and bushes beside you
Are not lost. Wherever you are is called Here,
And you must treat it as a powerful stranger,
Must ask permission to know it and be known.
The forest breathes. Listen. It answers,
I have made this place around you.
If you leave it, you may come back again, saying Here.
No two trees are the same to Raven.
No two branches are the same to Wren.
If what a tree or a bush does is lost on you,
You are surely lost. Stand still. The forest knows
Where you are. You must let it find you.

DAVID WAGONER

HALL OF OCEAN LIFE

Not from the unmapped valleys of darkness, nor
The milder regions of more clouded water
    Surrounding the summits of sunken
        Mountains, the forests of shallow oceans —

But within the great flapping of foamy wings,
On the glistening feathers of spume itself,
    The astonishing, changing surf that
        Breaks on the beaches of only water,

In the thin, breathing spray flung up against the
Hot emanations of sunlight mixed unseen

Among the gleamings, in singing air,
   Radiance, spinning at noontime, twisted

Out of the pungent methane, the dry stink of
Ammonia and generalities of
   Hydrogen, water and CO_2,
     The helical thread that we are strung on.

Was it that no generating Signal pierced
Darkening water, silencing depths, or that
   Only in those bright hurrahings of
     Accident could the rapid waves that were

Ever to flash with vision, ever to rise,
Dissolving into aspirations of their
   Own substance, carved in less than liquid,
     Returning light to the light, come to be?

JOHN HOLLANDER

THE SUN

The sun is the blind eyes of statues gilded
with lilies and fig leaves, the statues cast
of 20 carat gold, and the side frames
and pillars of gold, and the walls mirrors
recollecting gold and the flash bulbs flashing
to record the slaughter of the camera.

The Aurora Borealis Chimera
whirls into the furnace of its passion,
the twirling red disk of dawn whose semaphore
dots lavender pink and dashes the lame
animal to violet ashes flaking past
the sky-limb's fried foliage and gutted

scrapers, but it is merely the guided
sediment of reflections in the mirror

449

at Mt. Palomar. Palomino portions
of the early light crinkle across the lime-
stone tinfoil landscape of the pieced-
together jigsaw puzzle of the past,

and the sky clicks like an ancient camera,
crackles like celluloid and flames as fast.
A singed circle is left ringing the gilded
eye of the golden body behind the mirror.
It is the sun dissolving everything: Time,
Space and Fortune in its ferocious fashion.

ANDREW OERKE

ODE TO THE MEDIEVAL POETS

Chaucer, Langland, Douglas, Dunbar with all your
brother Anons, how on earth did you ever manage,
    without anaesthetics or plumbing,
    in daily peril from witches, warlocks,

lepers, The Holy Office, foreign mercenaries
burning as they came, to write so cheerfully,
    with no grimaces of self-pathos?
    Long-winded you could be but not vulgar,

bawdy but not grubby, your raucous flytings
sheer high-spirited fun, whereas our makers,
    beset by every creature comfort,
    immune, they believe, to all superstitions,

even at their best are so often morose or
kinky, petrified by their gorgon egos.
    We all ask, but I doubt if anyone
    can really say why all age-groups should find our

Age quite so repulsive. Without its heartless
engines, though, you could not tenant my book-shelves,

on hand to delect my ear and chuckle
my sad flesh. I would gladly just now be

turning out verses to applaud a thundery
jovial June when the judas-tree is in blossom,
    but am forbidden by the knowledge
      that you would have wrought them so much better.

W. H. AUDEN

CREMATORIUM

Where laurel hedges hide the coal and coke
    Our lawn-surrounded crematorium lies;
And every half-an-hour a puff of smoke
    Shows what we loved dissolving in the skies —
    Dear hands, dear feet, dear laughter-lighted eyes
And smiling lips which waited for a joke.

Now no one seems to know quite what to say:
    Friends are so altered by the passing years —
Well anyhow it's not so cold today
    And thus we try to dissipate our fears.
I am the Resurrection and the Life!
Strong, sly, and painful, doubt inserts its knife.

JOHN BETJEMAN

POETRY

The old forms are like birdhouses that
have been made homes so long they are
full of stuffing. Only the rarest birds
can squeeze in and out of the doorways. And
then they can't move around much inside, but
keep peeping the same sounds. Which the

451

stuffing almost entirely insulates. But
still they stay stuck, up on their poles.
And we keep listening hard for voices
to come out of them. And they do.

GREG KUZMA

NEGATIVE PASSAGE

Reading through your work tonight
As though it were autobiography,
I find your resonance . . .
"I shan't be yours forever; even this can't last."
How total the knowledge must have become,
As more you became yourself and us,
That we would know you less, and that
Apotheosis would have to be
A negative passage like Death . . .
Known as the nth of Doing to you
In that classical mode you invoked,
Over which, in an aerial entropy
Of mythical motion, You watched . . .
Known to us too, in a modified way,
Reciprocal also but monologic,
As an agon in which, to some lyric notion,
The creatured Image became the Likeness.

MICHAEL NEWMAN

THE VOWELS OF ANOTHER LANGUAGE

The road twisted through tongues of rock
And his mind kept changing yet he could not stop
To ask why he felt for these strangers
Feelings for which he had no name

TOM DISCH

EGO

Has thrust his nose under every board,
smelt out every wild carrot and white grub,
stucco'd the dirt with his tracks from side
to side, rubbed smooth the corner
posts, left his pink, red-bristled hide
on every barb of five strands of wire;

chewed the bark from the one scrub pine
that pitches a ghost of shade at noon,
bangs incessantly the metal trough-lid
at off-hours, chuffs down the white meal
raising a cloud around his ears, and cleans
each cob with the nicety of a Pharisee

tooth for tooth, squeezing contentedly
his small bagpipe voice as he mashes
corn with a slobbery leer and leaves
turds like cannonballs across a battlefield.
Meanwhile his little pink eye is
periscoped on the main chance —

the gate ajar, the slipped board,
the stray ducky that flusters through the wire —
saliva hanging from his mouth like a crown jewel.
His jowls shake with mirth under the smile
that made a killing on the market, won the fifth caucus,
took the city against all odds.

No wonder we shake at the thought of his getting out
of his square patch, electrify the wire,
(At night we hear him thump his dreams
on the corrugated tin hut and shudder,
the single naked bulb burning
through our sleep like his eye!),

take special dietary precautions against
his perpetual rut, except that March day

we drag the yearling sow to him
through mud up to his hocks. From that handseling
comes the fat litter — the white one for the Fair,
the spotted black to be slaughtered in November.

We don't show him to most neighbors — sometimes
to relatives, after picking them asparagus or straw-
berries. In June, framed by clover and bees
stringing out the sun under a blue sky
sugared with little clouds, he is, in his way,
quite grand, the enormous rusty blimp

of his body supporting intelligent
waggish ears, regally lidded eyes and
a pink, glistening snout
ready to shove up the privates of the world.

ROBERT SIEGEL

WAIT

Six beds in a square room: you give your name
And sleep for days. Then, the comeback — the shame,
The Thorazine, and long walks in the sun
As thought retreats from the oblivion
It took on trust. And through it all, you sense
Only your ruin and fatigue as dense
As sleep. What happened? They won't answer you,
But just solicit your submission to
The judgment they'll "in due time" formulate.
And till then? Get some rest. Be patient. Wait.

TIMOTHY STEELE

STONES: *Avesbury*

The alley of granite arkite pillars
    opens like a pathray in a long dead dream
        where the stone horses metamorphose into birds
            the instant we say: "It is a perfect horse."

I ascend into the world crystal among
   prisms and imprisoned gods who sing in the wind
     with mouths of giants: I O A. The Sun
       hearing its name, enters on silver wings.

Undefiled graffiti of gods which flow
   like water in the anchored rock: primal sculpture
     illimitably trapped in stone: chaos in the act
      of definition, the Word in formation.

Here I am, back in the mistletoe procession
   at the first familiar flaming revelation
     among the mirrors who can teach us who we are:
      anchored in bone, yet mobile voyaging juncture

between past and future: fluid, yet in tension
   between sun and moon: fire-conquered chaos in process:
     manifest mind and will: shadow casters confirming
       Him:
      bewitched gods tracking time toward our release in
      light.

DAISY ALDAN

A GARDEN OF SITUATIONS

Let there be no flowery banks,
No distractions.

Neither let trees
Cluster in a thicket,
But let a few stand tall,
Alone, and apart,
Like markers.

Let the statues be fat
And allegorical,
And set on high pedestals
That none may mistake them.

455

Let many paths be ruled
Near to each other
But with rare intersections,
And let them be gravel
That the walker may feel
Each step of his way.

So shall we know
Precisely where we are,
Precisely where we go,
That I am at this point,
Not that one, that you have reached
The point you have reached,
No other.

Here in these spaces
Perfect and dry,
Ours shall be a joy
Of lucid intervals
Like clarity in drunkenness,
Bounded on the near side
By uncertain ground
And on the far side by frenzy.

JACK ANDERSON

HISTORICAL MUSEUM, MANITOULIN ISLAND

After a while it dawns on us
we are intruders, in spite of the sign
and the box for donations. The knitted white
stockings, limp from too many washings,
droop before us like worn-out tongues
and still insist on their owner
(feet that wore them, hands that darned them),
her name and her yellow picture
— yes, but not yellow enough
that we should finger such secret parts.

We touch Mrs. Thompson's long cotton nightgown
and discover we are touching babies,
those that survived, and the two
in the graveyard beyond the wall.
We see that the golden snuffbox
and the doll with human hair
are dreams locked behind glass,
and when we come to the hard-eyed
tintype of Mr. and Mrs. Lewis
above their big double bed
and find beside it "Lucy Grey"
copied in violet ink,
we have forced another secret.

We're opening lives like lockets,
rummaging through possessions
stripped from still warm bodies.
Silence accuses us, level-eyed
like the poor who did not know they were poor,
the brave who did not know they were brave,
the enduring who endure in this room.
They had no right to call this a museum.
Not yet. We thank the lady
with tinted hair by the door
and re-enter our summery lives,
the ones they gave us: easy love,
warm rooms, soft speech, long years.

LISEL MUELLER

TERCE

Between the walls, the brim
Between the air and the water
Fits, presses where it can into

Corners, into cracks that freeze.
With its pressing into their sighs
It spares the walls

Nothing, sends them for breath
Into their own pains,
Into what they remember about being

One stone, breathing, the brim
Away somewhere, not pressing.
As it slips through their dark course

The seams that once bound them
Narrow and clutch, shudder to take
More, to take enough,

Coming and coming to be so close.
The brim curls at its edges, lapping.
The air and the water go their ways.

JAMES MC MICHAEL

DIDO: SWARMING

I am the ruined queen:
imperious, go down, go down.
I cling to trees till the black
clotted bodies open me,

and one thick circle. Swarm in the air.
The rich round honey jar
is empty now. The husk sloughs off.
I go where no bees are.

Sting one last time! They say
stabbed swans disguise their throats
with song. How inadvised
to choke on the first note,

buzzing in misery, to vibrate
in the throng like any fly.
Remind me I am queen
and warm me while I die

wrapped in my stiffened wings:
I should have had the globe!
Vein in the rigid wrist instead;
I harden like a scab.

KATHLEEN SPIVACK

MUSE

Cackling, smelling of camphor, crumbs of pink icing
Clinging to her lips, her lipstick smeared
Halfway around her neck, her cracked teeth bristling
With bloody splinters, she leans over my shoulder.
Oh my only hope, my lost dumfounding baggage,
My gristle-breasted, slack-jawed zealot, kiss me again.

DAVID WAGONER

N

Your body has moved to unstaunchable distance
In the years between death we will name this perspective

Now it is the paradigm to assure us there is doubt
The motion of these laws have their duty on the void

It requires all of my guile to edit this refusal
Even now you are the legion whereon night must depend

It is clear how time continues though the form has had
        enough
The light had prepared me and allowed you to be bound

The primordial radius had identified your lips
The tears had been at work for their multitude the diamonds

In the onslaught of this evidence my fantasy had held
You had been balanced again in the intention of the moon

Whoever had invented you the firmament repaid
This was the ending of my ecstasy The Past

In duplicity I recounted how the oceans were unformed
That this could have mattered gave a meaning to the clouds

It would have been believable to feel that another had been
    lost
Such is the illusion of the stones that challenge air

HUGH SEIDMAN

NEGATIVES

This is the light we dream in,
The milk light of midnight, the full moon
Reversing the balance like shapes on a negative:
The chalk hills, the spectral sky,
The black rose in flame,
Its odors and glittery hooks
Waiting for something to snag.

The mulberries wink like dimes;
Fat sheep, the mesquite and chaparral
Graze at their own sweet speed,
The earth white sugar;
Two miles below, and out,
The surf has nothing to add.

Is this what awaits us, amorphous
Cobalt and zinc, a wide tide
Of brilliance we cannot define
Or use, and leafless, without guilt;
No guidelines or flutter, no
Cadence to pinpoint, no no?

Silence. As though the doorway behind
Us were liquid, were black water;

As though we might enter; as though
The ferry were there,
Ready to take us across
— Remembering now, unwatermarked,
The blackout like scarves in our new hair.

CHARLES WRIGHT

TO D —, DEAD BY HER OWN HAND

My dear, I wonder if before the end
You ever thought about a children's game —
I'm sure you must have played it too — in which
You ran along a narrow garden wall
Pretending it to be a mountain ledge
So steep a snowy darkness fell away
On either side to deeps invisible;
And when you felt your balance being lost
You jumped because you feared to fall, and thought
For only an instant: that was when I died.

That was a life ago. And now you've gone,
Who would no longer play the grown-ups' game
Where, balanced on the ledge above the dark,
You go on running and you don't look down,
Nor ever jump because you fear to fall.

HOWARD NEMEROV

THE POET'S FAREWELL TO HIS TEETH

Now you are going, what can I do but wish you
(as my wife used to say) "every success
in your chosen field".

What we have seen together! Doctor X,
having gagged us, hurling his forceps to the floor
and denouncing our adolescent politics,

or the time we caught trench-mouth in Iowa City
and had to drive west slowly and haltingly,
spitting in all the branches of the Missouri.

Cigar-stained and tired of cavities, you leave.
It is time to go back to the pure world of teeth
and rest, and compose yourselves for the last eruption.

As to those things in a glass by the bathroom sink
they will never communicate with me as you have done,
fragile and paranoid, sensing the world around you

as wild drills and destructive caramel, getting even
for neglect by waking me into the pain of dawn,
that empty and intimate world of our bitter sharing.

Go, under that cool light. I will remember you:
the paper reports that people may still feel pain
in their missing teeth, as with any amputation.

I hope you relax by the shadowy root canals,
and thinking of me with kindness, but not regret,
toast me just once in the local anaesthetic.

WILLIAM DICKEY

PARABOLA

Year after year the princess lies asleep
Until the hundred years foretold are done,
Easily drawing her enchanted breath.
Caught on the monstrous thorns around the keep,
Bones of the youths who sought her, one by one
Rot loose and rattle to the ground beneath.

But when the Destined Lover at last shall come,
For whom alone Fortune reserves the prize,
The thorns give way; he mounts the cobwebbed stair;

Unerring he finds the tower, the door, the room,
The bed where, waking at his kiss she lies
Smiling in the loose fragrance of her hair.

That night, embracing on the bed of state,
He ravishes her century of sleep
And she repays the debt of that long dream;
Future and Past compose their vast debate;
His seed now sown, her harvest ripe to reap
Enact a variation on the theme.

For in her womb another princess waits,
A sleeping cell, a globule of bright dew.
Jostling their way up that mysterious stair,
A horde of lovers bursts between the gates,
All doomed but one, the destined suitor, who
By luck first reaches her and takes her there.

A parable of all we are or do!
The life of Nature is a formal dance
In which each step is ruled by what has been
And yet the pattern emerges always new:
The marriage of linked cause and random chance
Gives birth perpetually to the unforeseen.

One parable for the body and the mind:
With science and heredity to thank,
The heart is quite predictable as a pump,
But, let love change its beat, the choice is blind.
"Now" is a cross-roads where all maps prove blank,
And no-one knows which way the cat will jump.

So here stand I, by birth a cross between
Determined pattern and incredible chance,
Each with an equal share in what I am.
Though I should read the code stored in the gene,
Yet the blind lottery of circumstance
Mocks all solutions to its cryptogram.

As in my flesh, so in my spirit stand I
When does *this* hundred years draw to its close?
The hedge of thorns before me gives no clue.
My predecessor's carcass, shrunk and dry,
Stares at me through the spikes. O well, here goes!
I have this thing, and only this, to do.

                                    A. D. HOPE

WINTER DRIVE

Fallow fields, dark pewter sky,
Steely light on the wet plain,
Evening falls in freezing rain
With a promise and a lie.

Promise in the leaden sky,
In the sodden fields bleak shine,
In the slate vats full of wine,
In the knowledge that we die.

But the lie is in the soul,
And it rots the world we have
Till there's nothing left to save.

Dying world and deadened sky;
Traffic streams beyond control.
What is left to make us try?

                            JAMES MCAULEY

JULY 4TH

Gradual bud and bloom and seedfall speeded up
are these mute explosions in slow motion.
From vertical shoots above the sea, the fire
flowers open, shedding their petals. Black waves,

turned more than moonwhite, pink ice, lightning blue,
echo our gasps of admiration as they crash
and hush. Another bush ablaze snicks straight up.
A gap like heartstop between the last vanished
particle and the thuggish boom. And the thuggish
boom repeats in stutters from sandhill hollows
in the shore. We want more. A twirling sun,
or dismembered chrysanthemum bulleted up, leisurely
bursts, in an instant timestreak is suckswooped
back to its core. And we want more: red giant,
white dwarf, black hole dense, invisible, all in one.

                                    MAY SWENSON

PLAIN SONG TALK

I speak of the history of the world,
So deep there is no fathoming it,
At the depths of which one cannot speak,
Before which we whistle in the wind.

Our days and years are a vain attempt
To quell the meaning of the universe,
But we are worsted as the days go by,
We are shuffled into a bin of night.

I speak of the hopes we had in youth,
The diminishing powers we had as time went by,
Of sufferings old or new, and always doubt.
And of death the less said the better.

                            RICHARD EBERHART

DON'T FORGET

I was always called in early for dinner.
It was dusk usually, half an inning to go,
I'd hear my mother calling me to beat the dark,
everyone would mumble, I'd throw my glove down and
      leave.

At home, sitting at the table, I'd imagine the score,
and the speckled homework book seemed to watch me
until I opened it, stared at the numbers, and fell asleep.
Damp laundry rustled in the yards of the houses.

Everyone was punished like this because
our parents worried we'd fall, and missed us,
but we always got hurt anyway, or we'd sit for hours
sanding the wings of a wood fighterplane until they shined

like metal. We climbed walls until we slipped and our legs
    broke,
our first kisses were so murderous we almost fainted.
Don't forget, this is inside us every day.
We want everything, our hands stop too soon,

and who are we when a face whispers and opens to us
like a wave? The tame grasses of the head, the moist spiral
    ear,
some water nobody has crossed — you feel yourself leaving,
you can't lift your hands, you stand there, leaving.

STEPHEN BERG

SEAWEEDS

I know a little what it is like, once here at high tide
stranded, for them to be so attached to the bottom's
sarcophagus lids, up to their brown green gold wine
bottle necks in the prevailing booze, riding, as far
as we can see, like a picnic on a blanket.

Whatever plucks them from below the red horizon
like snapped pulleys and ropes for the pyramidal effort
of the moon, they come in, they come through the breakers,
heaps of hair, writing across the beach a collapsed
script, signers of a huge independence.

Melville thought them pure, bitter, seeing the fog-sized
flies dancing stiff and renaissance above. But I
have eaten nori and dulse, and to have gone deep
before being cast out leaves hardly a taste of loneliness.
And I take in their iodine.

SANDRA MC PHERSON

ABOUT THIS COURSE

We have been sailing in a certain small fountain,
    like physicists in toy boats.
Each craft bears a candle on its deck. We light the
    candles and the boats puff by
As if you were real, delightful. And we who have never
    been able to resist
The course of a new toy dream have spent much time
    watching the fun in the fountains.
And if we, in a sense, sink in that water,
    the goldfish, I am sure, will retain
Their silver dignity. We are fed beside the
    fountains
As the young are fed by the experiment and the
    results.
It confirms us; and now the whole water
    is silver;
A crucial step is taken, but years
    later,
The fountain is slowed down, as if controlled
    by your calm hands.

DAVID SHAPIRO

BURIAL

The old ones go to each other's funerals,
The old ones mourn themselves.
It is sometimes in perfection of the weather

In as now the ending summer
When shoe-darkening wetness of the grass of lawns,
And graveyards, does not dry or dull
Until about the tolling of the bell.
Not even the cleric thinks of heaven,
No one who's here has visions of a hell.
Glad that it's over, sons go off to their gravid
Wives or to their girls. And driving
Slowly home, in their expensive limousines,
The old ones mourn themselves.

GEOFFREY GRIGSON

LEAVING BUFFALO

Others, many others, must have known
That it was waiting for them at the center —
It was the weather. The weather made them certain
That at winter's core, wished on by the sun,

A revelation was waiting to occur:
Optimists, they took as their bright text,
"If not this year, why, surely then, the next."
They felt that waiting built strong character.

Season after season brought new dread,
For it was dreadful to be always waiting,
Enduring what they knew was past debating.
"Be patient as spiders," the Makers said.

Our lives are wrong, the Makers thought,
Picking at the scabs of old, unheeded
Warnings which they once thought were unneeded.
How can we tell them it was all for nought?

— What will survive of us are our manners.
They called abhorrent what was merely lewd,
But dreamt of applebreasted women: nude,
Bronze-skinned lovelies of the green savannas . . .

Elsewhere is fetching, *Elsewhere* tugs my sleeve —
My frenzied grin of departure gives me away!
Expecting nothing, I will leave today.
Others are waiting still, and still believe

That it will happen soon, that they were chosen
To be there when it happened, when the wind
Must search the dark streets for living trees to bend
Under its steep breath until their frozen

Hearts crack, and the wrenched-at houses flash their wrath,
Blazing from windows their secret dream of fire-
's deep red rose, uncurling everywhere,
Levelling the city in its path,

Spitting everything with sumptuous light!
Others are waiting, others still believe . . .
Given to the darkness of the grave
The Makers are burning in their shells tonight,

They rattle like peppercorns in their dark wood.
Above them, leafless, awkward branches touch
Each other dreadfully: the blighted Dutch
Elms they left as ornaments are dead.

CHARLES MARTIN

POEM

This beauty that I see
— the sun going down
scours the entangled
and lightly henna
withys and the wind
whips them as it
would ship a cloud —
is passing so swiftly
into night. A moon,
full and flat, and stars

a freight train passing
passing it is the sea
and not a train. This
beauty that collects
dry leaves in pools
and pockets and goes
freezingly, just able
still to swiftly flow
it goes, it goes.

JAMES SCHUYLER

IT IS THE STARS THAT GOVERN US

The stars are pinned against the sky,
pale and frozen in the ivory moonlight,
the constellations rigid as Monarchs.
Now become the dream; a human specimen.

Prod them with your eyes, let your fingers
trace the patterns of the dipper's handle,
drink deeply from the vessel's mouth;
how cold the moonlight feels on your tongue.

Turn it over, let the mercury run
down your veins until your body stiffens,
arms and legs are fastening in the sockets,
eyes light the way, turning like beacons.

Know that you are hollow to the core,
feel the certain fusion of your hemispheres.
Your life is being pulled into its course,
piercing through your skin the silver axis.

Your heart is hardening, feel its weight,
the valves are tightening slowly into place.
Now let them fix you with their icy stares;
now let them gaze at your great constellation.

MICHAEL MAGEE

FIRE-QUEEN

Unseen, snow slides from over-laden boughs.
Spume of flakes, flurry of light, cold smoke;
Kaleidoscope of crystal and lead and flame.
Then silence again as it sinks,
Weightless, lost, white into whiteness, down
To perma-frost encasing molten turbulence.

That core answers the sun-spots, flares
When her impotence most torments — she,
With her presumptions, her gestures, who has chosen
This place rather than any other
To expose herself to the gnawing ulcer
Of inertia, her own true nature.

Such is her kingdom — fire-queen
Of the absolute north, who rules by satire,
Inaction, disdain; touch blunted to ice,
Ears sealed, sight gone, reflection congealed, mirror
Shattered aeons ago, rather than see
Merely a pattern of line and colour, flat

As the diagram of what a face might be —
Which to recognise would mean to accept
That clamour of voices, imploring, complaining,
But silent, that rise from her brain like steam
From a tub-full of churning laundry.
But silent. Her thoughts — unspoken, ignored.

Their heat is the power that freezes, motor
Of her repression-machine, refrigerator
Of frightful patience, rigid mastadon throne,
Sealed and invisible ice-pyramid,
Red-hot iron-maiden of self-hatred
She's trapped inside by refusing to listen.

Screams settle like snow and never thaw.
Branches petrified under their burden

Of murdered desires. She sits like Lot's wife,
Beyond the need for praise or explanation,
Ambitionless as death, perfect, absorbed
Forever by her silent incantation.

RUTH FAINLIGHT

CREDO

My meaning passes like wild nightbirds
Whose cries are like the dew, risen
Or fallen, night's emanation, clear
Sayings of the unsystematized.

Clearer than crystal: plainer than day:
Simpler than absence when after hope
And memory — dream and empire — are blown
Away like cities we wake to the desert.

Doctrine has never sheltered this
Untamed belief that takes the whole
For its housing, heaven and earth and breath
And sleep, the undivided sphere.

BREWSTER GHISELIN

THE DESIRE OF WATER

Caught and composed, motionless blue, behind
the dam, the river and the rain appear
reserved, relying on a passing wind
to lick them back to life, that warps and moves
their welded surfaces against the sheer
wall with flowing room on its otherside.
But wavelets splashing cannot turn the tide
of emptiness enforced by concrete. Shove
as it might, surface water's only hope
is overflow, and that requires increasing

depth. Gradually, the billion rain drops
and bloated river combined, realizing
in their brooding blue depth the depth it takes,
rise toward the dam's lip too much for flood gates.

MARK JARMAN

PERVIGILIUM VENERIS

Like the white whale, born black, myself grows brighter
Year by year until at last my prime,
If it comes, should dazzle as a paradigm
Of transformation; or as if the night were
About to leave a pupal cave and light were
One instant signal to forget the time
Of the shamed slow-motion caterpillar climb,
I wait for wings that are more hale though slighter.

Winter-born by chance, my youth was frozen.
When will my sun shine? When will Apollo
Regard me here and let me know how long
Before that spring is coming that I've chosen?
When is the year I shall be as the swallow
That I may sing my one specific song?

SUZANNE NOGUERE

BREADTH. CIRCLE. DESERT. MONARCH.
MONTH. WISDOM.

(for which there are no rhymes)

Not as *height* rises into lightness
Nor as *length* strengthens — say, the accepting eye
Calmed by a longing of shoreline —

473

Breadth wields its increase over nothing, to the greater
Glory of nothing: our unwanted dimension,
Yet necessary.

What the *square* can share of its rightness
Extends a just plainness; the sure swerve of a
Curve continues beyond itself.
But O, the old closure! *Circle* of will returning
Inward to prison, wrenching all tangencies back,
Lest there be friendship

Even in clever touchings that the
City solders with pity or with desiring,
Or of *mountain's* unique bond with
The fountains gushing forth from it that cry out of high
Things. Solitariness of *Desert* ever
Stretches out in vain,

Lonely *Monarch* of all who survey
Its wearying inclusiveness, subject to
No true attachments as a *fool's*
To his toy tool, jingling self-image, nor object of
Blunderings that it keeps ever breeding — *wife* of
Self-created strife.

Sole rondures of *day* unrolling stay
The approach of stillness, and between them and
The larger wheel of *year* appear
The lunar counterturns in cold, reflected selfhood
Of *Month,* unbound to sun but only barely out
Of phase with its rounds.

These solitaries! whether bright or
Dim, unconstellated words rain down through the
Darkness: after *youth* has burned out
His tallow truth, and *love,* which above everything must
Cling to word and body, drains, *Wisdom* remains full,
Whole, unrhymable.

Intone them then: *Breadth Circle Desert*
Monarch Month Wisdom not for whatever spell
They generate but for their mere
Inexorable syntax. The eye's movement outward
Claims its huge dominions not by kinship, nor bond
Of common ending.

JOHN HOLLANDER

DEATH & EMPEDOCLES 444 B.C.

Glittering, adroit, the Sicilian wonder
Stepped from the sea, spoke to the crowds:
"I was first a girl, then a blundering boy,
Then a briery bush (Ankh into Crucifix!),
Then a bird, a fish: and last of all,
Your friend, Empedocles.
                            I come to greet you."
Scattered applause, then groans and hisses:
A woman's voice: "He was my lover.
He taught my hands to conquer snakes."
And other voices: "Take him away. His face
Has the look of death."
                            "The distant west
Turns green, then violet. There are tremors
In the earth and menstrual heat. People are warned:
There are ashes falling."
                            Some saw him leap
Deep into Aetna:
                    a roar of smoke, slow lava pouring —
(We found his sandal near the crater's lip) —
Smell of psychosis, metempsychosis in the air:
Earth and its caverns towering over him;
His way was lost in flames, a Mandrake forest —
He could not unkindle fire, unwind the spell.
He was neither Herakles, nor Ganymedes
While madness (hope of fame) walked at his side.

Streets had turned treacherous, and crowds fell quiet —
Each waiting for a comet in the sky.

HORACE GREGORY

SPIDER

Terror strikes lightly your stillness.
   Serene is your bed and your icebox.
Death is your neighbor calmly
   Surveying the scene as you strike.

The intruders, no more than inquisitive
   Guests, find adhesive your ladders:
Jacob's dream, mirrored, entices them in.
   They converge upon your constant hunger.

The struggle is short however frantic.
   What defeat that was not dealt
By you, ever lay in your net?
   A broom, a flame, a foot, a stronger mate.

THOMAS COLE

DECLENSION

In the chorus of memories a blessing in disguise.
The birds and the trees are satisifed. If these
Appear to grow smaller with distance how
Tell of the particulate the towering
Matter of the pine, its needles, or its osprey
Waiting magnanimous upon the sun
You saw from the curl of the bend back-rising there?

The tree, its mossed feet, the mane green:
Manor for whom, for what? The bird, or song
You had to ignore, heading on. A death?
Not knowing, you ignored the tree, the osprey.

What is not yours is that beyond the time
You do; or might be; or, "once upon a time . . ."

Spare, untouchable, the river bank. And there
White water, phrasing, races past you, back.
Particular roadside pines, coverging walls
Backing the head — to vanishing point. A sense
Of acrid pine musk that might have been there lingers,
Remembered. The graceful ornaments linger on
And overwhelm.
              How then will you get on
To what you know, as you must? The eggshell
On the garden path; the tanager's intent
In tapering branches? All this is what is not
For you, and the words rise outward toward your smile.

STEPHEN SANDY

IN A DREAM

a vacuum cleaner held over my head
is drawing out my brains through my nostrils,
blood running in a column straight up
into the vacuum bag whining like a jet engine.
I feel my intestines too beginning to move up
through my gullet and soon they will be pouring
through my nose. My bones quiver in their sockets,
my knees are shaking. I sit down,
emptiness is becoming me. I can no longer think,
I just listen to the sucking vacuum.
Here goes my heart, straight up into my throat
and choking me, pumping in my throat.
It is filling my mouth, it is forcing its way
between my teeth. The vacuum roars
and my mouth flies open and my heart is gone.

How is it I keep writing?
The vacuum roars and whines alternately,
my ears stick to my head but now my head
is rising, a wind is whistling through my skull.

My head is being lifted from my neck.
Take me altogether, great vacuum:
my arms, legs, sex, shoes, clothes,
my pen gripped in my whitened hand
drained of blood. Take me altogether
and I triumph, whirled in the vacuum bag
with my satellite heart, brain, bones and blood.

DAVID IGNATOW

CLOCK WITHOUT HANDS

The hands are being plated; they'll be brass.
Works are a quiet hive. And the hours pass.
Time's ticking here; the wheels keep even speed.
Only like heaven's own logic: hard to read.

JOHN FREDERICK NIMS

LAST DAYS

You roar over the meadow and roar.
Silence purrs in the grass. In what
a hungry bum told you was larch, a parked hawk
keeps quiet. Silence. You roar again.
You remember the bum begged food and you
turned him away. You turned girls who loved you
away. One wept and said "cold" in July.
And so on. You roar each morning. Mute hawk
in the larch, bum on the road, girls
going away. Some mornings, words. You roar words
over the meadow. "Clambake" and "fracas."
The song of the creek dries up. Beavers
head for the sky. And so on. Hawk on larch.
Bum on road. Girls gone. Creek dry. Beavers
in flight. You roar editorials into the sun.
And so on. The silent, the indifferent sun.

RICHARD HUGO

From COMPULSIVE QUALIFICATIONS

for Stewart Lindh

I

"Richard, May I Ask A Question? What Is An Episteme?"

A body of knowledge. As I know best now,
Regarding yours across the abyss between
    That chair and this one,
My ignorance the kind of bliss unlikely
To bridge the furniture without a struggle,
    A scene — mad or bad
Or just gauche. The known body is Greek to me,
Though I am said to have conspicuous gifts
    As a translator.
More likely the Bible is the right version:
All knowledge was probably gained at first hand
    And second nature;
To know the Lord was to be flesh of His flesh.
There was a God, but He has been dismembered;
    We are the pieces.

II

"Richard, What Do You Mean When You Say You're
    Writing Two-Part Inventions?"

The sense of invention is a coming-upon,
A matter of finding matter more than of fact,
    So that the finding matters.
And if invention is finding, all finding is
Finally choosing, and a choice is something made.
    Hence the sense of our saying
We "make" each other: because we choose that body
Over and above this one (ours), coming-upon
    Becomes more than just coming,
Becomes rather a coming-to, and to . . . ourselves.
Now in a two-part invention, the choosing works

Both ways, we exchange our parts
So we can be found by each other, and coming
Together, coming apart, not even coming,
    We shall have been invented.

III

"Richard, May I Ask You Something? Is Poetry Involved
    With Evil?"

If we follow Sade (as we do, from a distance —
After all, who could keep up?) the Law is crime's cause,
    Wedlock the source of divorce,
Nor can any Garden grow till we acknowledge
The weeds suffered outside, not sadistically,
    Just dialectically.
So much, then, for "involvement": no *Paradiso*
Without, in poetry at least, infernal parts.
    But let the word itself speak —
Evil, from Indo-European roots, flowers
Like a weed, meaning "up-from-under" and "over"
    (as *eaves* drop from above us),
Meaning also "supine," "thrown-backward" and "under,"
Meaning, as roots so often seem to mean, its own
    Opposite besides itself.
There we have it, as *I* would have it: infernal
Parts beside themselves, opposites supine, so that
    As even this four-letter
Old-English word means, *we* can be "extended forms
Which signify *exceeding the proper limit.*"
    Flowers of excess — O good!

XIII

"Richard, What Will It Be Like When *You* Ask The
    Questions?"

Like a landscape by night, and in summer, riding
480   The ghost of a road (or what you take for a road,

Wet still and hissing under your bicycle tires
     After an afternoon's rain)
But the ground keeps rising, the gray cumulus thins,
And there is the moon! round and sudden in the sky
Like an old sun casting a sort of dead daylight
     Upon the world's premises,
Cancelling shadowy promises of escape
At a slowed tempo of resignation, so that
There is no story left to tell yourself or me
     About the Day that Never
Or about the Night that Always — no story now
About what had been or what would be — it is how
You become a storyteller: there is no story,
     So you have to make it up.
Even the same actions differ when repeated;
This one will be the same, but with a difference
More interesting than the sameness, which is
     More significant than
The difference. You will find it matters little
Whether noon or the false noon of moonlight fastens
Your shadow to the macadam, whether you put
     Questions or are put to them;
Loser, you will find there is nothing to choose,
Whether you make others suffer or prefer them
To inflict suffering on you: it is always
     A god being crucified.

                    RICHARD HOWARD

PAGE

He turns to you, measly immortal page. Who will say the page
detested him? Who will say this page set fire to his house and
took away all that belonged to him? Sweet smelling page.
Steel-edged leaf, let him watch his fingers. He has to be careful
lest he find himself in a lost century believing in extinct prolif-
erations, lest he believe you say more than an ingenuous alpha-
bet, a cruel child of a language.

                    SANDRA MC PHERSON   481

SETTLER

The island was a word he woke upon,
Split by birth in two: one side dark
And carved or caved into peninsulas,

The other an extinct volcano, blown
Out, leaving a circle full of air.
The ground was nothing, but it was flat,

And by lying down things moved far away.
Hard beneath him, the island was a dot
He washed against, wishing he were drowned,

Gasping in the foam, coughing up
Other words, other islands, wreakage
Noisy and populous once: they crumbled

From his memory, no longer worked as sound.
But this beach, once he got back his breath,
His way of seeing in the dark, was his

Alone. There were no Friday's in the sand.
No vapor trails overhead, no smoke-stacks
Floating through the island silence. Only

The sound of him, map in mouth, exploring
Back and forth, forging the black rock
And giving it a name: No No No

STEWART LINDH

THE FOG DREAM

Out of the fog
the voice of the clairvoyant speaks
with the precision of a bird:
    You have a few years left.
    You will end in hope.

The listener in the fog is startled.
  I never asked a question.
  Why this answer?
His words hang in the air, unanswered,
  then drift away, slow feathers.

SANDRA M. GILBERT

BIRD AND THE MUSE

The Muse that stirs my blood,
In unforeseen control
Takes form becomes a bird
Blazing through realms of gold.

Leaves me so suddenly
I hardly know her gone
In worlds remote from me
She flies through land and sea.

Although the unwilling soul
Shrinks from her brilliant flight
She must fulfill her role
Resume her mythic part
Enter the sleeping heart.

Write then although the walls
Close in with never a sound,
She chides, inspires, recalls
The rarely trodden ground.

Learn patiently to paint,
The white face of your God
In the indifferent night
When all the senses faint.

She may again appear
Through heart and soul and mind
When your two eyes are blind
And days are dulled in fear.

483

Poor, lonely, her reward,
The angelic note of praise,
Your life must not record
Through all your days.

The Flying Victory
Lifts wounded wings and sings,
Part Goddess and part bird
I hear her passing sigh
Her final whisperings.

MARYA ZATURENSKA

From THE WAY DOWN

THEY RETURN

Long desired, the dead return.
— Saw our candle and were safe,
Bought from darkness by our care?
Light from ours has touched their eyes,
Blood of ours has filled their veins.
Absence, winter, shed like scales.

They return, but they are changed.
Armoured each in private shade,
Sullen, helmed against the light,
Their resentment fills our arms,
Sifting from their ribs like night.
Absence, winter, is their name.

Change comes slowly, where they were.
Pain, exclusion, long endured,
Ate their human places out,
Sold to darkness by our fear.
They, returning, bring us back
Absence, winter, what we gave.

JAY MACPHERSON

UNDER THE ARC DE TRIOMPHE: OCTOBER 17

The French clocks struck two-thirty, and above
autumnal Paris, itching with parades,
starlings darted in a blinding sky.
And you did not stare after. Nor did I.

Later that evening, in a chilly bed,
I slept, fatigued with seas I had not swum,
stone-battered on the shores of missed Calais,
and did not dream the air I had not flown
nor fall and wake, in still trying to run
late, panting, through the city. And the birds
that would have flown, had we been there to see
did not swoop down the sky that afternoon.
I cannot think with whom I spent the day
nor what I thought. I slept and woke alone.

MARILYN HACKER

EMPEDOCLES ON ETNA

In Agrigentum, earlier in Olympia,
I saw the crumbling temples with a tourist's eye,
    Presumed the lame chained to the village street;
    The dragon was never defeated of his prey.
    I thought of death as a descending path
    From which the landscape suddenly disappeared.

Taverns, brothels, circuses, narrow streets,
Raised voices in the low-beamed rooms:
    These for years I had accepted
    As`being the real, the tangible things.
    Motorways, lasers, mirvs and jets
    Would become miraculous accomplishments.

One habit, though, I was unable ever to break: 485
The reading of old books in search of wisdom.

There the lame walked, the dragon forsook
The naked heroine tied to the rock;
Temples shone and congregations sang
An audible version of the universe.

It was that woman. For days they thought her dead.
Resurrection was her wish, not magic of my own.
   But I was much censored in the city.
   Her house was profit for developers.
   Pity is no longer a natural attribute.
   If the dead are not dead, what remains true?

Citizens stood gaping at their windows.
They forgot the jargon which explained the sun.
   In ruined belfries iron tongues
   Licked against the palate of old bells;
   Brittle leaves echoed the green of Spring
And stagnant waters mirrored the memories of streams.

At the crater's rim I blame myself, not them.
There are frontiers only the centuries can extend
   After the vine has withered and been renewed,
   After the cities have been buried tier on tier.
   I was born too early as you, too, are born:
   My death has become a necessary myth.

H. B. MALLALIEU

WANDSWORTH COMMON

Geese in the pond are drifting, five
Angelic couples lie at rest
In scattered intervals. Above
A kite skips from its line by chance:
Walk by there slightly apart lest
   You stop short, hearing an absence.

Sly nature has quite clipped itself
To these smart accents which remain

Familiar, as if greened for golf.
How can it please the eye, this set
Emptied of flaws? Only the sane
   Make use of the lawns to forfeit —

Special sorrows for silly peace.
What should you do except look out
For something else? A ragged space
Tracked by a pandemonic mole
Or one dangerous tree without
   Its right plot, a stray oracle.

Yet why on earth deny the charm
Which is what keeps you there? All lights
Tell of this comfort, the sky warm
With a safe orange shade while clouds
Bulge faintly just where they should: nights
   Are kept smooth for dark promenades.

DAVID BROMWICH

A MAN OF WORDS

His case inspires interest
But little sympathy; it is smaller
Than at first appeared. Does the first nettle
Make any difference as what grows
Becomes a skit? Three sides enclosed,
The fourth open to a wash of the weather,
Exits and entrances, gestures theatrically meant
To punctuate like doubled-over weeds as
The garden fills up with snow?
Ah, but this would have been another, quite other
Entertainment, not the metallic taste
In my mouth as I look away, density black as gunpowder
In the angles where the grass writing goes on,
Rose-red in unexpected places like the pressure
Of fingers on a book suddenly snapped shut.

487

Those tangled versions of the truth are
Combed out, the snarls ripped out
And spread around. Behind the mask
Is still a continental appreciation
Of what is fine, rarely appears and when it does is already
Dying on the breeze that brought it to the threshold
Of speech. The story worn out from telling.
All diaries are alike, clear and cold, with
The outlook for continued cold. They are placed
Horizontal, parallel to the earth,
Like the unencumbering dead. Just time to reread this
And the past slips through your fingers, wishing you were
    there.

JOHN ASHBERY

ELEGY FOR YARDS, POUNDS, AND GALLONS

An unduly elected body of our elders
Is turning you out of office and schoolroom
Through ten long years, is phasing you
Out of our mouths and lives forever.

Words have been lost before: some hounded
Nearly to death, and some transplanted
With roots dead set against stone,
And some let slide into obscure senescence,

Some even murdered beyond recall like extinct animals —
(It would be cruel to rehearse their names:
They might stir from sleep on the dusty shelves
In pain for a moment).

Yet you, old emblems of distance and heaviness,
Solid and liquid companions, our good measures,
When have so many been forced to languish
For years through a deliberate deathwatch?

How can we name your colorless replacements
Or let them tell us for our time being
How much we weigh, how short we are,
Or how little we have left to drink?

Goodbye to Pounds by the Ton and all their Ounces,
To Gallons, Quarts, and Pints,
To Yards whose Feet are inching their last Mile,
Weighed down, poured out, written off,

And drifting slowly away from us
Like drams, like chains and gills,
To become as quaint as leagues and palms
In an old poem.

DAVID WAGONER

WORLD OF DARKNESS

The animals live in darkness. We
Call it "filtered light" but they know
It to be darkness and live in it as if
There were no light at all, their own
Night fenced by white bulbs
Lit to make them stay in ours.

The animals live in darkness we
Call "artificial nocturnal habitat"
And god, we ought to know,
We are the species which knows . . . but
For my part I know less and less.
When I was twenty I knew who
I was, who my friends were,
What I had to do and what
I loved. Now I am nearly thirty
And I know only what I love.
My hand holds the hand of a little
Boy who is afraid of snakes.

The animals live in darkness. We
Call this darkness "night" and we move
Along its railing. Our eyes dilate
And we see the snakes. The world
Ends. We enter the world of daylight
Blind and unable to find home.

ROBERT CHATAIN

From SONGS OF THE TRANSFORMED

SIREN SONG

This is the one song everyone
would like to learn: the song
that is irresistable:

the song that forces men
to leap overboard in squadrons
even though they see the beached skulls

the song nobody knows
because anyone who has heard it
is dead, and the others can't remember.

Shall I tell you the secret
and if I do, will you get me
out of this bird suit?

I don't enjoy it here
squatting on this island
looking picturesque and mythical

with these two feathery maniacs,
I don't enjoy singing
this trio, fatal and valuable.

I will tell the secret to you,
to you, only to you.
Come closer. This song

is a cry for help: Help me!
Only you, only you can,
you are unique

at last. Alas
it is a boring song
but it works every time.

MARGARET ATWOOD

VOWEL MOVEMENTS

Take a statement: the same as yesterday's dictation:
   Lately pain has been there waiting when I awake.
Creative despair and failure have made their patient.
   Anyway, I'm afraid I have nothing to say.
Those crazy phrases I desecrated the paper
   With against the grain . . . Taste has turned away her face
Temporarily, like a hasty, ill-paid waitress
   At table, barely capable but very vague.
Mistaken praise and blame degrade profane and sacred
   Places so strange you may not even know their names.
Vacant the gymnasium where words once played naked
   Amazing games that always used to end in mate.

Better, then, the effort than preterite perfection,
   I guess. Indeed, I envy the eminent dead
The special effects I am ready to inherit
   Less than their sentiments and impenitent sense
Of aesthetic gesture. Unpleasant and pretentious,
   The Western hemisphere has plenty to forget.
The mess men might yet make of themselves, given present
   Events! Are many content to accept the best?

Precious as sex is, flesh, perennially wretched
  Begs the bread of heaven, blessing nevertheless
The unexpected sender's address on a letter.
  Every breathless sentence says not yet to death.

The past cannot matter except as an abstraction,
  A flattering caricature of happy lands
Wherein many a grand, imaginary castle
  In fact turns out to be a tourist trap at last,
A vast palace that adrastic phantoms inhabit.
  Maps of madness characteristically blank
Ask vatic questions, exact a magic answer:
  The family photograph album at a glance,
Granny, Dad, Aunt Sally, that dissatisfied madame
  Who manages passion's incalculable acts —
Paris, everyman's romantic trash and tarry —
  Abracadabra, and the vanished cast comes back!

(If civilization isn't a silly gimmick,
  Is it the wit to wish, the will to make it stick?
The mathematical vision which built this system
  Figures the width of a minute within an inch.
Primitive physics, a sophisticated fiction,
  Insists that in principle everything is fixed.
Visitors picnic amid pretty *Chichén Itzá,*
  With its sacrificial pit, artificial hills
And cricket pitch wherein the winner is the victim.
  To think an instinct like iniquity exists!
Hidden riches fill big individual middens;
  In the Wizard's Pyramid little lizards live.)

Specious sweets we reach for eagerly with Eve's evil
  Greed recede like the fleeting details of a dream.
It seems that we have been a brief season in Eden:
  Chic unreal estates where immediately green
Trees repeated in completely meaningless series
  Briefly yield to the weaker tyranny of weeds
Even as we seek relief in a secret clearing.
  Prehistory can be too recent; need we read
These steles' queried speech? Here undefeated peoples

Experienced deceit; here scenes of deepest grief
Teach us to weep the cheap and easy tears of reason;
  Here the sea of being sleeps, a period peace.

Frustration, fuss, and lust are love's unlucky colours.
  Thunderstruck, the muscular monuments look dumb.
Judged by the numbers that once flourished in the jungle
  In hundreds of miles of dull undercover scrub,
Unless somebody was insufferably ugly
  Mistrust of one another must be in the blood.
Unsuccess in a dozen tough struggles instructs us
  Justice is a mother-fucker. Suffering's fun
For a month, but in a millennium no wonder
  One becomes somewhat disgusted. Unsubtle skull,
The mysteries of dust are nothing to live up to.
  Insulted by a touch, one mutters, "Summer sucks."

Undone by the siesta and by sudden showers
  Is it uncomfortable in the hungry South?
Now cowed by Kulkulkan's geometrical scowl,
  Now smitten by classic brown faces in a crowd,
You falter at mounds memorial to a thousand
  Bleeding hearts in a single holiday cut out,
Submitted to the sun, insatiable flesh-flower
  Of the universe, all-devouring powerhouse,
Confounded by our sound of pronounceable vowels.
  (Myths, as the guide allows, are handed down by mouth.)
Though mood and voice and person, gender, tense and
    number
  Predicate a verb, its cases explain a noun.

Proper noun or pronoun, indubitably human,
  Whose beautiful excuse is, usually, youth,
Doomed to the brutal usufructu of the future,
  Consumed by the illusions of jejune amours.
You used to choose the rules with superfluous humour,
  Tuned to the influential movements of the moon
Whose smooth translucent route through roofless rooms
    illumines
  From dewy moonrise unto lunar afternoon

Tulum and its improvements, tumulus and ruins,
  Poorly reproduced, a too crudely stupid view.
Who knew nude truth from rumour, amusement from music
  Soon would prove a fool. Beauty, useless, is a wound

On and off; the impossible is honour's motto,
  Monotony the awful drawback of my song.
What was lost was often all we had got in common,
  Our quasi-comic quandary depended on
Qu'en dirai-je? chronic, colossal hypochondry,
  Neurotic complication or hypnotic calm.
Gods begotten of loss, not bronze nor terra cotta
  Haunt the province of law, of cause and conscious wrong.
Following the Long Count a lot has been forgotten:
  Positive nonsense, fraud, false plots and hollow talk,
Soporific concepts toppled by Fall or Conquest,
  The cosmos as a model watch that wants to stop.

At any moment the doors of the soul may open
  And those reproachful ghosts invoked from the remote
Coasts of tomorrow begin to impose the order
  Of bone and trophy, home and the odour of smoke.
O mornings that broke on the slopes of cold volcanoes,
  Almost frozen, golden and old-rose, like a scroll
Slowly unfolded, or a brocade robe thrown over
  The throne of the mountains, cloaking their cones in snow!
How, an emotion swollen by every omen,
  No psychotrope, only a semi-precious stone,
Topaz or opal, adorns the close of the strophe.
  Woe wrote these notes in a code also known as prose.

Ode: this leafy, streamless land where coy waters loiter
  Under the embroidered soil, subterfluous coin
Of another culture destroyed by lack of moisture,
  Spoiled by the unavoidable poison of choice.
Archaeological lawyers exploit the foibles
  Of a royalty that in time joined *hoi polloi:*
History's unemployed, geography's anointed
  Unlike the orchids of the forests, spin and toil.
Imperfectly convinced of final disappointment,

Persuaded of the possibility of joy,
Pen poised for the pointless impressions of those voices
    That boil up like bubbles on the face of the void,

Finally I try to define why divine silence
    Underlies the tidy designs of paradise.
Priceless as the insights of the inspired psyche,
    Blind, violent as a geyser, right as a rhyme,
Fine ideas likely to undermine the idle
    Mind divided between the types of fire and ice,
"Highly stylized" politely describes the bright eyesores
    Shining like diamonds or rhinestones in the night sky,
Lifelike, provided life survives its vital cycle
    And the tireless indictment of time's diatribe,
While mankind, sightless, frightened, like a child in twilight
    Dies of the devices it was enlightened by.

Amazing games that always used to end in mate!
Precious as sex is, flesh, perennially wretched
    In fact turns out to be a tourist trap at last.
The mathematical vision which built this system
    Of the universe, all-devouring power-house
(The mysteries of dust are nothing to live up to!)
    Briefly yields to the weaker tyranny of weeds.
You used to choose the rules with superfluous humour:
    Monotony, the awful drawback of my song,
Slowly unfolded, like a brocade robe thrown over.
    Persuaded of the possibility of joy,
Finally I tried to define why divine silence . . .

DARYL HINE

NARCISSUS: TO HIMSELF

What of these verses that I write,
Imperfect, yet in which I see
Fictions and truths, noble and trite,
That sometimes show what's left of me!

DAVID GALLER

495

LOOK TO THE BACK OF THE HAND

It is a water hand, this right one,
changed by the will and actions;
fingers long and tapering, palm
not thick or calloused, skin
clear, yet slightly flushed with emotion:
the hand, perhaps, of an artist.
Do not look at the back of this hand.

The finger of Apollo reaches long
into creativity: seeker who never finds self.
The thumb rises strong, supple
with generosity, stretching toward ambition.
Benevolence, platonic love,
devotion are read in the mounts.
Do not turn this hand over.

It is an atlas surrounded by lakes,
full of paths and roads, hills valleys plains.
Lines intersect, fork off,
chain — yet the signs remain.
It erodes with years, wears
my signature and I cannot change it.
"Hair on the back of the hand
denotes extreme cruelty in a woman."

JUDITH MINTY

From THE JOY OF COOKING

CONSERVES

Season, ending, makes no sign, but the wind
And the light which rake across the vine change,
Fall away, bring the months to mind in chains
Of figures round its iron calender;
Rise and set of years sheds remembered light,
No other, while in this raw hour, outside,

A season writhes along the shaken vine,
Dies, and drags to its death some fruitless pride.

Fruit which comes away light from the main stalk,
Bearing no blemish, will last a winter
In still, cool places. Fruit which holds the stalk
May be cankered or green, do not force it,
Crude hands make a sour stomach. Fruit fallen
Will be bruised, though none show: it rots or stews.

There is no ideal time for canning.

DAVID MUS

ODE TO PORNOGRAPHY

Hail mer-
ry, tricky, and clandestine
art! the schoolboy's peek at what might follow
first pubic hairs and acne, toy
for the worldly, secret vice
for the prim and proper, scorned

by priest,
proscribed by censor, you still
bear a socially redeeming message:
through photos, drawings, films, and books
you show jocund multitudes
eager, active (and passive),

going
at it in couples, threesomes,
and jampacked gangbangs, smooching and licking
whatever's in sight and rolling
around naked on beds, fur,
bearskin rugs, and haybarn floors

humping

non-stop any man, woman,

or friendly beast as fancy prompts, happy
  to tempt us with, over here, some
    curious devices and, there,
    touch of lace or leather.

   high heels
  or creamy salves: the orgy
just keeps going — recoupling in every
  known position while inventing
    fresh ones, these people are as
    simple and classic as those

   in farce,
  and their action is as com-
plicated, yet it all comes out all right —
  Pornography! you make us want
    to romp at large, consenting
    adults where choice is free and

   easy
  and no one blushes, suffers
guilt, hurts, or gets hurt, and if your world can't
  fit yet within our cramped confines
    you prod us into gasping
    for plenitudes ruddier than

   our pinched
  morality — I rise now,
I swell to climax! — as judges judge you
  wanton, I praise you, knowing how
    our species can be best and
    blessed when we are most at play.

JACK ANDERSON

ANGELS

Most are innocent, shy, will not undress.
They own neither genitals nor pubic hair.

Only the fallen of the hierarchy
make an appearance these secular days.

No longer useful as artists' models,
dismissed by theologians, morale tends
to be low — even high class angels grumble
as they loiter in our empty churches.

Neutered, they hide when a gothic door opens.
Sudden light blinds them, footsteps deafen,
Welsh hymns stampede their shadows entirely.
Still their stink lingers, cold stone and incense.

But the fallen dare even 10 Downing Street,
astonish, fly through walls for their next trick;
spotlit, enter the dreams of the important,
slowly open their gorgeous, Carnaby wings.

DANNIE ABSE

THE POEM

I had never heard of the whiteness
Of such poetry — of that sweet blank of paper
You called "The Compassionate Buddha."

He lives by himself in that poem
Which bid me — and like that page, in time
I have come to rest beneath its sheer net.

DAVID SCHLOSS

THE MIRROR

Here is a child who is leaning over a paper,
A pencil in hand. And what he seems to be doing
is drawing or thinking to draw. Or perhaps he is writing,
Writing or drawing a summer he stands by the sea.

He is drawing or writing a child leaning over a paper
Who is perfectly through with the summer, through with
    the sea.

And that is the world. The world is what he is writing
Or drawing perhaps. The world is the drawing or
    writing,
Perhaps is the child, perhaps the summer and sea.

JOHN N. MORRIS

THE DAY YOU ARE READING THIS

The planet of Nothing fills the sky, and
a philosopher goes out and admires that
greatest of all discoveries in the heavens.

Even the rest of us, now and then we
fall outward and on into that glorious
hole where all of us really are.

But mostly we look steadily at the
stars, and when we meet someone
we say, "Have a good day."

WILLIAM STAFFORD

SIGNS

Threading the palm, a web of tiny lines
Spells out the lost money, the heart, the head,
The wagging tongues, the sudden deaths, in signs
We would smooth out like imprints on a bed,

In signs that can't be helped, geese heading south,
In signs read anxiously, like breath that clouds
A mirror held to a barely open mouth,
Like telegrams, the gathering of crowds —

The plane, an X in the sky spelling disaster:
Before the whistle and hit, a tracer flare;
Before rubble, a hairline crack in plaster
And a housefly's panicked scribbling on the air.

GJERTRUD SCHNACKENBERG

HOMAGE TO THE CARRACCI

Limp as unwatered flowers, the grey limbs
And academic heads of vanquished caryatides
Droop from the illusory ledge, casting
Satisfying shadows on the ovolo, the astragal,
The egg-and-dart. This round tribune supports,
As well, a whole encyclopaedia of engines
And machineries devised to pull down
The dome on top of us. Some of the pulleys
Already are in place, ropes taut, the frescoed
Laborers straining at the winches.
A crack's perceptible across
The cloud on which a god's superior anatomy
Reposes. He smiles, not oblivious
But as though from the first stroke
Of his natal brush he's been aware that
He, his pantheon, the cloud, the crack, and all this
Foreshortened, revolutionary crew were nothing
But paint and plaster, ingenious and untrue.
God of this ceiling, let us worship you!

TOM DISCH

THE PLEASURE OF RUINS

We cannot walk like Byron among Ayasoluk's ruined
mosques, kicking the heads off yellow iris and eating
cold lamb, but still we never envy the Bedouin

for whom no city dies because any wall will brace
against a sand-struck wind. A heat rash or hotel dream,
with luck a capital's stone egg, or the rippled trace

of arches under water, perhaps a sketch, are all we take
back each week. If the statues were painted and the floors
were squared to scale, we would have no taste to make

the slow sacrifice to knowledge and learn the tomb
was always a gate, its prayers were only warnings
or directions for strangers towards the storeroom

we had made a court for our regret: that lizards
keep the place of lions in the garden, tracking
the sun across stones cut by history's haphazard

rearrangements, or the initials of a need to stay
beyond ourselves on columns. The prophets were right.
Babylon is "an astonishment and an hissing," afraid

to be seen in ropes and rails only guides dare cross.
So long quarried or fortified, the past is portioned now
to front the digs that sift what leaves us at a loss.

We frieze our hurts to watch them rubbed smooth
by tourists, and these reliefs are stunned in glass,
case studies scattered in city museums to approve

our pleasure at the site. Pleasure? The sight survives
its defeat and holds sea and cliff to a coast of pines
aligned like pillars to shade what gods may yet arrive.

J. D. MC CLATCHY

SATYR

My horny feet are cutting through the fog,
Which is no fog to me; my medium,
My element is their ambiguous

Relation to the other. Who are they?
I know and you know they are those who need
Just what I have to give them at this moment.
I concentrate the fog to clarity,
I hold them in the motions of one will.
If, afterwards, they drift in fog again,
Or if they don't remember, who could care,
Who has regrets, knowing the joys that rise
The more intense for being unregarded?
Listen, my hooves are sharp upon the stones —
The sounds are questions, opportune, intent.
Assuage your curiosity! You need
Their answers in the fundamental act.

CHARLES GULLANS

A RAIN OF RITES

Sometimes a rain comes
slowly across the sky, that turns
upon its grey cloud, breaking away into light
before it reaches its objective.

The rain I have known and traded all this life
is thrown like kelp on the beach.
Like some shape of conscience I cannot look at,
a malignant purpose in a nun's eye.

Who was the last man on earth,
to whom the cold cloud brought the blood to his face?
Numbly I climb to the mountain-tops of ours
where my own soul quivers on the edge of answers.

Which still, stale air sits on an angel's wings?
What holds my rain so it's hard to overcome?

JAYANTA MAHAPATRA

AN ASTRONOMER'S JOURNAL

Even in sleep my eyes are on the elements.
My eyes are pencils being perpetually resharpened
puzzling out the sky's connecting dots
one almost expects to be accompanied by numbers,
jig-saw animal shaped constellations,
bear, bent dipper, wed fish in repose,
crowding out the angels who I suppose
must be stacked up tier on tier
as in the horseshoe of the opera house.
Each night the sky splits open like a melon
its starry filaments
the astronomer examines with great intensity.
Caught in his expensive glass eye
more microscope than telescope,
it is his own eye he sees, reflected
and possessed, a moon-disc in a lake,
safe, even to himself, untouchable;
and so his notion of himself must be corrected:
"Actually, the universe is introspective".

JANE SHORE

From ESSAY ON PSYCHIATRISTS

XIV. THEIR SPEECH, COMPARED WITH WISDOM AND POETRY

Terms of all kinds mellow with time, growing
Arbitrary and rich as we call this man "neurotic"
Or that man "a peacock." The lore of psychiatrists —

"Paranoid", "Anal" and so on, if they still use
Such terms — also passes into the status of old sayings:
Water thinner than blood or under bridges; bridges

Crossed in the future or burnt in the past. Or the terms
Of myth, the phrases that well up in my mind:
Two blind women and a blind little boy, running —

Easier to cut thin air into planks with a saw
And then drive nails into those planks of air,
Than to evade those three, the blind harriers,

The tireless blind women and the blind boy, pursuing
For long years of my life, for long centuries of time.
Concerning Justice, Fortune and Love

There may be wisdom, but no science and few terms:
Blind, and blinding too. Hot in pursuit and flight,
Justice, Fortune and Love demand the arts

Of knowing and naming: and, yes, the psychiatrists, too,
Patiently naming them. But all in pursuit and flight, two
Blind women, tireless, and the blind little boy.

ROBERT PINSKY

BORDERING MANUSCRIPT

I am alert to these letters in extraordinary numbers: perhaps
   from grass heavy-headed with seed, flickering a's and r's
under pressure of sun that I recognize as holy and intended —
   while a bird of indecipherable mind is scrolling margins of
     air.
A gold, illegible word rests on the left hand of vision.
   Illusions of its spelling leaf from the lacquer of hedges past
exits of buildings. Women removed across hundred-foot
     stretches
   of chained grass evoke vowels with their liftings of hair,
but let me confess: the name could be a man's as well as a
     woman's.
   People printed with my children and wife in the foreground,
     though
accurate and clear, seem from a sufficient, forgetful distance
   to twine into the gigantic characters which fit no speech.
Places redolent with heat and resinous pines of meetings
   perhaps ten years ago form amber in retrospect.

The puzzle I see has thousands of pieces, each poor day
   hiding its two or one. Had I all the days permanently
     together,
I could assemble the jig-sawed chips in a lifetime. This
     thought
   chills me close to a water-like stillness, tea-colored and
     brackish
with vacations on rivers, as if a plane of focus shimmering
     behind
   the tear in a photograph, or body of air from all fields
inhabiting a music. Behind my lips, tipping my unknown
   tongue, she waits in her surface, her name my speech's
     mistress.

JAMES APPLEWHITE

A YOUNGER POET

No more exercises of style for him

He watches the energies that once fueled them
Dissolve in acids of self-suspicion

The tricks and glamors of favorite past masters
He has either assimilated or must discard now

His mode, for better and worse, seems set

He can now set about evading self-parody

How to be true to, though disappointed in, his art
Has become his major care
And actual subject matter, however couched

Should it bother him that those who read him
Understand things he didn't think he'd written?

It doesn't, he's grateful for any attention

But the more he tries to be clear, the more stupid
He seems to himself, the more stupid his readers seem

Stupidity coats the Earth like a vegetable invasion
In one of his inexpressible visions
— Or does it pour from the Earth itself, like lava?
In any case, it covers everything

He pokes at it obsessively
With the instrument of his chastened line

PETER SCHJELDAHL

INFLATION

There was a time (such songs begin this way)
When every jewel that graced a pocket, each
Pebble and shell, keepsake of thought's delay
Over some bit of world, had a private speech,
The stored-up, light, long story of a day.

But now there greet the fingers, when they reach
Their refuge, in place of something that might relate
The feel of summer, searchings of a beach,
Car, house, and office on a chain, a weight
Of paper, a half-handful of silver speech.

CHARLES O. HARTMAN

DOME POEM

Not, of course, the monster hunched downtown
    with its rigid paws coiled into purchase
        where it seems to take a quiet shit,
    though it is certainly attractive enough,
with Parian marble and stained glass slits,

    to tell us something if we looked close instead
        of up, dizzying ourselves until we forget

507

what it was we were looking at it for or
where we are. But no, not that Whitmanian
lump of what is bigger and better than other

such creations. What we must have is so simple
it constantly sits there like a shadow's
shadow on water, bones and tendons slyly
hidden so only the maker knows how it is
done, and it smiles and says simplify, simplify.

It is so much like America, too, that anyone
inside looks out uninhibited on the stars
which suddenly become real and intense
like the rain beating wherever we are
until it is a waterfall of original innocence,

even though there may be a syphilitic finger
gouging a tender trench. What matters to
us is the words it can nourish, hold,
even generate like scribes in slow sweat,
row on row distilling the King James that no

one of them thought more worthy than his poems.
But a poem is a kind of country, full
of tent stays and lines you always kick
at night, politicians and old women with
old eyes loving the transparent, cheap silk

anybody can use to set up one of those lean-to
lily-pads. The good thing about a dome
is the way the principle reduces, extends
one drop of water to its proto-shape, one
wounded round atom smashing back in vengeance

it has never conceived in its watery head.
Splitting the atom reveals the absence
neither heart nor mind can bear, air,
whose stout shell the dome leans on, that
darkness in and out of rooms, mouths, words.

DAVE SMITH

1975

SENTIENCE

"The female genital, like the blank page anticipating the
     poem,
is an absence, a not me, which I occupy.
By occupying absence, I experience myself becoming more
than what I was. The blank page and this genital
are an appeal to being. By being where I was not,
I am no longer self-contained: I experience myself
in the dimensions, contours, textures of my mate.
When she is naked like lava undressed of pine
I not only feel her but see her. She is wrinkled.
I am poor; I will take even the wrinkled.
High country, faceless, rough on the feet, swindling the
     lungs.
I am poor but igneous landscape asks nothing of me
nor gives me anything I want but myself."

SANDRA MC PHERSON

WAITING ROOMS

What great genius invented the waiting room?
Every sublime idea no doubt is simple, but
Simplicity alone is never enough.
A cube sequestered in space and filled with time,
Pure time, refined, distilled, denatured time
Without qualities, without even dust . . .
Dust in a sunbeam between Venetian blinds
Where a boy and his mother wait . . . Eternity!
But I am straying from the subject: waiting rooms.

All over the globe, in the great terminals
And the tiny rooms of disbarred abortionists,
For transport, diagnosis, or divorce . . .
Alas! Maybe this mighty and terrible theme
Is too much for me. But wait! I have an idea.

You've heard it said, of course, that anything
May instantly turn into everything
In this world secreting figures of itself
forever and everywhere? How wonderful
That is, how horrible. Wherever you wait,
Between anticipation and regret,
Between the first desire and the second
Is but the razor of a moment, is
Not even time; and neither is motion more,
At sixty miles an hour or six hundred,
Than an illusion sent by devils to afford
Themselves illusory laughs at our expense
(we suffer, but they become no happier).

Think how even in heaven where they wait
The Resurrection, even in the graves
Of heaven with the harps, this law applies:
One waiting room will get you to the next.
Even your room, even your very own,
With the old magazines on the end tables,
The goldfish in the bowl below the window
Where the sunbeam falls between Venetian blinds . . .
And in the downstairs hall there is your mailbox,
One among many gathering paper and dust,
A waiting room in figure, summing up
Much in a little, the legendary box
Where hope only remains. You wait and see.

HOWARD NEMEROV

THE WAITING-ROOM

I sit thinking of a rowing-boat I saw
at rest on transparent water, not
quite at rest, testing its rope, testing
the weight that kept it steady and weightless.

Something from Beethoven goes on and on
at the side of my mind, like a bad-tempered neighbour.

Strange how so much impatience
won through to such inhuman calm.

I wait. A fan drones away. It's so
monotonous the room could be in flight.
I sit staring at a mirror. All it shows
is the reflection of a pale barred window.

ROBIN FULTON

WINTER REPORT

The world is several billion years of age
   and I am thirty. Last year's grass
comes up like whiskers through the snow
   and the shovel leans against the barn.
And I am weary, weary of metaphor,
   of making from the residue of thought
a gathered whole. And what is gathered?
   Surely not the fantasies that spring
from a pile of bricks imagined as a building,
   nor the memories that cling
to padlocks, stumps, old cable. All
   is wrapped, tied, presented whole
to those who believe in wholes, or wish to.
   And the voices speaking quietly
backstage, the doubts and questions rising in
   the mind, remain unheard
by any reader. This fine deception
   can't go on. The bright sunlight falls
on the ice at the peak of a roof
   but doesn't melt it. The roof itself
is bent. And the thing which only a moment ago
   I'd thought to say, is already fled and gone.

BEN HOWARD

DIEHARD

At first blush, discomfiting
to turn so beyond belief
credulous no time after the creed
failed than which anything

must have seemed less
unbelievable — Yeti, UFO
spacecraft, witchcraft,
monster in Loch Ness —

till time told why
any world's more likely
than one whose truths all
always meet the eye.

JUDITH MOFFETT

DECEPTION

Someone fits a flute to his lips, and
The reprise begins: your hand in mine,
Distance to be negotiated, full course
Of days, shrugging off the differences,
Moving on parallel runways of glass.
From my side you also went transparent,
Lace of your veins outlining a form
In the root-system of the arbor vitae,
Devouring time itself devoured.

Nothing predicted tonight, the zero air,
Old ironies newly pointed in cascade
Down the fire-escape, broken water
On the pavement treacherous underfoot.
No hour passes but lets fall a token
Of hope or denial. The statue, whose
Blue damages suggest a man of snow,

Comes back to life to witness its death —
And now gives up that ghost of form only
A child or a fool would try to restore:
Try and fail, try and fail and try.

ALFRED CORN

"CAN I TEMPT YOU TO A POND WALK?"

1

Tender fingers ran up my ankle
I was tempted and I fell
into a muddy stroll along
a field path of matted grass
to unreflecting water and
an unfinished, abandoned house
(cement blocks), a bombed-out building.

2

A hedgerow, trees grow in wild file.
Behind a scrim of cloud, a smudge
was mother, father, brother, sister sun.
A distant sound of shots: hunters.
I have nothing to say.

3

No, nothing to say. Tears
for my lost youth? Nope, not
even those. Soon a moon
full or almost full will rise
behind those clouds that hover,
forever, over Long Island. It
is almost New Year. May it
be better than the last. One
makes it so, of course, oneself.

Oh, I don't know about that,
nor why yesterday was sunny
and today was not. "Can I
tempt you to a pond walk?"
I have nothing to say; but, well, yes.

JAMES SCHUYLER

FROM THE RIGHTEOUS MAN EVEN THE
WILD BEASTS RUN AWAY

O take me to the sullen flats
Where I may linger through the day
Appeased, though riven by each sense,
And gather to a certitude.
There I belong. Only today
A much-feared wolf retreated at
My scholar's eye: the temperate man
Admits no hunger not his own.
(Send him the hard beatitude
Of one sun in the place-locked sky.)

Ample journey if the soul
Flung what it took and could not help
— That going, brimming, everywhere —
To lighten in a sudden small
And lucid elementary globe,
Improbable, unstemmed, at rest,
And white on who receives its gaze.
(In that new land where the old trees
Are shattered to an unmeant shade,
I'd be imposed upon by things.)

Until each falling look obeyed
Line that wore to an edge. How close
These solemn feintings into sight,
How proper to the exile of
Large simulacra: so the reign

Of objects sorted one by one,
The mountain at horizon-lip,
Aspens divulging endlessly.
(Discreet yet lively in all touch
Who shall dare to settle here?)

I'd lean to rubbled things that make
Below the harvest they survive
A clarifying signature,
Rapt and unwelcome. Quartz maybe;
Obsidian that burned to live
Unsorrowing, conditional;
Or else some stone just isolate.
(The steady hills call out a name.
Over and over they must speak
The water's cadences alone.)

DAVID BROMWICH

THE DUMP

The field of poetry ends here
and I have come to this point
and looked over into the hollow
where no two things match up,
and there are no levels on levels
of meaning among the garbage.
It is a shock to see how much
of this is mine, the thrown out,
the once-let-slip now gone. Here
is an epigraph, and over there,
under a pillow swollen with tears
or rain, a dream of waking up alone,
or sad, the theme gone undeveloped
in my later poems. And other
things as well. All, all come
to reside here, a great indigestible,
the cooked and the uncooked,

the drowsy and the rock dead,
simile between whose items
the strands are frayed or the
clasp half gone. A bracelet
on an arm, but the arm detached.
A frying pan full of skylarks,
a Buick with its license plate
taped over the windshield,
and all the scenes from childhood
stranded single on their flaps
of paper photographs, faded,
or with oil saturated. And none
of the faces matching the faces
I had placed back when I
knew these people, never looked
at them. It must have been
that poetry goes on without
the facts. So much retouching
and reconstructing goes into it,
so much it is the magic show
of the undisclosed: the dream
brought nervously to light once,
and looked upon out of half-open eyes,
displacing the actual leg and nose.
This is clearly far from the tower.
Clearly the end of some road.
Or the edge of the mind's city,
against which it works and pushes.
Here the painful actual, that
which no rising meter can free,
the chaff of a life, the most of it,
its miscellaneous debris.

GREG KUZMA

TRANSLATION

Lost: the Original, its Reason and its Rhyme,
Words whose meanings do not change through time,

"The soul in paraphrase", the heart in prose,
Strictures or structures, meter, *les mots justes*;
"The owlet umlaut" when the text was German,
Two hours of sleep each night, hapax legomenon,
A sense of self, fidelity, one's honor,
Authorized versions from a living donor.

Found in translation: someone else's voice:
Ringing and lucid, whispered, distant, true,
That in its rising accents falls to you,
Wahlverwandtschaft, a fortunate choice,
A call to answer, momentary grace,
Unbidden, yours; a way to praise.

RIKA LESSER

FRAGMENTI

O tender-heartedness right bitter grown
Because they knew thee not in all the world
Nor would, that gentleness thou hast to give.

•

And are chevaliers in the court of Him
Who reigneth ever where the stars grow dim
Beyond our sight.

•

Marble smooth by flowing waters grown.

EZRA POUND

TO EARTH

Churning the compost, dazed
    by reverie, I've forked some bit,
face china-white, or hand like ivory.
    Recollections in fragments turn up

517

as leaves seem sifting earthward
   farther than the surface, snowing
into an unlighted place like birds
   migratory to the back of a mirror
as *here* stands reversed about
   a stump-root in-rotting by rings:
tree like a glove full of shadow
   inverted into land below the mind.

Straightening, I consider dissolution:
   this nitrogen, carbon, oxygen,
hydrogen, bark-bits and blossoms,
   cat's bird shrouded in leaves, fishes
aground, in shallows I see through,
   to spines still aligned in harps
and arrowing beyond, toward fields
   at home, houses which have flaked
to loam burying teacup fragments. Faces
   gleam with sun on tombstones.
I am haunted by the crumbled attics,
   handle feelings like Civil War swords:
metal for an elemental forge.

JAMES APPLEWHITE

THE ICE-CREAM WARS

Although I mean it, and project the meaning
As hard as I can into its brushed-metal surface,
It cannot, in this deteriorating climate, pick up
Where I leave off. It sees the Japanese text
(About two men making love on a foam-rubber bed)
As among the most massive secretions of the human spirit.
Its part is in the shade, beyond the iron spikes of the fence,
Mixing red with blue. As the day wears on
Those who come to seem reasonable are shouted down
(*Why you old goat!* Look who's talkin'. Let's see you
Climb off that tower — the waterworks architecture, both
   stupid and

Grandly humorous at the same time, is a kind of mask for
  him,
Like a seal's face. Time and the weather
Don't always go hand in hand, as here: sometimes
One is slanted sideways, disappears for awhile.
Then later it's forget-me-not time, and rapturous
Clouds appear above the lawn, and the rose tells
The old old story, the pearl of the orient, occluded
And still apt to rise at times).
                              A few black smudges
On the outer boulevards, like squashed midges
And the truth becomes a hole, something one has always
  known,
A heaviness in the trees, and no one can say
where it comes from, or how long it will stay —

A randomness, a darkness of one's own.

                                        JOHN ASHBERY

PRINCESS ELIZABETH OF BOHEMIA, AS PERDITA

The delicate girl was eager to air
her virgin flower-de-luce held tight held
high in her fist as a poodle's nose, rare
as a garnished mushroom on a jewelled
Stuart's table. The startling innocence
of her eyes made the sky a rumpled bed,
her white skin was refined as th' excremence
of that delicious bird: the dove. Like Ed
walks o'er fresh fields in Scottish tweed, her stroll
widened the sense of heather. Negligence,
too, was her tour de force. A barcarolle
restored to each heart her adolescence:
    caught in her eyes the late years wept, seeing
    th' impossibility of her being.

                              FRANK O'HARA   519

THE RING

I carry it on my keychain, which itself
is a big brass ring
large enough for my wrist,
holding keys for safe deposit box,
friends' apartments,
My house, office and faithless car.

I would like to wear it,
the only ornament on my plain body,
but it is a relic,
the husband gone to other wives,
and it could never be a symbol of sharing,
but like the gold it's made of, stands for possession, power,
the security of a throne.

So, on my keyring,
dull from resting in my dark purse,
it hangs, reminding me of failures, of beauty I once had,
of more ancient searches for an enchanted ring.

I understand, now, what that enchantment is, though.
It is being loved.
Or, conversely, loving so much that you feel loved.
And the ring hangs there
with my keys,
reminding of failure.

This vain head full of roses,
crystal, bleeding lips,

a voice doomed to listen, forever,
to itself.

DIANE WAKOSKI

THE DEATH OF THE MOON

Through the long death of the moon, we drank her light
As slowly as snow-melt, bearing her funeral
Against the turn of the earth by nights like flares
As she fell westward, trailing a torn shroud
Across the mountains, over the ashen water.

Our feet washed pale as shell, we faltered
After her, naming all she could answer,
But she turned her cold, lopsided face
Further away than we could follow.

She shrank to half a skull,
Sinking as if to sleep
At the salt edge of her grave.

Then her white knife,
Her closing eyelid.

Her darkness.

DAVID WAGONER

HERE AND NOW

The waters of earth come and go
like the waters of this sea
broken as it is out of the dust
of other men. Don't ask me why
I came down to the water's edge —
hell, I was young, and I thought
I knew life, I thought I could
hold the darkness the way a man
holds a cup of coffee before
he wakens, the way he pulls
at a cigarette and wonders

how he came to this room, the walls
scarred with the gray brush
of years, how he travelled so long
to waken this sagging bed, and takes
up his damp socks one by one
and the heavy shoes smelling of oil,
and doesn't cry out or even sigh
for fear he will hear. So I stood
and let the waves climb up
the dark shore. The village
slept behind me, my wife,
my kids, still dreaming of home,
and I, the dog of the house,
prowled the darkened streets
which lead here and to silence,
the first cold light smearing
the eastern sky and the Levante
blowing its warm salt breath
in my face. If I had commanded
the sun to stand still the day
would have come on moment
by moment climbing the white walls
of the town, if I'd cursed the air
it would've lightened before
my eyes at last a fire
at the tip of each wave, and in
its depths the sea turning from gray
to a dense blue. So I said
nothing, but when my eyes filled
slowly with the first salted
rains of sorrow, I let them
come believing I wept for joy
at the gift of one more day.
I suppose the wind still blows
at ease across the sleeping face
of the village I fled all those years
ago, and some young man comes
down to the sea and murmurs a word,
his name, or God's or a child's,

or maybe just the sea's. Let him
be wiser than I, let him fight back
the tears and taste only the sea's salt,
let him take what he can —
the trembling of his hands,
the silence before him, the slow
awakening of his eyes, the windows
of the town opening on first light,
the children starting suddenly
from their twisted sheets with a cry
of neither victory or defeat,
only the surprise of having come back
to what no one promised, here and now.

PHILIP LEVINE

TWININGS ORANGE PEKOE

The gas ring's hoarse exhaling wheeze,
Voice of blue flamelets, licks the kettle's
Copper underbelly, which crouches
Closer, concentrates, by degrees

Begins spellbound to match that pressure
And dragon tone. Breath crowds the slim
Tranced throat that cannot close or scream;
It spouts a rushing *whooo* of pleasure.

The brown potbellied pot, top doffed,
Reveals its scalded insides' tender
Nursery blue, from which a cloud
Exudes, and from its spout a slender

Curl. It sweats and loves the *tch*
A lid makes popping off a tin.
The fragrance deep as leafmold, rich
As pipe tobacco, coffee, cocoa;

Loves the spoon's dry *scroop,* the skin-
Tight leafheap scattered in its breast
(A tannic prickle); the swift boiling
Flashflood, spoonswirl, settling flight; loves best

The steeping in the dark: blind alchemy:
Tap water, and an acid that cures leather
Stains cups and eats through glazes, pregnantly
Stewing together,

To arch forth in a stream as brown and bright
And smoky as an eye, strain marbling up
Through milk and sugar in a stoneware cup,
White white on white.

                                        JUDITH MOFFETT

ELEGY

The pages of history open. The dead enter.
It is winter in the spine of the book
where they land, inexplicable texts,
and a small rain falling, a mist of promises,
disjointed sentences, woes, failures.

The dead are puzzled:
was it for this they left
the land of grammar, the syntax of their skin?
We turn the pages. We read.
Sometimes, in moments of vertigo,

we notice that they are speaking.
Tiny whinings and murmurings arise,
as of insects urging their rights, their dissatisfactions,
invisible insects dwelling uncomfortably
in the margins, in the white spaces around words.

SANDRA M. GILBERT

LIST OF THE EDITORS
OF *POETRY*

CREDITS

INDEX

———————————

The Editors of *Poetry*
and the dates of their tenure

Harriet Monroe, October 1912–September 1936

Morton Dauwen Zabel, October 1936–October 1937

George Dillon, November 1937–August 1942

Peter De Vries, September 1942–April 1946
(with Jessica Nelson North, Marion Strobel, John
Frederick Nims, and others)

George Dillon, May 1946–April 1949
(with Marion Strobel, Peter De Vries, John Frederick
Nims)

Hayden Carruth, May 1949–January 1950

Karl Shapiro, March 1950–September 1955
(with Henry Rago, Acting Editor,
February–September 1955)

Henry Rago, October 1955–March 1969
(with Daryl Hine, Visiting Editor,
October 1968–March 1969)

Daryl Hine, April 1969–December 1977

John Frederick Nims, January 1978–

CREDITS

Dannie Abse: "Near the Border of Insanities." Reprinted by permission of the author; Léonie Adams: "Counsel to Unreason." Reprinted in *High Falcon and Other Poems,* The John Day Company, 1929. Reprinted by permission of the author, from *Poems: A Selection,* Funk and Wagnalls, 1954; Mortimer J. Adler: "The Fearless." Reprinted by permission of the author; Conrad Aiken: "Discordants IV" ("Discordants III") and "Multitudes Turn in Darkness" ("The House of Dust, Part III"), from *Collected Poems 1916–1970* by Conrad Aiken. Copyright © 1953, 1970 by Conrad Aiken. Reprinted by permission of Oxford University Press, Inc.; Richard Aldington: "Images." Copyright © 1976 by Catherine Guillaume. Reprinted by permission of Rosica Colin Limited; Hervey Allen: "Upstairs Downstairs." Reprinted by permission of Richard F. Allen; Patrick Anderson: "Sestina in Time of Winter," from *The Colour as Naked* by Patrick Anderson. Reprinted by permission of the Canadian publisher, McClelland and Stewart Limited, Toronto; Sherwood Anderson: "A Visit" (from "Mid-American Songs"). Copyright 1918 by John Lane Company. Copyright renewed 1945 by Eleanor Copenhaver Anderson. Reprinted by permission of Harold Ober Associates Incorporated.

A. R. Ammons: "Close-up," reprinted from *Collected Poems, 1951–1971* by A. R. Ammons, with the permission of W. W. Norton & Company, Inc., New York, N.Y. Copyright © 1972 by A. R. Ammons; John Ashbery: "Grand Abacus," from *Some Trees,* copyright © 1956 by John Ashbery. All rights reserved. Reprinted by permission of the author and Georges Borchardt, Inc. "To Redouté," from *The Tennis Court Oath,* copyright © 1957, 1959, 1960, 1961, 1962 by John Ashbery. All rights reserved. Reprinted by permission of the author and Georges Borchardt, Inc.; W. H. Auden: "Journey to Ice-

529

531

"A Morning Letter." Published by Oyez (Berkeley) in *The Years As Catches,* 1966. Reprinted by permission of Robert Duncan. "Returning to Roots of First Feeling." Published by New Directions in *The Opening of the Field.* Reprinted by permission of New Directions Publishing Corporation; Clifford Dyment: "Sanctuary." Reprinted in *Collected Poems,* under the title "Secret Idiom." Reproduced by permission of J. M. Dent & Sons Ltd, London; Richard Eberhart: "Under the Hill" (from "Things Unknown"). Reprinted by permission of Richard Eberhart. "The Spider," from *The Quarry* by Richard Eberhart. Reprinted by permission of Chatto and Windus Ltd, London. "The Spider," from *Collected Poems: 1930–1976* by Richard Eberhart. Copyright © 1960, 1976 by Richard Eberhart. Reprinted by permission of Oxford University Press, Inc.

Loren Eiseley: "The Deserted Homestead." Reprinted by permission of Mable Langdon Eiseley, Executrix of the Estate of Loren C. Eiseley; Paul Eldridge: "To a Courtesan a Thousand Years Dead." Reprinted from *Cobwebs and Cosmos,* by Paul Eldridge, with the permission of Liveright Publishing Corporation. Copyright 1930 by Horace Liveright, Inc. Copyright renewed 1957 by Paul Eldridge, c/o Liveright Publishing Corporation; T. S. Eliot: "The Love Song of J. Alfred Prufrock." Copyright 1915 by Harriet Monroe. "Aunt Helen." Copyright 1916 by Harriet Monroe. "La Figla Che Piange," "Mr. Apollinax," and "Morning at the Window." Copyright 1916 by Harriet Monroe. Published by Harcourt Brace Jovanovich, Inc., in *Collected Poems 1909–1962* by T. S. Eliot. Reprinted by permission of Harcourt Brace Jovanovich, Inc.; William Empson: "Reflection from Rochester." Copyright 1936 by Harriet Monroe. "Bacchus III" ("The god who fled down with a standard yard"). Copyright 1940 by The Estate of Harriet Monroe. "Bacchus IV" ("The herm whose length measured degrees of heat"). Copyright 1942 by The Modern Poetry Association. Published by Harcourt Brace Jovanovich, Inc., in *Collected Poems of William Empson.* Reprinted by permission of Harcourt Brace Jovanovich, Inc.; Paul Engle: "Moving In," from *Embrace: Selected Love Poems* by Paul Engle. Reprinted by permission of Random House, Inc., and Alfred A. Knopf, Inc.

Arthur Davison Ficke: "III. The Wave Symphony" (from "Four Japanese Paintings") and "Perspective of Co-ordination" (from "Three Sonnets"). Reprinted by permission of Mrs. Stanhope B. Ficke; Leslie A. Fiedler; "No Ghost Is True" (from "Thou Shalt Surely Die . . ."). Reprinted by permission of Leslie A. Fiedler; Robert Finch: "Words." Reprinted by permission of The Macmillan Company of Canada Limited; Dudley Fitts: "Southwest Passage." Reprinted by permission of Cornelia H. Fitts; Robert Fitzgerald: "Midsummer," "Metaphysician," and "Metaphysical." Reprinted in *Spring Shade (Poems 1931–1970)* by Robert Fitzgerald. Copyright © 1971 by Robert Fitzgerald. Reprinted by permission of New Directions Publishing Corporation; John Gould Fletcher: "The Monadnock" (from "Chicago Poems"). Reprinted by permission of Booker Worthen and Ben Kimpel. Literary Executors of the Estate of Charlie May Fletcher; Hortense Flexner: "Contemporary." Reprinted by permission of Mrs. Maxwell Schubert; Robert Francis: "Part for the Whole." Reprinted by permission of The University of Massachusetts Press. "Cold." Reprinted by permission of Wesleyan University Press; Robert Frost: "The Code — Heroics" (retitled "The Code"), "The Flower-Boat," and "At Woodward's Gardens," from *The Poetry of Robert Frost,* edited by Edward Connery Lathem. Copyright 1928, 1930, 1939, © 1969 by Holt, Rinehart and Winston. Copyright 1936, © 1956, 1958 by Robert Frost. Copyright © 1964, 1967 by Lesley Frost Ballantine. Reprinted by permission of Holt, Rinehart and Winston, Publishers.

Roy Fuller: "Sonnet" ("The crumbled rock of London is dripping under") and "Soliloquy in an Air-Raid." Reprinted by permission of Dufour Editions, Inc., Chester Springs, PA 19425; Brewster Ghiselin: "Headland." Republished in *Against the Circle,* copyright 1946 by E. P. Dutton & Co., Inc. Reprinted by permission of Brewster Ghiselin; William Gibson: "Circe." Reprinted by permission of the author; Louis Ginsberg; "Hymn to Evil." Reprinted by permission of Edith Ginsberg; Francis Golffing: "The Higher Empiricism." Reprinted by permission of the author; Paul Goodman: "Dreams are the Royal Road to the Unconscious" and "Stanzas" ("thought I woke: the midnight sun"). From *Collected Poems,* by Paul Goodman. Reprinted by permission of Random House, Inc., and Alfred A. Knopf, Inc. "Little Ode." Reprinted by permission of Sally Goodman, Executrix of the Estate of Paul Goodman; W. S. Graham: "The Constructed Space." From *Malcolmn Mooney's Land,* Faber & Faber, 1970. Reprinted by permission of W. S. Graham; Robert Graves: "In the Beginning Was a Word." Copyright 1926 by Harriet Monroe. "The Cool Web," "Return of the Goddess Artemis," "The Foreboding," and "From the Embassy." Published in *Collected Poems of Robert Graves,* Doubleday, 1955. Copyright © 1955, by Robert Graves. All Rights Reserved. Reprinted by permission of Curtis Brown, Ltd.; Geoffrey Grigson: "The Professionals." Reprinted by permission of the author; Thom Gunn: "High Fidelity" and "The Unsettled Motorcyclist's Vision of His Death." Published in *The Sense of Movement,* Faber & Faber, Ltd., London. Reprinted by permission of Thom Gunn; Donald Hall:

Chester Kallman: "A Romance." Reprinted by permission of Curtis Brown Ltd. Copyright 1954 by Chester Kallman; Weldon Kees: "Henry James at Newport" and "Small Prayer." Reprinted from *The Collected Poems of Weldon Kees,* by permission of the University of Nebraska Press. © 1943, 1947, 1954 by Weldon Kees; © 1960 by John A. Kees; © 1962, 1975 by the University of Nebraska Press; X. J. Kennedy: "Nude Descending a Staircase." Reprinted from *Nude Descending a Staircase,* Doubleday, copyright © 1961 by X. J. Kennedy, with permission of the author; Francis King: "Séance." Reprinted by permission of the author; Galway Kinnell: "Braemar." Reprinted by permission of the author; A. M. Klein: "Upon the Heavenly Scarp," from *The Collected Poems of A. M. Klein,* edited by Miriam Waddington. Copyright © 1974. Reprinted by permission of McGraw-Hill Ryerson Limited.

Kenneth Koch: "Poem for My Twentieth Birthday," "Schoolyard in April," and "Permanently." Reprinted by permission of Grove Press, Inc., and Kenneth Koch; Alfred Kreymborg: "To W.C.W. M.D." Reprinted by permission of Dorothy Kreymborg, Executrix of the Estate of Alfred Kreymborg; Stanley Kunitz: "Prophecy on Lethe," Copyright 1929 by Stanley Kunitz; "Goose Pond," copyright © 1956 by Stanley Kunitz; and "Approach to Thebes," copyright © 1957 by Stanley Kunitz. From *Selected Poems 1928–1958* by Stanley Kunitz. Reprinted by permission of Little, Brown and Co., in association with Atlantic Monthly Press; Dilys Bennett Laing: "Eros Out of the Sea." Reprinted by permission of David Laing; V. R. Lang: "The Suicide." Copyright © by Bradley Phillips. Reprinted by permission of Bradley S. Phillips; D. H. Lawrence: "Green," "Illicit" ("On the Balcony"), "Nostalgia," "Moonrise," and "Don Juan," from *The Complete Poems of D. H. Lawrence* edited by Vivian de Sola Pinto and F. Warren Roberts. Copyright © 1964, 1971 by Angelo Ravagli and C. M. Weekley, Executors of the Estate of Frieda Lawrence Ravagli. Reprinted by permission of The Viking Press; Denise Levertov: "To the Snake," reprinted in *With Eyes at the Back of Our Head.* Copyright © 1959 by Denise Levertov Goodman. Reprinted by permission of New Directions Publishing Corporation; Cecil Day Lewis: "Winter Night," "Condemned" (from "The Magnetic Mountain"), from *Collected Poems 1954* by C. Day Lewis. Reprinted by permission of the Executors of the Estate of C. Day Lewis, Jonathan Cape Ltd, and the Hogarth Press.

Janet Lewis: "At Carmel Highlands." Reprinted by permission of Janet Lewis Winters; Nicholas Vachel Lindsay: "General William Booth Enters into Heaven," from *Collected Poems of Vachel Lindsay.* Copyright

537

INDEX

Abse, Dannie, *Near the Border of Insanities,* 260; *Angels,* 498

Adams, Léonie, *Counsel to Unreason,* 101

Adler, Mortimer J., *The Fearless,* 75

Aiken, Conrad, *From* DISCORDANTS: "Dead Cleopatra lies in a crystal casket," 29; *Multitudes Turn in Darkness,* 63

Aldan, Daisy, *Stones: Avesbury* 454

Aldington, Richard, *Images,* 31

Allen, Hervey, *Upstairs Downstairs,* 81

Ammons, A. R., *Close-Up,* 353; *Gravelly Run,* 371; *Transaction,* 426; *Play,* 439

Anderson, Jack, *A Garden of Situations,* 455; *Ode to Pornography,* 497

Anderson, Jon, *In Sepia,* 442

Anderson, Patrick, *Sestina in Time of Winter,* 304

Anderson, Sherwood, *A Visit,* 51

Applewhite, James, *Bordering Manuscript,* 505; *To Earth,* 517

Ashbery, John, *Grand Abacus,* 327; *To Redouté,* 338; *If the Birds Knew,* 390; *A Man of Words,* 488; *The Ice-Cream Wars,* 519

Atwood, Margaret, *Siren Song,* 490

Auden, W. H., *Journey to Iceland,* 177; "O who can ever praise enough," 179; *Voltaire at Ferney,* 197; "He watched with all his organs of concern," 213; *The Shield of Achilles,* 299; *Ode to the Medieval Poets,* 450

Avison, Margaret, *The Party,* 266; *Stray Dog, Near Ecully,* 347

Barker, George, *Sequence,* 181; *Ode Against St. Cecilia's Day,* 277; "Keelhauled across the star-wrecked death of God," 307

Barnard, Mary, *Shoreline,* 150

Beach, Joseph Warren, *Horatian Ode,* 310

Bell, Marvin, *The Music of the Spheres*, 428

Benedikt, Michael, *Fraudulent Days*, 409

Berg, Stephen, *Don't Forget*, 465

Berry, Wendell, *September 2*, 430

Berryman, John, *The Traveler*, 270; *The Cage*, 282; *Snow Line*, 391

Betjeman, John, *Crematorium*, 452

Bishop, Elizabeth, *Paris, 7 A.M.*, 183; *A Miracle for Breakfast*, 184; *From the Country to the City*, 186; *Song*, 186

Bishop, John Peale, *The Hunchback*, 76; *Hunger and Thirst*, 131; *The Ancestors*, 142

Bishop, Morris, *Dementia Praecox*, 90

Blackmur, R. P., *Resurrection*, 133; "Three silences made him a single word," 143

Blake, Howard, *Argent Solipsism*, 156

Bly, Robert, *Hurrying Away from the Earth*, 410; *After Long Busyness*, 444

Bock, Frederick, *Aubade: The Desert*, 351

Bogan, Louise, *Knowledge*, 83; *Hypocrite Swift*, 123; *Putting to Sea*, 175; *After the Persian*, 301

Booth, Philip, *Seeing Auden Off*, 394

Bottrall, Ronald, *Mating Answer*, 180; *Darkened Windows*, 192

Bowers, Edgar, *The Astronomers of Mount Blanc*, 381

Bowles, Paul, *Extract*, 127

Boyle, Kay, *Monody to the Sound of Zithers*, 84; *To a Seaman Dead on Land*, 100

Brinnin, John Malcolm, *At the Band Concert*, 224; *Angle Eye of Memory*, 256

Bromwich, David, *Wandsworth Common*, 485; *From the Righteous Man Even the Wild Beasts Run Away*, 514

Brooke, Rupert, *Nineteen-fourteen*, 21

Brooks, Gwendolyn, "Still Do I Keep My Look, My Identity . . . ," 242; *The Children of the Poor*, 275; *We Real Cool*, 362

Bryher, Winifred, *Blue Sleep*, 73; *Thessalian*, 91

Bunting, Basil, *The Word*, 121; *Fearful Symmetry*, 129; *Fishermen*, 147; *To Violet*, 222

Burford, William, *On the Apparition of Oneself*, 299

Bynner, Witter, *Grieve Not for Beauty*, 6; *Lines to Do With Youth*, 333

Carruth, Hayden, *From* CONTRA MORTEM, 398

Carnevali, Emanuel, *Walt Whitman*, 61

Carroll, Jim, *The Distances*, 415

Cassity, Turner, *Chronology*, 317; *Technique on the Firing Line*, 385; *The Gardens of Proserpine*, 395

Chatain, Robert, *World of Darkness*, 489

Ciardi, John, *First Snow on an Airfield*, 240; *Journal*, 246; *Death's the Classic Look*, 388

Clark, Tom, *The Greeks*, 422

Cole, Thomas, *Spider*, 476

Comfort, Alex, *The Lovers*, 232

Corn, Alfred, *Deception*, 512

Cowley, Malcolm, *Danny*, 68; *Nocturnal Landscape*, 85; *The Streets of Air*, 99

Crane, Hart, *At Melville's Tomb*, 98; *O Carib Isle!*, 104; *From* THE URN, 136

Creeley, Robert, *Song*, 365

Cullen, Countee, *For Amy Lowell*, 94

cummings, e. e., ")when what hugs stopping earth than silent is," 194; "anyone lived in a pretty how town," 206; "what if a much of a which of a wind," 236; "if(touched by love's own secret)we,like homing," 266; "how many moments must(amazing each," 375

Cunningham, J. V., *Sonnet on a Still Night*, 130; *Epigram*, 304; *Miramar Beach*, 392

Dahlberg, Edward, *Kansas City West Bottoms*, 120

Daiches, David, *Ulysses' Library*, 215; *Notes for a History of Poetry*, 379

Daryush, Elizabeth, *The Look*, 273

Davie, Donald, *Autumn Imagined*, 391

Davis, H. L., *Stalks of Wild Hay*, 70

Davison, Edward, *The Owl*, 94

de la Mare, Walter, *Things*, 208; *Antiques*, 208; *Immanent*, 224

Deutsch, Babette, "Tak for Sidst," 81; *Memory*, 218; *The Poem*, 284

De Vries, Peter, *Mirror*, 195

Dickey, James, *The Landfall*, 359; *Inside the River*, 372; *After the Night Hunt*, 381; *Venom*, 418

Dickey, William, *Teaching Swift to Young Ladies*, 359; *The Poet's Farewell to His Teeth*, 461

Dillon, George, *The Hard Lovers*, 97

Disch, Tom, *The Vowels of Another Language*, 452; *Homage to the Carracci*, 501

Dobyns, Stephen, *Counterparts*, 427

D., H. (Hilda Doolittle), *Epigram*, 6; *Moonrise*, 20; *Birds in Snow*, 109; *In Time of Gold*, 346

Dos Passos, John, *Crimson Tent*, 96

Drinkwater, John, *Invocation*, 41; *Reciprocity*, 51

Dugan, Alan, *Aside*, 242; *Niagara Falls*, 262; *Prison Song*, 307; *From Heraclitus*, 387

Duncan, Robert, *A Spring Memorandum*, 229; *A Morning Letter*, 344; *Returning to Roots of First Feeling*, 363; *After a Passage in Baudelaire*, 387

Dyment, Clifford, *Sanctuary*, 155

Eberhart, Richard, *Under the Hill*, 106; *The Spider*, 362; *Plain Song Talk*, 465

Eiseley, Loren C., *The Deserted Homestead,* 112

Eldridge, Paul, *To a Courtesan a Thousand Years Dead,* 91

Eliot, T. S., *The Love Song of J. Alfred Prufrock,* 24; *Aunt Helen,* 31; *La Figlia Che Piange,* 39; *Mr. Apollinax,* 40; *Morning at the Window,* 40

Empson, William, *Reflection from Rochester,* 173; *Bacchus III,* 204; *Bacchus IV,* 227

Engle, Paul, *Moving In,* 202

Fainlight, Ruth, *Fire-Queen,* 471

Ficke, Arthur Davison, *The Wave Symphony,* 41; *Perspective of Co-ordination,* 76

Fiedler, Leslie A., *No Ghost Is True,* 258

Finch, Robert, *Words,* 221

Finkel, Donald, *Metaphysic of Snow,* 397

Fitts, Dudley, *Southwest Passage,* 113

Fitzgerald, Robert, *Midsummer,* 122; *Metaphysician,* 144; *Metaphysical,* 336

Fletcher, John Gould, *The Monadnock,* 52

Flexner, Hortense, *Contemporary,* 103

Forbes, Calvin, *Gabriel's Blues,* 432

Ford, Ford Madox. *See* Hueffer

Francis, Robert, *Part for the Whole,* 246; *Cold,* 312

Frost, Robert, *The Code — Heroics,* 10; *The Flower-Boat,* 87; *At Woodward's Gardens,* 162

Fuller, Roy, "The crumbled rock of London is dripping under," 202; *Soliloquy in an Air-Raid,* 219

Fulton, Robin, *The Waiting-Room,* 510

Galler, David, *Narcissus: To Himself,* 495

Ghiselin, Brewster, *Headland,* 197; *Credo,* 472

Gibson, William, *Circe,* 278

Gilbert, Sandra M., *The Fog Dream,* 482; *Elegy,* 524

Ginsberg, Louis, *Hymn to Evil,* 103

Glassco, John, *For Cora Lightbody, R. N.,* 446

Glück, Louise, *The Magi,* 444

Golffing, Francis C., *The Higher Empiricism,* 249

Goodman, Paul, "Dreams Are the Royal Road to the Unconscious," 263; *Stanzas,* 275; *Little Ode,* 287

Graham, W. S., *The Constructed Space,* 350; *The Beast in the Space,* 408

Graves, Robert, *In the Beginning Was a Word,* 101; *The Cool Web,* 102; *Return of the Goddess Artemis,* 268; *The Foreboding,* 295; *From the Embassy,* 306

Gregory, Horace, *On a Celtic Mask by Henry Moore,* 377; *Death & Empedocles 444 B.C.,* 475

Grigson, Geoffrey, *The Professionals,* 224; *Burial,* 467

Gullans, Charles, *Satyr,* 502

Gunn, Thom, *High Fidelity,* 317; *The Unsettled Motorcyclist's Vision of His*

Death, 340; *The Messenger,* 429

Hacker, Marilyn, *Under the Arc de Triomphe: October 17,* 485

Hall, Donald, *T. R.,* 349

Hammond, Mac, *In Memory of V. R. Lang,* 394

Harris, Sydney J., *I Come to Bury Caesar,* 160

Hartman, Charles O., *Inflation,* 507

Hayakawa, S. I., *To One Elect,* 147

Heap, Jane, "Where go the birds when the rain," 51

Hecht, Anthony, *Alceste in the Wilderness,* 286

Heffernan, Michael, *The Table,* 422

Hemingway, Ernest, *Champs d'Honneur,* 84; *Chapter Heading,* 85

Heyen, William, *The King's Men,* 414

Heyward, DuBose, *The Equinox,* 87

Hill, Geoffrey, *Wreaths,* 343

Hine, Daryl, *Vowel Movements,* 491

Hollander, John, *For the Passing of Groucho's Pursuer,* 378; *Swan and Shadow,* 406; *Hall of Ocean Life,* 448; *Breadth. Circle. Desert. Monarch. Month. Wisdom,* 473

Hope, A. D., *The School of Night,* 419; *Parabola,* 462

Hoskins, Katherine, *Baucis and Philemon,* 445

Howard, Ben, *Winter Report,* 511

Howard, Richard, *Landed: A Valentine,* 327; *Secular Games,* 406; *Aubade: Donna Anna to Juan, Still Asleep,* 420; *From Compulsive Qualifications,* 479

Hoyem, Andrew, *Circumambulation of Mt. Tamalpais,* 441

Hueffer, Ford Madox, *The Sanctuary,* 54

Hughes, Langston, *Sailor,* 124; *Dust Bowl,* 221

Hughes, Ted, *After Lorca,* 392

Hugo, Richard, *Skykomish River Running,* 352; *Last Days,* 478

Ignatow, David, *In a Dream,* 477

James, Thomas, *Reasons,* 441

Jarman, Mark, *The Desire of Water,* 472

Jarrell, Randall, *The Ways and the Peoples,* 199; *The Emancipators,* 237; *Losses,* 241; *The Sleeping Beauty: Variation of the Prince,* 272; *Aging,* 314

Jeffers, Robinson, *Grass on the Cliff,* 107; *The Bloody Sire,* 214; *The Beauty of Things,* 291

Johnston, George, *Indoors,* 445

Jones, David, *The Wall,* 320

Jones, LeRoi, *Like Rousseau,* 396

Jong, Erica, *Climbing You,* 447

Joyce, James, *Night Piece,* 44; *On the Beach at Fontana,* 52

Justice, Donald, "Time and the weather wear away," 380; *About My Poems,* 396

Kallman, Chester, *A Romance,* 310; *Dead Center,* 425

Kees, Weldon, *Henry James at*

Newport, 223; *Small Prayer*, 268

Kennedy, X. J., *Nude Descending a Staircase*, 364

King, Francis, *Séance*, 245

Kinnell, Galway, *Braemar*, 330

Kizer, Carolyn, *To a Visiting Poet in a College Dormitory*, 374

Klein, A. M., *Upon the Heavenly Scarp*, 228

Koch, Kenneth, *Poem for My Twentieth Birthday*, 249; *Schoolyard in April*, 262; *Permanently*, 331

Koethe, John, *Mission Bay*, 423

Kreymborg, Alfred, *To W. C. W. M. D.*, 69

Kumin, Maxine, *The Masochist*, 417

Kunitz, Stanley, *Prophecy on Lethe*, 111; *Goose Pond*, 328; *The Approach to Thebes*, 339

Kuzma, Greg, *Poetry*, 451; *The Dump*, 515

La Follette, Melvin Walker, *Didactic Sonnet*, 311

Laing, Dilys Bennett, *Eros out of the Sea*, 239

Lang, V. R., *The Suicide*, 277

Lattimore, Richmond, *Remorse*, 377

Lawrence, D. H., *Green*, 9; *Illicit*, 10; *Don Juan*, 19; *Moonrise*, 56; *Nostalgia*, 59

Lee, Agnes, *The Ilex Tree*, 73

Lehman, David, *For David Shapiro*, 439

Lesser, Rika, *Translation*, 516

Levertov, Denise, *To the Snake*, 350; *The Illustration — A Footnote*, 376; *Invocation*, 424

Levine, Philip, *He Faces the Second Winter*, 374; *The Reply*, 384; *Here and Now*, 521

Lewis, C. Day, *Winter Night*, 128; *From* THE MAGNETIC MOUNTAIN, 139

Lewis, Janet, *At Carmel Highlands*, 189

Lindh, Stewart, *Settler*, 482

Lindsay, Vachel, *General William Booth Enters into Heaven*, 4; *The Horrid Voice of Science*, 63

Logan, John, *Lines for a Young Wanderer in Mexico*, 358

Lowell, Amy, *Venus Transiens*, 21; *Desolation*, 43

Lowell, Robert, *The Ghost*, 252; *The Fat Man in the Mirror*, 264

MacCaig, Norman, *Beach Talk*, 316

MacLeish, Archibald, *Ars Poetica*, 95; *Epistle to the Rapalloan*, 110

MacNeice, Louis, *Perdita*, 205; *The Springboard*, 235

Macpherson, Jay, *From* THE ARK, 335; *They Return*, 484

Magee, Michael, *It Is the Stars That Govern Us*, 470

Mahapatra, Jayanta, *A Rain of Rites*, 503

Mallalieu, H. B., *Epilogue*, 200; *Empedocles on Etna*, 485

Malley, Jean, *Untitled*, 428

Martin, Charles, *Leaving Buffalo*, 468

Marz, Roy, *Vittoria Colonna*, 293

Masters, Edgar Lee, *In Memory*

of Bryan Lathrop, 36; *Keats to Fanny Brawne,* 74; *Mind Flying Afar,* 89

Mayo, E. L. *The Word of Water,* 309

McAlmon, Robert, *For Instance,* 92

McAuley, James, *Winter Drive,* 464

McClatchy, J. D., *The Pleasure of Ruins,* 501

McCloskey, Mark, *Too Dark,* 431

McLaughlin, Kathy, *Suicide Pond,* 297

McMichael, James, *Terce,* 457

McPherson, Sandra, *Seaweeds,* 465; *Page,* 481; *Sentience,* 509

Mead, Margaret, *Misericordia,* 113

Meredith, William, *Iambic Feet Considered as Honorable Scars,* 389

Merrill, James, *The Green Eye,* 249; *The Broken Bowl,* 259; *Hotel de l'Universe et Portugal,* 294; *Angel,* 366; *The Mad Scene,* 389; *The Black Mesa,* 444

Merton, Thomas, *The Dark Morning,* 229

Merwin, W. S., *Variation on the Gothic Spiral,* 269; *The Sapphire,* 311; *The Highway,* 339; *Divinities,* 412; *Sunset after Rain,* 432

Mezey, Robert, *Vetus Flamma,* 378

Miles, Josephine, *On Inhabiting an Orange,* 146; *Sunday,* 168; *Dream,* 356

Millay, Edna St. Vincent, *From*

FIGS FROM THISTLES, 55; *Recuerdo,* 62; "Women have loved before as I love now," 119; *The Snow Storm,* 196

Minty, Judith, *Look to the Back of the Hand,* 496

Moffett, Judith, *Diehard,* 512; *Twinings Orange Pekoe,* 523

Monro, Harold, *Birth,* 38

Monroe, Harriet, *The Pine at Timber-Line,* 28; *In High Places,* 83; *A Farewell,* 176

Moore, Marianne, *That Harp You Play So Well,* 24; *The Hero,* 132; *No Swan So Fine,* 135; *The Buffalo,* 148; *Pigeons,* 157; *Walking-Sticks and Paperweights and Watermarks,* 170; *Then the Ermine,* 303

Moore, Merrill, *Transfusion,* 111

Moore, Nicholas, "Fivesucked the features of my girl by glory," 205

Morris, John N., *The Mirror,* 499

Morse, Samuel French, *Song in the Cold Season,* 167

Moss, Howard, *A Game of Chance,* 238; *The King's Speech,* 342

Mott, Michael, *Islanders, Inlanders,* 430

Mueller, Lisel, *Historical Museum, Manitoulin Island,* 456

Muir, Edwin, *Then . . . ,* 209; *The Finder Found,* 222

Mus, David, *Conserves,* 496

Nemerov, Howard, *Sigmund Freud,* 236; *Holding the Mirror*

Up to Nature, 345; *The Dragonfly,* 380; *To D--, Dead by Her Own Hand,* 461; *Waiting Rooms,* 509

Nerber, John, *Castaway,* 250

Newman, Michael, *Negative Passage,* 452

Nims, John Frederick, *Parting: 1940,* 208; *Conclusion,* 292; *Clock Without Hands,* 478

Noguere, Suzanne, *Pervigilium Veneris,* 473

Oerke, Andrew, *The Sun,* 449

O'Hara, Frank, *Chez Jane,* 313; *Radio,* 329; *In Favor of One's Time,* 366; *Homosexuality,* 431; *Princess Elizabeth of Bohemia, as Perdita,* 519

Oppen, George, *Population,* 371

Orlovitz, Gil, *Art of the Sonnet: LVI,* 346

Page, P. K., *Stories of Snow,* 247

Patchen, Kenneth, *Empty Dwelling Places,* 145; *O Now the Drenched Land Wakes,* 315

Pettingell, Phoebe, *Ode on Zero,* 440

Pinsky, Robert, *From* ESSAY ON PSYCHIATRISTS, 504

Pitchford, Kenneth, *Lobotomy,* 306

Plath, Sylvia, *Metamorphosis,* 333; *The Death of Myth-Making,* 361; *Stars over the Dordogne,* 383

Porter, Fairfield, *The Island in the Evening,* 314

Pound, Ezra, *To Whistler, American,* 3; *Tenzone,* 7; *From* LUSTRA, 8; TO ΚΑΛΌΝ, 18; *The Coming of War: Actaeon,* 19; *O Atthis,* 37; *The Lake Isle,* 37; *From* THREE CANTOS, 45; *From* PROPERTIUS, 60; *From* CANTO LXXX, 254; *Fragmenti,* 517

Prokosch, Frederic, *The Gothic Dusk,* 164

Rago, Henry, *The Monster,* 291

Raine, Kathleen, *The Instrument,* 298

Rakosi, Carl, *The Memoirs,* 141

Reed, John, *Proud New York,* 61

Reeve, F. D., *Hope,* 433

Reznikoff, Charles, *Winter Sketches,* 137

Richardson, Dorothy M., *Message,* 104

Ridge, Lola, *Chicago,* 90

Riding, Laura (Gottschalk) (Jackson), *Head Itself,* 93

Ridler, Anne, *On a Picture by Michele Da Verona, of Arion as a Boy Riding Upon a Dolphin,* 292

Robinson, Edwin Arlington, *Eros Turannos,* 16

Rodman, Selden, *Time of Day,* 140

Roethke, Theodore, *Bound,* 134; "Long Live the Weeds," 168; *The Reckoning,* 193; *Second Shadow,* 218; *Dolor,* 238; *The Return,* 251

Rosenberg, Harold, *Epos,* 154

Rosenberg, Isaac, *Break of Day in the Trenches,* 42

Rosten, Norman, *Aesthetic,* 188

Rukeyser, Muriel, *Time Exposures,* 165; *Motive,* 259; *The Place at Alert Bay,* 297

Sandburg, Carl, *Chicago,* 14; *In*

Tall Grass, 44; *Falltime,* 58; *Alice Corbin Is Gone,* 364

Sandy, Stephen, *Declension,* 475

Sarton, May, *Fruit of Loneliness,* 119

Savage, D. S., *Fall of Leaves,* 166

Scarfe, Francis, *The Grotto,* 261

Schjeldahl, Peter, *A Younger Poet,* 506

Schloss, David, *The Poem,* 499

Schnackenberg, Gjertrude, *Signs,* 500

Schuyler, James, "This beauty that I see," 469; "Can I Tempt You to a Pond Walk?," 513

Schwartz, Delmore, "Old man in the crystal morning after snow," 182; "In the naked bed, in Plato's cave," 189; *The Self Unsatisfied Runs Everywhere,* 283; *The Heart Flies Up, Erratic as a Kite,* 283; *Swift,* 354

Scott, Tom, *The Real Muse,* 337

Scott, Winfield Townley, *The First Reader,* 146; *Uses of Poetry,* 411

Seidman, Hugh, *N,* 459

Seiffert, Marjorie Allen, *Cubist Portrait,* 77

Sexton, Anne, *The Black Art,* 385; *The Wedding Night,* 401

Shapiro, David, *About This Course,* 467

Shapiro, Harvey, *Provincetown, Mass.,* 281

Shapiro, Karl, *Necropolis,* 213; *October 1,* 225; *The Dirty Word,* 264; *The Alphabet,* 309;

"I swore to stab the sonnet with my pen," 412

Shore, Jane, *An Astronomer's Journal,* 504

Siegel, Robert, *Ego,* 453

Sitwell, Edith, *Elegy for Dylan Thomas,* 318

Sitwell, Osbert, *Maxixe,* 82

Smith, David, *Dome Poem,* 507

Smith, Sidney Goodsir, *Cokkils,* 330

Smith, Stevie, *Here Lies . . .,* 396

Smith, William Jay, "Abruptly All the Palm Trees," 239; *Nightwood,* 305

Snyder, Gary, "There is another world above this one; or outside of this one," 402

Sorrentino, Gilbert, *Handbook of Versification,* 425

Spacks, Barry, *October,* 405

Spencer, Theodore, *Return,* 232

Spender, Stephen, *The Marginal Field,* 195

Spivack, Kathleen, *Dido: Swarming,* 458

Stafford, William, *Shepherd,* 347; *After Plotinus,* 367; *Priest Lake,* 408; *The Day You Are Reading This,* 500

Steele, Timothy, *Wait,* 454

Stein, Gertrude, *Stanzas in Meditation,* 201

Stephens, James, *Dark Wings,* 18

Stevens, Wallace, *Sunday Morning,* 32; *The Indigo Glass in the Grass,* 64; *Anecdote of the Jar,* 65; *The Curtains in the House of the Metaphysician,*

65; *Tea at the Palaz of Hoon,*
79; *Of the Manner of
Addressing Clouds,* 79; *Of
Heaven Considered as a Tomb,*
80; *The Sense of the Sleight-of-
Hand Man,* 199; *The Ultimate
Poem is Abstract,* 267; *From*
THINGS OF AUGUST, 279
Stone, Ruth, *Private Pantomime,*
332
Strand, Mark, *Black Maps,* 433
Strobel, Marion, *Pastoral,* 86
Swenson, May, *Fire Island,* 423;
July 4th, 464
Symons, Arthur, *Dreams,* 58
Symons, Julian, *Hart Crane,*
226
Tagore, Rabindranath, *From*
EPIGRAMS, 38
Tate, Allen, *From* SONNETS OF
THE BLOOD, 124; *The Wolves,*
127
Teasdale, Sara, *September
Midnight,* 15; *The Answer,* 30;
Song, 64; *Epitaph,* 90
Thomas, Dylan, "When all my
five and country senses see,"
191; "O make me a mask
and a wall to shut from your
spies," 191; "Not from this
anger, anticlimax after," 191;
"The spire cranes. Its statue
is an aviary," 192; *Poem in
October,* 243; *Out of a War of
Wits,* 326
Thompson, Francis, *To My
Friend,* 7
Todd, Ruthven, *Upon This
Rock,* 271
Tomlinson, Charles, *The Door,*
404; *The Chances of Rhyme,*
413

Trudell, Dennis, *Hotel in Paris,*
425
Turbyfill, Mark, *Benediction,* 57
Tyler, Parker, *Anthology of
Nouns,* 194; *Nijinsky,* 298
Untermeyer, Louis, *End of the
Comedy,* 62
Urdang, Constance, *Birth of
Venus,* 332
Van Doren, Mark, *Apple Hell,*
99; *Slowly, Slowly Wisdom
Gathers,* 412
Van Duyn Mona, "The Wish
to Be Believed," 403; *Open
Letter from a Constant Reader,*
417
Viereck, Peter, *Graves Are
Made to Waltz On,* 206
Wagoner, David, *Marsh Leaf,*
274; *The Words,* 393; *Lost,*
448; *Muse,* 459; *Elegy for
Yards, Pounds, and Gallons,*
488; *The Death of the Moon,*
521
Wakoski, Diane, *The Ring,* 520
Waley, Arthur, *The Orphan,* 53
Warren, Robert Penn,
Watershed, 130; *The Limited,*
139; *The Garden,* 155; *Bearded
Oaks,* 187; *Terror,* 216
Watkins, Vernon, *Demands of
the Muse,* 348; *Cwmrhydyceirw
Elegiacs,* 413
Weiss, T., *The Fire at
Alexandria,* 356
Wescott, Glenway, *The Poet at
Night-fall,* 78; *The Summer
Ending,* 199
Wheelock, John Hall,
Beethoven, 32
Wheelwright, John, *Canal
Street,* 135

Wilbur, Richard, *The Death of a Toad*, 268; "A World Without Objects Is a Sensible Emptiness," 285; *Marginalia*, 309

Williams, Oscar, *The Golden Fleece*, 77

Williams, Thomas Lanier (Tennessee), *My Love Was Light*, 183

Williams, William Carlos, *Slow Movement*, 23; *Marriage*, 42; *Le Médecin Malgré Lui*, 56; *The Lonely Street*, 80; *4th of July*, 143; *To an Elder Poet*, 174; *River Rhyme*, 216; *Lear*, 270

Wilson, Edmund, *Not Here*, 73

Winters, Yvor, *Hawk's Eyes*, 74; *Static Autumn*, 86; *A Nocturne for October 31st*, 190; *Night of Battle*, 257

Wright, Charles, *Nightletter*, 435; *Negatives*, 460

Wylie, Elinor, *Atavism*, 75; *Lament for Glasgerion*, 108

Yeats, William Butler, *Fallen Majesty*, 4; *To a Friend Whose Work Has Come to Nothing*, 17; *The Magi*, 18; *The Hawk*, 35; *The Scholars*, 36; *A Prayer for My Daughter*, 65; *Meru*, 150

Zabel, Morton Dauwen, *Journal to Stella*, 108

Zaturenska, Marya, *Bird and the Muse*, 483

Zukofsky, Louis, *Of Dying Beauty*, 88; "*Mantis*," 152; *1892–1941*, 234